Edexcel

AS
Geography

Sue Warn • Cameron Dunn • David Holmes • Bob Hordern
Simon Oakes • Michael Witherick

Philip Allan Updates, an imprint of Hodder Education, an Hachette UK company, Market Place, Deddington, Oxfordshire OX15 0SE

Orders
Bookpoint Ltd, 130 Milton Park, Abingdon, Oxfordshire OX14 4SB
tel: 01235 827827
fax: 01235 400401
e-mail: education@bookpoint.co.uk

Lines are open 9.00 a.m.–5.00 p.m., Monday to Saturday, with a 24-hour message answering service. You can also order through the Philip Allan Updates website: www.philipallan.co.uk

© Philip Allan Updates 2008

ISBN 978-0-340-94929-0

Impression number   9 8
Year   2014   2013   2012

This material has been endorsed by Edexcel and offers high quality support for the delivery of Edexcel qualifications.

Edexcel endorsement does not mean that this material is essential to achieve any Edexcel qualification, nor does it mean that this is the only suitable material available to support any Edexcel qualification. No endorsed material will be used verbatim in setting any Edexcel examination and any resource lists produced by Edexcel shall include this and other appropriate texts. While this material has been through an Edexcel quality assurance process, all responsibility for the content remains with the publisher.

Copies of official specifications for all Edexcel qualifications may be found on the Edexcel website — www.edexcel.org.uk.

Front cover photographs reproduced by permission of TopFoto, Thomas Kelly/ Still Pictures.

All Office for National Statistics material is Crown copyright, reproduced under the terms of PSI Licence Number C200700185.

Printed in Dubai.

Hachette UK's policy is to use papers that are natural, renewable and recyclable products and made from wood grown in sustainable forests. The logging and manufacturing processes are expected to conform to the environmental regulations of the country of origin.

P01899

Contents

Unit 2 Geographical investigations

Extreme weather

Unequal spaces

Rebranding places

Introduction

This book has been written for students of Edexcel AS Geography by a team of senior examiners.

It is organised to reflect the structure of the AS specification — each chapter covers one subsection of a topic. Within a chapter, each specification enquiry question is addressed and there is full coverage of what the specification indicates that students need to learn. Case studies prescribed by the specification are included and compulsory case studies are highlighted.

Other useful features include:

➤ definitions of **key terms** to assist you in developing your use of geographical terminology
➤ **key concept** boxes to explain important ideas
➤ **skills focus** features to develop your primary fieldwork and research skills
➤ a range of photographs, maps and graphs to develop your data-response skills
➤ information on useful websites
➤ self-testing **review questions** at the end of each chapter to enhance understanding of key ideas and provide extension activities

The online material (**www.hodderplus.co.uk/philipallan**) provides examination advice and sample questions for Units 1 and 2, with the questions in the same style as the real examination questions. Answers, mark schemes and examiners' tips for success accompany the questions to help you improve your performance.

Edexcel AS Geography

The AS specification consists of two units, which provide you with an opportunity to study aspects of physical, human and environmental geography.

Unit 1 Global challenges consists of two compulsory topics:
➤ World at risk
➤ Going global

The unit focuses on the issues of global hazards and globalisation at the broad scale. However, it also provides smaller-scale case studies and opportunities to explore how your life interacts with these global challenges.

Unit 2 Geographical investigations provides opportunities to develop your fieldwork and research skills. Four topics are offered and you must choose *one* physical and *one* human topic.

Physical topics
➤ **Extreme weather** looks at the threats from abnormal or severe weather events.
➤ **Crowded coasts** reveals how increasing development is testing our ability to manage valued coastal environments.

Human topics

➤ **Unequal spaces** explores the causes and consequences of rural and urban disparities and how to manage them.
➤ **Rebranding places** focuses on the need to reimage and regenerate rural and urban places, using appropriate strategies.

Each topic focuses on local, small-scale investigations, mainly in the UK, but also drawing on parallel examples from around the world.

Assessment Objectives

In common with all other geography specifications, there are three Assessment Objectives in Edexcel AS Geography. Candidates should be able to:

1 Demonstrate knowledge and understanding of content, concepts and processes.
2 Analyse, interpret and evaluate geographical information, issues and view-points, and apply their understanding in unfamiliar contexts.
3 Select and use a variety of methods, skills and techniques (including new technologies) to investigate questions and issues, reach conclusions and communicate findings (Unit 2 emphasises this objective).

Scheme of Assessment

More details of this are available online at **www.hodderplus.co.uk/philipallan**.

	Assessment weighting for A-level (AS)	Exam format	Marks	Time
Unit 1 Global challenges	30% (60%)	Written paper in two sections Section A Six compulsory resource-based short structured questions Section B Choice of one resource-based longer essay question from four	65 + 25 = 90	1½ hours
Unit 2 Geographical investigations	20% (40%)	Four resource-based questions, one for each option. Student to choose one physical and one human question. Each question tests fieldwork and research skills and is a structured essay question	35 + 35 = 70	1 hour

Unit **1**
Global challenges

World at risk

Global hazards

What are the main types of physical risk facing the world and how big a threat are they?

By the end of this chapter you should have:

➤ *learnt how the major types of hazard — especially drought, floods and storms — and the impacts of global warming can combine to increase physical risk*

➤ *understood how the disaster risk equation has worsened as a result of increased numbers of hazards (especially hydro-meteorological) and rising numbers of vulnerable people with limited capacity to cope*

➤ *considered why global warming may be the greatest threat to humanity*

Context hazard Widespread (global) threat due to environmental factors such as climate change.

Geophysical hazard A hazard formed by tectonic/geological processes (earthquakes, volcanoes and tsunamis).

Hazard A perceived natural event which has the potential to threaten both life and property.

Hydro-meteorological hazard A hazard formed by hydrological (floods) and atmospheric (storms and droughts) processes.

Vulnerability A high risk combined with an inability of individuals and communities to cope.

The nature of hazard

A natural event such as a tsunami only becomes a **hazard** if it threatens humans. There are many different types of hazard. Environmental hazards are specific events like earthquakes or floods, usually classified into:

➤ *natural processes*, where the hazard results from an extreme **geophysical** or **hydro-meteorological** event, such as a flood or volcanic eruption

➤ *natural-technological disasters* (na-tech), where natural hazards trigger technological disaster (e.g. flooding causes a dam to burst)

➤ *technological accidents*, such as Chernobyl nuclear power plant exploding

As can be seen from Figure 1.1, environmental hazards are related in varying degrees to **context hazards** which operate at a global or continental scale.

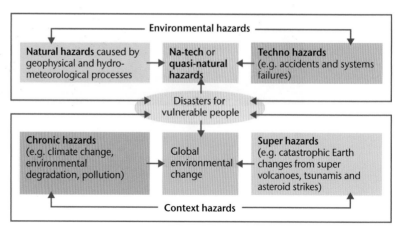

Figure 1.1 Environmental and context hazards

Chronic hazards such as global warming and the El Niño–La Niña cycle may increase the threat from environmental hazards: for example, a sea-level rise increases the risk of coastal floods.

Some key features of environmental hazards make them a huge threat:

➤ The warning time is normally short and onset is rapid (apart from drought).
➤ Humans are exposed to hazards because people live in hazardous areas through perceived economic advantage or over-confidence about safety.
➤ Most direct losses to life or property occur within days or weeks of the event, unless there is a secondary hazard.
➤ The resulting disaster often justifies an emergency response, sometimes on the scale of international humanitarian aid.

Some socioeconomic characteristics, such as high population density, high poverty level or corrupt and inefficient government increase people's **vulnerability** and amplify the risks, particularly of death, from environmental hazards.

Types of natural hazard

We have seen that there are many ways of classifying hazards. We will focus on natural hazards, using the classification of the Emergency Events Database (EM-DAT):

➤ **Geophysical hazards** result from geological or geomorphological processes (e.g. volcanoes, earthquakes and tsunamis).
➤ **Hydro-meteorological hazards** result from atmospheric or hydro-logical processes (e.g. floods, storms and droughts).

> ### Key terms
>
> **Disaster** A hazard becoming reality in an event that causes deaths and damage to goods/ property and the environment.
>
> **Risk** The probability of a hazard event occurring and creating loss of lives and livelihoods.

Other hazards, such as those resulting from mass movement (e.g. snow avalanches and landslides), could be placed in either group, as both types of process are involved. For example, an avalanche is formed from snow and ice (atmospheric conditions), yet the mass movement is a geomorphological process.

The risk of disaster

Figure 1.2 shows how a hazard event can become a **disaster**, especially when it occurs in areas where environments and people are vulnerable.

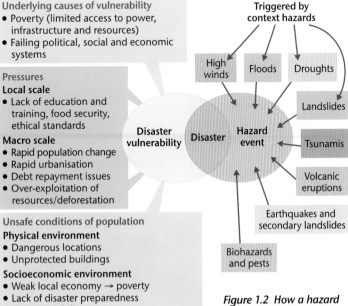

Underlying causes of vulnerability
• Poverty (limited access to power, infrastructure and resources)
• Failing political, social and economic systems

Pressures
Local scale
• Lack of education and training, food security, ethical standards
Macro scale
• Rapid population change
• Rapid urbanisation
• Debt repayment issues
• Over-exploitation of resources/deforestation

Unsafe conditions of population
Physical environment
• Dangerous locations
• Unprotected buildings
Socioeconomic environment
• Weak local economy → poverty
• Lack of disaster preparedness
• Hunger and disease

Triggered by context hazards

Disaster vulnerability — Disaster — Hazard event

High winds · Floods · Droughts · Landslides · Tsunamis · Volcanic eruptions · Earthquakes and secondary landslides · Biohazards and pests

Figure 1.2 How a hazard becomes a disaster

What is risk?

The types of **risk** from global hazards are listed below in order of decreasing severity.

Hazards to people
> death and severe injury
> disease, stress

Hazards to goods
> economic losses
> infrastructure damage
> property damage

Hazards to the environment
> pollution
> loss of flora and fauna
> loss of amenity

Exposure to a hazard is not always unavoidable. People may consciously place themselves at risk. As Table 1.1 shows, there are huge areas of the world and billions of people exposed to one or more hazard risks.

Why do people remain exposed to hazard risks?

Photograph 1.1 Flooding of the River Avon, July 2007

Changing risks
It is difficult to predict when or where an event may occur or what the magnitude will be. Natural hazards vary in space as well as time because of changing human

Thinking Media/Environment Agency

activities and changing physical factors, such as tectonic plate movements. The rise in sea level means that low-lying coastal plains that were once safe places to live are now more prone to storm surge and flood. Deforestation of watersheds leads to less interception of rain and more flashy hydrographs, increasing the frequency and magnitude of flood events.

Table 1.1 Summary of hazard risks

	Hazard type	Occurrence	Rank for deaths	Deaths, 1980–2000
HYDRO-METEOROLOGICAL	**Drought** Frequently includes extreme heat, wildfires and secondary hazard of famine	Defined as rainfall of 50% less than the 3-month median. 40% of world's land surface, containing 70% of population and worth 70% of agricultural production, is exposed to drought. Areas include west and midwest USA, central America, northeast Brazil, sub-Saharan Africa, Horn of Africa, southern Spain and Portugal, northwest India, northeast China, southeast Asia and southern Australia.	1 including secondary deaths from famine; 6 for heatwaves	563,701 mainly from famine + 19,249 extreme heat + 1,046 wildfires
	Floods	Coastal, river and flash flooding occurs in over one-third of world's land areas, affecting 82% of world's population (high population densities in river basins and coastal plains); 10% of land surface is very flood prone and contains 40% of the world's people. Areas include midwest USA, coastal South America, Bangladesh, Europe, river basins of China, India, the Philippines and east Africa.	3	170,010 (rising rapidly)
	Storms Cyclones, can include temperate storms and tornadoes	Concentrated in tropical belts, especially coastal areas, covering 6.7% of world's land area but 24% of world's population. Areas often developed and contain much infrastructure and GDP. Areas include Caribbean, southern USA, southeast Asia and northeast Australia.	2	251,384 (varies according to cycles)
GEOPHYSICAL	**Landslides** Including snow avalanches	Affect 5% of world's population, largely in mountainous areas. Many are secondary hazards from earthquakes, floods and tsunamis.	7	18,200
	Earthquakes	About 7.5% of world's total land area, containing 20% of world's population, is highly earthquake prone. Distribution of earthquakes concentrated along mobile plate boundaries, including Japan, Philippines, west USA and South America, New Zealand, Indonesia, India, Iran and Turkey.	4	158,551
	Volcanoes	Spatially concentrated, affect only 0.5% of world's land surface mainly in Japan, Philippines, Indonesia, west USA, Mexico, central America and Iceland. Associated with mobile plate boundaries or hotspots (Hawaii).	5	25,050 (explosive eruptions comparatively rare)
	Large tsunamis	Associated with earthquakes and only affect coastal areas (e.g. Hawaii and Indonesia).	8	3,000

Note: As tsunami-prone areas are densely populated, large tsunamis such as the 2004 south Asia event could distort statistics.
Sources: International Research Institute for Climate Prediction (IRI), Climate Data Library, Dartmouth Flood Observatory, World Atlas of Large Flood Events, UNEP GIS covered by Global and Regional Integrated Data, Norwegian Geotechnical Institute (NGI), Global Seismic Hazard Program (GSHAP), Worldwide Volcano Database from National Geophysical Data Centre

*Photograph 1.2
Slums on a hillside
in Rio de Janeiro*

Lack of alternatives

Often the world's poorest, most vulnerable people are forced to live in unsafe locations such as hillsides or floodplains, or regions subject to drought, owing to shortage of land or lack of knowledge of better alternatives (Photograph 1.2).

Benefits versus costs

People may subconsciously weigh up the benefits versus the costs of living in high-risk areas. The benefits of fertile farming land on the flanks of a volcano for example, may outweigh the risk from eruptions.

Risk perception

People tend to be optimistic about the risk of hazards occurring. They are comforted by statistics which show that the risk of death from hazard events is far lower than that from influenza or car accidents. They also believe that if a high magnitude event has occurred, they may be safe for the next few years, although this is not true. Figure 1.3 shows how the risk perception process works.

Figure 1.3 The risk perception process

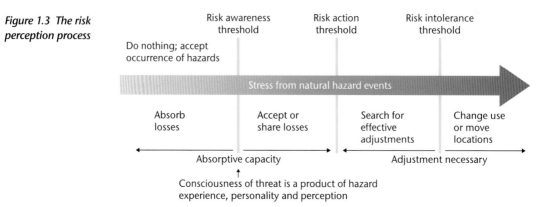

Measuring risk

The key concept box below explains the **risk equation**. People living in areas of high physical exposure to hazards and with high levels of human vulnerability will be the most at risk and these people are largely found in the poorest countries of the world (Figure 1.4).

High risk, high security (e.g. California)	High risk, low security (e.g. Haiti, Bangladesh, Somalia, Mali)
Low risk, high security (e.g. UK)	Low risk, low security (e.g. Bolivia, Angola)

Physical exposure to hazards (risk) →

Human vulnerability to disaster (insecurity) →

Figure 1.4 Vulnerability quadrant

The risk equation

Key concept

The **risk equation** measures the level of hazard risk for an area:

$$risk = \frac{\text{frequency or magnitude of hazard} \times \text{level of vulnerability}}{\text{capacity of population to cope}}$$

If we look at each of these elements in turn, we can see that the risk equation for the future is gloomy.

Frequency or magnitude of hazard is increasing

Use of fossil fuels is warming the planet. The resulting change in climate is increasing the frequency and severity of weather-related hazards (e.g. floods, droughts, windstorms) and expanding the range of disease carriers.

Level of vulnerability is increasing

Hazards become disasters only when people get in the way. Unsustainable development involves poor land use (e.g. building on floodplains, unstable slopes and coasts) and environmental degradation (e.g. bleaching of coral reefs, destruction of coastal mangroves, deforestation of water catchments). This is increasing the vulnerability of millions of people.

Capacity to cope is decreasing

Communities need skills, tools and money to cope with the effects of climate change. However, debt repayments, unfair trade arrangements, selective foreign investment, and rich countries directing aid funds towards politically strategic regions rather than the most needy mean that the poorest and most vulnerable communities lack these resources. Rural–urban migration is also undermining traditional coping strategies.

The future

The most affected areas will be the poorest countries and communities in the world, particularly in sub-Saharan Africa, parts of southeast Asia, and many of the small island developing states (see Chapter 5). The future risk equation emphasises how the development gap between rich and poor countries is actually widening.

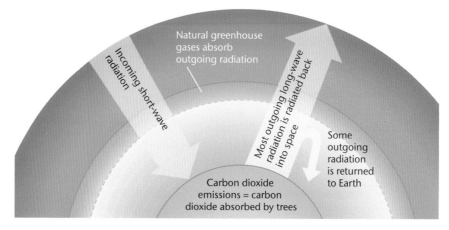

Figure 1.5 The greenhouse effect

Labels in figure:
Incoming short-wave radiation
Natural greenhouse gases absorb outgoing radiation
Most outgoing long-wave radiation is radiated back into space
Some outgoing radiation is returned to Earth
Carbon dioxide emissions = carbon dioxide absorbed by trees

Global warming: our greatest hazard?

The greenhouse effect

The **greenhouse effect** is a natural phenomenon. It is the process by which the so-called greenhouse gases — water vapour (the biggest contributor), carbon dioxide, methane, CFCs, nitrous oxide and ozone — absorb outgoing long-wave radiation from the Earth and send some of it back to the Earth's surface, which is warmed (Figure 1.5). This sustains life on Earth by raising temperatures to a global average of 15°C. Without the greenhouse effect the Earth would be up to 30°C cooler.

Concentrations of carbon dioxide and other greenhouse gases were constant at about 280 parts per million (ppm) until the early nineteenth century. In 2007, however, they stood at 430 ppm as a result of emissions from human activities, particularly the burning of **fossil fuels** such as oil and coal. Most scientists agree that these increased levels of greenhouse gases mean that an **enhanced greenhouse effect** (Figure 1.6) is now

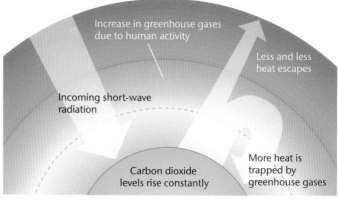

Labels in figure:
Increase in greenhouse gases due to human activity
Less and less heat escapes
Incoming short-wave radiation
Carbon dioxide levels rise constantly
More heat is trapped by greenhouse gases

Figure 1.6 The enhanced greenhouse effect

Ingram

*Photograph 1.3
The impacts of
global warming are
complex. Melting of
sea ice not only
reduces habitat for
polar bears, it also
affects ocean
currents and how
much solar
radiation is
reflected back
into space*

occurring. In time, this will lead to an increase in temperatures affecting all parts of the world. A concentration of over 450 ppm is expected to lead to a rise of 2°C in the Earth's temperature, which is regarded by many scientists as the global **tipping point** for dangerous **climate change** to occur.

Why is global warming important?

Climate change is believed by many to be the most important issue we face.
➤ It is a global problem affecting all areas of the world.
➤ It is a chronic hazard with an enormous range of direct impacts. Rising temperatures can make other environmental problems worse.
➤ Changes in climate will affect ecology and wildlife, and could lead to the spread into new areas of diseases such as malaria.
➤ Rising ocean temperatures may cause an increasing frequency and magnitude of hurricanes (this is investigated in Chapter 2) and are responsible for widespread damage to coral reefs.
➤ The Earth consists of a number of interlocking systems which can impact on each other via positive and negative **feedbacks**. For example, as glaciers and ice sheets melt, oceans become diluted by fresh water, which impacts on ocean circulation. Moreover, ice has a high **albedo** and as it melts more heat from the sun will be absorbed, which will raise the temperature further and make the remaining ice melt quicker.
➤ Global warming has many *indirect* impacts too, as thermal expansion of the oceans leads to rising sea levels.

> **Key term**
>
> **Feedback mechanism**
> Where the output of a system acts to amplify (positive) or reduce (negative) further output (e.g. the melting of Arctic permafrost leads to the release of trapped methane which leads to further global warming).

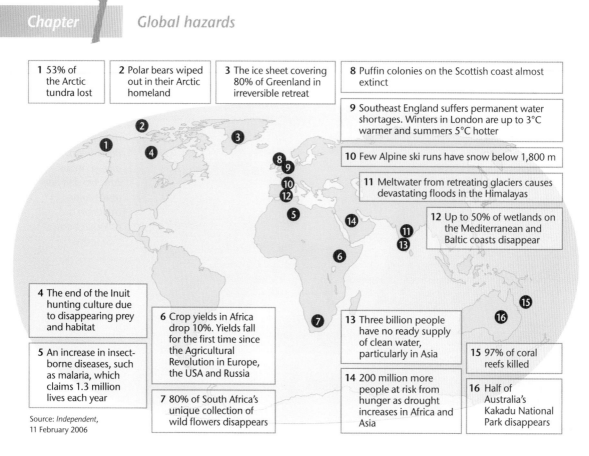

1 53% of the Arctic tundra lost

2 Polar bears wiped out in their Arctic homeland

3 The ice sheet covering 80% of Greenland in irreversible retreat

8 Puffin colonies on the Scottish coast almost extinct

9 Southeast England suffers permanent water shortages. Winters in London are up to 3°C warmer and summers 5°C hotter

10 Few Alpine ski runs have snow below 1,800 m

11 Meltwater from retreating glaciers causes devastating floods in the Himalayas

12 Up to 50% of wetlands on the Mediterranean and Baltic coasts disappear

4 The end of the Inuit hunting culture due to disappearing prey and habitat

5 An increase in insect-borne diseases, such as malaria, which claims 1.3 million lives each year

6 Crop yields in Africa drop 10%. Yields fall for the first time since the Agricultural Revolution in Europe, the USA and Russia

7 80% of South Africa's unique collection of wild flowers disappears

13 Three billion people have no ready supply of clean water, particularly in Asia

14 200 million more people at risk from hunger as drought increases in Africa and Asia

15 97% of coral reefs killed

16 Half of Australia's Kakadu National Park disappears

Source: *Independent*, 11 February 2006

Figure 1.7 Socioeconomic impacts of a 2°C global temperature change

➤ Global warming is not just an environmental problem, but has a huge range of social and economic impacts. Figure 1.7 shows a sample of the problems that could occur if there is a 2°C increase in temperature worldwide.

➤ Vulnerable poor people in less developed countries are most likely to suffer the effects of climate change, such as increased drought in sub-Saharan Africa and more frequent flooding in low-lying Bangladesh. At the same time, the biggest contribution to climate change is being made by the richest developed countries, which emit most greenhouse gases. This is unfair and increases the gap between rich and poor.

Solving the problem of global warming is difficult and complex for two main reasons:

➤ it is hard to make accurate predictions about the nature and impacts of global warming

➤ tackling the problem requires international agreement to cut greenhouse gas emissions and this is politically and economically unacceptable for many countries

In conclusion, a word of caution: global warming is not responsible for all the extreme weather hazards across the globe (see case study). Many of these are the result of short-term climate change induced by atmospheric or oceanic oscillations (e.g. El Niño Southern Oscillation, p.19).

Case study: 2006: a year of wild weather

The hazard calendar in Table 1.2 shows how 2006 was a year of wild weather, breaking a number of records. Although this seems to be part of a trend towards unpredictability, it is hard to believe that the incidents shown are independent of each other and not part of climate change. The same more extreme pattern has also been shown by UK weather in recent years.

Table 1.2 Hazard calendar

Month	ENSO	Droughts	Floods	Storms	Extreme temperatures
January	Weak La Niña	Drought in east Kenya	Flooding and mudslides in abnormally wet Indonesia (weak La Niña)	Cyclone Clare strikes northwest Australia. Cyclone in Fiji causes widespread flooding	Heavy snow, 4 m, north Japan. Snow in east Europe −30°C in Ukraine and Russia
February			Major flooding in Bolivia		
March		Drought persists in Spain and Portugal	Spring flooding along Danube highest since 1895 (150 deaths)	Cyclone Larry hits Queensland	Arctic has warmest spring on record
April		Persistent anticyclone drought in southeast England after warm dry summer 2005. Droughts in west and north China and Afghanistan lead to crop losses and water shortage	Rain inundates Kenya and Somalia	Cyclone Monica hits Queensland coast (most intense ever in southern hemisphere)	
May					
June				Catastrophic storms hit southeast China	High temperature in Europe leads to loss of cereal production in southern France
July		Drought in southwest China and Horn of Africa	Heavy rains in Sahel lead to flooding in Niger	Typhoon Saomai, category 5 (250 deaths)	Hottest summer on record in UK
August			Widespread flooding in Hunan province, China (612 deaths)	Tropical storm Bils hits southeast China (600 deaths)	Severe heat across USA (warmest since 1895)
September	Moderate El Niño develops	Great Australian drought, worst in modern times. Massive wildfires (El Niño induced)	Monsoonal floods in Asia, especially Thailand (154 deaths) and Rajasthan, India (200 deaths)	Four category 4 storms strike Philippines — flooding and landslides	Warmest autumn on record over most of Europe
October			Deluge of rain in Ethiopia	Tornado in Saroma Hokkaido, Japan (9 deaths)	Heatwave in Australia nationwide 40°C+ in NSW
November			Flooding in Somalia and Kenya (150 deaths) Floods in Indonesia (Sumatra) and Malaysia (worst in a century)	Typhoon Durion hits Philippines (1,200 deaths)	
December			Flash floods hit Melbourne, Australia	Severe winter storms and damaging tornadoes in Kilburn, London	Very cold in Victoria and New South Wales, Australia, in December

Review questions

1 Explain, with the help of examples, the difference between hazards and disasters.

2 Study the vulnerability quadrant (Figure 1.4). Redraw the quadrant and select and justify further examples of countries in each of the four categories.

3 a Explain with examples how unsustainable development increases the risk equation.

   b Referring to the risk equation, suggest reasons why there will be even more disasters in the future.

4 Read the case study '2006: a year of wild weather'. How much impact do you think global warming may have had on world weather?

Global hazard trends

How and why are natural hazards becoming seen as an increasing global threat?

By the end of this chapter you should understand:

➤ *the extent to which some types of hazard, notably hydro-meteorological hazards, are increasing in both magnitude and frequency, and having greater impacts on people*

➤ *why hazard events develop into disasters as a result of physical factors (context hazards) and human factors (increased social and economic vulnerability)*

➤ *why on a global scale hazard-related deaths are falling, whereas the numbers affected and economic losses are escalating*

Hazard trends

Understanding global hazard trends is not simple. First, there are concerns over the nature and reliability of the statistics — even from the most widely used sources, such as the Emergency Events Database (EM-DAT) (see skills focus, p. 14). Second, the definition of hazard events and their classification into types causes ambiguities.

This book adopts the twofold classification of natural hazards — hydro-meteorological and geophysical — and focuses on the 'big six': droughts, storms, floods, earthquakes, volcanoes and slides (including snow avalanches and landslides).

The terms 'hazard' and 'disaster' are often used interchangeably, in spite of there being a clear distinction between a hazard as a *potentially threatening event*, and a disaster as the *realisation of a hazard event*. As we shall see, different measures are used by different agencies to indicate when a hazard event merits the status of a disaster.

Interpreting disaster statistics

The different sources of disaster data often produce very different statistics. Always consider the source of the data you analyse, and whether it is reliable.

How good are disaster statistics?

Like health and population trends, disaster statistics are reported by governments to UN agencies. They are only as good as the methods used to collect them. There are several reasons to question the data obtained:

➤ There is no universally agreed definition of a disaster. Equally, there is no universally agreed numerical threshold for designating an event as a disaster, such as 25 or 100 deaths, or 1% of the population affected, or 1% of annual GDP lost, or a combination of these.

> Reporting of disaster death numbers depends on whether direct (primary) deaths only or indirect (secondary) deaths from subsequent hazards or associated diseases are counted.

> Location is significant. Events in remote places away from the media spotlight are frequently under-recorded. Around 10% of all data from the last 10 years are missing even on the CRED (Centre for Research on the Epidemiology of Disasters) database.

> Declaration of disaster deaths and casualties may be subject to political influences. The impact of the 2004 tsunami in Myanmar (Burma) was

Skills focus

The website for the International Strategy for Disaster Reduction (ISDR) presents the most complete record of disasters (**www.unisdr.org/ disaster-statistics/introduction.htm**). Statistics are provided for three time periods: 1900–2006, 1970–2006 and 1991–2006.

The data on EM-DAT (**www.emdat.net**) are freely accessible, unlike those of the other two main global database providers, Munich Re (Nat Cat **www.munichre.com**) and Swiss Re (Sigma **www.swissre.com**), which are used by the insurance industry. Table 2.1 shows how using different criteria and providing for different audiences means that there are huge discrepancies in the data.

Table 2.1 Data on disasters in selected countries using different databases, 1970–2006

	EM-DAT (CRED)	Nat Cat (Munich Re)	Sigma (Swiss Re)
Honduras			
Number of disasters	14	34	7
Total killed	15,121	15,184	9,760
Total affected	2,892,107	4,888,806	0
Total damage ($m)	2,145	3,982	5,560
India			
Number of disasters	147	229	120
Total killed	58,609	69,243	65,058
Total affected	706,722,177	248,738,441	16,188,723
Total damage ($m)	17,850	22,133	68,854
Mozambique			
Number of disasters	16	23	4
Total killed	105,745	877	233
Total affected	9,952,500	2,993,281	6,500
Total damage ($m)	27	112	2,085
Vietnam			
Number of disasters	55	101	36
Total killed	10,350	11,114	9,618
Total affected	36,572,845	20,869,877	2,840,748
Total damage ($m)	1,915	3,402	2,681
Total number of disasters	232	387	167
Total killed	189,825	96,418	84,669
Total affected	756,139,629	277,490,405	19,035,971
Total damage ($m)	21,937	29,629	79,180

ignored by its government, but in Thailand, where many foreign tourists were killed, the impact was initially overstated and then played down to conserve the Thai tourist industry.

➤ Statistics on major disasters are complex to collect, especially in remote rural areas of developing countries (e.g. the Kashmir earthquake of 2005, Photograph 2.1) or densely populated squatter settlements where statistics on population are inaccurate.

➤ Time-trend analysis, which involves interpreting historical data to produce trends (see Figure 2.1), can be difficult. Much depends on the intervals selected and whether the means of data collection have remained constant. Trends can be upset by a cluster of mega disasters, as in 2005–06.

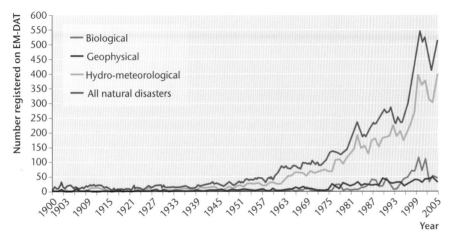

Photograph 2.1
The Kashmir earthquake caused devastation in Pakistan

Analysis of hazard trends

Figure 2.1 shows that the number of reported disasters has grown significantly in recent years. In a globalised world more disasters will be reported as a result of improved access to information technology. Equally, with a world population of over 6 billion and rising, there will be increasing numbers of vulnerable people living in poverty, especially in Africa.

However, these facts alone do not account for the rising trends. Figure 2.1 shows that the occurrence of hydro-meteorological hazards has increased dramatically since the 1960s, with a knock-on effect on the overall rising trend. In contrast, the number of geophysical disasters (earthquakes, volcanoes and

Figure 2.1
Hazard trends, 1900–2005

tsunamis) shows fluctuations (known as timescale variations) but no overall rising trend. Biological disasters (infestations and diseases) show a slightly rising trend from the 1990s onwards, possibly linked to climate change.

Magnitude and frequency

Key concept

Figure 2.2 explores the relationships between magnitude and frequency in hazard events.

Magnitude

Magnitude is the size of a natural hazard event and so represents the amount of work done (e.g. the energy given off during a volcanic eruption). Magnitude scales categorise events according to size/energy and enable people to understand the processes and to model the likely impacts. Scales include:

➤ hurricanes: Saffir–Simpson scale (1–5)
➤ earthquakes: Richter scale (1–10 log scale)
➤ tornadoes: TORRO or Fujita intensity scales
➤ volcanic eruptions: explosivity index

Low-magnitude events, such as an earth tremor of Richter scale 2.5, have less impact on people than high-magnitude events, such as the earthquake which caused the 2004 south Asia tsunami, measuring 9.1 on the Richter scale.

Frequency

Frequency is the number of events of a given magnitude that occur over a period of time. Low-magnitude events are likely to have a more frequent recurrence level, and therefore to present more frequent but less devastating risks.

Figure 2.2 The relationship between magnitude and frequency

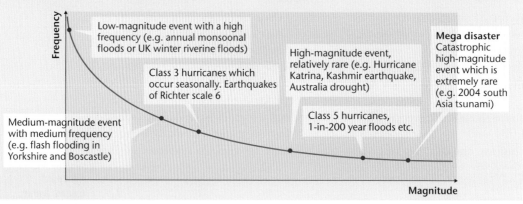

Key terms

Frequency How often an event of a certain size (magnitude) occurs. For example, a flood of 1 m height may occur, on average, every year on a particular river, while a 2 m flood may only occur about every 10 years. The frequency is called the recurrence interval.

Magnitude The size of the event (e.g. force of a gale on the Beaufort scale or size of an earthquake on the Richter scale).

Contrasting trends

Figure 2.3 looks at recent decades in detail and emphasises the contrasting trends between hydro-meteorological and geophysical hazards.

If we look at geophysical hazards first (Figure 2.3a), the variations over time can be accounted for by the clustering of events along mobile (usually destructive) plate boundaries. There have been a number of earthquakes (including the one that caused the 2004 south Asia tsunami) off the coast of

Indonesia, where the Indian plate is being subducted beneath the Burma plate. Other mobile active zones include Iran and Turkey. However, there is no solid evidence that the frequency or magnitude of earthquakes or volcanic eruptions is increasing. Nevertheless, geophysical activity remains a huge killer.

(a) Geophysical

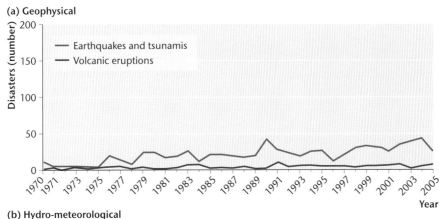

Fluctuating trend
Rare but devastating

(b) Hydro-meteorological

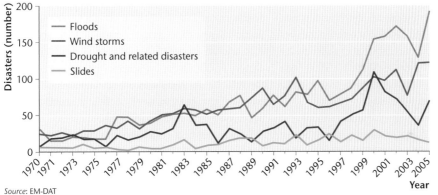

Rapidly rising trend of flood events

Rising trend of hurricanes, typhoons tornadoes, etc.

Increasingly wide-spread drought, affecting millions of people

Fluctuating trend usually linked to other hazards

Source: EM-DAT

Figure 2.3 Number of natural disasters by type, 1970–2005

In contrast, part (b) of Figure 2.3 shows that the number of reported hydro-meteorological events is definitely on the increase. This is likely to be associated with climate change. It is predicted that global warming will increase the frequency, magnitude and impact of hydro-meteorological disasters.

Another explanation for the increased frequency of such disasters lies in the context hazard of increased environmental degradation caused by population pressure. Deforestation and other loss of land cover, for example, as people cut down trees for firewood or clear forest to grow crops, can lead to flash flooding. Ecosystems undamaged by human impact provide protection against natural disasters (e.g. mangroves protect coasts against tsunamis). We cannot be sure that damage to the environment *causes* disasters, but it is clear that it makes the impacts of natural hazards worse. The case study on p. 18 considers whether hurricanes are increasing, and if climate change is contributing to this. Short-term fluctuations in climate caused by El Niño Southern Oscillation also have an impact on hydro-meteorological disasters and these are explained on p. 19.

Are hurricanes increasing as a result of climate change?

This case study explores three complex issues:

- What evidence is there to suggest that hurricanes and related storm types are increasing in frequency and/or magnitude?
- If there are changes, to what extent can these be linked to global warming, or to short-term climate change (e.g. El Niño Southern Oscillation, p. 19)?
- How accurate are the records of hurricanes? It could be that new satellite technology records more hurricanes than was possible before 1970, and this may explain the rise in the number of hurricanes recorded.

At a basic level, the relationship shown in Figure 2.4 seems straightforward. Scientists have found that greenhouse gas emissions have contributed to a rise in (a) global average temperatures, and this has had a knock-on impact on (b) sea-surface temperatures (SSTs). Increasing SSTs provide ideal conditions for (c) spawning more and stronger storms. Higher SSTs pump up an existing storm's power and greater evaporation rates add to its rainfall.

Research into the incidence of tropical storms and hurricanes (severe tropical storms) using North Atlantic records dating back to 1880 has identified three major trends. From 1905 to 1930 there was an annual average of 6 tropical storms/hurricanes. From 1931 to 1994 the number jumped to an average of 9.4 and remained steady until 1995. From 1995 there was a 10-year period with an annual average of 15 tropical storms, of which 8 were hurricanes. In 2004, the 'year of savage storms', a series of hurricanes criss-crossed the Caribbean, and in 2005, the year of Katrina, Rita and Wilma, there were so many storms that they ran out of names.

If it was a straightforward case of global warming heating the oceans, then 2006 should have continued the trend, but it had only 8 tropical storms and nothing above category 3. However, the Pacific had a year of record storms. This suggests that there might be an oscillation between the Atlantic and the Pacific.

The key concepts box opposite explains El Niño Southern Oscillation (ENSO). This is basically a fluctuation in sea-surface temperature in the Pacific, but it is known that El Niño events (warming of the eastern Pacific Ocean) reduce hurricane frequency in the Atlantic. As 2006 was the start of an El Niño, this may be the reason why so few tropical storms occurred in the Atlantic that year.

Most scientists conclude that global warming is contributing to storms of greater magnitude, but that ENSO has an important impact on frequency.

Figure 2.4 Global warming and North Atlantic storms

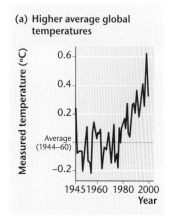

(a) **Higher average global temperatures**

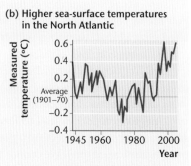

(b) **Higher sea-surface temperatures in the North Atlantic**

Sea-surface temperatures vary slightly year to year, but since 1994 they have been far higher than the average.

(c) **More storms per year in the North Atlantic**

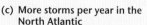
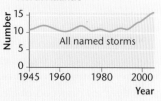

Since the mid-1990s the number of named tropical storms and hurricanes in the North Atlantic has been high. Aircraft observance of storms began in 1944 and satellite tracking in the 1970s

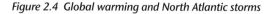

Source: Scientific American, July 2007

El Niño Southern Oscillation

The Pacific Ocean contains huge amounts of circulating warm and cold water. El Niño and La Niña are changes in this circulation, linked with changes in atmospheric processes. They are part of a continually oscillating climatic pattern called the El Niño Southern Oscillation (ENSO).

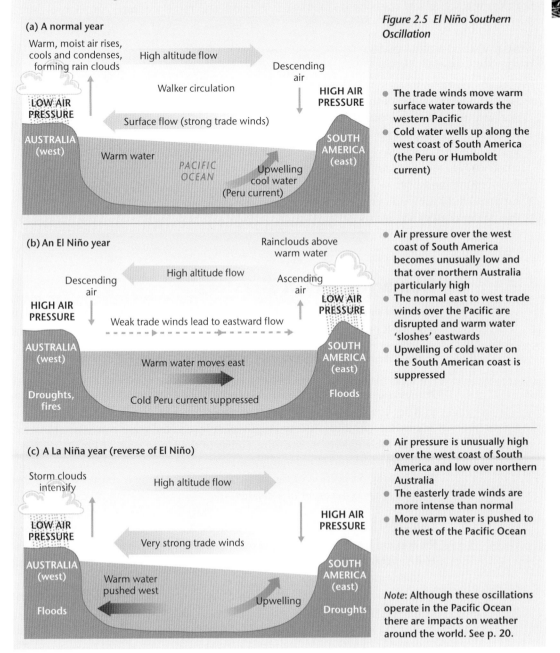

Figure 2.5 El Niño Southern Oscillation

(a) A normal year

Warm, moist air rises, cools and condenses, forming rain clouds

High altitude flow

Descending air

Walker circulation

HIGH AIR PRESSURE

LOW AIR PRESSURE

Surface flow (strong trade winds)

AUSTRALIA (west)

Warm water

PACIFIC OCEAN

SOUTH AMERICA (east)

Upwelling cool water (Peru current)

- The trade winds move warm surface water towards the western Pacific
- Cold water wells up along the west coast of South America (the Peru or Humboldt current)

(b) An El Niño year

Rainclouds above warm water

High altitude flow

Descending air

Ascending air

HIGH AIR PRESSURE

LOW AIR PRESSURE

Weak trade winds lead to eastward flow

AUSTRALIA (west)

Warm water moves east

SOUTH AMERICA (east)

Droughts, fires

Cold Peru current suppressed

Floods

- Air pressure over the west coast of South America becomes unusually low and that over northern Australia particularly high
- The normal east to west trade winds over the Pacific are disrupted and warm water 'sloshes' eastwards
- Upwelling of cold water on the South American coast is suppressed

(c) A La Niña year (reverse of El Niño)

Storm clouds intensify

High altitude flow

HIGH AIR PRESSURE

LOW AIR PRESSURE

Very strong trade winds

AUSTRALIA (west)

Warm water pushed west

SOUTH AMERICA (east)

Floods

Upwelling

Droughts

- Air pressure is unusually high over the west coast of South America and low over northern Australia
- The easterly trade winds are more intense than normal
- More warm water is pushed to the west of the Pacific Ocean

Note: Although these oscillations operate in the Pacific Ocean there are impacts on weather around the world. See p. 20.

This affects the weather around the world and is therefore a context hazard.

Figure 2.5 shows the conditions experienced during El Niño and La Niña. These events happen every 2–7 years and last 1–2 years. It is not clear whether global warming is changing the frequency or intensity of El Niño events..

How ENSO contributes to a more hazardous world

During an El Niño:

➤ rainfall is reduced in southeast Asia, New Zealand, Australia and India, leading to drought, crop failure and wildfires
➤ heavy rain in California, Mexico and the coasts of Peru and Ecuador often results in flooding and mudslides
➤ suppression of the cold current in the east Pacific devastates fish catches off the west coast of South America

➤ unusually strong winds in the Atlantic shear off the tops of clouds preventing convection cells forming so there are fewer severe hurricanes in the USA and Caribbean
➤ tornadoes in the USA are reduced
➤ there are more cyclones in Hawaii and Polynesia but fewer in north Australia
➤ southern Africa may experience drought while there may be floods in east Africa

During a La Niña:

➤ rainfall is higher than normal in Indonesia and the Philippines and lower than normal on the west coast of South America
➤ southern Africa and southeast Australia may experience floods
➤ eastern Africa, California and South America may experience drought
➤ there are more hurricanes in the Caribbean and USA

Human factors in disasters

Physical factors such as ENSO contribute to the growth in hazards, but human behaviour plays a part too because it leads to increased vulnerability.

Rapid population growth

Growing world population means:

➤ pressure on land which leads to people living in high-risk areas, such as low-lying flood-prone land in Bangladesh
➤ growing numbers of very elderly people, e.g. there are concerns about the vulnerable elderly in hazardous areas of the world such as Japan (prone to earthquakes) and Florida (hurricanes)
➤ a growing proportion of the very young in developing countries who are also vulnerable in the event of a disaster

Deforestation and land degradation

Pressure on land from growing populations also leads to:

➤ deforestation to gain farmland, which can cause flooding and soil erosion and contributes to climate change
➤ destruction of mangroves as coastal areas are developed, which leads to coastal erosion and flooding
➤ farming in marginal areas and deforestation for firewood, which leads to desertification

Urbanisation

Rural–urban migration and rapid uncontrolled growth of cities lead to:
➤ the development of squatter settlements on areas at risk of landslides or flooding.

Informal housing like this is also vulnerable to earthquakes.

Poverty and politics

Disasters tend to have a greater impact in poorer countries:
➤ earthquakes have much higher death tolls in less developed countries which cannot afford the technology to build earthquake-proof buildings
➤ developing countries may not be able to afford to prepare for emergencies (e.g. Bangladesh relies on foreign aid to provide flood and cyclone shelters)
➤ if populations are poorly educated and have little access to communications technology it is harder to prepare them for disasters
➤ it is difficult to get aid to remote areas with poor infrastructure such as roads and bridges
➤ corrupt governments may misuse resources, making disasters worse (see the case study on Hurricane Jeanne) or prevent international aid reaching their populations (e.g. Myanmar (Burma) following the 2004 Asian tsunami)

The case study below on the Haitian floods shows how both physical and human factors made the hazard event of Hurricane Jeanne into a disaster in September 2004. Hurricane Jeanne was the weakest of the four 'savage storms' that year (see p. 23) and led to a major disaster only in Haiti.

Case study — Hurricane Jeanne, Haiti, 2004

In September 2004 more than 3,000 Haitians died in the flooding that followed Hurricane Jeanne even though it was only category 3 in strength. Seven months earlier the country's elected president had been deposed in a US-backed coup and armed uprising that left 300 dead.

A quarter of a million Haitians were left homeless and starving by the hurricane. Efforts to get food, water, blankets and medicines to them were hampered by remaining floodwaters or mudslides blocking the country's main north–south road.

Kofi Annan, the UN secretary general, called it a 'natural disaster', but this was largely a manmade catastrophe. The same storm killed only 20 people in Dominican Republic, which still has its forests. Haiti was once a lush tropical paradise, but poverty has forced Haitians to chop down tens of thousands of trees a year to make charcoal as their only affordable fuel. With no trees and no topsoil, there was nothing to stop rainwater from flooding down on to low-lying areas.

In the 1950s, 25% of Haiti was covered in thick verdant forest. Now, it is less than 2%. The country could be desert by the end of the decade unless the government takes reforestation seriously. There is a reforestation plan, but for every tree planted in recent years, seven were chopped down.

Much of the blame must go to the Duvalier family that ruled Haiti from the 1950s to the 1980s. Backed by successive US governments as a stabilising, anti-Communist influence within 160 km of Cuba, the Duvaliers created a society in which the wealthy lived in luxury and the poor had to chop down trees to survive.

*Figure 2.6
The relationship
between hazard,
disaster and
vulnerability*

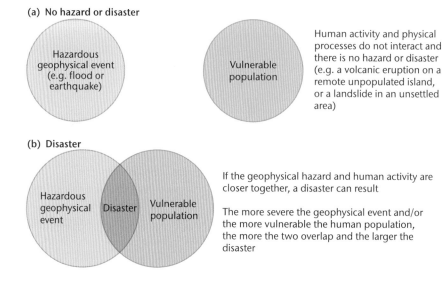

(a) No hazard or disaster

Hazardous geophysical event (e.g. flood or earthquake)

Vulnerable population

Human activity and physical processes do not interact and there is no hazard or disaster (e.g. a volcanic eruption on a remote unpopulated island, or a landslide in an unsettled area)

(b) Disaster

Hazardous geophysical event | Disaster | Vulnerable population

If the geophysical hazard and human activity are closer together, a disaster can result

The more severe the geophysical event and/or the more vulnerable the human population, the more the two overlap and the larger the disaster

Figure 2.6 reinforces the idea from Chapter 1 that a hazard only exists when *people* are threatened by an event, and that a disaster is the realisation of a hazard. Figure 2.7 shows the factors that lead to a hazard becoming a disaster. Note that many of these are human, not physical, factors.

*Figure 2.7
Processes
influencing the
development of a
hazard into a
disaster*

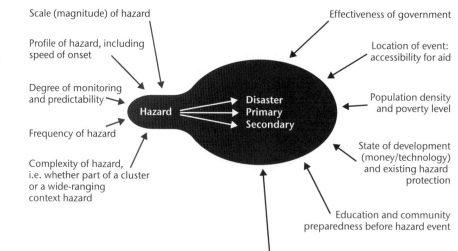

Scale (magnitude) of hazard

Profile of hazard, including speed of onset

Degree of monitoring and predictability

Frequency of hazard

Complexity of hazard, i.e. whether part of a cluster or a wide-ranging context hazard

Hazard → Disaster Primary Secondary

Effectiveness of government

Location of event: accessibility for aid

Population density and poverty level

State of development (money/technology) and existing hazard protection

Education and community preparedness before hazard event

Management during hazard event

Trends in human costs of disasters

Reported deaths

The number of people reported killed by disasters fell dramatically in the twentieth century because better prediction techniques and protection measures were developed (see the case study below for examples). As Figure 2.8 shows, the death rate has levelled off in recent years in spite of better disaster management. This is largely because of increasing numbers of hydro-meteorological hazard events which became disasters. There is a fluctuating but steady rate of around 25,000–40,000 deaths per year. However, some years are exceptions. Several huge disasters made 2004–05 unforgettable: the south Asia tsunami which killed an estimated 250,000, two record hurricane seasons, and the Kashmir earthquake which claimed 75,000 lives.

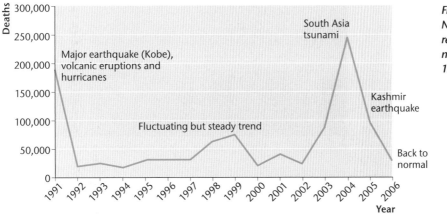

Figure 2.8
Number of people reported killed by natural disasters, 1991–2005

The case study below compares the responses of four countries to the 'savage storms' of 2004 — a series of hurricanes that crisscrossed the Caribbean. They range from Cuba, which combined the political efficiency of a totalitarian state with sound technology and outstanding community preparedness, to Haiti (the poorest Caribbean country) where, as described in the more detailed case study on p. 21, a political vacuum worsened the poor response.

Case study Caribbean 'savage storms', 2004

In 2004 the Caribbean was hit by a series of tropical storms including Hurricanes Charley, Fran, Ivan and Jeanne. Four responses to these disasters are described below.

Cuba

- Civil defence is part of national security.
- Cuba has a world-class meteorological institute which produces computer models and reaches people through all types of media.
- Within 48 hours of the storm arriving, the vulnerable can be contacted and escape routes planned.
- Within 12 hours, people can be evacuated to shelters using public transport.

- The population is educated about hurricane dangers.
- Cuba has well-organised systems at national, regional and local government levels.
- During Hurricanes Charley and Ivan, only four people died.

Jamaica

- Since Hurricane Gilbert in 1988, preparedness has paid off. In each parish, there are community disaster-response officers and plans.
- Maps have been drawn up showing resources and the homes of most vulnerable people.
- There are trained Red Cross emergency helpers,

well-equipped wardens and designated shelters.

■ 'Gilbert anniversary' practice drills and earthquake awareness events are held. However, this is a voluntary system so requires persuasion.

■ 14 people were killed in Hurricane Ivan.

Haiti

■ Haiti suffers problems with floods and landslides (see the case study on p. 21).

■ Political instability including a coup in 2004 has led to a lack of local government organisation.

■ Extreme poverty has led to a lack of resources (e.g. at the national meteorological centre).

■ The poor level of education makes it difficult to develop effective communications.

■ Up to 3,000 people were killed in Hurricane Jeanne.

Dominican Republic

■ The Dominican Republic is trying hard to respond to weather hazards.

Photograph 2.2 Sea front houses in Jamaica damaged by Hurricane Ivan

■ It has delivered maps and organised visits from Red Cross outreach workers to communities.

■ It has introduced a new civil defence system based on churches.

■ As the main threat is hurricanes, defences focus on wind hazards. But the main problem in Hurricane Jeanne was flooding (100 mm rain in 24 hours).

■ The country lacks short-wave radios and key equipment.

■ 20 people drowned during Hurricane Jeanne.

Number of people affected

The number of people *affected* by hazards and disasters shows an overall rising trend since 1991 (see Figure 2.9). Being 'affected' means surviving the disaster but losing your home, crops and animals, livelihood or health for a designated

Figure 2.9 Number of people reported affected by natural disasters, 1991–2005

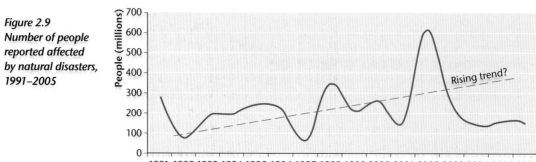

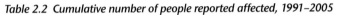

Table 2.2 Cumulative number of people reported affected, 1991–2005

Level of development	Flood	Wind storm	Drought*	Slide	Earthquake and tsunami	Volcanic eruption	Total
OECD	2,680,209	14,565,498	18,004,502	12,482	921,522	78,420	37,723,852
FSU and east Europe	8,823,124	4,051,295	11,416,841	71,801	1,285,530	0	25,848,223
Developing countries	1,885,951,169	382,712,627	736,645,786	2,630,620	43,198,839	2,127,117	3,035,655,591
Least developed countries	142,590,313	34,724,961	183,930,893	291,063	739,085	410,406	368,673,811
Countries not classified	398,961	891,082	607,940	511	111,527	0	2261,484
Total	2,0144,443,776	436,945,463	950,605,962	3,006,477	46,256,503	2,615,943	3,470,162,961

* Includes extreme temperatures.
Note: OECD: Organisation for Economic Cooperation and Development includes 30 developed countries.
FSU: Former Soviet Union

period (often 1–3 months). On average, 188 million people per year are affected by disasters — six times as many as are affected annually by conflicts.

There is a clear relationship between the numbers affected and the level of social and economic development in a country. Table 2.2 shows that the vast majority of people affected are in developing and least developed countries. The reasons for this, such as vulnerability of shanty towns in developing world cities, and the inability of poorer countries to prepare for disasters, were discussed earlier in this chapter. The table also shows how significant drought, floods and tropical storms (hurricanes) are.

Economic losses

Economic losses from disasters have grown exponentially (Figure 2.10), nearly tripling between 1980–89 and 1990–99. This is a far greater rate than the growth in the number of disasters. Note how insured losses have increased less dramatically than total economic losses.

*Figure 2.10
Economic losses in major natural disasters, 1950–2002*

Hurricane Andrew, Kobe earthquake

> 167

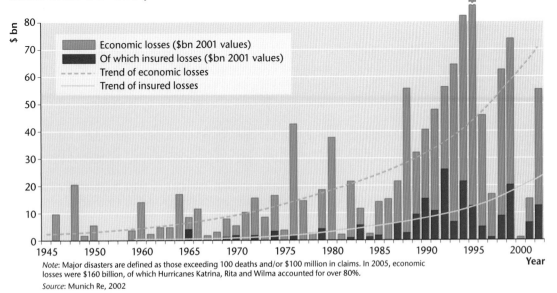

Note: Major disasters are defined as those exceeding 100 deaths and/or $100 million in claims. In 2005, economic losses were $160 billion, of which Hurricanes Katrina, Rita and Wilma accounted for over 80%.

Source: Munich Re, 2002

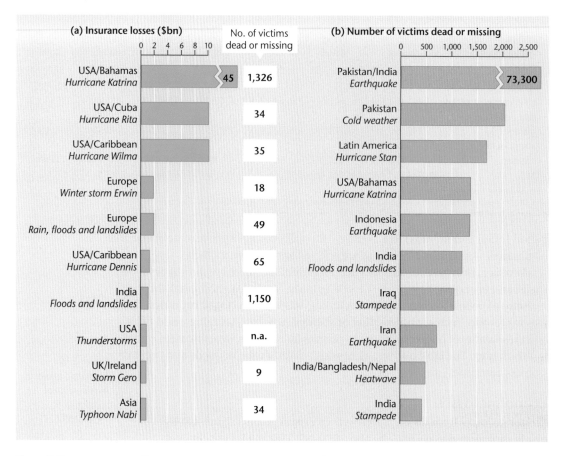

Figure 2.11
(a) Insurance losses
and (b) human
costs of recent mega
events

Figure 2.11 compares insurance losses and human costs of recent mega disasters. Note how the rankings of various events are completely different in the two graphs, reflecting the different impacts in developed and less developed countries.

However, it is too simple to say that developing countries suffer the greatest number of deaths and developed countries the greatest economic impact of disasters. The economic losses appear greater in richer countries because of the value of their economies and the cost of making good the damage. For example the insurance costs of repairing a house damaged by flood in the UK may be great, but in Bangladesh it is not uncommon for people to lose their crops, houses, and all their possessions in a flood, none of which will have been insured. Many developing countries depend on cash crops or tourism for their income, and both of these can be devastated by a natural disaster. Economic losses in poorer countries may be smaller in actual figures but far greater as a proportion of their annual GDP.

Economic losses are increasing faster than number of disasters, largely because of the growing economies of many recently and newly industrialising countries, especially in Asia.

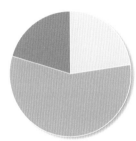

| Number of disasters | Number of people killed | Number of people affected | Estimated damage |

	High human development
	Medium human development
	Low human development

Global disaster trends: a summary

The main global trends discussed in this chapter are summarised in Figure 2.12, which shows the close link to levels of development. Natural disasters are more common in countries with a low and medium level of development. Many of these countries are in tropical areas which have monsoon rainfall or hurricanes.

Disasters cause more death and disruption in poor countries, which lack the resources and funds to develop high-tech prevention and prediction systems.

Damage in absolute economic terms remains highest in high-income countries, but in relative terms it is much more devastating for poorer countries.

Figure 2.12 Disasters related to human development levels

Review questions

1 Use the case study of Haiti to explain how physical and human factors contributed to 2004 becoming a year of disasters.

2 Describe and suggest reasons for the pattern shown in Figure 2.12.

3 Use Table 2.3 to examine the relationship between the magnitude of the 15 deadliest earthquakes since 1990 and the number of deaths they caused.

4 Make a hazard log for a term of your AS course. Record the type of event, its location and its impacts in terms of death and damage. What pattern of hazard occurrence do you notice? How and why do death tolls vary?

Table 2.3 Magnitude and death toll of 15 earthquakes, 1990–2005

Date	Location	Magnitude	Deaths
1990	Philippines	7.7	1,621
1990	Iran	7.4	50,000
1991	Northern India	6.8	2,000
1992	Flores, Indonesia	7.8	2,519
1993	India	6.2	9,748
1995	Kobe, Japan	6.9	5,530
1997	Northern Iran	7.3	1,572
1998	Afghanistan/Tajikistan	6.6	4,000
1999	Taiwan	7.7	2,297
1999	Turkey	7.6	17,118
2001	India	7.7	20,023
2002	Afghanistan	6.1	1,000
2003	Southeast Iran	6.6	30,000
2004	Offshore Indonesia	9.0	283,106
2005	Northern Sumatra, Indonesia	8.7	1,313

Global hazard patterns

Why are some places more hazardous and disaster-prone than others?

By the end of this chapter you should have:
➤ *analysed the distribution of the world's major geophysical and hydro-meteorological hazards*
➤ *understood that disaster hotspots develop where two or more hazards occur in vulnerable places — this understanding is supported by two compulsory case studies of the Philippines and the Californian coast*
➤ *assessed how hazard prone your local region is*

The distribution of geophysical hazards

The three main geophysical hazards are earthquakes, volcanoes and tsunamis. A knowledge of **plate tectonics** is fundamental to understanding the occurrence of geophysical hazards (see the key concepts box).

Earthquakes

*Figure 3.1
Distribution of
earthquakes*

As can be seen from Figure 3.1, the main earthquake zones are clustered along plate boundaries. The most powerful earthquakes are associated with destructive or conservative boundaries.

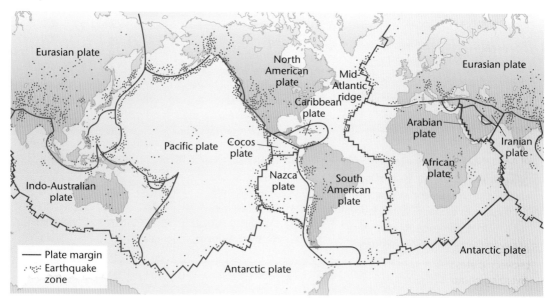

Plate tectonics

According to plate tectonics theory the **lithosphere** or Earth's crust is divided into seven major sections or **plates**, and a number of smaller ones (Figure 3.1). Some plates are oceanic (e.g. the Pacific plate), others continental. These plates float on the underlying semi-molten mantle known as the **asthenosphere**. There are three major types of plate boundary — constructive, destructive and conservative — each of which has particular geophysical hazards associated with it.

Hotspots from within the asthenosphere generate thermal convection currents which cause **magma** (molten material) to rise towards the Earth's surface. This continuous process forms new crust along the line of **constructive boundaries**, where the plates are diverging.

At the same time, older crust is being destroyed at **destructive boundaries**, where plates converge. The type of activity here depends on whether both plates are continental, both plates are oceanic or (as in Figure 3.2) an oceanic plate is being subducted or dragged down beneath a lighter continental plate.

At **conservative boundaries**, two plates slide past each other and there is no creation or destruction of crust.

The type of movement and the degree of activity at the plate margins almost totally controls the distribution, frequency and magnitude of earthquakes and volcanic eruptions.

Figure 3.2 Cross-section across oceanic/continental plate convergence at a destructive plate boundary

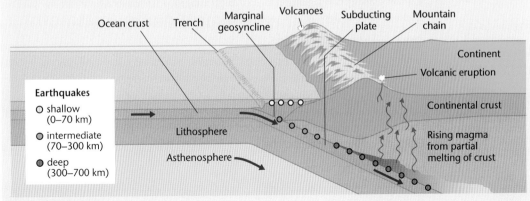

Earthquakes
○ shallow (0–70 km)
◓ intermediate (70–300 km)
● deep (300–700 km)

Labels: Ocean crust, Trench, Marginal geosyncline, Volcanoes, Subducting plate, Mountain chain, Continent, Volcanic eruption, Continental crust, Rising magma from partial melting of crust, Lithosphere, Asthenosphere

Destructive plate boundaries

Destructive boundaries where oceanic crust is being subducted beneath a continental plate (Figure 3.1 and Philippines case study, p. 38), or where two oceanic plates collide, produce a full range of earthquake types (shallow, intermediate and deep). The force of compression as the plates meet causes stresses in the crust, and when the pressure is suddenly released, the ground surface immediately above shakes violently.

The point at which pressure release occurs within the crust is known as the earthquake focus, and the point immediately above that at the Earth's surface is the epicentre.

At destructive boundaries where two continental plates are colliding to produce fold mountains, shallow, highly damaging earthquakes occur. These present a hazard risk over a wide area in countries such as India and Iran.

Constructive plate boundaries

Constructive boundaries (where oceanic plates are moving apart) are associated with large numbers of shallow, low-magnitude earthquakes as magma rises. Most are submarine (except in places like Iceland) and so pose little hazard to people.

Conservative plate boundaries

Conservative boundaries, where there is lateral crust movement, produce frequent shallow earthquakes, sometimes of high magnitude: for example, along the San Andreas fault system of the western USA (see California case study, p. 38).

Other earthquakes

A small minority of earthquakes occur *within* plates, usually involving the reactivation of ancient fault lines, for example the Church Stretton fault in Shropshire.

Occasionally earthquakes can result from human actions such as dam and reservoir building, which increase the weight and therefore stress on the land. These occur where there is no record of earthquakes. In Killari, northern India, in 1993, an earthquake caused by a dam killed 10,000 people.

Earthquake hazards

➤ *Primary hazards* result from ground movement and ground shaking. Surface seismic waves can cause buildings and other infrastructure (e.g. pipes for water and gas supply) to collapse.
➤ *Secondary hazards* include soil liquefaction, landslides, avalanches, tsunamis and exposure to adverse weather. These can add significantly to the death toll.

Volcanic eruptions

The world's active volcanoes are found in three tectonic situations: at constructive and destructive plate boundaries, and at hotspots. The type of tectonic situation determines the composition of the magma and therefore the degree of explosivity of the eruption, which is a key factor in the degree of hazard risk.

Figure 3.3 shows the global distribution of active volcanoes, although hazard risk can also come from dormant volcanoes which have not erupted in living memory (e.g. Mt St Helens).

Constructive plate boundaries

Most of the magma that reaches the Earth's surface wells up at oceanic ridges such as the mid-Atlantic. These volcanoes are mostly on the sea floor and do not represent a major hazard to people except where they emerge above sea level to form islands such as Iceland. Rift valleys occur where the continental crust is being 'stretched'. The East African rift valley has a line of 14 active volcanoes, some of which can produce dangerous eruptions (e.g. Mt Nyragongo in the Democratic Republic of Congo, 2002).

Destructive plate boundaries

Some 80% of the world's active volcanoes occur along destructive boundaries. Soufrière Hills in Montserrat, West Indies is an example of a volcano formed where two ocean plates collide. When oceanic plates are subducted beneath continental plates, explosive volcanoes such as Mt St Helens are formed. The 'ring of fire' around the Pacific has many such volcanoes (see the Philippines case study, p. 38).

Photograph 3.1 Mt St Helens erupting in 1980

Figure 3.3 Global distribution of active volcanoes

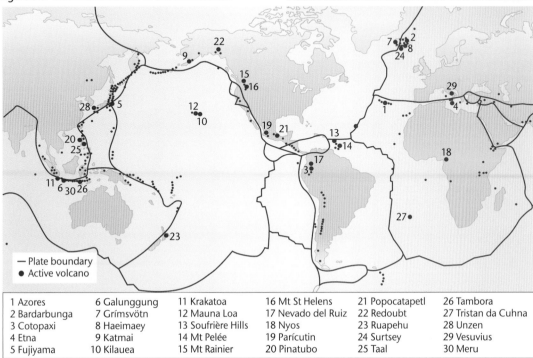

1 Azores	6 Galunggung	11 Krakatoa	16 Mt St Helens	21 Popocatapetl	26 Tambora
2 Bardarbunga	7 Grímsvötn	12 Mauna Loa	17 Nevado del Ruiz	22 Redoubt	27 Tristan da Cuhna
3 Cotopaxi	8 Haeimaey	13 Soufrière Hills	18 Nyos	23 Ruapehu	28 Unzen
4 Etna	9 Katmai	14 Mt Pelée	19 Parícutin	24 Surtsey	29 Vesuvius
5 Fujiyama	10 Kilauea	15 Mt Rainier	20 Pinatubo	25 Taal	30 Meru

Hotspots

Hotspots are localised areas of the lithosphere which have an unusually high heat flow, and where magma rises to the surface as a **plume**. Hawaii is an example. As a lithospheric plate moves over the hotspot, a chain of volcanoes is created.

Volcanic hazards

Apart from the local impacts of lava flows the most catastrophic impacts of volcanoes are pyroclastic flows, ash falls, tsunamis and mudflows.

The distribution of slides

Slides include a variety of rapid mass movements, such as rock slides, debris flows, snow avalanches, and rainfall- and earthquake-induced landslides.

Landslides

Landslides are the seventh biggest killer with over 1,400 deaths per year, ranking above both volcanoes and drought. Areas prone to landslides are shown in Figure 3.4. Most are mountainous, and experience landslides after abnormally heavy rain and/or seismic activity.

Human factors also play a part. Deforestation of hillsides in southeast Asia and building on hillslopes in Hong Kong have both led to widespread slides following rain.

Figure 3.4
Global distribution of landslide hotspots

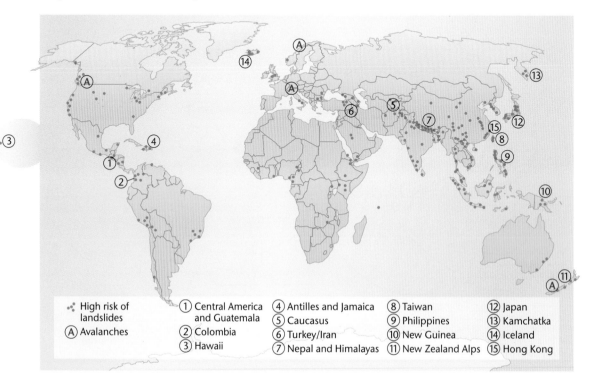

•⁚ High risk of landslides	① Central America and Guatemala	④ Antilles and Jamaica	⑧ Taiwan	⑫ Japan
Ⓐ Avalanches	② Colombia	⑤ Caucasus	⑨ Philippines	⑬ Kamchatka
	③ Hawaii	⑥ Turkey/Iran	⑩ New Guinea	⑭ Iceland
		⑦ Nepal and Himalayas	⑪ New Zealand Alps	⑮ Hong Kong

Snow avalanches

Snow avalanches are concentrated in high mountainous areas such as the Southern Alps of New Zealand or the Rockies of North America (see Figure 3.4). Avalanches tend to occur on slopes steeper than 35°.

An average of 40 deaths a year in Europe and over 100 in North America are caused by avalanches. Recent research has suggested that global warming may be increasing avalanche occurrence, although trends in deaths have slowed because of effective management.

The distribution of hydro-meteorological hazards

These extreme weather hazards are widespread in their distribution, growing in frequency and increasingly unpredictable in their locations.

Drought

Drought has a dispersed pattern — over one-third of the world's land surface has some level of drought exposure (see Figure 3.5). This includes 70% of the world's people and agricultural value, which means that drought has an effect on global food security.

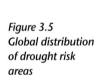

Key term

Inter-tropical convergence zone
A zone of low atmospheric pressure near the equator. This migrates seasonally.

Causes of drought

The causes of drought include the following:
➤ *Variations in the movement of the* **inter-tropical convergence zone** *(ITCZ). As the ITCZ moves north and south through Africa, it brings a band of seasonal rain. In some years, high-pressure zones expand and block the rain-bearing*

Figure 3.5
Global distribution of drought risk areas

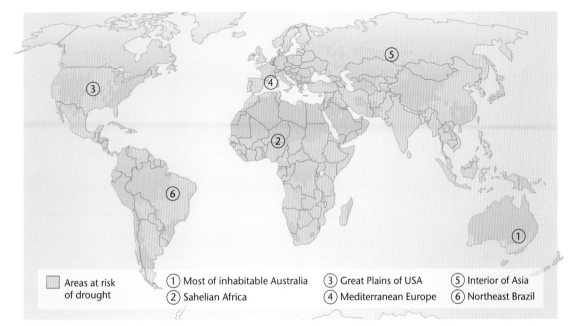

▦ Areas at risk of drought	① Most of inhabitable Australia	③ Great Plains of USA	⑤ Interior of Asia
	② Sahelian Africa	④ Mediterranean Europe	⑥ Northeast Brazil

winds. In southern Ethiopia and Somalia, where farmers depend for food on rain-fed agriculture, famines may result if the summer rains never arrive.

➤ *El Niño* can bring major changes to rainfall patterns (see p. 19). In particular (as in 2006), it can bring drought conditions to Indonesia and Australia.

➤ *Changes in mid-latitude depression tracks.* In temperate regions, depressions bring large amounts of rainfall. However, if blocking anticyclones form and persist, depressions are forced to track further north, leading to very dry conditions. Droughts in the UK and France (1976, 1989–92, 1995, 2003 and 2006) as well as in the US midwest in the 1930s were all related to this cause.

Drought hazards

Drought leads to failure of crops and loss of livestock, wildfires, duststorms and famine. It has economic impacts on agriculture and water-related businesses in developed countries.

Flooding

Flooding is a frequent hazard and is evident in some 33% of the world's area, which is inhabited by over 80% of its population (Figure 3.6). Regional-scale, high-magnitude floods are frequent events in India/Bangladesh and China.

Causes of flooding

➤ By far the most common cause is excessive rainfall related to atmospheric processes, including monsoon rainfall and cyclones. In temperate climates, a series of depressions sometimes brings prolonged high rainfall.

➤ Intense rainfall sometimes associated with thunderstorms can lead to localised flash flooding. These sudden floods can have a devastating impact.

Figure 3.6
Global distribution of flood risk areas

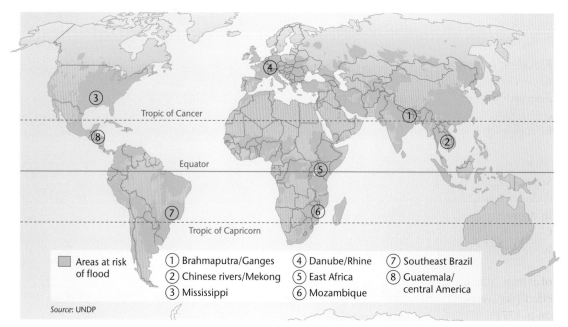

Areas at risk of flood

① Brahmaputra/Ganges ④ Danube/Rhine ⑦ Southeast Brazil
② Chinese rivers/Mekong ⑤ East Africa ⑧ Guatemala/central America
③ Mississippi ⑥ Mozambique

Source: UNDP

Pers-Anders Petterson/UNEP/Still Pictures

▶ The El Niño Southern Oscillation can bring devastating floods, as in Mozambique in 1997 and 2006 (Photograph 3.2).

▶ Rapid snowmelt can add water to an already swollen river system.

Photograph 3.2
Flooding in
Mozambique

Flooding hazards

In developing countries flooding may lead to deaths by drowning and disease, destruction of food crops and infrastructure and loss of homes. In developed countries it disrupts transport and infrastructure, damages livelihoods and creates high insurance costs.

Storms

Storms include tropical cyclones, mid-latitude storms and tornadoes. Tropical cyclones (hurricanes in the Atlantic) are violent storms between 200 and 700 km in diameter. They occur in the latitudes 5–20° north and south of the equator. Once generated, cyclones tend to move westward and are at their height of destruction in the locations shown in Figure 3.7.

Tropical cyclones or hurricanes will only occur over warm ocean (over 26°C) of at least 70 m depth at least 5°N or 5°S of the equator in order that the Coriolis effect (very weak at the equator) can bring about rotation of air (see Figure 15.8 on p. 177).

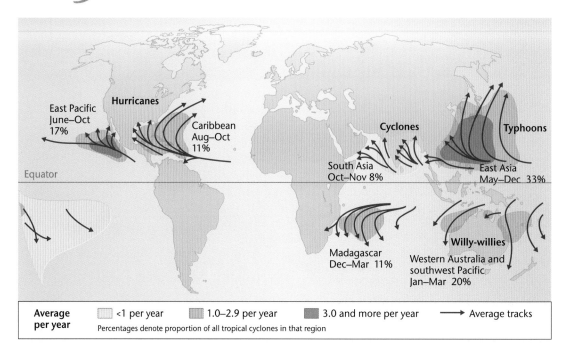

Average per year ☐ <1 per year ▨ 1.0–2.9 per year ▧ 3.0 and more per year → Average tracks

Percentages denote proportion of all tropical cyclones in that region

Figure 3.7
Global distribution
and seasons of
tropical cyclones

Tropical storm hazards

Storms cause damage in several ways, including heavy rain (leading to floods and mudslides), high wind velocity and very low central pressure (leading to storm surges and coastal flooding). They can be devastating (e.g. Hurricane Katrina).

Disaster hotspots

Identifying and defining hazard hotspots

Figure 3.8
Identification of a
hazard hotspot

In 2001 the World Bank's Disaster Management Facility (now the Hazard Management Unit) together with the Center of Hazard and Risk Management at Columbia University began a project to identify disaster hotspots, not only at a country level but within a country. These hotspots are multiple hazard zones.

Exposure to risk from two or more hazard groups (may be from one or more types within a group)

Result
Hotspots are likely to be where plate boundaries intersect with major storm belts in areas of high human concentration in low or medium developed countries.

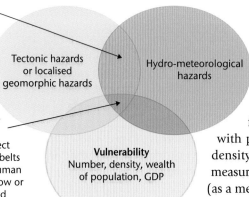

The project assessed the risk of death and damage. The level of risk was estimated by combining exposure to the six major natural hazards (earthquakes, volcanoes, landslides, floods, drought and storms). Historical vulnerability (from data for the last 30 years) was combined with potential vulnerability based on size, density and poverty of the population (as measures of mortality) and GDP per unit area (as a measure of potential economic damage). Figure 3.8 summarises this.

The World Bank's global risk analysis was noteworthy for its use of geographic information systems (GIS) techniques. Grid squares of 2.5 minutes of latitude and longitude were used as a base for various estimates of hazard probability, occurrence and extent, and these were then related to the economic value of the land, its population and population density, and vulnerability profiles. As the aim was to identify disaster as opposed to hazard hotspots, only cells with a minimum population of 105 or densities above 5 per km^2 were entered on the database of around 4 million cells.

When answering questions on multiple hazard zones, it is sensible to select data for a country that is compact and uniform in terms of hazard risk and vulnerability, such as the Philippines (see the compulsory case study on p. 38).

Table 3.1 lists the countries most at risk from multiple hazards.

Table 3.1 Top ten countries most at risk from multiple hazards

Risk of mortality	Risk of economic losses (as % of GDP)
Taiwan	Taiwan
El Salvador	Dominican Republic
Costa Rica	Jamaica
Philippines	El Salvador
Dominica	Guatemala
Guatemala	Japan
Japan	Costa Rica
Indonesia	Philippines
Jamaica	Colombia
Bangladesh	Bangladesh

Source: World Bank

Managing a hazard hotspot

The identification of multiple hazard zones has major implications for development and investment planning, and for disaster preparedness and loss prevention.

However, many hazard-prone areas have long lists of priorities more immediate than risk management, such as poverty reduction or fighting HIV/AIDS, and may be unable to afford the technology required to cope with multiple hazards.

Figure 3.9 locates some of the key disaster hotspots. The two compulsory case studies which follow illustrate the features of multiple hazard zones.

Figure 3.9 Location of areas subject to multiple hazard risk

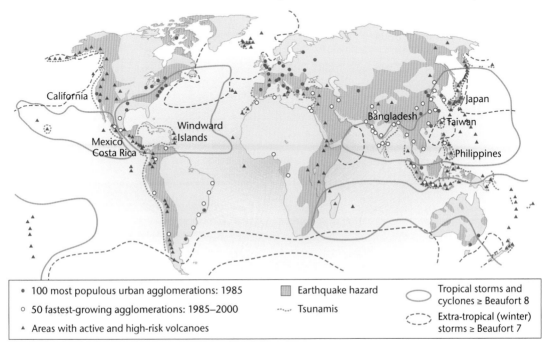

- • 100 most populous urban agglomerations: 1985
- ○ 50 fastest-growing agglomerations: 1985–2000
- ▲ Areas with active and high-risk volcanoes

▨ Earthquake hazard
⋯ Tsunamis

⬭ Tropical storms and cyclones ≥ Beaufort 8
⬭ Extra-tropical (winter) storms ≥ Beaufort 7

Disaster hotspots: the Philippines

The Philippines, an island arc in southeast Asia, consists of over 7,000 islands, many very small, concentrated at latitudes between 5 and 20°N of the equator. It lies in a belt of tropical cyclones (typhoons), and astride an active plate boundary. The dense oceanic Philippines plate is being subducted beneath the Eurasian plate. The country experiences a tropical monsoon climate and is subject to heavy rainfall. Flooding can lead to landslides because of the deforestation of many hillsides.

The Philippines is a lower-middle-income country which is developing fast. With a rapidly increasing young population, average population densities for the whole country are high at 240 people per km^2, with up to 2,000 people per km^2 in the megacity of Manila. Many of these people are very poor and live on the coast, making them vulnerable to locally generated tsunamis and typhoon-generated storm surges. On average, about ten typhoons occur each season, especially in Luzon.

In response, the government has established several organisations to carry out forecasting, warning, hazard risk assessment, disaster training and education. These include the National Disaster Co-ordinating Council; Philippine Atmospheric, Geophysical and Astronomical Services; and the Philippine Institute of Volcanology and Seismology. Land-use planning and building regulation, and structural programmes of defences help people to survive the huge range of hazards facing them.

Table 3.2 Disasters in the Philippines, 1905–2007

	Number of events	Total killed	Total injured	Homeless total	Affected total	Damage ($m)	Example
Drought	6	8	0	0	6 million	64,000	April 1998, 2.5 million severely affected
Earthquake	21	9,580	13,051	3,985	2.25 million	844,485	Manila (1990) 6,000 killed
Flood	72	2,716	570	500,000	11.25 million	446,361	July 1972 2.7 million affected
Slide	25	2,604	381	23,000	310,663	12,258	February 2006 1,126 killed
Volcano	20	2,996	1,188	79,000	1.5 million	23,961	Taal (July 1911) 1,335 killed Pinatubo (July 1991) 700 killed
Tsunami	5	69	0	0	5,250	6,000	Worst tsunami in 1976
Typhoon	241	35,983	29,178	6.25 million	86 million	9,018,574	November 1991 6,000 killed

Disaster hotspots: the California coast

The state of California contains nearly 40 million people and has an economy the size of a high-income country. However, it suffers from a vast range of hazards, including huge risks from geophysical hazards (especially earthquakes) as well as a range of atmospheric hazards such as fog, drought and associated wildfires, and major impacts from the El Niño Southern Oscillation. The hazardous zone is concentrated along the San Andreas fault, which runs parallel to the coast.

Table 3.3 Hazards of the California coast: summary

Hazard	Causes	Impacts
Earthquakes (Figure 3.10)	A network of active faults (e.g. San Andreas fault) underlies the Los Angeles region and the San Francisco Bay Area (e.g. Hayward and San Gregoria faults).	The soft basin sediments in Los Angeles lead to rapid shaking. Five major earthquakes were recorded in the last 100 years. The San Francisco Bay Area has experienced several large earthquakes too.
River flooding	Winter storms, especially during El Niño years, lead to floods in the Los Angeles and San Gabriel rivers, exacerbated by deforested hillsides.	Rivers are now heavily channelised, but floods can still take place, usually between October and January.
Coastal flooding	The area around Long Beach, which is subsiding, sometimes floods in heavy storms.	Increasing threat with rising sea levels in the future.
Drought	A potential summer problem in Mediterranean climate especially in southern California, but more marked in La Niña years.	Exacerbated by lack of water supplies in Los Angeles for the rising population.
Wildfires/ bushfires	As Los Angeles expands into rural areas, wildfires are a major hazard, especially during the dry Santa Ana wind periods.	Likely to be an increasing hazard as people move out to hills on the fringe of Los Angeles and south of San Francisco.
Landslides/ mudslides	Landslides take place in heavy winter storms where hillsides have been burnt by wildfire and eroded. Also a risk along the coast near Malibu and Santa Monica.	A growing risk as climate becomes more unpredictable in all coastal areas.
Fog and smog	Advection fog occurs when cool air from cold offshore current drifts inland and meets warm air (especially in summer). Climate conditions combine with car pollution to generate photo-chemical smog, which collects in the basin.	A mega city-wide hazard, especially in late summer and autumn.

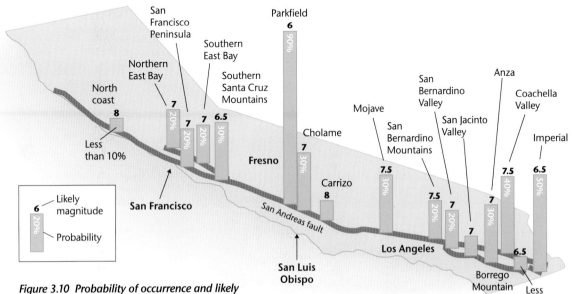

Figure 3.10 Probability of occurrence and likely magnitude of earthquakes on the California coast

California is home to the megacity of Los Angeles, San Francisco and San Diego. Much of the coastline is 'crowded' as various land uses compete for prime space. This human–physical interface increases the danger from hazards, and only sophisticated management prevents California from becoming a disaster zone (recent major events such as the Lomo Prieta earthquake of 1989 led to very few deaths). Nevertheless California contains an underclass of around 3.5 million people, many of them semi-legal migrants, a large proportion of whom live in hazardous locations.

Table 3.3 summarises the range of hazards experienced along the Californian coastal zone.

Investigating the hazard risk of your local area

The UK is one of the most hazard-free parts of the world, but research in your local area may still yield a surprising number of past hazard events. You can research the history of hazard events in your local area using historic newspapers (the public library may have a local history archive), searching online and interviewing older residents. Look for evidence of past hazard events in the local environment, and consider how climate change might affect your local area.

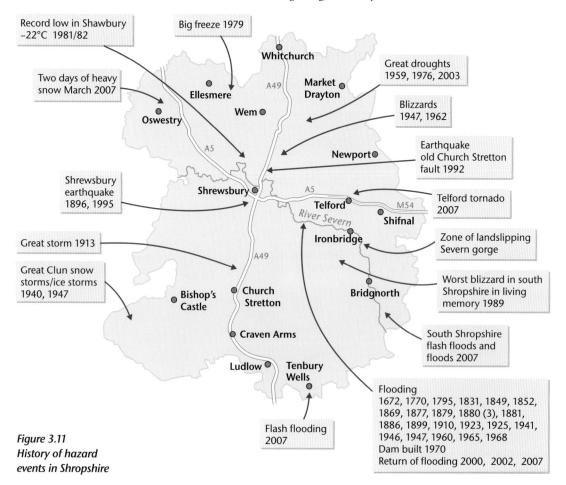

Figure 3.11
History of hazard events in Shropshire

Researching the history of local hazard events

Figure 3.11 shows the result of a survey of hazard events in historic newspapers and other documents at the Shropshire County Records Office. The county is not hazard prone and certainly could not be considered a multiple hazard zone, but the research revealed a surprising range of events.

The hazards are essentially of four main types:

➤ *Flooding* from major rivers such as the Severn is and always has been a major hazard in Shropshire. It has traditionally occurred in a measured sequence, with up to 18 hours' warning, in October and November (see the case study on p. 201). Between 1970 and 2000 flooding was eliminated by catchment management in the upper Severn (the building of Clyweddog dam and Melverley Washlands basin). However, the floods returned with a vengeance in 2000, and in summer 2007 flooding affected the whole county. A series of flash floods (e.g. Tenbury Wells) and small stream floods (e.g. the Corve at Ludlow) resulted from torrential rainfall of up to 20 mm in 3 hours, and river flooding followed. Associated land slipping along the Severn gorge also occurs at regular intervals.

➤ *Earthquakes* ranging from 4 to 5 on the Richter scale result from movement along historic fault lines, such as the Church Stretton fault. These minor earthquakes cause damage to a few buildings and occasional minor injury but no deaths.

➤ *Snowstorms and droughts.* Shropshire's continental position within the UK leads to harsh winters and severe snowfalls. Shawbury is renowned for its record cold temperatures. Shropshire also experiences heatwaves and droughts in summer, often (as in 1976) when the whole of the country falls under the influence of a blocking high or anticyclone. The extremely cold winters seem to be a waning hazard, although in March 2007 there were heavy snowfalls for 2 days.

➤ *Storms and tornadoes.* The decline of the previous group of hazards may be linked to the expansion of other groups of hazards associated with climate change. These include the violent storms and flash flooding in Tenbury Wells (summer 2007) and the Telford tornado.

Review questions

1 Explain how plate tectonics can help our understanding of the distribution of either earthquakes or volcanic eruptions.
2 Which of the three hydro-meteorological hazards do you think threatens the greatest disasters: drought, floods, or tropical cyclones and storms? Give your reasons.
3 Compare and contrast the two disaster hotspots of the Philippines and the Californian coast in terms of their range and management of hazards.
4 Identify hazard events which have occurred in your local area. Which hazard event is most likely to be repeated? How do you rate the risks of such an event?

Climate change and its causes

Is global warming a recent short-term phenomenon or should it be seen as part of long-term climate change?

By the end of this chapter you should have:
- ➤ *examined the evidence for long-, medium- and short-term climate change*
- ➤ *explored both natural and human causes of climate change*
- ➤ *assessed the evidence for and against the view that current climate change (global warming) is unprecedented, and largely the result of human activity*

Key terms

Climate The average conditions of precipitation, temperature, pressure and wind measured over a 30-year period.

Climate change Any long-term trend or shift in climate detected by a sustained shift in the average value for any climatic element (e.g. rainfall, drought, storminess).

Back in time: long-term climate change

Ice cores

The best evidence of long-term **climate change** comes from Greenland and Antarctic ice cores. Cores removed from ice sheets reveal layers going down through the ice. Rather like tree rings, each layer records a season of snowfall, buried and compressed by later falls.

The 3,200 metre East Antarctic core records the **climate** of the last 800,000 years. Air bubbles trapped in the ice contain atmospheric carbon dioxide and the ice itself preserves a record of oxygen isotopes. Figure 4.1 illustrates how low concentrations of carbon dioxide occur naturally during glacial (cold) periods, and high concentrations during interglacial (warm) periods (like the one we are in now). It is clear that atmospheric carbon dioxide levels are higher now (in the Holocene interglacial) than at any time for over half a million years. Based on this evidence alone, can we really expect our climate to stay the same?

Figure 4.1 Atmospheric carbon dioxide concentration measured from the Vostok ice core, also from East Antarctica

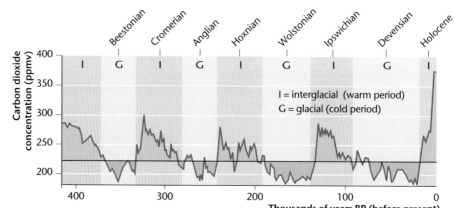

Edexcel AS Geography

Climate timescales

Climate change can be assessed across short, medium and long timescales. Short-term (recent) climate change has been measured over the last few decades using sensitive, accurate equipment such as satellites and ocean temperature buoys. The medium-term (historical) timescale covers changes over the last few thousand years. Since around 1850, direct measurements of climate variables have been made using thermometers and rain gauges, but prior to this most climate data come from proxies, which indicate climate but do not directly measure it. Long-term climate change has occurred on geological timescales, over several hundreds of thousands to millions of years. Evidence for this most often comes from ice cores. Figure 4.2 illustrates these three timescales of climate change.

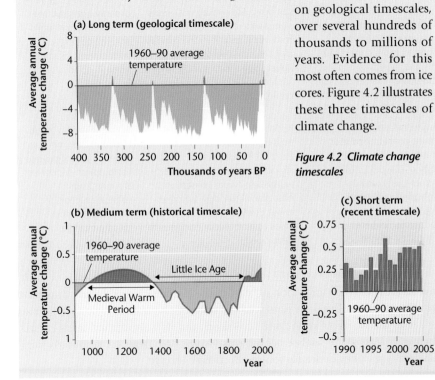

Figure 4.2 Climate change timescales

Oceans

The world's oceans play a key role in climate regulation. Oceans act as carbon dioxide sinks, removing carbon dioxide from the atmosphere. Evaporation from oceans is vital for cloud formation, and maintaining precipitation levels. Ocean currents transfer warm water from the equator towards the poles, and this 'evens out' temperature extremes between the poles and the equator. Surface currents are driven by winds, as part of the global circulation. Deep ocean currents form the **thermohaline circulation** which flows between the oceans.

Key term

Thermohaline circulation
A global system of surface and deep-water ocean currents, driven by differences in temperature (thermo-) and salinity (-haline) between areas of the oceans. An alternative name is the ocean conveyor (see p. 52).

Table 4.1 Summary of evidence for long-term climate change

Evidence	How the technique works	Past climate?	Reliability?
Carbon dioxide levels	Carbon dioxide is sampled from bubbles trapped in ice cores, from Greenland and Antarctica. This allows a time series of carbon dioxide levels in the atmosphere to be reconstructed.	Carbon dioxide levels have varied naturally between 180 ppm and 280 ppm over the last 800,000 years. The 2007 level, 383 parts per million, is unprecedented over the last 800,000 years.	The number of carbon dioxide sequences that correlate well with each other suggests that this is a reliable record.
Oxygen isotope record	Oxygen isotopes are sampled from ice cores and ocean sediment cores. The ratio of oxygen 16 to oxygen 18 isotopes is a good indicator of past sea levels. During glacial periods, oxygen 16 was evaporated more easily from the oceans, which became enriched with oxygen 18. Ice from glacial periods is enriched with oxygen 16.	The oxygen isotope record and carbon dioxide record correlate well. When carbon dioxide levels were low, so was sea level. Around 20,000 years ago, as ice sheets reached their maximum extent in the glacial climate, sea level was 130 m lower than today. Landforms such as raised beaches also record past sea levels.	As with carbon dioxide sequences, the number of oxygen isotope records that broadly agree on sea-level changes is high, and the correlation with carbon dioxide levels is good.
Pollen	Pollen, extracted from sediment cores in peat bogs and lake beds, records the ecology of the past. Pollen grains are preserved in waterlogged sediments. Different plant species have characteristic pollen shapes, which can be identified.	Pollen sequences show that ecosystems have changed in the past in response to climate change. In the UK, tundra ecosystems were present in past glacial periods, whereas forest gradually colonised areas as interglacial conditions developed.	Accurate pollen reconstructions rely on good preservation of pollen. Long pollen sequences are rare, and vegetation change may 'lag' behind climate change.

Ocean currents, especially the role of the Gulf Stream and North Atlantic Drift, have recently become an important part of the climate change debate. The 2004 film *The Day After Tomorrow* portrayed the northern hemisphere plunged into an ice age as the North Atlantic Drift 'turned off' and its warming influence ceased. There is at least some science behind this (see p. 52). Table 4.1 summarises the different types of evidence for long-term climate change.

Medium-term climate change

Historical and palaeo-environmental evidence

Proxy records are used to reconstruct climate before the start of instrumental records. These include paintings, poems, record books, diaries and journals which record weather at the time. The Thames froze over regularly between 1500 and 1850, as shown in Photograph 4.2.

Since the mid-fourteenth century, the date of the grape harvest in the Burgundy region of France has been

Key terms

Little Ice Age A cool period in Europe (and possibly globally), in which many Alpine glaciers advanced. It lasted from around 1400 until 1850.

Medieval Warm Period A period of unusually warm North Atlantic climate lasting from around 800 to 1400.

Photograph 4.1 A frost fair on the Thames in 1677

TopFoto

scrupulously recorded. This historical sequence of grape ripening dates is a proxy record, and has been used to indicate past climate (see Figure 4.3). The graph shows evidence of significant warming since 1900, as well as the **Little Ice Age** and **Medieval Warm Period**.

Table 4.2 Summary of evidence for medium-term climate change

Evidence	How the technique works	Past climate?	Reliability?
Historical records	Analysing paintings, photo-graphs and sequences such as the grape harvest data in Figure 4.3. Written accounts, such as the Greenland sagas, are also useful records.	These records may indicate past climates. Evidence points to both a colder period (the Little Ice Age) and a warmer period (the Medieval Warm Period) in the historical past.	These sources did not set out to record climate, and must be used with care. They are usually local, and it is difficult to use them to generalise.
Tree rings	Many trees are sensitive to annual changes in temperature, sunlight and precipitation. The thickness of annual growth rings records climatic conditions.	Wide rings reflect good growing conditions, narrow rings periods of climate stress. Long-term sequences of tree rings can be obtained from living trees, such as the Bristlecone Pines of the western USA (some specimens are 4,500 years old).	The accuracy of the tree ring record is good, but it is localised. It is difficult to determine the relative importance of temperature, precipitation, sunlight and wind.
Retreating glaciers	Valley glaciers, in areas such as the Alps, grow and shrink in response to climate. These changes can be tracked by examining old paintings, photographs and maps, and taking direct measurements of snout or moraine positions.	Evidence suggests that the majority of glaciers reached their most recent maximum extent in 1850. This correlates well with the Little Ice Age, and the colder temperatures in the seventeenth and eighteenth centuries. Most glaciers have retreated since 1850.	Reliable measurements extend back to around 1880; before this the record is patchy and relies more on proxy historical records.

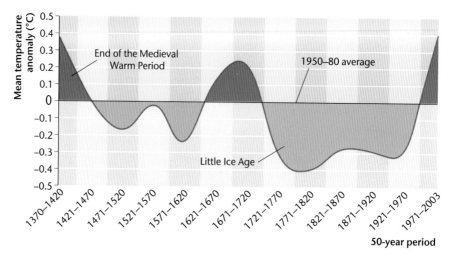

*Figure 4.3
A climate proxy:
temperature
anomalies
reconstructed from
grape harvest dates,
Burgundy, France,
1370–2003*

Proxy records need to be used with care. The date of the grape harvest could have been affected by non-climate factors such as conflict or diseased vines. It may also be hard to know the relative importance of temperature, precipitation, sunlight hours or a combination of factors in influencing grape harvest dates.

Table 4.2 on p. 45 summarises the evidence for medium-term climate change.

Global warming? Recent climate change

The instrumental record

Instrumental records from weather stations exist for the last 100 years or so. They show that near-surface air temperatures rose by 0.74°C between 1900 and 2000. The warming trend has been almost constant since 1960, and 11 of the world's 12 hottest years since 1850 occurred in the decade 1995–2006.

The oceans have warmed to depths of 3,000 m. Warmer oceans cause problems for temperature-sensitive organisms such as coral. There is growing concern about ocean acidification. Measurements suggest that the pH of the oceans has decreased from 8.25 to 8.14 since 1750. The most likely cause is increased levels of dissolved carbon dioxide.

The instrumental record also demonstrates that global sea level has risen. Between 1961 and 2003 it rose by 1.8 mm per year, rising to 3.1 mm per year between 1993 and 2003. Most of this rise is attributed to **thermal expansion**, with water from melting glaciers and ice caps, so far, having a lesser impact on sea level.

> **Key term**
>
> **Thermal expansion**
> The increased volume of the oceans as a result of their higher water temperature, leading to sea-level rise. It accounted for about 60% of sea-level rise in the late twentieth century.

Ice response

Ice is a key indicator for climate scientists. Ice is found in many forms — as valley glaciers in the Alps, as ice caps on mountain ranges, as ice sheets in Greenland and Antarctica, as floating ice shelves, and as sea ice that forms in winter in high latitudes. In a warming world, ice might be expected to melt. Figure 4.4 summarises recent evidence of ice response to climate change.

Melting of Greenland ice sheet has increased by 16% since 1979. NASA satellites measured record melting in 2006: 239 km³ of ice. Many glaciers, which drain the ice sheet, have doubled speed of flow since late 1990s

NASA satellite data show floating Arctic sea ice declining by 8.5% per decade. Arctic Ocean could be ice free in summer by 2060 if trends identified since 1979 continue

Valley glaciers thinning by more than 1 m yr⁻¹

World Glacier Monitoring Service reported in 2007 that 30 valley glaciers in nine mountain ranges were melting three times faster than in the 1980s. Many valley glaciers are 50% smaller than in 1850. Since 2000, Alpine glaciers have thinned by an average of 1 m per year. Similar rates observed in Andes, Patagonia, the Cascades range and Himalayas

Evidence of melting ice in Antarctica less clear than for Arctic. Some small ice shelves in Antarctic Peninsula have collapsed: 1,600 km² Larsen A in 1995, 1,100 km² Wilkins in 1998 and 13,500 km³ Larsen B in 2002. In 2005 British Antarctic Survey found that 85% of Antartic Peninsula glaciers had retreated by an average of 600 m since 1953

Figure 4.4 Recent changes in global ice cover

Drivers of climate change

There is no single cause of climate change. On the very long timescales of glacial–interglacial cycles, the most common explanation is the variation in the Earth's orbit around the sun. On timescales of hundreds to thousands of years, variations in the sun's solar output may fit observed climate trends. The warming that the Earth has experienced in the last few decades (global warming) is increasingly seen as driven by human pollution of the atmosphere. There is also evidence that volcanic activity can alter climate, but usually only for a few years.

Astronomical forcing

A Serbian, Milutin Milankovitch, developed the theory of astronomical **climate forcing** in 1924. He argued that the surface temperature of the Earth changes over time because the Earth's orbit and axis tilt vary over time. These variations lead to changes in the amount and distribution of solar radiation received by the Earth from the sun. Over a timescale

> **Key term**
>
> **Climate forcing** Any mechanism that alters the global energy balance and 'forces' the climate to change in response.

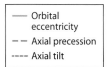

— Orbital
  eccentricity

– – Axial precession

---- Axial tilt

Figure 4.5
Interaction of the
three Milankovitch
cycles

Source: J. J. Lowe and
M. J. C. Walker,
Reconstructing Quaternary
Environments, Longman,
1992

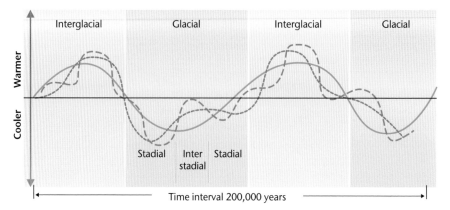

of 100,000 years, the Earth's orbit changes from circular to elliptical and back again (orbital eccentricity). This changes the amount of radiation received from the sun. On a timescale of 41,000 years, the Earth's axis tilts from 21.5° to 24.5° and back again (axial tilt). This changes the seasonality of the Earth's climate. The smaller the tilt, the smaller the difference between summer and winter. In addition, on a 22,000-year timescale, the Earth's axis 'wobbles' and this changes the point in the year that the Earth is closest to the sun (axial precession). Figure 4.5 shows the combined effects of these three cycles.

In support of Milankovitch's theory is the fact that ice ages (glacials) have occurred at regular 100,000-year intervals. However, the actual impact of orbital changes on solar radiation amount and distribution is small — probably no more than enough to change global temperature by 0.5°C. We know, from the evidence of past climate change, that ice ages were about 5°C colder than interglacials. Many scientists argue that Milankovitch cycles may have been just enough to *trigger* a major global climate change, but that climate feedback mechanisms (see the key concept box below) are needed to *sustain* it.

Climate feedback

Feedback effects are those than can either amplify a small change and make it larger (positive feedback), or diminish the change and make it smaller (negative feedback).

An example of positive feedback is snow and ice cover. Small increases in snow and ice dramatically raise surface albedo (reflectivity), so more solar energy is reflected back into space. This contributes to further cooling, which might encourage further snowfall. This may be how the 0.5°C cooling identified by Milankovitch is amplified into a 5°C global cooling.

An example of negative feedback is cloud cover. As global warming occurs, more evaporation will occur and this may increase global cloud cover. Increasingly cloudy skies could reflect more solar energy back into space, and diminish the effect of the warming.

Solar output

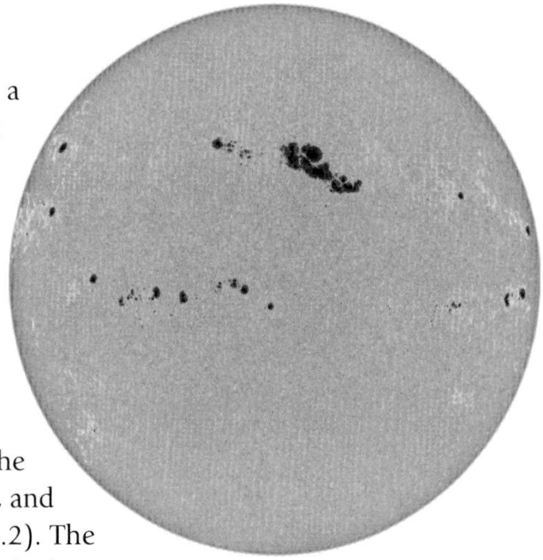

The amount of energy emitted by the sun varies as a result of sunspots (Photograph 4.2). These are dark spots that appear on the sun's surface, caused by intense magnetic storms. The effect of sunspots is to blast more solar radiation towards the Earth. There is a well-known 11-year sunspot cycle, as well as longer cycles. The total variation in solar radiation caused by sunspots is about 0.1%. Sunspots have been recorded for around 2,000 years, and there is a good record for around 400 years.

A long period with almost no sunspots, known as the Maunder Minimum, occurred between 1645 and 1715, and this is often linked to the Little Ice Age (see Figure 4.2). The Medieval Warm Period (also on Figure 4.2) has been linked to more intense sunspot activity, although it is unclear whether the Medieval Warm Period was a global event. Some scientists have suggested that around 20% of twentieth-century warming may be attributed to solar output variation.

Photograph 4.2
Sunspots

Volcanic and cosmic causes

Volcanic activity can alter global climate. Major eruptions eject material into the stratosphere, where high-level winds distribute it around the globe. Volcanoes eject huge volumes of ash, sulphur dioxide, water vapour and carbon dioxide. Tambora, Indonesia, in 1815 ejected 200 million tonnes of sulphur dioxide; in 1991 Mt Pinatubo in the Philippines ejected 17 million tonnes. High in the atmosphere, sulphur dioxide forms a haze of sulphate aerosols, which reduces the amount of sunlight received at the Earth's surface.

The eruption of Tambora led to the 'year without a summer' in 1816 as global temperatures dipped by 0.4–0.7°C. Temperature falls followed the Pinatubo eruption. These changes are short-lived, as the sulphate aerosols persist only for 2–3 years. Similar cooling effects would be felt following a major asteroid strike on the Earth as dust and debris thrown up by the impact blanketed the planet. Cooling would be short term unless feedback mechanisms occurred to amplify the change.

Atmospheric forcing

The prime cause of recent climate change is the enhanced greenhouse effect. This is described in Chapter 1 (p. 8). It is the way in which human-induced pollution of the atmosphere is causing it to trap more heat at the Earth's surface.

Global dimming?

Recently a new forcing mechanism, global dimming, has entered the debate. Atmospheric pollutants like soot (suspended particulate matter) and sulphur dioxide reflect solar energy back into space and so have a net cooling effect. Greenhouse gases reflect outgoing radiation back to Earth and so have a net warming effect. It is possible that human pollution is both warming and cooling the planet at the same time, and that some pollutants are actually reducing the full impact of global warming. In North America and Europe, soot and sulphur dioxide pollution has fallen dramatically since 1990, as a result of attempts to reduce acid rain. Is it a coincidence that the global warming trend has accelerated at the same time?

Unprecedented global warming?

The observed widespread warming of the atmosphere and ocean, together with ice mass loss, support the conclusion that it is extremely unlikely that global climate change of the past fifty years can be explained without external forcing, and very likely that it is not due to known natural causes alone.   (IPCC 4th Assessment, 2007)

This quote, from the United Nations Intergovernmental Panel on Climate Change (IPCC), sums up the current state of play in the global warming debate. The overwhelming majority of scientists are certain that human pollution of the atmosphere is responsible for recent rising global temperatures. The recorded rise, especially since 1990, is not questioned. However, some groups and individuals question whether temperature rises are beyond what might be considered 'natural' variations, and the extent to which humans are to blame. It is, for instance, difficult to separate the impact of solar variations from the enhanced greenhouse effect.

Skills focus

In the exam, it is important that you give a balanced view of global warming, but what does 'balanced' mean? First, there is no question that our climate is changing. The modern instrumental record shows these changes. Being able to quote key facts and figures is important, as this will show that you have factual knowledge to support your claims about global warming. There are uncertainties, however. We do not know how our climate will change in the future for a number of reasons:

- The level of greenhouse gases in the future cannot be known today.
- The role of feedback mechanisms is uncertain.
- The influence of processes such as global dimming requires further research.
- The interaction of natural processes (volcanic activity, solar output, orbital changes) and human pollution is not clear.

In the exam, you can provide 'balance' by showing that you are aware of these uncertainties.

The key question is whether global warming is unprecedented in historical terms, and outside the natural variations examined earlier in this chapter. There is overwhelming evidence to suggest that our current climate is different from that of previous human experience:

- The level of carbon dioxide in the atmosphere is far above the 'natural' level, and continues to rise.
- Eleven of the 12 warmest years on record occurred between 1995 and 2006. There is very little variation from this warming trend.
- The period from 1950 to 2000 in the northern hemisphere was the warmest 50-year period for 1,300 years, and 0.65°C of the 0.74°C degree rise in temperature since 1901 occurred from 1950 onwards.
- Temperature rises have been recorded on all

continents since 1970 — there is little regional variation.

- Satellite observations since 1993 suggest an annual rise in sea level of 3.1 mm, and a decline in Arctic sea ice of 2.7% per decade.
- Extreme weather events may be increasing. For 2003 the World Meteorological Organization reported that in May there were more tornadoes in the USA than ever before, temperatures in France in June were 5–7°C above normal, Switzerland's summer was the hottest in 250 years and monsoon temperatures in India peaked at 45°C. 'Weird weather' seems to be ever more 'normal'.

The complexity of the climate system makes it hard to predict change. The role of the oceans as a carbon sink, and the importance of ocean circulation to climate, is not fully understood. It is unclear to what extent some feedback mechanisms might speed up climate change, or dampen down its impact.

Review questions

1 Assess the reliability of proxy records, such as harvest dates and old paintings, in the study of medium-term climate change.
2 Select five pieces of evidence that you think support the view that today's climate is hotting up. Rank your evidence in terms of its reliability. Justify your order.
3 Write a brief statement, of no more than 150 words, to try to convince a 'climate sceptic' that recent climate change is 'unprecedented'.
4 Outline three of the theories put forward to explain climate change. Which one do you think provides the best explanation of recent climate change?

Chapter

5

The impacts of global warming

What are the impacts of global warming and why should we be concerned?

By the end of this chapter you should have:

➤ *understood the range of direct environmental, social and economic impacts of global warming by focusing on two compulsory case studies of the Arctic and Africa*

➤ *evaluated the indirect impacts such as rising sea levels*

➤ *assessed the complexities of modelling the impacts of climate change*

➤ *weighed up the evidence which suggests that global warming could lead to catastrophic, irreversible changes*

Direct impacts

The distribution of temperature and rainfall changes means that climate change will affect different geographical locations in different ways.

The Arctic: climate change and its impacts

In the past few decades, average Arctic temperatures have risen at twice the rate of the rest of the world (3–4 °C in the last 50 years in Alaska and northwest Canada). Over the next 100 years they could rise a further 3–5 °C over land and up to 7 °C over the oceans. This is already leading to melting of the Greenland ice sheet,

Figure 5.1 Effect of melting Arctic ice on ocean currents

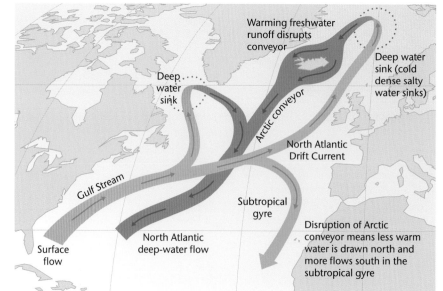

glaciers and sea ice. Ice and snow reflect a lot of solar energy, so when they melt more energy is absorbed and warming increases. In addition:

➤ Figure 5.1 shows how the melting of ice could make the Arctic Ocean less saline and warmer. This would weaken the formation of the Arctic conveyor, which draws the warm Gulf Stream current northwards. The loss of the warm Gulf Stream would cause dramatic cooling of the climate in northwestern Europe.

➤ Water from melting ice sheets and glaciers will contribute to rising sea levels globally (see pp. 56–59).

The case study below looks at the impact of these changes on the Arctic environment.

Case study — Impact of climate change on the Arctic region

Climate change in the polar regions is likely to be among the largest and most rapid of any on Earth, with major environmental and eco-logical impacts, and knock-on socioeconomic effects, especially in the Arctic. Note, however, that both positive and negative im-pacts can be seen.

Photograph 5.1 Inuits will be badly affected by Arctic climate change

Corel

Impacts on natural systems
Vegetation shifts
Vegetation zones are pre-dicted to shift northwards, with coniferous forests encroaching on tundra and on ice deserts. This shift will destabilise existing food webs. The longer, warmer growing season will be a benefit to Arctic agriculture although soils will be a limiting factor.

Thawing of permafrost
Up to 40% of total **permafrost** is expected to thaw, especially in Siberia. This will release large quantities of methane — itself a greenhouse gas. In some areas, lakes and rivers will drain as the frozen ground beneath them thaws, while rising river flows could create new wetlands in other places. These changes will have an impact on species, particularly freshwater fish such as the Arctic char and lake trout.

Key terms

Habitat The environment of plants and animals, in which they live, feed and reproduce.

Permafrost Permanently frozen ground.

Increasing fires and insects
Global warming will increase forest fires and insect-caused tree death, which may have an impact on old-growth forest, a valuable **habitat** that is rich in lichens, mosses, fungi and birds such as wood-peckers. Alien species may invade.

Ultraviolet impacts
Increased ultraviolet (UV) radiation will reach the

Earth's surface as snow and ice cover is lost. Many freshwater ecosystems are highly sensitive to UV radiation, which destroys phytoplankton at the base of the marine food chain.

Carbon cycle changes

The replacement of Arctic vegetation with more forests will lead to higher primary productivity and increased carbon dioxide uptake, but methane emissions from warming wetlands and thawing permafrost could counterbalance this positive impact.

Other impacts

Increased coastal erosion as thawing permafrost weakens the coast, and there are more waves and storm surges as the protection of sea ice is lost.

Impacts on animal species

Northward species shifts

Species will shift north with forests. Some species are likely to suffer major decline.

Marine species

Marine species dependent on sea ice, including polar bears, ice-living seals, walruses and some birds, will decline. Some may face extinction. Birds like geese will have different migration patterns.

Land species

Land species adapted to the Arctic climate, including lemming, vole, Arctic fox, snowy owl and caribou are at risk.

Impacts on society

The ecological and environmental changes described above will mean:

- loss of hunting culture and decline of food security for **indigenous** peoples (e.g. Inuits) (Photograph 5.1)
- need for herd animals (e.g. reindeer) to change their migration routes
- decline in northern freshwater fisheries (e.g. threatened Arctic char), but enhanced marine fisheries (e.g. arrival of cod and herring due to warmer water).
  - increasing access for marine shipping, but disruption of land-based transport because of permafrost thawing
  - enhanced agriculture and forestry
  - as large areas of snow and ice melt, exposing new land and open sea, the Arctic will become more accessible, and vulnerable to exploitation for oil, gas, fish and other resources

The key changes are summarised in Figure 5.2.

Source: Arctic Impact Assessment 2004, www.acia.uaf.edu

Figure 5.2 Arctic region: summary of key changes

— Present summer sea-ice extent	— Present tree-line	— Present permafrost boundary
⋯ Projected summer sea-ice extent	⋯ Projected tree-line	⋯ Projected permafrost boundary

USA · RUSSIA · CANADA · GREENLAND · North pole

Key term

Indigenous Native.

Africa: climate change and its impacts

Africa is the continent that makes the least contribution to global warming, yet it is the most vulnerable to climate change. Much of its population is dependent on climate-sensitive resources such as local water and ecosystems, and has a limited ability to respond to changing climate because of poverty.

It is predicted that temperatures in Africa overall will rise by 3–4°C above the mean global change. Rainfall is likely to increase in the equatorial region but decrease to the north and south of that band.

COMPULSORY Case study Impact of climate change on the continent of Africa

Figure 5.3 summarises Africa's vulnerability to global warming.

Water issues

Life in Africa is regulated by access to water for agriculture, domestic use and hydroelectric power. Many of the larger rivers are internationally shared (e.g. River Nile), creating potential for conflict between water users.

Demand outstrips supply of water for 25% of Africans. However, enough water is available in most parts of Africa. Poverty is the key reason why millions have no access to safe and reliable water supplies. Water stress could lead to wars, global migrations and famine.

Food insecurity

Seventy per cent of the population are subsistence farmers, many of whom will not be able to feed themselves should water supplies dry up, pasture quality deteriorate or crops fail. Increased locust plagues may also threaten food supplies.

Natural resources

Poor people, especially those living in marginal environments, depend directly on wild plants and animals to support their way of life. Loss of biodiversity due to climate change will threaten them.

Health

Vector-borne diseases (e.g. malaria) and water-borne diseases (e.g. diarrhoea) could increase with climate change. Moreover, 80% of health services rely on wild plants for remedies, which are under threat.

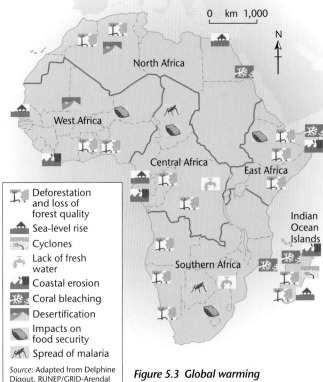

Deforestation and loss of forest quality
Sea-level rise
Cyclones
Lack of fresh water
Coastal erosion
Coral bleaching
Desertification
Impacts on food security
Spread of malaria

Source: Adapted from Delphine Digout, RUNEP/GRID-Arendal

Figure 5.3 Global warming vulnerability in Africa

Development of coastal zones

Movement of environmental refugees from the countryside puts pressure on the coastal zones, especially of north and west Africa. Refugees set up home in shanty towns in cities such as Accra, Freetown and Lagos. Sixty per cent of Africans live in coastal zones, many of which are at risk of coastal erosion and flooding. The threat from these is likely to increase as a result of rising sea level. If the coastal zones were flooded, much of the continent's infrastructure of roads, bridges and buildings would also be lost.

Desertification

Desertification is a major destroyer of grasslands. It is increased by unreliable or decreasing rainfall.

Poverty

At the root of Africa's vulnerability is poverty. Two thirds of least developed countries are located in Africa. The problem is made worse by conflicts (e.g. in Darfur in the Sudan, where pastoralists are fighting arable farmers). An unjust trading system forces many countries to sell their exports (e.g. Mali cotton) at a low price to compete with subsidised European and North American products. Above all, the burden of unpayable debt means that no money is available for the mitigation of climate impacts and the introduction of adaptive strategies.

Potential extent of flooding in areas predicted to be at risk

Figure 5.4 Possible effect of rising sea levels on England and Wales

Source: Environment Agency/Science Media Centre

Indirect impacts: rising sea levels

Modelling the rise in sea level

A worst-case scenario of a 15 m rise in sea level by 2100 would put many of the world's great cities in peril, including London (Figure 5.4), New York and Tokyo. To reach this estimate, the following calculations were made:

Melting of West Antarctic ice sheet	5 m rise
Complete melting of Greenland ice sheet	7 m rise
Collapse and melting of world's glacier systems	2 m rise
Continued thermal expansion of oceans	1 m rise

Such a rise equates to around 15 m this century or 1.5 m per decade.

The reality is that predicting **eustatic** sea-level rise is complex. Most models predict a rise of up to 1 m by 2100, unlike the worst-case scenario above. Reasons for this uncertainty are:

➤ the difficulty of estimating future greenhouse gas emissions
➤ whether the model adopts a 'business as usual' or a sustainable scenario
➤ the difficulty of predicting the impact of the thermal expansion of oceans and melting of ice sheets and glaciers

Part of sea-level rise to 2100 will be from thermal expansion of the oceans (expansion of the water as it warms). Even if greenhouse gas emissions stabilised, sea level would continue to rise due to the continued warming of deep oceans.

Modelling the contribution from melting ice sheets and glaciers is complex. It has been suggested that Antarctic ice sheets might increase in size with climate change, because warming could lead to increased snowfall, but recent satellite observations suggest that atmospheric and ocean warming are leading to melting in both Greenland and Antarctica.

Key terms

Eustatic change Change in sea level due to change in the amount of water in the oceans.

Isostatic change Movement of land in response to loss or gain of mass (e.g. melting ice sheets leads to uplift).

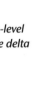

Sea-level rise is a worldwide process, but the rise of sea level in different places may vary as there will be localised land movements caused by tectonics and **isostatic change** from changing sediment or ice-sheet pressure. As the oceans have different temperatures thermal expansion will not be uniform.

Vulnerable areas

Three types of area are vulnerable to sea-level rise:

➤ the world's large river deltas (e.g. Brahmaputra–Ganges, Nile, Mississippi)
➤ areas that lie close to sea level and are already defended (e.g. the Netherlands, parts of eastern England)
➤ small, low-lying islands (usually coral atolls) in the Pacific and Indian Oceans

Bangladesh and Egypt

In Bangladesh, rising sea water is already destroying mangrove swamps. Some 70% of the country consists of floodplains less than 6 m above sea level. Bangladesh could lose up to 20% of its land, displacing up to 40 million people. By 2050 the local sea level could have risen 1 m (70 cm as a result of subsidence and groundwater removal). Rising sea level threatens to reduce supplies of food and fresh drinking water and damage agricultural land in a country where 65% of the rapidly growing population are subsistence farmers. Bangladesh is a multiple hazard zone (river floods, coastal floods, storm surges, typhoons) and climate change is likely to make things worse. Solutions are complex as the coast is too long to defend.

A similar situation exists in the Nile delta in Egypt, where local subsidence exacerbates the impact of the rising sea level (see Figure 5.5). A 1 m rise in sea level

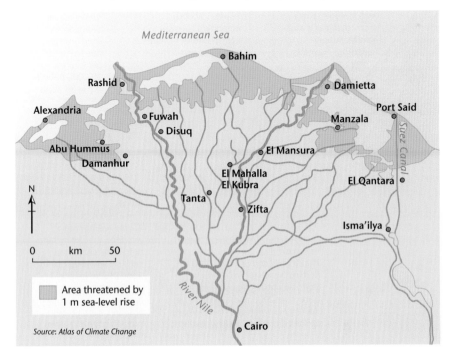

Source: Atlas of Climate Change

Figure 5.5
Impact of sea-level rise in the Nile delta

could affect 15% of Egypt's habitable land (7 million people). Other examples include the Mekong delta in China and the Mississippi delta in the USA.

The Netherlands

In contrast to Bangladesh, the Netherlands is one of the richest countries of the world. It is largely made up of coastal lowlands, over 50% of which are polders (reclaimed land), below present sea level. This densely populated, heavily developed area is defended by a complex system of dykes and coastal sand dunes. It is estimated that a 1 m rise in sea level would cost the Netherlands $12,000 million (at 2005 prices) to defend.

Pacific islands

Low-lying small islands are already feeling the effects of sea-level rises (Figure 5.6). Islands like those in the Pacific have common vulnerabilities:

➤ small physical size — there is nowhere to flee to
➤ low elevation (coral atolls) and vulnerability to rising sea level
➤ prone to natural disasters, especially hurricanes (e.g. the hurricane on Niue in 2005, which caused the whole population to migrate to New Zealand)
➤ dense and growing populations, with some rapid urbanisation (e.g. on Fiji)
➤ increasing degradation of natural environments (e.g. coral reef and mangrove destruction on Fiji)
➤ vulnerability of groundwater to contamination by sea water
➤ wide geographic distribution and remoteness

Figure 5.6
Islands threatened
by rising sea levels

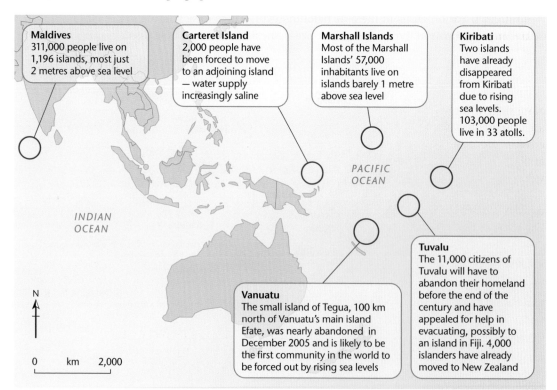

Maldives
311,000 people live on 1,196 islands, most just 2 metres above sea level

Carteret Island
2,000 people have been forced to move to an adjoining island — water supply increasingly saline

Marshall Islands
Most of the Marshall Islands' 57,000 inhabitants live on islands barely 1 metre above sea level

Kiribati
Two islands have already disappeared from Kiribati due to rising sea levels. 103,000 people live in 33 atolls.

PACIFIC OCEAN

INDIAN OCEAN

Vanuatu
The small island of Tegua, 100 km north of Vanuatu's main island Efate, was nearly abandoned in December 2005 and is likely to be the first community in the world to be forced out by rising sea levels

Tuvalu
The 11,000 citizens of Tuvalu will have to abandon their homeland before the end of the century and have appealed for help in evacuating, possibly to an island in Fiji. 4,000 islanders have already moved to New Zealand

N

0   km   2,000

Photograph 5.2 Pacific islands will be the first to suffer from sea-level rise

➤ limited resources — many are among the least developed countries and the cost of protection is therefore far beyond them

Note that, while coral atolls are vulnerable and liable to erosion from storms, coral atoll growth can keep pace with *slowly* rising sea levels.

Figure 5.7 shows the key elements of managing risks like sea-level rise.

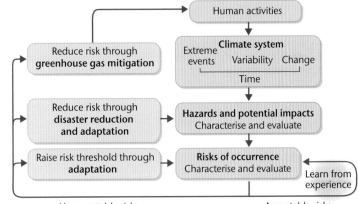

*Figure 5.7
An integrated
approach to risk
management*

Predicting emissions and their impacts

How climate will change during the twenty-first century is a critical question that the Intergovernmental Panel on Climate Change (IPCC) and climate change scientists are addressing. Simulations are used to create climate change models. Predictions rely on three main scenarios — low, medium and high greenhouse gas emissions — which produce different global warming outcomes. Best estimates range from 1.8°C to 4°C. Obviously, higher emissions lead to higher temperatures.

Projected growth of greenhouse gas emissions

Key concept

- In 2007, greenhouse gas (GHG) levels stood at 430 ppm (parts per million) carbon dioxide. Before the Industrial Revolution they were 280 ppm.
- Annual emissions are still rising. In a 'business as usual' scenario with no attempt at reduction they will reach 550 ppm by 2035. Possible projections are given in Table 5.1.
- Most future emissions growth will come from developing countries. India and China will contribute 75% of the increase.
- The link between economic development and growth of GHG emissions could be broken by use of green technologies.
- Despite increasing scarcity, supplies of fossil fuels exist to fuel emissions growth to well beyond 800 ppm, including oil sands, oil shales and coal.

Table 5.1 Greenhouse gas emissions, 1990–2050

	Emission source	Current emissions	Rank	Description and projection
ENERGY	Electricity and heat	24%	1	Fastest-growing source, especially with rapidly growing population and economic development in China, India and middle east.
	Transport	14%	3 =	High emissions from road transport and growing contribution for aviation. Second fastest growing source associated with globalisation and economic development.
	Industry	14%	3 =	Major contribution from NICs, rest declining because of technology and diversified economies. Several GHGs, especially nitrous oxide from heavy industry.
	Buildings (heating, lighting, cooking, etc.)	8%	6	Will increase by two-thirds between 2000 and 2050 because of larger population and development (especially urbanisation) in developing countries.
NON-ENERGY	Deforestation	17%	2	Deforestation (loss of carbon sink) is mainly occurring in Indonesia and Brazil. Projected to fall, so potential damage limited in future.
	Agriculture	14%	5	Fertiliser use and livestock each account for one-third of current emissions. There will be a steady rise largely because of the key role of intensive farming in feeding the growing world population.

Why the uncertainty?

Projections of emissions levels and their impacts are difficult, because it is hard to predict the following:

- the level and nature of economic development, particularly in countries like India and China, which will determine greenhouse gas (GHG) emissions
- what degree of international action will be taken to reduce emissions
- the inertia in the system — even if GHG emissions stabilise, climate change will continue
- the impact of positive feedback, for example as permafrost areas thaw due to

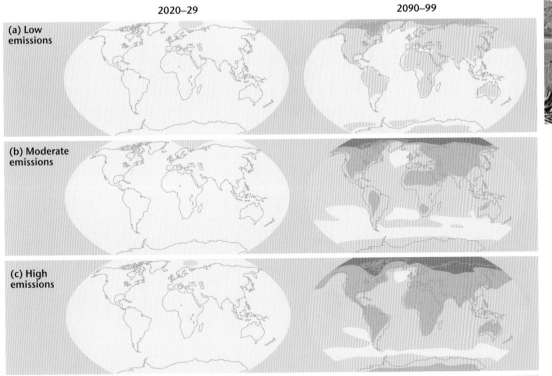

Figure 5.8 *Projected temperature changes relative to 1980–99 based on three economic scenarios that assume no new emissions policy*

Temperature increase (°C)

☐	0–2
☐	2–4
☐	4–6
☐	>6°C

global warming the powerful GHG methane will be released, increasing warming still further

A more hazardous world?

Emissions predictions range from 'business as usual' (no attempt at reduction) to a more sustainable approach. Figure 5.8 shows the projected global temperature changes based on low, moderate and high emissions. Scientists are reasonably confident that the pattern of regional change will mirror the changes observed over the last 50 years (i.e. greater warming over land than ocean and extreme changes in the Arctic). It is the *size* of the changes which is unknown.

Table 5.2 looks at predicted impacts of different levels of global warming. The impacts become disproportionately more damaging and disrupting with more warming. Reaching the 'tipping point' (see key concepts box) could trigger abrupt changes on a regional scale, which are likely to be irreversible. These could lead to mass migration from badly hit areas to relatively stable areas (e.g. from Africa to Europe), and to large-scale conflicts over water and food security (see Chapter 7).

Global warming could also herald a more hazardous world, with sudden shifts in weather patterns, leading to a crisis over water availability, floods and drought. It could even lead to a collapse of the West Antarctic and Greenland ice sheets, causing a 15 m sea-level rise and threatening the lives of millions.

Table 5.2 *Effects of different global temperature rises, according to the Stern Review*

Temperature rise (°C)	Water	Food	Health	Land	Environment	Abrupt and large-scale impacts
1	Small glaciers in the Andes disappear, threatening water supplies for 50 million people.	Modest increases in cereal yields in temperate regions.	At least 300,000 people each year die from climate-related diseases (e.g. diarrhoea, malaria) and malnutrition. Reduction in winter mortality in cold countries.	Permafrost thawing damages buildings and roads in parts of Canada and Russia.	At least 10% of land species facing extinction. 80% bleaching of coral reefs, including Great Barrier Reef.	Atlantic thermohaline circulation starts to weaken.
2	Potential 20–30% decrease in water availability in some vulnerable regions (e.g. southern Africa, Mediterranean).	Sharp declines in crop yield in tropical regions (5–10% in Africa).	40–60 million more people exposed to malaria in Africa.	Up to 10 million more people affected by coastal flooding each year.	15–40% of species facing extinction. High risk of extinction of Arctic species.	Potential for Greenland ice sheet to begin melting, irreversibly, accelerating sea-level rise and leading to an eventual 7 m sea-level rise.
3	In southern Europe, serious droughts occur once every 10 years. 1–4 billion more people suffer water shortages. 1–5 billion gain water, which may increase flood risk.	150–550 additional millions at risk of hunger. Agricultural yields in temperate latitudes likely to peak.	1–3 million more people die from malnutrition.	1–170 million more people affected by coastal flooding each year.	20–50% of species facing extinction, including 25–60% of mammals, 30–40% of birds and 15–70% of butterflies in South Africa.	Rising risk of abrupt changes to atmospheric circulations (e.g. the monsoon).
4	Potential 30–50% decrease in water availability in southern Africa and Mediterranean.	Agricultural yields decline by 15–35% in Africa. Entire regions out of production (e.g. parts of Australia).	Up to 80 million more people exposed to malaria in Africa.	7–300 million more people affected by coastal flooding each year.	Loss of around half of the Arctic tundra.	Rising risk of collapse of West Antarctic ice sheet.
5	Possible disappearance of large glaciers in Himalayas, affecting one-quarter of China's population and hundreds of millions in India.	Continued increase in ocean acidity, seriously disrupting marine ecosystems and fish stocks.		Sea-level rise threatens small islands, low-lying coastal areas (e.g. Florida) and major world cities (e.g. New York, London, Tokyo).		Rising risk of collapse of Atlantic thermohaline circulation.

The latest science suggests that the Earth's average temperature will rise by even more than 5 or 6°C if emissions continue to grow and positive feedbacks amplify the warming effect of greenhouse gases. The level of global temperature rise would be equivalent to the amount of warming that occurred between the last ice age and today — and is likely to lead to major disruption and large-scale movement of population. Such 'socially contingent' effects could be catastrophic, but are hard to predict with current models as the temperatures involved are so far outside human experience.

Tipping point

The **tipping point** is reached when climate change occurs irreversibly and at an increasing rate. Scientists originally agreed this was at a certain level of greenhouse emissions (450 ppm carbon dioxide) and a threshold temperature rise of 2°C. Increasingly, they are talking about visible manifestations of the tipping point, such as the loss of the massive Greenland ice sheet, the melting of the West Antarctic ice sheet, the destruction of the Amazon forest, and the collapse of the global ocean current system (known as the thermohaline circulation), all of which would lead to catastrophic changes.

Review questions

1 Contrast the Arctic region and Africa in terms of the likely impacts of global warming.

2 Summarise the physical and human features which make Bangladesh and the Pacific Islands so vulnerable to sea-level rise.

3 Why it is difficult to make accurate predictions about the impacts of global warming?

4 Use a world map to show five locations that are expected to benefit in different ways from the impacts of global warming. For each of the locations, provide some boxed commentary identifying the exact nature of the benefit.

5 Discuss the view that those countries contributing least to global greenhouse emissions are likely to suffer most from the impacts of global warming.

Coping with climate change

What are the strategies for dealing with climate change?

By the end of this chapter you should have:

➤ *examined the role of adaptation and mitigation strategies in coping with climate change*
➤ *explored the views and roles of different 'players' in managing climate change, such as governments, businesses, NGOs and individuals*
➤ *evaluated the costs and benefits of strategies and policies at a range of different scales, from local to global*

Mitigation or adaptation?

There is global agreement that the climate change threat needs to be addressed, but much less agreement on how to achieve this. There is also a key difference between human and natural systems, and how they would respond to mitigation or adaptation:

➤ For human systems like the economy, mitigation would involve an upfront cost, to reduce atmospheric pollution to 'safe' levels. Adaptation might mean that costs were spread over a longer time scale and were more gradual.
➤ For natural systems like ecosystems, mitigation could limit damage. Adaptation might condemn natural systems which could not 'adapt' to a changing climate. Species might become extinct, and biodiversity be degraded as threats to ecosystems increased.

The value of natural systems (ecosystems and the hydrological cycle) is a strong argument for acting now to reduce the worst impacts of climate change. In addition, although the wealthy developed world may have the resources to adapt to a changing climate, parts of the poorer developing world lack the **adaptive capacity** to cope. Increasing adaptive capacity here would require:

➤ reducing poverty to meet the costs of adaptation
➤ increasing access to resources including energy resources and materials

Figure 6.1
Scales of mitigation

Increasingly large scale →

Individual	Local	National	Global
Lifestyles and consumption choices	Local government strategies on planning, recycling, transport	Government policies and national tax frameworks	International agreements for global action

➤ improving education and skills to develop understanding of the challenges and ability to change

➤ improving health — malnutrition, malaria and HIV/AIDS all reduce adaptive capacity

➤ improving infrastructure such as roads, energy supply and communications

Photograph 6.1
Local councils provide recycling boxes to households

Ability to adapt is linked to level of development. Most adaptation strategies will be local in scale, as adaptations need to be tailored to local impacts of climate change. Mitigation can occur at a range of scales from local to global (Figure 6.1). On a global scale, international agreements are important, but individual governments must decide how agreements should be implemented.

In most cases, it falls to local agencies (e.g. local councils) to decide on the actions needed, and to 'persuade' individuals to make the correct choices. Recycling is a good example. The UK government target is for 30% of domestic waste to be recycled by 2010. This is one way of reducing waste and helping to meet the Kyoto Protocol target. The UK national government funds advertising campaigns to persuade us to recycle, but your local council provides the recycling bins, boxes and skips — and might even fine you if you refuse to recycle (Photograph 6.1). This local infrastructure is the crucial part of the jigsaw — hence the phrase 'think global, act local'.

Figure 6.2 illustrates a range of climate coping strategies, across a spectrum from adaptation (minimal greenhouse gas reductions) to mitigation (reductions in greenhouse gas emissions). All strategies have costs and benefits.

Figure 6.2
The spectrum of climate change coping strategies

Adaptation					Mitigation
None ——————————— Reduction in greenhouse gas emissions ——————————— Significant					
Land-use planning	**Agricultural technology**	**Geo-engineering**	**Sustainable development**	**Carbon capture technology**	**Carbon-neutral development**
Preventing development on floodplains and vulnerable coasts. Removal of urban scrubland to prevent the spread of fire.	Drought-tolerant crops, no-tillage systems, water harvesting technology, the use of urban waste water on fields.	Orbiting solar shields to reflect incoming solar radiation, ocean iron seeding to increase algal growth and sequester carbon.	Reduced resource consumption, increased recycling of materials, locally sourced foodstuffs, alternative transport.	Large-scale carbon capture technology applied to power stations and industry, deep-sea or geological burial.	Offsetting of all carbon emissions through afforestation, wholesale switching to renewable energy supplies.
✔ Reduces vulnerability to extreme weather events.	✔ Much of the technology already exists, and could be adopted quickly.	✔ Could provide a 'one-off' solution and avoid need for lifestyle changes.	✔ Is known to work, and some aspects (e.g. recycling) have already been accepted by the public.	✔ Technology is advanced and removes the problem at source.	✔ Has the most fundamental impact on emissions.
✗ Costly to implement, and may be opposed by existing residents and businesses, small scale only.	✗ Costs may be prohibitive in the developing world, where the need is greatest.	✗ Huge costs and untried technology, side-effects largely unknown.	✗ Lifestyle changes may be opposed, and the changes are slow to take effect.	✗ High costs passed on to consumers. Encourages continued unsustainable use of finite resources.	✗ Could prevent development; public opposition to land-use and lifestyle changes.

Mitigation and adaptation

Key concept

Mitigation and adaptation are different strategies for coping with climate change.

Mitigation means reducing the output of greenhouse gases and increasing the size of greenhouse gas sinks. Examples of mitigation are:
➤ setting targets to reduce carbon dioxide emissions
➤ switching to renewable energy sources, such as wind power
➤ 'capturing' carbon emissions from power stations and storing them, for instance in spent oil wells

Adaptation means changing our lifestyles to cope with a new environment rather than trying to stop climate change. Examples of adaptation are:
➤ managed retreat of coastlines vulnerable to sea-level rise
➤ developing drought-resistant crops
➤ enlarging existing conservation areas to allow for shifting habitat zones

Many scientists argue that climate change would occur *even if* humans stopped polluting the atmosphere now, so 100% mitigation would still require some adaptation.

Adaptation involves a range of strategies. The United Nations Environment Programme (UNEP) recognises eight possible adaptation options, which are evaluated in Table 6.1. Most of these options depend on resources (money, land, expertise), which many developing nations lack. Some are discussed in the case study on Tuvalu on the next page.

*Table 6.1
UNEP adaptation
strategies to climate
change*

Strategy	Description	Appraisal
1 Bear the loss	As costs occur (e.g. due to increased flooding), they are absorbed.	The costs may become unbearable if they occur too frequently.
2 Share the loss	As costs occur, relief is provided by governments, aid agencies and insurers.	The costs may become too large for society and economy to cope with.
3 Modify the threat	The costs are reduced by some form of protection (e.g. a flood barrier).	If the threat grows, further costly investment may be needed.
4 Prevent	One response to increased drought could be to develop a new water source such as drip-fed irrigation.	The investment costs are likely to be high.
5 Relocate	Abandon areas for less risky locations.	This assumes there are new areas available.
6 Research	Investigating the problem and developing new technological solutions (e.g. drought-tolerant crops)	This requires technical expertise, funding and infrastructure.
7 Change use	Changing crops grown in response to changing climate, or developing hill-walking holidays in a former ski resort.	This involves long-term planning and reinvestment costs.
8 Change behaviour	Education, for example to encourage people to conserve water.	A long-term option; producing lifestyle change is notoriously difficult.

Case study: Adapting to climate change on Tuvalu

Tuvalu is a small island state in the Pacific Ocean, between Australia and Hawaii. It gained independence from the UK in 1978. In 2005 the population was 10,500, spread over nine tiny islands, none of which is more than 5 m above sea level. As Tuvalu is too remote for significant tourism, its economy relies on semi-subsistence farming and fishing, plus foreign aid.

Like many small island states, such as the Maldives and Kiribati, Tuvalu is on the climate-change front line. As sea levels rise by 1–2 mm per year, the low-lying islands are being flooded more frequently by the highest tides and tropical storms. The porous coral atolls flood from below as water levels rise, pushing salt water up through the ground in numerous small springs. This poisons the *pulaka* pits in which Tuvaluans grow starchy tubers, an important food crop.

Poor coastal management and beach mining for building materials worsen the problem, and road-building projects have stripped valuable land of vegetation. How can Tuvalu adapt to the threat? It has several options:

- *Relocate.* In 2001, New Zealand agreed to accept 75 Tuvaluans per year, as environmental refugees, possibly until 2050.
- *Change behaviour.* In 2000, Tuvalu joined the United Nations with the aim of bringing its climate-change plight to the world's attention. It hoped that other countries would take action to mitigate.
- *Modify the threat.* Beach mining is being regulated to reduce erosion risk.
- *Prevent the loss.* Salt-tolerant crops to replace traditional *pulaka* may be an option.

Tuvalu lacks adaptive capacity. It is a developing nation, with a tiny GDP of around $12 million. High fertility rates (2.8 per woman in 2005), poor environmental management and reliance on foreign aid do not suggest a good future. If sea levels do rise by 18–59 cm as the IPCC predicted in 2007, much of the country will be uninhabitable.

Globally, attempts to mitigate climate change have centred on the 1997 Kyoto Protocol. There were good reasons to suggest that this agreement might work. The 1987 Montreal Protocol set limits on CFC emissions, which damage the ozone layer. CFC levels fell as developed countries phased them out. Funds were provided to encourage developing countries to switch to less damaging alternatives. This experience demonstrates that, faced with an international environmental problem, governments can cooperate and find a solution.

However, the experience around Kyoto has been different. The case study explores the reasons for this.

Case study: The Kyoto Protocol

At the 1992 Earth Summit in Rio de Janeiro, the United Nations Framework Convention on Climate Change (UNFCCC) was agreed. This framework aims to 'achieve stabilization of greenhouse gas concentrations in the atmosphere at a low enough level to prevent dangerous anthropogenic interference with the climate system'. This treaty was signed by 190 countries including the USA and negotiations began on a protocol, which was adopted at a UNFCCC conference in Kyoto in 1997.

During negotiations the treaty became increasingly complex. For instance:

- In order for the treaty to enter into force, 55 countries had to ratify it, including enough countries to account for 55% of global carbon dioxide emissions in 1990. This was only achieved in 2005 when Russia signed.
- Emissions reduction targets are country specific. The EU target is 8%, the USA 6%, Iceland 10% and Russia 0%.
- Complex systems were introduced allowing 'trading' of carbon credits: that is, buying unused emissions from other countries or businesses.
- Carbon sinks, such as planting forests, were allowed, so that countries can 'offset' emissions. Critics argue that both this and carbon trading allow polluters to continue to pollute.
- The protocol was undermined in 2001, as the USA withdrew, stating that the cost of meeting the Kyoto targets was too high, and would damage the US economy.

Kyoto has not been a huge success in reducing emissions of GHGs. Reductions are likely to be in the order of 0.5% by 2012. Some countries will do better, such as the UK and Sweden, but others, like Germany, Spain and Japan, are currently off target. China's emissions have increased by over 50% since 1990. In December 2007 a UN climate-change convention in Indonesia produced the 'Bali roadmap', which started a 2-year process of negotiations on a new set of emissions targets. Even governments like the USA that were reluctant to change have now recognised that climate change is a threat.

Key players in climate change

Businesses

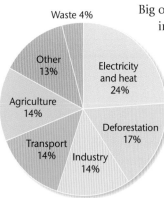

Figure 6.3
Global greenhouse gas emissions by economic sector, 2000

Big oil companies and car manufacturers may seem to have a vested interest in polluting. Cleaning up pollution costs money, while polluting costs nothing (at least in the short term).

For many years, businesses argued that reducing pollution would cost money, profits and jobs (the economics of climate change are examined in the key concept box 'Putting a price on climate' on the next page). Transnational corporations (TNCs), such as Exxon-Mobil, BP, Shell, Ford and General Motors, funded the Global Climate Coalition (GCC) between 1989 and 2002. This opposed action on climate change, and funded research to counter the warnings about global warming.

Companies began to leave GCC in 1997, and it was wound up in 2002. Visit the websites of some major TNCs now and their 'greenness' is surprising. This change in attitude is important. Figure 6.3 shows global greenhouse gas emissions in 2000 by economic sector. Companies of all sizes control many of the emissions, and therefore need to be 'on board' if mitigation strategies are to work. The changing attitudes of businesses can be explained by a range of factors:

➤ moral and public pressure to protect, not destroy, the environment
➤ fears about energy supply, linked to high oil prices
➤ increased moves by governments towards taxing carbon emissions
➤ demands from investors, such as pension funds, that companies are environmentally sound
➤ new technologies, such as renewable energy, hybrid cars and energy-efficient appliances, which represent new markets

Putting a price on climate

Key concept

How much might climate change cost? In 2006 Sir Nicholas Stern (for the UK Treasury) attempted to answer this. The *Stern Review* concluded that, if climate change is allowed to continue unchecked, it could cost at least 5% and possibly 20% of global annual GDP. If the world decided to mitigate climate change, the cost would be about 1% of GDP per annum. Many economists broadly agree with this. Central to Stern's argument is that it is more sensible to invest in mitigation today than to 'do nothing' and face spiralling costs, and global recession, in the future. Table 6.2 outlines some of the 'costs'.

Table 6.2
The costs of climate change

Mitigation costs (the costs of preventing climate change now)	'Do nothing' costs (the costs of coping with climate change in the future)
• Implementing energy-efficient technology in homes and buildings.	• Increased cost of farming and food.
• Switching to renewable energy sources, such as wind, solar and biomass.	• Migration, and dealing with environmental refugees.
• Investing in public transport systems to reduce car use and investing in low-emission transport technology.	• Increased water costs in areas where supply runs short.
• Taxes on carbon emissions for businesses and individuals.	• Increased aid if climate damages food security.
• Capturing, and storing, some carbon emissions.	• Increased healthcare costs; dealing with spreading diseases such as malaria.
	• Infrastructure such as coastal and flood defences.
	• Higher insurance premiums in a more hazardous climate.

The change in business attitudes is illustrated by the establishment, in 2007, of the US Climate Action Partnership. This is a group of businesses calling for 'a pathway that will slow, stop and reverse the growth of US emissions while expanding the US economy'. Members of the group include BP America, General Motors, Ford and Shell.

Climate change might bring some benefits, such as fewer deaths from hypothermia, new crops for some areas, or increased tourism in others. Stern argues these benefits will be tiny compared to the eventual costs. Equally there could be some benefits of mitigation. Renewable energy, hybrid cars, public transport and energy-efficient buildings require research and development, and will provide new jobs and opportunities for economic growth. Is the change in the attitude of businesses due to the realisation that climate change might damage their profits, while acting to prevent it might actually increase them?

National strategies

One conclusion of the Stern Review was that emissions should be stabilised at between 450 and 550 ppm carbon dioxide, and that this 'would require global emissions to peak in the next 10–20 years, and then fall at a rate of at least 1–3% per year'. This call for urgent and significant mitigation action is in tune with the

Table 6.3 Current and potential national climate change policies

Country	Aim	Strategy	Evaluation
UK	Reduce carbon dioxide emissions by 60% by 2050.	10% of electricity supply to come from renewable sources by 2010, rising to 20% by 2020. The majority is likely to come from onshore and offshore wind farms.	The key issue is land-use planning. Where do wind turbines go? Protests against turbines are frequent, and offshore turbines are costly. Wind is not 100% reliable, so other power sources need to be kept as standbys.
USA	An 18% reduction in greenhouse gas emission intensity by 2012 (from 183 tonnes of carbon dioxide per million dollars of GDP to 151 tonnes).	A key strategy is subsidising farmers to grow maize and other crops, to make **biofuel**. This can be used in cars and trucks, either 'neat' or mixed with fossil fuels to reduce dependency on fossil fuel oil and reduce carbon emissions.	Biofuel crops 'fix' carbon, reducing emissions. However, growing biofuels instead of food crops has led to shortages of food and rising food prices. A quadrupling of the maize price led to riots in Mexico in 2007. The energy used converting the crop to useable fuel (ethanol) reduces the carbon saving.
Norway	Exceed the Kyoto agreement and cut 1990 emissions levels by 30% by 2020.	Norway began storing carbon dioxide in exhausted oil fields in 1996. It plans to capture 1.5 million tonnes of carbon dioxide from gas-fired power plants, and store it underground by 2014.	Artificial carbon sequestration is new and untested on a large scale. Fears are that carbon dioxide will leak out of the deep geological structures it is buried in. Costs are high, and it requires no lifestyle change, but it may be a useful short-term fix.
China	The National Action Plan on Climate Change (June 2007) could reduce carbon emissions by 1.5 billion tonnes if fully implemented.	China aims to increase renewable energy from 7% to 10% by 2010, using wind, nuclear and hydroelectric power and to improve the efficiency of coal-fired power stations.	China is the world's largest emitter of carbon dioxide. Its National Action Plan contains no clear target for carbon dioxide reductions. 70% of China's electricity is produced from coal and this is not expected to decline significantly.

widely held belief that climate change above 2°C will be 'dangerous' (see Table 5.2 in Chapter 5), and that this is likely above 550 ppm carbon dioxide.

International climate change agreements after 2012 might set a 550 ppm target. It will be up to national governments to decide on strategies to achieve it. Table 6.3 outlines some current and potential strategies.

Key term

Biofuels Fuel such as ethanol extracted from plants.

Taxing and trading

Many countries use their tax system to raise the costs of polluting. In the UK, car tax is priced by carbon dioxide emissions (Photograph 6.2), for example:

Tax band B cars, e.g. Vauxhall Corsa 1.0 litre = £35
Tax band D cars, e.g. Ford Focus 1.6 litre   = £145
Tax band G cars, e.g. BMW 550 4.8 litre   = £400
(2008 figures)

Choosing to drive a large car costs more, as it pollutes more. Air travel is likely to be taxed more in the future. Carbon credit cards would give each person a 'carbon budget' which would be debited as resources were bought (flights, petrol, food,

Volkswagen

*Photograph 6.2
The VW Polo
BlueMotion,
designed to fall into
the lowest tax band
for emissions*

household energy). Any carbon use above your personal budget would have to be paid for — effectively a carbon tax. This idea is politically controversial and would take a long time to implement.

In 2005 the EU began a carbon trading system called EU ETS (European Union Emission Trading Scheme). It is the world's only compulsory example of a 'cap and trade' system — a mechanism that sets a limit on the emission of a pollutant (cap) but allows companies that are within the limit to sell credits to companies that need to pollute more (trade). This covers around 50% of all EU carbon emissions. The power generation, steel, cement and other large, heavily polluting industries are part of the scheme. Figure 6.4 explains how the ETS works.

As an alternative to buying carbon credits, EU countries can purchase Certified Emission Reduction credits (CERs) by investing in environmentally friendly projects in developing nations.

There has been criticism of the ETS, in particular that caps were too lenient at first. A key issue in carbon trading is effective monitoring to ensure that caps are realistic, efficiency gains are real, and investment in projects in the developing world has actually reduced emissions.

*Figure 6.4
The EU ETS*

EU target emissions set at 6,572 million tonnes (mt) of carbon dioxide for 2005–07 ➡ UK 'share' set at 736 million tonnes — the UK's 'cap' ➡ 1,078 UK installations, such as power stations and cement works, are included in the scheme. Each is given its own 'cap'

Factory A
Cap = 1 mt

Emissions = 1 mt
No action needed

Factory B
Cap = 0.5 mt

Emissions = 0.6 mt
Must either increase efficiency, or buy carbon credits

Factory C
Cap = 0.8 mt

Emissions = 0.6 mt
Sells 0.2 mt to the EU carbon market = profit

- The EU cap, national caps and installation caps are set to achieve the Kyoto targets
- Phase 1 ran from 2005 to 2007
- Phase 2 will run from 2008 to 2012

Local action

Local action is critical in tackling climate change. Local Agenda 21 (or LA21) emerged from the 1992 Rio Earth Summit. It calls on governments to encourage local authorities (councils in the UK) to implement sustainable strategies to improve the environment, and reduce carbon emissions. Without local strategies, it is hard for individuals to 'do their bit'. The case study of London below shows how local action might help to mitigate the climate threat.

Case study — London's climate change strategy

In 2007 the mayor of London launched the 'Action Today to Protect Tomorrow' plan for London. The plan commits the city to reducing its carbon dioxide emissions to 30% of 1990 levels by 2025.

How can such an ambitious target be achieved? Various initiatives are proposed:

- the Green Homes Programme — subsidised or free home insulation; improving energy efficiency in existing council houses
- setting and enforcing new building standards for energy efficiency
- investing in local, small-scale renewable energy schemes such as solar and wind power

- encouraging 'waste to energy' schemes as an alternative to landfill
- providing clean, efficient public transport (converting all 8,000 London buses to diesel electric hybrids), raising the London congestion charge to £25 for heavily polluting vehicles, and encouraging cycling
- promoting the purchase of low-carbon goods and services by council offices and other bodies

Further research

www.london.gov.uk/mayor/environment/climate-change/docs/ccap_fullreport.pdf

Climate change and you

Your own role in climate change mitigation is critical. Your personal carbon footprint (see the skills focus box) and ecological footprint can be reduced by:

➤ walking, cycling or taking the bus instead of using the car
➤ buying locally produced food
➤ switching your energy supplier to one using renewable sources
➤ energy efficiency in the home, such as using energy-efficient light bulbs (70% less energy and therefore carbon dioxide than standard bulbs)

These actions may sound simple and small scale but when added up over millions of people and households they can be significant. Switching every light bulb in London to an energy-efficient one would save 575,000 tonnes of carbon dioxide emissions per year.

However, there are problems with the footprint approach. Asking everyone to reduce their footprint could be seen as unfair, as some people consume far less than the average. Millions of people in the developing world do not consume enough to have even a reasonable quality of life — surely they need to consume more, not fewer, resources? Squaring this difficulty has led to the development of the 'contraction and convergence' model (Figure 6.5).

Contraction and convergence allows poorer countries to increase their emissions, while developed countries, with their resources and technology, reduce

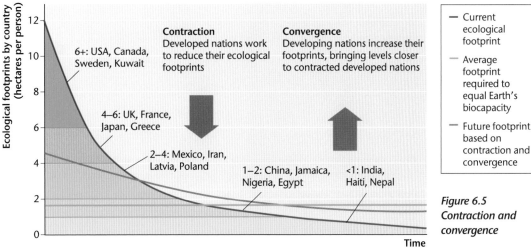

Figure 6.5 Contraction and convergence

theirs. Long term, it is envisaged that the poorer countries would convert to 'greener' forms of energy and consumption as their development allowed. This model has certain advantages:

➤ It would allow countries such as China and India to continue to develop, and perhaps overcome their objections to limiting their own emissions.

➤ It implies that resources need to be shared out more fairly, with the expectation that quality of life must improve for the least developed.

➤ It recognises that over-consuming nations need to reduce their footprints.

Skills focus

Your 'carbon footprint' is the amount of carbon dioxide you emit in a year. The term can also refer to all the carbon emitted during the life cycle of a product (the manufacture, use and disposal of a car, for instance). Examples of carbon footprints for selected countries are given in Figure 6.6.

Task

1 Briefly compare the data in Figure 6.6, and suggest reasons for the differences between countries.

2 Use a carbon calculator on the internet to determine your own carbon footprint.

3 Calculate the average footprint for your class, then scale this up to calculate it for your whole school or college.

4 Using an internet carbon calculator, explore the best way to reduce your school or college carbon footprint using a combination of:

■ carbon offsetting
■ changes to transport
■ changes to consumption
■ energy efficiency gains

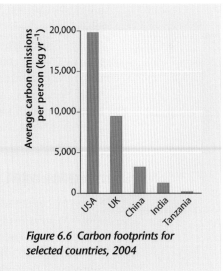

Figure 6.6 Carbon footprints for selected countries, 2004

Climate crusaders

Key concept

The individuals and groups who keep climate change in the news might be called 'climate crusaders'. They have a number of common characteristics:

➤ They are usually already famous.
➤ They are passionate about climate change.
➤ They often use climate change as a 'selling point' for some other purpose.

This last point may sound cynical, but is it wrong to link a serious message about climate change to some other purpose? A good example is the band Coldplay. When they launched their album, *A Rush of Blood to the Head*, in 2002 they bought 10,000 mango trees for villagers in India, to offset the carbon emitted in making and selling their CDs. Coldplay want to sell music; why not sell it *and* send out a powerful message?

High-profile converts to the climate cause include Al Gore (former US vice president and presidential candidate). His film, *An Inconvenient Truth*, had a major impact on public opinion in the USA. Arnold Schwarzenegger, film star and governor of California, has strong green credentials — an important lever when you run a state whose economy is the eighth largest in the world.

Well-known campaign groups include WWF, Greenpeace, Friends of the Earth and the Sierra Club.

Crusaders make fringe activities, such as carbon offsetting, seem mainstream and this encourages wider participation. They also change the political agenda. The popularity of Al Gore's message has made ignoring it politically difficult. They can make real change. Wal-Mart's Sustainability 360 programme, driven by its 'green' chief executive, H. Scott Lee, pledges to cut carbon dioxide emissions in existing stores by 20%, and to build new stores that are 25–30% more energy efficient. It aims to make its 7,000 trucks 50% more energy efficient by 2015, and to reduce packaging by 5% by 2013. This could be seen as a public relations exercise. On the other hand, if Wal-Mart benefits through lower energy costs, and the environment benefits through lower emissions, should we not applaud the move?

Incremental progress

Progress on coping with climate change is likely to be incremental: that is, gradual and slower than many would like. The situation can be summarised as follows:

➤ There is now a scientific consensus, backed by convincing data, that global warming is occurring and that action needs to be taken. There is general agreement that 550 ppm carbon dioxide represents a concentration beyond which climate change is likely to be 'dangerous'.
➤ There is a political consensus that action is required. Even in the USA, which has dragged its feet on climate change, many local mayors, states and cities are beginning to take action, independent of the federal government.

Why is progress on mitigation not faster? What are the barriers preventing action?

➤ *Uncertainty.* We cannot say for sure how the climate will change in the future. The counter-argument is that uncertainty makes it all the more important to act, and apply the 'precautionary principle' of minimising unknown risks.

➤ *Costs.* The costs of mitigating are high, and would damage economic growth. Against this we have evidence such as the *Stern Review*, which suggests that the costs of mitigation will be lower than those of doing nothing.

➤ *Political inertia.* Mitigation policies, such as carbon taxes, are vote losers. This is one reason why progress is likely to be gradual, and based on a consensus.

➤ *Economic systems.* Business and industry inevitably pollute. Major investment is needed to implement clean systems and businesses are reluctant to invest in something which does not make profit for them.

➤ *International agreements.* These take time to negotiate, and not all countries agree. However, the Montreal and Kyoto agreements have partially worked. Does every country in the world need to sign up for an agreement to work? China, the USA and the EU account for over 50% of all carbon emissions.

Many economists, scientists and politicians now believe that decisive mitigation has to occur by 2020 if dangerous climate change is to be avoided. We shall see.

Review questions

1 Using examples from your own research, write illustrated definitions of 'mitigation' and 'adaptation'.
2 Explain how pressure from consumers might persuade a business, such as a supermarket, to 'go green'.
3 Using examples, explain the phrase 'think global, act local'.
4 Draw up a brief five-point plan setting out your ideas for a post-2012 'Son of Kyoto' international climate action agreement.

Chapter 7

The challenge of global hazards for the future

How should we tackle the global challenges of increasing risk and vulnerability in a hazardous world?

By the end of this chapter you should be able to:
- ➤ *evaluate the enormity of the challenge facing a world at risk from water shortages, food insecurity, escalating health problems and conflicts*
- ➤ *explain how innovative, sustainable strategies may help countries to mitigate and adapt to climate change and its hazardous impacts*
- ➤ *understand that at all scales, from global to local, the focus of solutions should be on the underlying issues of risk and vulnerability*

The enormity of the challenge

Climate change has implications for economic growth, human security and social wellbeing, especially for the poorest and most marginalised people. Figure 7.1 shows the vicious cycle of problems generated by climate change.

Figure 7.1
Vicious cycle of climate change

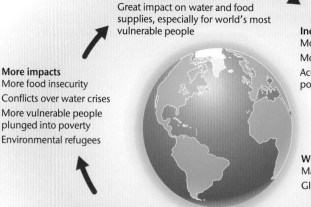

Higher temperatures
More hazardous world
Great impact on water and food supplies, especially for world's most vulnerable people

Increased evaporation
More water vapour
More ice sheet and glacier melt
Accelerating changes because of positive feedbacks

Worsening greenhouse effect
Major issue of rising sea levels
Global warming impacts

More uncertainty
More extreme weather with more uncertainty
Rising temperatures and changing precipitation patterns
Growing incidence of drought and flood events
Growing incidence of severe storms

More impacts
More food insecurity
Conflicts over water crises
More vulnerable people plunged into poverty
Environmental refugees

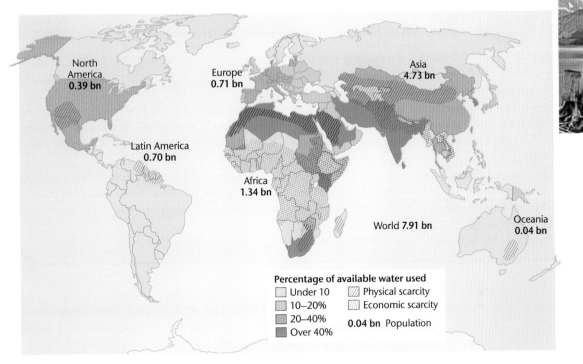

North
America
0.39 bn

Europe
0.71 bn

Asia
4.73 bn

Latin America
0.70 bn

Africa
1.34 bn

World **7.91 bn**

Oceania
0.04 bn

Percentage of available water used
- Under 10
- 10–20%
- 20–40%
- Over 40%
- Physical scarcity
- Economic scarcity

0.04 bn Population

Figure 7.2
Global water usage,
2025

Water shortages

Populations are increasing and placing demands on water supplies for agriculture and industry. Estimates suggest that water demands could rise by 50%, especially in far eastern countries.

Figure 7.2 shows the global situation. The World Bank estimates that as much as 50% of the world's population, concentrated in Africa, the middle east and southern Asia, will face severe water shortages by 2025. Around 2.8 billion people currently experience water stress (i.e. lack of safe, reliable supply).

Around 1.2 billion experience stress because of *physical* scarcity (i.e. lack of available supplies to meet demand). This could reach 1.7 billion by 2100. However, 1.6 billion people experience *economic* water scarcity because of poverty and poor governance. For example, some countries have allowed private water companies to supply water to their large cities, with disastrous results for the urban poor. The problem is not caused by global warming, but is made worse by climate change issues such as high temperatures in cities, unreliable supplies of rain for agriculturalists, and deteriorating pastures for nomadic herders.

In the High Andes and Himalayas, the disappearance of glaciers means that people can no longer rely on glacial meltwater as a water source. This is a particular problem in Colombia and Bolivia in South America.

Rapid changes in weather patterns leave people little time to adapt. For example, central American indigenous peoples are suffering badly from climate change but are the least equipped to act, as the case study on Miskito Indians on the next page shows.

Climate change is having a devastating effect on the Miskito Indians who live in wooden huts in Nicaragua's western territories. They subsist on crops planted on a few hectares of land and food hunted from the jungle and rivers.

Ten years ago, Marciano Washington could harvest 60 bags of rice a hectare from his 3 hectares of land. Last year he managed seven.

Environmental researchers are warning that the effect of climate change is likely to hit indigenous communities like the Miskito the hardest. The livelihoods of these isolated communities depend on nature and on predicting the weather, making them vulnerable to increasingly unstable weather patterns.

Temperatures across central America are expected to rise by 1–3°C and rainfall will decrease by 25% by 2070. Droughts, hurricanes and unseasonal flooding will increase.

The Miskito are isolated from modern farming techniques and hampered by poverty from years of economic neglect and discrimination.

Source: *Guardian*, 29 May 2007

Food insecurity

Food security means populations having access to enough food for an active, healthy life. Food insecurity results either from a lack of available food due to physical factors such as climate, or when there is adequate food available but the community or individual is too poor to access it.

Corel

Photograph 7.1 Subsistence farmers in Africa will be badly hit by extreme events

The impact of global warming on food security is complex, as it depends on a combination of the following factors:

➤ Higher temperatures stress crops and reduce yields, yet prolong growing seasons and allow a wider range of crops to be grown.
➤ A higher concentration of carbon dioxide speeds plant growth and increases resilience to water stress. Up to a certain level, this could be favourable for the midwest USA and parts of southeast Asia.
➤ Certain areas (e.g. equatorial and east Africa) will have more rainfall.
➤ Higher temperatures can promote the growth of crop pests and diseases.

In theory, agriculture is adaptable to global warming. There are many innovative techniques — some very high tech, and others appropriate to subsistence farmers — which can overcome water stress, so at a global level, food production and therefore food security should not be adversely affected by climate change except perhaps indirectly.

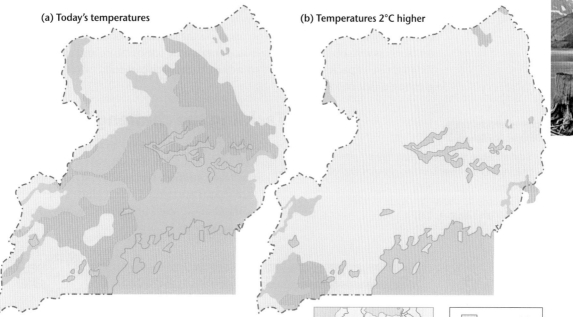

(a) Today's temperatures
(b) Temperatures 2°C higher

	Not suitable
	Less suitable
	Suitable

*Figure 7.3
Coffee-growing
areas in Uganda*

However, in reality there will be both winners and losers. Recent research has suggested that harvests of rice, wheat and corn (vital food crops) could plummet by a third over the next 20 years. Studies have shown that crop yields could drop by up to 10% for every 1°C temperature rise in some areas of Asia. Studies in east Africa predict a dramatic decrease in the land area suitable for growing cash crops like tea and coffee (Figure 7.3).

Subsistence farmers, particularly in Africa, will be badly affected by drought and extreme events, and malnutrition is likely to get worse.

The challenge

How countries cope with climate change will depend on wealth. Poverty leads to poor health, malnutrition and an inability to cope with extreme weather events. These interconnecting factors are summarised by the poverty bomb (Figure 7.4). Climate change is just one of the detonators.

A United Nations report in June 2007 concluded that the Darfur conflict in Sudan is driven by climate change and environmental degradation, which

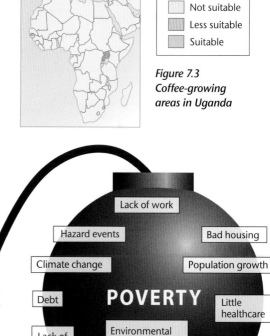

Possible detonator

Lack of work
Hazard events
Bad housing
Climate change
Population growth
Debt
POVERTY
Little healthcare
Lack of water
Environmental degradation and context hazards
Famine
Low income
Illiteracy

Figure 7.4 The poverty bomb

threaten to trigger a succession of new wars across Africa. The vulnerability of a community to climate change depends upon the sensitivity of the systems it relies on (such as agriculture) to changes in, for example temperature and rainfall, and its adaptive capacity, or ability to adjust to new circumstances (for example growing different food crops).

Tackling the challenge

So far, this book has concentrated on the dangers of global warming. This section looks at the range of sustainable strategies available to combat and cope with global warming. These include **sustainable development** at all levels and 'green' strategies such as renewable energy.

Sustainable development strategies   Key concept

Frameworks for sustainable development include the sustainability quadrant (Figure 7.5).

Many sustainable development strategies are applicable across the whole range of development levels. In addition, many schemes are sustainable in more than one part of the sustainability quadrant.

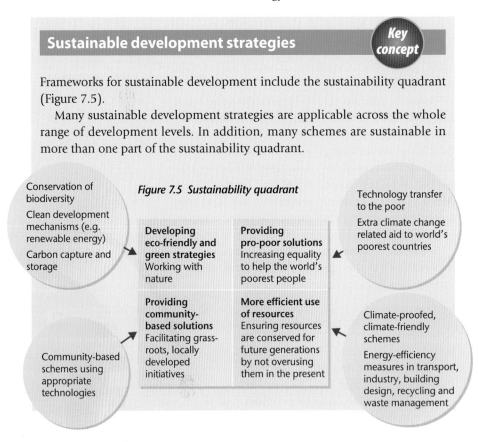

Figure 7.5 Sustainability quadrant

Conservation of biodiversity

Clean development mechanisms (e.g. renewable energy)

Carbon capture and storage

Developing eco-friendly and green strategies Working with nature

Providing pro-poor solutions Increasing equality to help the world's poorest people

Providing community-based solutions Facilitating grass-roots, locally developed initiatives

More efficient use of resources Ensuring resources are conserved for future generations by not overusing them in the present

Technology transfer to the poor

Extra climate change related aid to world's poorest countries

Climate-proofed, climate-friendly schemes

Energy-efficiency measures in transport, industry, building design, recycling and waste management

Community-based schemes using appropriate technologies

Green strategies

Tree planting

Trees take in carbon dioxide and 'fix' it in the form of hydrocarbons. However, in the first 10 years of its life, a growing tree releases more carbon dioxide than it absorbs, especially if the ground is cleared beforehand for forest planting.

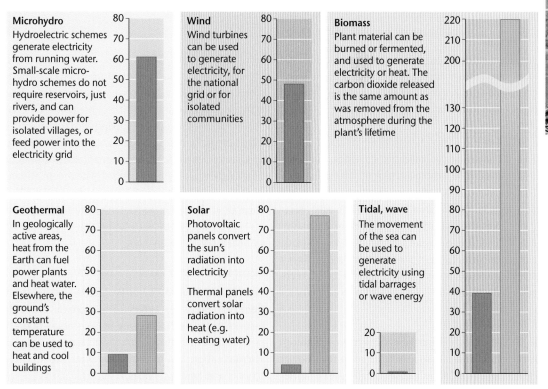

Figure 7.6 Renewable energy generation

Source: Atlas of Climate Change

Gigawatts produced, 2004
■ Electricity
▨ Heat

Under the Kyoto Protocol, countries are not prohibited from deforestation, yet they can claim carbon credits for new planting, while in reality releasing large amounts of carbon dioxide.

Renewable energy projects

Renewable energy projects are important, but again the costs and benefits of each scheme must be weighed up.

Large-scale renewable energy projects such as the Three Gorges dam in China have all kinds of environmental negatives as well as the obvious benefits of providing large quantities of 'green' electricity (fewer coal-fired power stations) and controlling floods on the River Yangtze. Biofuel crops provide renewable energy but take up huge areas of land that could be used for foodstuffs. In addition, deforestation in order to grow biofuel crops, which is happening in several South American countries, increases carbon dioxide emissions.

Wind farms generate 'green electricity' yet cover large areas of countryside and coast. In terms of power generated per unit of land occupied, photovoltaic cells which generate electricity using sunlight appear to be the most effective renewable energy source (see Figure 7.6).

The case study on the next page looks at a selection of renewable energy schemes.

Case study — Renewable energy schemes

This case study summarises a range of successful local renewable energy schemes. Many of these use intermediate technology which is cheap and easy to build using local materials.

Community hydropower in Kenya

Two community hydroelectric schemes, Kathama and Thima (in the remote areas of Mt Kenya), provide lighting, radio and telecommunications to over 200 households. For chicken farmers in the area, electricity provides warmth and therefore increased productivity. It also saves 42 tonnes of carbon dioxide emissions each year, as no kerosene is needed. This is an example of appropriate (intermediate) technology developed by Practical Action in east Africa.

The solar island

In 1996 the West Bengal Renewable Energy Development Association began a medium-scale solar power development in Sagan Island. It now uses a stand-alone photovoltaic power plant that provides grid-quality electricity to homes, shops, businesses and rural cooperatives as well as schools and health services. Diesel-powered generators have been replaced by this scheme.

Biomass cooking

More than 2.5 billion people burn biomass (wood, charcoal, dung, etc.) for cooking and heating. Biomass energy accounts for 80% of the current global renewable energy supply. Working with communities in countries including Sudan and Kenya, NGOs are providing cleaner fuels and more efficient stoves to improve the quality of cooking and health. In Sudan, the fuel used is liquefied petroleum gas, which is cheaper and cleaner than charcoal. In Kenya, wood fuel is still used, but with fuel-efficient stoves and smoke hoods for cleaner air.

Jepirachi Wind Power Project

The Jepirachi Wind Power Project in northeastern Colombia aims to build 15 windmills on land belonging to the Wayun, one of Colombia's poorest peoples. The energy generated will be used to power a desalination plant providing water to homes, schools and health services.

Further research

Details of renewable energy schemes can be obtained from websites such as www.itdg.org (Practical Action), www.neweconomics.org and www.iied.org.

Community-based solutions

Community-based solutions work well because they are 'bottom up' — developed by local people for local people instead of being imposed by government. They are applicable to all aspects of mitigating and adapting to climate change in countries at all stages of development. The two schemes in the case study below are completely different in focus, but contain elements of the bottom-up model.

Case study — Community-based green strategies

Low Carbon Wolvercote, Oxfordshire

Wolvercote is a village with a strong community spirit, consisting of original villagers and newcomers. A group of people including the vicar, local artists and the founder of ClimateXchange Oxfordshire (www.climatex.org) has acted as a catalyst in

creating the following schemes to lower the village's carbon footprint:
- ➤ Each road has waste champions who organise rubbish swaps of unwanted items and take the surplus to a recycling centre.
- ➤ Information is circulated on the ten most effective

Photograph 7.2

Ian Curtis

Ian Curtis

ways to reduce carbon dioxide emissions (e.g. composting, home insulation, solar panels, cutting food miles).

➤ Green transport strategies have been introduced, including car shares for work and supermarket shopping, safe cycling and promotion of the local bus service.

➤ Older residents have been asked for advice on how to live simply (e.g. growing your own vegetables and saving on fuel).

➤ Cloth bags are available to cut down on the use of plastic bags.

Photograph 7.3

Machakos and Makueni, Kenya

In Machakos and Makueni districts, Kenya, Christian Aid is working with its local NGO partner, the Benevolent Institute of Development Initiatives, on a capacity-building scheme to help local farmers who are suffering from water shortages due to the melting of Kilimanjaro's glaciers. The scheme aims to identify 'faithful, available and teachable' people and train them to mobilise volunteers in each community to assess needs and tackle key issues. So far over 100 local smallholders are looking at initiatives such as:

➤ building fences to contain water and combat soil erosion

➤ developing composting skills

➤ constructing rain-fed irrigation systems via tanks and gullies

➤ experimenting with new 'crops' such as gravillea trees which put nitrogen back into the soil

Energy efficiency

Energy efficiency not only reduces emissions, it also cuts costs and local pollution. It is therefore a popular solution. However, developing countries feel that the cost of developing energy-saving technology should be shared or borne entirely by the more economically developed countries (see the case study on India and China below).

Methods of increasing energy efficiency include:

➤ remodelled factories with cleaner industrial processes and optimum energy use
➤ redesigned houses with modern boiler systems and full insulation
➤ green transport using new or greener fuels (hydrogen or hybrid technology)
➤ greener power stations with lower emissions

Many companies, including General Electric and 3M, have found that growth based on green principles is profitable.

Case study: India and China

China and India, because of their size (a combined population of 2.5 billion) and rapid economic growth (6–10% per year), have a critical role to play in controlling emissions.

Photograph 7.4 People struggling to breathe in dense air pollution in China

■ India's greenhouse gas emissions could rise by 70% by 2025.
■ The increase in China's emissions from 2000 to 2030 will nearly equal the increase from the entire industrialised world.
■ China's total electricity demand will rise by an

estimated 2,600 GW by 2050, which is the equivalent of adding four 300 MW power plants every week for the next 45 years.

■ India's energy consumption rose by 280% between 1980 and 2001, even faster than China's, and nearly half the population still lacks regular access to electricity.

These statistics suggest nightmare projections for greenhouse gases even if the developed countries all cut their emissions drastically. Both India and China are desperate for energy to fuel their economic expansion, as this is pulling their citizens out of poverty. Despite considerable investments in nuclear power (India), hydroelectric power (China) and renewables, most of the new energy will need to come from coal (an abundant resource in both countries). China builds one new coal-fuelled power station every day.

Environmental concerns inevitably lag behind the need for growth. However, both China and India see climate change policy as a way to address some immediate problems, such as energy shortages, energy inefficiency and severe atmospheric pollution. They can get the international community to pay for improvements using mechanisms established at Kyoto.

The Special Climate Change Fund (SSCF) and the Clean Development Mechanism (CDM) allow developed countries to sponsor greenhouse-gas-cutting projects in developing countries in exchange for carbon credits that can be used to meet their own emissions targets (e.g. the UK has made huge investments in scrubbers for Chinese power stations).

A more hazardous world

Urgent priorities for managing future global hazards are summed up by the Hyogo Framework for Action, 2005–15, developed in 2005 by the World Conference on Disaster Reduction in Kobe, Japan. Figure 7.7 shows how closely disaster risk

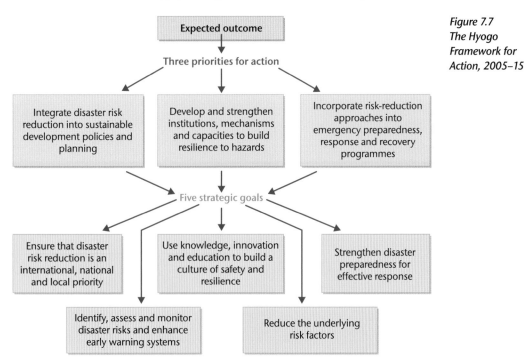

Figure 7.7
The Hyogo Framework for Action, 2005–15

reduction is linked to poverty alleviation. Building resilience to disaster should therefore be at the heart of all development policies.

The framework can be applied at all scales from local to international. At a local scale, an examination of the impact of a recurring hazard event such as flood risk could be used, perhaps contrasting the 2007 floods in the UK with those in southern Asia. At a regional scale, the persistence of poverty in most African countries could be considered. At a global scale, a mega disaster such as the 2004 south Asia tsunami could be researched and evaluated using the Hyogo framework.

Useful websites include www.panda.org, www.fiacc.net and www.climate network.org.

Review questions

1 Explain the difference between:
  a physical water scarcity and economic water scarcity
  b food availability deficit and food entitlement deficit.
2 Referring to Figure 7.4, show how climate change is linked to the other detonators of poverty.
3 Discuss the view that renewable energy sources are rarely completely environmentally friendly. Which source do you think is the least friendly? Give your reasons.
4 Examine the usefulness of the Hyogo Framework (Figure 7.7) for managing disasters at (two) contrasting scales.

Unit 1
Global challenges

Going global

Chapter 8

Globalisation

What is globalisation and how is it changing people's lives?

By the end of this chapter you should have:

➤ *explored the key concepts, processes and terminology relating to globalisation and the associated processes of population change and migration*

➤ *identified key factors in the spread of globalisation, including the growth of trans-national corporations and the establishment of international organisations such as the International Monetary Fund*

➤ *examined the impact of globalisation on population movements*

What is globalisation?

The word 'globalisation' only came into common usage during the 1990s. Prior to that, geographers mainly talked about 'the global economy'. However, there was a growing recognition that economic changes were accompanied by important cultural, demographic (population), political and environmental changes on a worldwide scale (and at an ever-accelerating pace). The umbrella term 'globalisation' is now used to describe the many ways in which places and people are becoming ever more closely linked (Photograph 8.1).

Some of the global changes are exciting and bring new possibilities. Wealth is spreading to more, although by no means all, people. Cultures are mixing and becoming more diverse. In the UK, people routinely consume food, films and music from all over the world. However, there are downsides to globalisation too. A world in which people are more free to move across borders — as is now happening in the EU — is not to everyone's taste. There are serious issues about how it is possible for goods and resources to be moved around the world so easily while many people still go hungry. Finally, people everywhere look set to bear the heavy costs of the worst environmental impacts of globalisation, as described in Chapters 5–7.

Photograph 8.1 Coca Cola in Morocco. Globalisation describes the way cultures are ever more closely linked

Corel

Globalisation

Globalisation is sometimes described as being 'nothing new', in the sense that people, countries and continents have always been connected in economic, cultural and political ways, through:

➤ trade — especially after 1492 when Columbus reached the Americas and the traditional world economy began to take shape

➤ colonialism — by the end of the nineteenth century, the British empire directly controlled one-quarter of the world and its peoples

➤ cooperation — since the First World War ended in 1918, international organisations similar to today's United Nations have existed

What makes modern (post-1940s) globalisation different is:

➤ a *lengthening* of connections between people and places, with products sourced from further away than ever before (in one extreme case, bottled water is now brought to the UK from Fiji, 16,000 km away)

➤ a *deepening* of connections to other people and places in more areas of our lives

Study a laptop and see where the parts originated (Figure 8.1). Think about the food you eat each day and the places from which it is sourced. It is more or less impossible *not* to be connected to other people and places through the products we consume.

This sense of connection is not true for everyone in the world. Some nations (e.g. Chad) experience a much more 'shallow' form of integration (Figure 8.2). In other cases, there can be great unevenness among a country's citizens in their experience of globalisation. For instance, many people living in Brazil's core cities of Rio de Janeiro and São Paulo are connected to the rest of the world as producers of goods or as consumers — even favela dwellers may follow the fortunes of Real Madrid or listen to US rock bands. However, the Korubo people, in Brazil's Amazon rainforest, have almost no knowledge of the outside world, and are in no sense connected socially or economically to other places. Even so, their environment may soon be at risk because of logging or global climate change.

Figure 8.1 The global origins of the parts of a Dell laptop

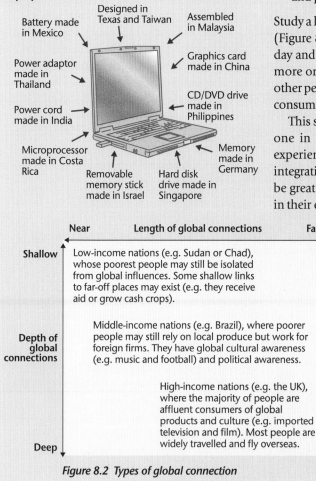

Figure 8.2 Types of global connection

Globalisation, population change and migration

Demographic (population) changes are an important aspect of globalisation. Economic growth usually triggers an increase in the number of people living in a region. This is due to changes in the **birth rate**, **death rate** and level of **natural increase** over time. Accompanying this growth in overall population numbers, the proportion of people living in urban areas also increases over time as a result of **internal migration** of **economic migrants**. Greater levels of international migration are another aspect of the strong influence that globalisation has on population dynamics.

Push and pull factors are usually identified to explain migration flows. These factors are the reasons why people are repelled by, or attracted to, different places. Globalisation can concentrate wealth in some places, for instance when businesses set up factories or offices in the world's major cities, making them more attractive to economic migrants. At the same time, rural areas usually modernise in ways that reduce job opportunities (mechanisation of farming, for instance). Mass population movements are generated, some of which cross territorial borders.

In the past, **intervening obstacles** such as political barriers often meant that such migration could not take place. However, globalisation sometimes removes these obstacles. Citizens of the 27 EU member countries can now move freely and can, in most cases, take up work wherever they please in the EU. For instance, between 2004 and 2006, 650,000 Polish people gained UK work permits. Many were young and their arrival has noticeably modified the population pyramids of those cities where they have settled.

Sometimes, **intervening opportunities** can interrupt a migration flow. For instance, young Polish migrants heading to Ireland via London may not complete their original planned journey if they find work in London.

Key terms

Birth rate The number of births per 1,000 people per year in a region (a measure of fertility, although actual fertility rates are highly dependent upon population structure, with youthful populations having much higher fertility than greying populations).

Death rate The number of deaths per 1,000 people per year in a region (a measure of mortality).

Economic migrant A migrant whose primary motivation is to seek employment. Migrants who already have jobs may set off in search of better pay, more regular pay, promotion or a change of career.

Internal migration The movement of people between different regions within the same nation. Hundreds of millions of people in the world's poorer nations have made an internal movement from the countryside to cities in recent decades, in response to differing levels of economic opportunity.

Intervening obstacle Barrier to a migrant such as a political border or physical feature (e.g. the Mediterranean for north Africans heading to Europe). Obstacles can include family pressures and travel costs.

Intervening opportunity An alternative migration destination that exists between the migrant's place of origin and intended destination.

Natural increase The difference between the birth rate and the death rate, usually converted into a percentage. A negative figure suggests deaths exceed births and may be described as 'natural decrease'.

Population growth over time

Since Europe's Industrial Revolution in the eighteenth century, societies around the world have experienced a fall in death rate followed by a fall in birth rate. This has occurred as the benefits of modern healthcare, sanitation, nutrition and education have spread between countries. The resulting changes in natural increase and total population sizes are described by the demographic transition model (Figure 8.3).

In almost all cases, economic growth — as it has spread around the world — has been accompanied by a period of pronounced population growth. The UK was the first nation to industrialise and its population increased from 5 million in 1750 to around 40 million by 1900 (it has now reached 60 million). In countries such as India and Brazil changes are still taking place, and on an even larger scale. India, whose population was already large at 300 million in 1940, is predicted to reach a staggering 1.5 billion by 2030.

High rates of population growth occur when a society enters a stage in which death rate falls but birth rate does not. This happens when the benefits of modern health, medicine and food technology result in a fall in mortality, but there is a time lag before economic and cultural preferences for fewer children become established. This is currently the situation in much of Africa, where populations are expected to double over the next 30 years. In contrast, the European nations that experienced early economic growth now have near-zero population growth, as birth rates fell to the same low level as death rates some decades ago.

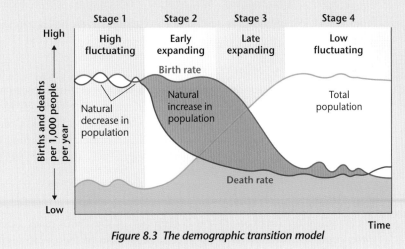

Figure 8.3 The demographic transition model

The evolution of globalisation

A number of factors have been responsible for the lengthening and deepening of the interconnections between places that define globalisation. Some factors are continuations of much older processes, such as the growth of international air travel, while others are entirely new, such as the internet.

The period that concerns us most begins in 1945, the year when the Second World War ended, worldwide economic reconstruction began (notably for

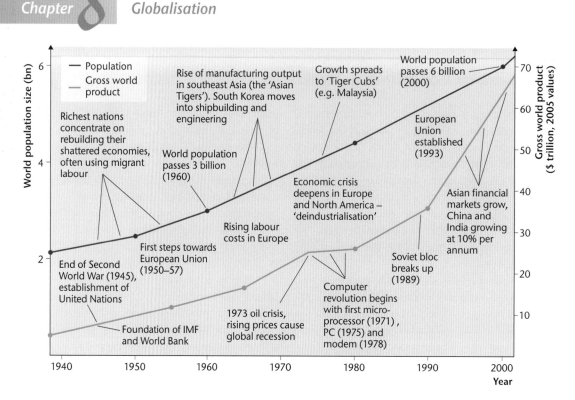

*Figure 8.4
The postwar
globalisation
timeline*

Japan and Germany) and the International Monetary Fund (IMF) was set up
(Figure 8.4). We will look at several key influences on globalisation throughout
the postwar decades.

Transnational corporations

Transnational corporations (TNCs) are firms with operations spread across the
world, operating in many nations as both makers and sellers of goods and services.
Instantly recognisable 'global brands' such as Coca-Cola, McDonald's and the BBC
(a special case, as it is partly funded by the UK government) have brought cultural
as well as economic changes to places where products are made and consumed
(Photograph 8.2).

Transport

The arrival of the intercontinental Boeing 747 in the 1960s made international
travel more commonplace, while recent expansion of the cheap flights sector
(e.g. Ryanair and easyJet) has brought air travel to the masses in richer nations.
The growth in containerised shipping since the 1940s is another important factor.
Around 200 million individual container movements are thought to take place
each year.

Computer and internet technology

Computers have had a profound effect on how businesses operate and where they
can locate. Computer-aided design and manufacturing (CAD and CAM) have
revolutionised manufacturing processes. They help make manufacturing more

Photograph 8.2 Global brands have brought cultural changes: McDonald's in Shanghai

flexible and less reliant on human labour, allowing some firms to become more footloose. Information and communications technology (ICT) allows managers of offices and plants which are geographically distant to keep in touch more easily (e.g. through e-mail and video-conferencing). This has allowed TNCs to expand into new territories, either to make or to sell their products.

International organisations

International organisations grew in power and influence throughout the twentieth century. The most important of these 'brokers' of globalisation is the IMF. Based in Washington, it channels loans from the world's richest nations to countries that apply for help. In return, the governments that receive loans must agree to run free-market economies that are open to investment from outside. This means TNCs can enter these countries more easily, further promoting globalisation. IMF rules and regulations are sometimes controversial, especially **structural adjustment programmes** (SAPs). For example, in Tanzania, water services to shanty towns in the capital Dar es Salaam were cut off when the country was required to privatise its water services as a condition of receiving $143 million debt relief.

Other important organisations that work alongside the IMF include the World Trade Organization (WTO) and the World Bank. Non-governmental organisations (NGOs), such as Oxfam and Christian Aid, also have a major transglobal influence, working to connect places and people through flows of aid or debt relief.

> ### Key term
>
> **Structural adjustment programmes** Strict conditions imposed on countries receiving loans from the IMF and the World Bank. Receiving governments may be required to cut back on healthcare, education, sanitation and housing programmes.

Markets

Markets are on the rise globally. More and more people living in major world cities have enough wealth to be significant consumers of goods and services. In 2007, China already had an estimated 30 million affluent consumers, and it is predicted to become the world's largest market for consumer goods by 2015. The growth of major stock markets (where shares of companies are traded and vast amounts of wealth are generated) has also been an important influence. Since 1945, several new stock exchanges have opened, notably Shanghai (China) in 1990.

 Case study **Globalisation and Christmas**

According to a recent estimate, the ingredients of a typical UK Christmas lunch collectively travel around 130,000 km. In the past, Christmas meals — as well as the presents given — would probably have originated locally within the UK. Now, food and toys are transported from all over the world by plane, lorry or container ship. For example, a Christmas dinner might include:

- frozen turkeys flown into the UK from Thailand
- wine flown into the UK from New Zealand
- runner beans flown into the UK from Zambia

Of course, it is still possible to obtain ingredients locally. A London family could source an organic free-range goose from Norwich as well as wine and sprouts from Kent. However, these products might well cost more — costs of production in less developed countries are lower. Efficient transport systems also help to keep prices down. Large container ships move enormous volumes of produce. The unit cost of food items and manufactured toys barely rises, even when goods have travelled all the way from China to the UK (Figure 8.5). Transnational corporations help drive this change, looking for the cheapest possible location to grow food or assemble manufactured goods for the Christmas market.

For instance, one of the most popular items on UK high streets for Christmas 2005 was a toy called

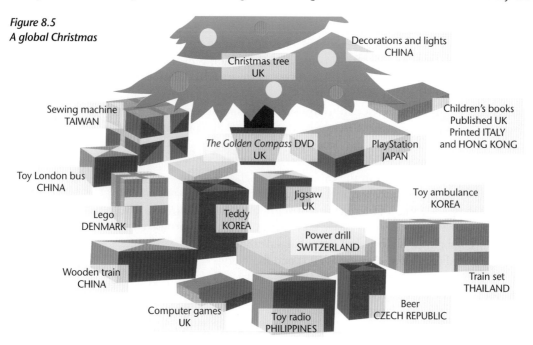

Figure 8.5
A global Christmas

Decorations and lights
CHINA

Christmas tree
UK

Sewing machine
TAIWAN

Children's books
Published UK
Printed ITALY
and HONG KONG

The Golden Compass DVD
UK

PlayStation
JAPAN

Toy London bus
CHINA

Jigsaw
UK

Toy ambulance
KOREA

Lego
DENMARK

Teddy
KOREA

Power drill
SWITZERLAND

Wooden train
CHINA

Train set
THAILAND

Computer games
UK

Toy radio
PHILIPPINES

Beer
CZECH REPUBLIC

Roboraptor. Selling at around £80, the product was manufactured by a Chinese company, Wah Shing Toys, using very cheap labour. The city of Dongguan, where Wah Shing is based, is known as 'Santa's workshop' because so many of the world's toys are made there. Working 24 hours a day, 7 days a week, the Dongguan factory produced 1.5 million Roboraptors in the run-up to Christmas 2005. The workforce was more than doubled, from 3,000 to 7,000, during this period. The firm employs many rural migrants and prefers women, who are more dextrous.

The globalisation of Christmas does not finish at the end of the holiday season. The UK government-sponsored Recycle Now organisation estimates that 1 billion Christmas cards, 8 million Christmas trees, 750 million extra bottles and 500 million jars need to be disposed of each year. Much of this waste is now sent back to China for recycling, as it is far cheaper to process materials there than in the UK.

Globalisation and population movements

Globalisation can make us think of the world as a potentially borderless place. The photograph 'Earth-rise' was taken by *Apollo 11* astronauts in 1969 (Photograph 8.3). It was the first time people living on Earth had seen the world as a single entity. This iconic image helped assist the process of globalisation and also raised environmental awareness.

People are increasingly thinking of themselves as 'global citizens', visiting and often relocating to distant places. This is especially true of the international **elite** (Figure 8.6). These affluent people, whose

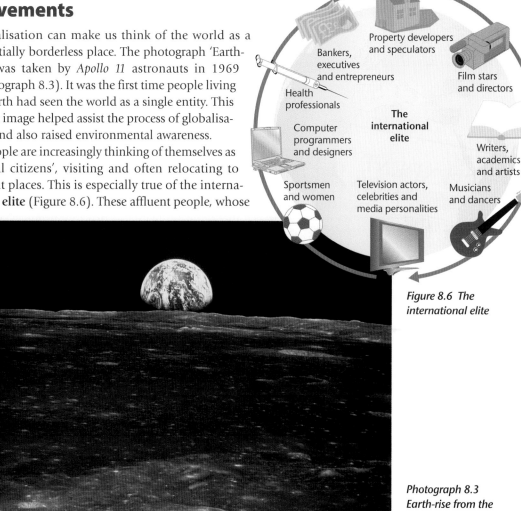

Figure 8.6 The international elite

Property developers and speculators
Bankers, executives and entrepreneurs
Film stars and directors
Health professionals
The international elite
Computer programmers and designers
Writers, academics and artists
Sportsmen and women
Television actors, celebrities and media personalities
Musicians and dancers

Photograph 8.3 Earth-rise from the Moon (1969)

NASA/SPL

Key terms

Elite A group of people who are economically and socially powerful. Their money may be inherited or entrepreneurial in origin (e.g. Bill Gates has earned over $50 billion from his company Microsoft).

Foreign direct investment A financial injection made by a TNC into a nation's economy, either to build new facilities (factories or shops) or to acquire or merge with an existing firm there.

Rural–urban migration A movement of population from rural to urban areas. Typically, it is a young (15–30 years) migration and often male-dominated, although in Asian nations (notably China and Thailand) there is a balance between men and women.

skills or financial resources are highly prized, may find few obstacles to prevent them from moving between countries for work or residency. For example, there are around 200,000 Americans living in the UK, even though the USA is not part of the EU.

As well as international migration, internal movements between different regions of a single country have increased. Large-scale **rural–urban migration** is taking place in many of the world's poorest and emerging economies on a scale never seen before. Some 3.3 billion people now live in urban areas. Two important reasons for this shift are:

➤ Television and radio (helped by satellite), as well as printed books and newspapers, can be received even in remote and impoverished rural areas in poor countries. For instance, mobile cinemas and satellite dishes have penetrated even into the remotest parts of rural India. Such knowledge of other places can trigger migration of the young.

➤ The **foreign direct investment** (FDI) that TNCs make in urban areas of poorer countries greatly boosts the employment opportunities on offer, thereby attracting rural migrants.

Globalisation may mean easier movement of goods and money, but this is not always the case for population migration. Since 11 September 2001, when terrorists destroyed the World Trade Center, rich countries have started introducing new immigration rules and restrictions. It has become harder to gain a visa to enter the USA, which was often described in the past as an 'immigrant nation', and kept its doors open for tens of millions of people in the nineteenth and early twentieth centuries.

Heightened fears about terrorism and national security have accompanied the most recent phase of globalisation. Conflicts between different values and attitudes have been brought into increasingly sharp focus. Meanwhile, the world's poor continue to gain greater knowledge of the affluent conditions in rich countries, while their own countries suffer drought (e.g. sub-Saharan Africa) and flood (e.g. Bangladesh) as a result of climate change. European policy-makers are toughening their stance towards migration as increasing numbers of hungry refugees from poor African nations such as Somalia attempt to cross the Mediterranean into Europe in unsafe, leaky boats (Photograph 8.4).

The Independent

Photograph 8.4 African migrants cling to a tuna net in the Mediterranean

Skills focus

It is probably unwise to take your laptop or mobile apart to see where the parts come from. However, it is possible to deconstruct ('take apart') art, music or films — artefacts that we can tell are a product of globalisation because they show signs of different cultural influences. Much popular music is a combination of European and African musical forms. Food is another good example — the ingredients of 'fusion' cuisine are drawn from many different places.

Following this line of inquiry, study Image 3 of 'Spiderman India' at **www.gothamcomics.com/spiderman_india**. This version of the popular American superhero — owned by the New York transnational corporation, Marvel Entertainment Group — was 're-imagined' for a young Indian audience by a firm based in Bangalore. The following task involves decoding the image to find signs of how a local culture has redesigned a global icon.

Task

1 Record the characteristics that appear to be Indian, rather than American.
2 Decide what overall message the image sends about globalisation. Is globalisation a simple 'exporting' of American products?
3 Decide if this illustration could best be described as an example of cultural or economic globalisation — or both.

> **Tip** You may need to refer back to the original American 'Spiderman' to see what changes have been made to the character. A Google Image search will help you find the original. You can also find additional information at **www.geographyinthenews.rgs.org/news/article/?id=325**.

Review questions

1 Study Figure 8.1. Using an atlas, estimate the total kilometres that the parts of the laptop have travelled, assuming it is finally assembled for sale in Malaysia.
2 Draw a table with two columns headed '1900' and '2000'. List the leading transport and communications technologies associated with each time period.
3 Compare recent global trends in internal and international migration.
4 Describe the varied characteristics of elite groups and suggest reasons why these people find it relatively easy to move between nations.
5 Using examples at a range of scales, outline the main factors responsible for globalisation.

Global groupings

What are the main groupings of nations and what differences exist in levels of wealth and power?

By the end of this chapter you should have:

➤ *developed an awareness of the various ways in which geographers classify and categorise nations according to their levels of wealth and power*

➤ *researched the voluntary political groupings (trade blocs) to which most nations belong*

➤ *studied the geography of one transnational corporation*

➤ *analysed the role that transnational corporations play in building links between nations*

Key terms

Development gap The difference in levels of economic and social well-being between the richest and poorest people on the planet.

Gross domestic product A measure of the financial value of the goods and services produced within a territory (including foreign firms located there). It is often divided by population size to produce a per capita figure for the purpose of making comparisons.

Human development index A United Nations measure of economic and social development that takes into account income per capita, life expectancy and adult literacy.

Poverty A lack of wealth. *Absolute* poverty describes income levels below what is needed to maintain an adequate diet. *Relative* poverty describes income levels that are below average for a region.

A useful starting point when studying the disparities in wealth and power is to group nations into different categories. These might be based on wealth, the provision of basic needs, or political considerations (such as the power and influence a nation has).

In the past the world was crudely divided into two categories, using the labels 'developed' and 'developing'. However, such an approach no longer works well. The distribution of people living in **poverty**, as well as of elite groups, has become more complex in the era of globalisation. In particular:

➤ A large number of previously poor nations are now relatively wealthy, in terms of national annual income (e.g. average earnings or per capita gross domestic product, GDP). These middle-income countries include Malaysia, Egypt, Brazil and China.

➤ The presence of rich elites in many countries makes it harder to generalise about rich and poor nations as a whole. Despite being in middle-income countries with a relatively low **human development index** (HDI), cities like São Paulo, Beijing and Bangalore are home to millions of people who have affluent lifestyles, complicating the analysis once again. Does it still make sense to talk of a **development gap** between nations, or is the gap just between groups of people? City landscapes in such countries do not immediately suggest poverty (Photograph 9.1), although it will certainly be found on the urban fringes.

Economic groupings and political groupings

Geographers use two types of grouping to study nations in a global context. These
are economic groupings and political groupings.

Economic groupings

Nations can be categorised according to their overall levels of wealth and the
power that this brings. Several important groupings are described below, all of
which are used either by researchers or by agencies such as the United Nations
(UN). Sometimes there is overlap between groupings (Figure 9.1).

Least developed countries (LDCs)

The term 'least developed countries' can be used to refer to the world's poorest
low-income nations. This group of around 50 states (out of the world total of
192 countries formally recognised by the UN) has sometimes been described as
'Fourth World' nations to emphasise their bleak conditions and their populations'

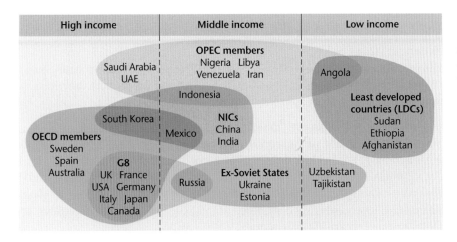

*Figure 9.1
Economic
groupings of
nations, with
examples of
member countries*

❶ Haiti	❿ São Tomé & Príncipe	⓭ Democratic Republic of the Congo	㉗ Djibouti	㊱ Yemen
❷ Cape Verde	⓫ Equatorial Guinea	⓴ Angola	㉘ Eritrea	㊲ Maldives
❸ The Gambia	⓬ Senegal	㉑ Zambia	㉙ Madagascar	㊳ Afghanistan
❹ Guinea-Bissau	⓭ Mauritania	㉒ Tanzania	㉚ Lesotho	㊴ Bhutan
❺ Guinea	⓮ Burkina Faso	㉓ Mozambique	㉛ Malawi	㊵ Nepal
❻ Sierra Leone	⓯ Mali	㉔ Sudan	㉜ Comoros	㊶ Myanmar
❼ Liberia	⓰ Niger	㉕ Ethiopia	㉝ Burundi	㊷ East Timor
❽ Togo	⓱ Chad	㉖ Somalia	㉞ Rwanda	㊸ Laos
❾ Benin	⓲ Central African Republic		㉟ Uganda	㊹ Cambodia

(additional column: ㊺ Solomon Islands, ㊻ Bangladesh, ㊼ Tuvalu, ㊽ Kiribati, ㊾ Vanuatu, ㊿ Samoa)

Figure 9.2
The world's 50 least developed countries

lack of engagement with globalising forces (Figure 9.2). A number of these nations, such as Sudan and Afghanistan, are frequently described as 'failed states' by politicians.

Newly industrialised countries (NICs)

NICs are middle-income nations where exports and average earnings have risen at unprecedented rates since the 1970s. Brazil, Mexico and Argentina are often placed in this category, but the most famous are the 'Asian Tigers' (Hong Kong, Singapore, South Korea and Taiwan). They have recently been joined by many more in a second wave that includes the rising superpower economies of India and China. These are sometimes called recently industrialised countries (RICs) to distinguish them from the first wave of NICs.

Ex-Soviet states

The break-up of the Soviet Union in 1989 (re)created 15 ex-Soviet states, many of which score poorly in GDP and HDI figures, and are usually described as middle-income (e.g. Russia) or low-income (e.g. Kazakhstan).

Organisation of Petroleum Exporting Countries (OPEC)

Since the 1960s, many of the world's major oil producers have belonged to this organisation. The **petrodollar** earnings of states like Saudi Arabia make it one of the wealthiest countries in the world, with a GDP of around $350 billion in 2007. However, although most OPEC members display well above average levels of wealth, it is often unevenly distributed among citizens (notably in Nigeria, an OPEC member where life expectancy is just 44 years).

Organisation for Economic Cooperation and Development (OECD)

In contrast to OPEC, the OECD is an organisation of 30 nations where high levels of wealth are far more evenly distributed among citizens and the typical standard of living is good. This grouping includes all the world's high-income nations. The most powerful seven (or eight) of these are known as the G7 (or G8) and they are the USA, Canada, the UK, Germany, France, Italy, Japan (and Russia).

The groupings described above tell us that, as well as high-income OECD countries and low-income LDCs, there are now large numbers of middle-income countries consisting of ex-Soviet states, NICs (and RICs) and OPEC states. Any simple twofold grouping of the world's nations has become too much of an oversimplification.

> **Key term**
>
> **Petrodollars** Money derived from selling oil. Since the formation of OPEC, states such as Saudi Arabia, the United Arab Emirates (UAE, including Dubai) and Venezuela have experienced significant increases in levels of national wealth.

Political groupings (trade blocs)

To complicate matters further, countries have formed trade blocs (Figure 9.3). These differ from economic groupings (such as NICs) in two important ways:

➤ To trade freely, agreements have to be drawn up that allow national boundaries to be crossed by flows of goods, money and sometimes workers. National laws have to be amended, which is why these can be described as political groupings (despite having an economic purpose).

➤ Trade blocs can contain nations at varying levels of economic development. For instance, Mexico and the USA are both part of the North American Free Trade Agreement (NAFTA). This makes sense because Mexico has a cheap labour force, while the USA has management and research expertise. It allows American

Figure 9.3 Selected regional trade bloc groupings

NAFTA
Canada
USA
Mexico

CARICOM
Antigua and Barbuda
Bahamas
Barbados
Belize
Dominica
Grenada
Guyana
Jamaica
Montserrat
St Kitts and Nevis
St Lucia
St Vincent and the Grenadines
Suriname
Trinidad and Tobago

MERCOSUR
Argentina
Brazil
Paraguay
Uruguay

EU
Austria
Belgium
Bulgaria
Cyprus
Czech Republic
Denmark
Estonia
Finland
France
Germany
Greece
Hungary
Ireland
Italy
Latvia
Lithuania
Luxembourg
Malta
Netherlands
Poland
Portugal
Romania
Slovakia
Slovenia
Spain
Sweden
UK

COMESA
Angola
Burundi
Comoros
Dem. Rep. of the Congo
Djibouti
Egypt
Eritrea
Ethiopia
Kenya
Madagascar
Malawi
Mauritius
Namibia
Rwanda
Seychelles
Sudan
Swaziland
Tanzania
Uganda
Zambia
Zimbabwe

ASEAN
Brunei
Cambodia
Indonesia
Laos
Malaysia
Myanmar
Philippines
Singapore
Thailand
Vietnam

transnational corporations (TNCs) to exploit the human resources of both nations, cheaply manufacturing goods in branch plants in Mexico (*maquiladoras*) that are designed and marketed by white-collar staff in the USA. Geographers describe this as a **spatial division of labour**.

With the exception of the European Union (EU), where the free movement of people is also permitted, trade blocs usually make only the movement of goods and money easier. They do not allow unrestricted migration of people, and in some cases they make it harder. For instance, the USA wants the global benefit of free access for US firms to Mexican labour within Mexico, but sees unrestricted movement of Mexicans into the USA as a global challenge — and refuses to allow it. Huge numbers of guards are deployed on the border to stop Mexicans illegally entering the USA.

Why do nations belong to trade blocs?

Key concept

Trade blocs are voluntary international organisations that exist for trading purposes, bringing greater economic strength and security to the nations that join. Free trade is encouraged by the removal of internal tariffs (the taxes that are paid when importing or exporting goods and services between countries). Trade blocs can also protect members by establishing a common external tariff for foreign imports. The EU has integrated even further, with a common currency (the euro) and some shared political legislation (Table 9.1).

Table 9.1 EU timeline

Year	Events
1950	Schuman Plan proposes a European Coal and Steel Community (ECSC).
1952	ECSC is created.
1957	Treaty of Rome establishing the European Economic Community (EEC) is signed by Belgium, France, Germany, Italy, Luxembourg and the Netherlands.
1958	EEC comes into operation.
1962	Common Agricultural Policy (CAP) is agreed.
1968	Customs union completed.
1973	UK, Ireland and Denmark join the EC.
1979	European Monetary System established; first direct elections to the European Parliament.
1986	Spain and Portugal join the EC.
1993	European Union (EU) is established as the Maastricht Treaty comes into force.
1995	Austria, Finland and Sweden join the EU, which now has 15 members.
2002	Euro notes and coins come into circulation in 12 of the 15 EU member states.
2004	Ten new member states join the EU — Cyprus, Czech Republic, Estonia, Hungary, Latvia, Lithuania, Malta, Poland, Slovakia and Slovenia; EU Constitutional Treaty agreed.
2007	Romania and Bulgaria join the EU.
2008	Kosovo declares independence supported by EU.

The removal of internal tariffs brings a number of benefits to member states:

➤ Markets grow. For instance, when ten new nations joined the EU in 2004, UK firm Tesco gained access to 75 million extra customers.

➤ Firms that have a comparative advantage in the production of a particular product or service should prosper. French wine-makers, thanks to their advantageous climate and soil, produce a superior product that is widely consumed throughout a tariff-free Europe.

➤ An enlarged market increases demand, raising the volume of production and lowering manufacturing costs per unit. This improved economy of scale means that products can be sold more cheaply and sales rise even further for the most successful firms.

➤ Smaller national firms within a trade bloc can merge to form TNCs, making their operations more cost-effective.

In the special case of the EU, members are eligible for EU Structural Funds to help develop their economies, while agricultural producers in all countries of the European Union benefit from farm subsidies issued under the Common Agricultural Policy.

The EU is also sometimes said to bring political stability to the continent. European economic integration at the end of the Second World War was in part driven by a desire to avert any future pan-European conflict.

Further research

The BBC provides an excellent interactive link for studying the major groupings of nations: http://news.bbc.co.uk/hi/english/static/special_report/1999/11/99/seattle_trade_talks/defaultapec.stm.

See also: www.geographyinthenews.rgs.org/news/article/?id=484.

Transnational corporations

Transnational corporations (TNCs) can be described as 'architects' of globalisation, helping to build bridges between nations. They bolt together different economies and societies through their supply chains and marketing strategies. TNCs have their roots in the colonial businesses of the eighteenth and nineteenth centuries, such as the UK's East India Company. Today, they have evolved into complex organisations:

➤ TNCs may build their businesses up by buying foreign firms in mergers or acquisitions. For instance, the Irish beer manufacturer Guinness is now part of the drinks giant Diageo.

➤ Much of the manufacturing work is subcontracted to third parties. This makes it hard to enforce good working conditions in factories where global brands are made.

➤ Most manufacturing TNCs are **assembly industries**, relying upon a chain of suppliers. Some suppliers may be independent subcontractors; some may be owned by the parent company. For instance, the Mini factory in Oxford is owned by the German firm BMW. An amazing 2,500 different suppliers provide parts to assemble the Mini (Figure 9.4 on the next page). Some of these are within the EU (to avoid import tariffs). However, some engines are brought all the way from a Brazilian factory that is part-owned by BMW.

Key terms

Assembly industries Manufacturing operations that take the products of many different industries and fit them together to make finished goods.

Transnational corporation A company that has operations in more than one country.

Key terms

Branch plant A factory built in a country by a TNC which has its headquarters elsewhere.

Consumption The purchase and use of commodities (both food and goods) as well as services. Even landscapes can be commodified and consumed (if one pays to visit them).

Glocalisation The local sourcing of parts by TNCs in places where they assemble their 'global products' close to markets. At the same time, they are able to customise their products to meet local tastes or laws.

Parent company The original business that a global TNC has developed around, and whose directors still make decisions that affect the organisation as a whole. For instance, the Walt Disney Company owns several television networks, animation studios (such as Pixar) and 11 theme parks.

Tertiary sector Also known as the service sector, this consists of businesses that produce no physical product. Instead, they sell the products of manufacturing or agricultural industries, or offer a service such as education or tourism.

Figure 9.4 The Mini: an example of an assembly industry

Windscreen
Made in: Belgium
Company headquarters: France

Wing mirrors
Made in: Germany
Company headquarters: Canada

Bonnet
Made in: Netherlands
Company headquarters: Austria

Radiator
Made in: Germany
Company headquarters: Germany

Exhaust system
Made in: UK
Company headquarters: USA

Wheels
Made in: Italy, Germany
Company headquarters: USA

Front and rear bumpers
Made in: UK
Company headquarters: Canada

Engine
Made in: Brazil
Company headquarters: Brazil

Table 9.2 Locating the headquarters of selected TNCs

World rank (by 2006 revenue)	Company	Country of headquarters
1	Exxon Mobile	USA
2	Wal-Mart	USA
3	Royal Dutch/Shell	Netherlands/UK
4	BP	UK
7	DaimlerChrysler	Germany/USA
8	Toyota	Japan
13	ING Group	Netherlands
23	Sinopec	China
25	Carrefour	France
46	Samsung	South Korea

All of this makes it hard to map the geography of a TNC. The largest firms have **branch plants** (factories or offices) in almost every country in the world, while also entering into business partnerships with local companies in the countries they operate in (**glocalisation**). Their products are consumed in countries across the world.

With such complex networks of production and consumption, it is surprising to learn that TNCs can still 'belong' to particular places. However, the **parent company** has to register its profits in a particular place (Figure 9.5 and Table 9.2).

TNCs also promote common patterns of **consumption**. In 2005, Burger King opened its first Chinese store, while Time Out launched *Time Out Delhi* in 2007. Thanks to TNCs, global brands become recognisable in all parts of the world. However, products are often adapted to local tastes and preferences (Cadbury makes its Chinese chocolate sweeter). This is another aspect of glocalisation.

You must study *one* TNC. The case study of Tesco shows how you can do this.

In which nation is the bulk of assets and senior staff located?

In which nation is the TNC as a whole taxed on its worldwide earnings?

What is the nationality of the board of directors and decision-makers?

To which nation would the group turn for diplomatic protection and support?

What is the legal nationality of the parent company?

Figure 9.5 Investigating which country a TNC belongs to

Case study — Transnational Tesco

Tesco began life in 1919 as a grocery stall in the East End of London, run by Jack Cohen (his first day's profit was £1). By 1956, the first Tesco self-service supermarket had opened in a converted cinema in Maldon. Throughout the 1970s and 1980s success followed success in the UK market. Key to the firm's growth has been a strategy of diversification into new markets, becoming a 'one-stop' shop for electrical goods, toys and home products in addition to its traditional business of food. Tesco products are usually manufactured in low-wage countries.

For instance, Tesco sold Value Jeans for just £3 in 2007. Low-cost items like this are sourced via Tesco agents in Hong Kong, which use suppliers in China,

Figure 9.6 Countries in which Tesco had stores, 2007

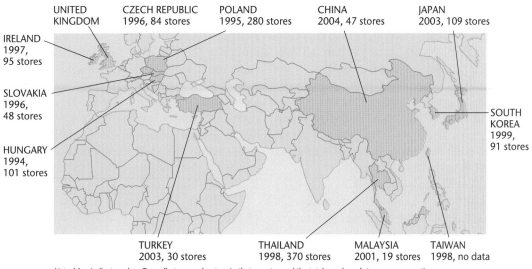

UNITED KINGDOM

CZECH REPUBLIC 1996, 84 stores

POLAND 1995, 280 stores

CHINA 2004, 47 stores

JAPAN 2003, 109 stores

IRELAND 1997, 95 stores

SLOVAKIA 1996, 48 stores

HUNGARY 1994, 101 stores

SOUTH KOREA 1999, 91 stores

TURKEY 2003, 30 stores

THAILAND 1998, 370 stores

MALAYSIA 2001, 19 stores

TAIWAN 1998, no data

Note: Map indicates when Tesco first opened a store in that country and the total number of stores now operating

Thailand, Mauritius, Bangladesh, Sri Lanka and India (where Shivam, a garment manufacturer based in Fairidabad, produces clothes for the super-market chain). Average hourly wages are only around 50p in China and India, and even less in Sri Lanka, which explains why products can be sold so cheaply in the UK, driving up sales and profits.

The UK is no longer Tesco's only market. The firm increasingly sees overseas nations not just as places to source goods from, but as *markets to sell its products to*. After opening eastern European stores in Hungary and Poland, entry into Asian markets began in 1998. In South Korea, Tesco set up a joint venture with Korean TNC Samsung to found a chain of stores called HomePlus. In 2004 the first Tesco stores opened in China, where rising wealth among the elite means that there is a growing number of affluent consumers. In 2007 it moved into the USA.

Sixty per cent of Tesco's international profits now come from Asia. In total, the firm has over 1,250 overseas stores and employs more than 450,000 people. Over the last 10 years it has quadrupled its profits to become the UK's leading retailer and a major TNC. Worldwide sales topped £47 billion in 2006, resulting in an amazing £2.7 billion profit. Technology has also played a role, with the advent of online shopping.

Is Tesco exploiting people in Asia, or helping spread wealth? The issues are complex. Wages in factories are low, but so are living costs and many of Tesco's overseas employees are shop managers who receive good wages.

Photograph 9.2 A Thai Tesco supermarket

Does Tesco damage the environment? Shipping goods around the world on this scale makes the firm a huge emitter of greenhouse gases, but it has pledged to reduce its impact by cutting the pack-aging on its own-label products. The firm's chief executive has acknowledged that 'these issues are of growing importance to our customers. It is sound business sense.'

Is Tesco responsible for eroding local cultures by making people all over the world buy identical products? The company claims not, saying that it makes sound business sense to pay attention to local customers' cultures and to use local supply chains. For instance, Thai customers are used to shopping at traditional 'wet' vegetable markets, rummaging through piles of produce to choose what they want. Rather than forcing the European approach of neatly packaged, convenient portions, Tesco stores in Thailand contain a 'wet' market.

Further research
www.tescocorporate.com
www.corporatewatch.org/?lid=1825#where

World's top five TNCs (2006)		2006 GDP of selected nations		
TNC	Revenue ($bn)	Country	GDP ($bn)	Rank
Exxon Mobile	377	Thailand	206	34
Wal-Mart	351	Nigeria	115	48
Royal Dutch/Shell	318	Pakistan	128	45
BP	274	Bangladesh	65	57
General Motors	207	Zimbabwe	5	131

Table 9.3
How the wealth of TNCs compares with that of nations

Table 9.4 Opposing views about TNCs

The case against TNCs	The benefits TNCs can bring
• *Tax avoidance.* TNCs may avoid paying full taxes in the countries where they operate, through transfer pricing and tax concessions. This means that governments find it harder to raise revenues, provide services and respond to the demands of local people.	• *Raising living standards.* TNCs invest in the economies of developing countries. They are sometimes active in raising wages and can help spread wealth globally. FDI has helped China overtake the UK and France to become the world's fourth biggest economy. (China is the world's largest recipient of FDI, with around half a million foreign-funded enterprises.)
• *Limited linkages.* FDI does not always help developing world economies. If links are made with local firms (e.g. in the sourcing of raw materials) then more wealth may be generated, but this does not always happen.	• *Transfer of technology.* TNCs can be responsible for the transfer of technology and managerial know-how. For instance, South Korean firms such as Daewoo and Samsung have learned to design, make and sell their own products to foreign markets.
• *Growing global wealth divide.* By selectively investing in certain regions (e.g. southeast Asia) while largely bypassing others (e.g. sub-Saharan Africa), TNCs are active agents in creating a new geography of 'haves' and 'have-nots'.	• *Political stability.* In eastern Europe and China, investment by TNCs has contributed to economic growth and political stability. This may be contrasted with conditions in much of Africa, where instability, civil war and distance from markets has made the investment environment less favourable.
• *Environmental degradation.* TNCs are often a major cause of environmental degradation, which has the greatest impact on the poor. One of the most notorious cases of this occurred on 2 December 1984, when poisonous methyl isocynate gas was emitted from the pesticide plant in Bhopal, India, owned by the US TNC Union Carbide. This led to the deaths of thousands of Indian people living close to the plant.	• *Raising environmental awareness.* Because large TNCs have a corporate image to uphold, they sometimes *do* respond to criticism. Many large firms are now trying to establish their 'green credentials' and are starting to address issues around packaging, transport and carbon emissions, while also increasing their fair trade commitment (the UK's Co-operative Group and Waitrose are leaders in this field).

How do TNCs affect global wealth?

Do TNCs help or hinder the spread of global wealth? The profits of the world's largest firms are greater than the GDPs of many middle-income and low-income nations (Table 9.3). This leads critics of TNCs to suggest that firms exploit workers in poor countries in the pursuit of profit. They argue that in a fairer world TNCs would pay workers in low-income nations better. However, supporters of globalisation believe that some benefits are still felt by the poor (Table 9.4).

TNCs bring foreign direct investment (FDI) to nations. Even if wages are low by UK standards, workers will still spend money after they have been paid, thereby stimulating the growth of other local services. For instance, workers at the Dyson plant in Malaysia are paid around £3 per hour, far more than Malaysian workers earned in the past.

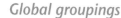

Skills focus

An **impact assessment** is a way of analysing information in order to make a balanced judgement about whether overall effects are positive or negative.

Figure 9.7 Possible impacts of TNCs

Maintaining gender inequality in the workplace — firms may be happy to pay women less money than men

Ecosystem damage — TNCs may have a poor record of looking after the environment (e.g. Shell's oil spills in Nigeria)

Worker health damage — TNCs only have to meet local health and safety laws, which may be weak, rather than those set in their country of origin

Literacy improvement — workers may be trained by the TNCs that hire them

Increasing income inequality — by paying high wages to local middlemen and managers while keeping average 'sweatshop' wages down

More money for local markets — once local people are receiving pay from TNCs, local firms benefit from increased custom

Hybrid products — exciting new products emerge as TNCs adapt their products to local tastes and fashions

Air miles — products are shipped over great distances, creating pollution

Global products favoured over local ones — traditional clothes and foods may be abandoned as a result of the influence of TNCs

Luring workers away from farming — if too many migrants head to cities to work for TNCs, this can result in food shortages

Worker exploitation — employees may be forced to work long hours and be banned from joining trade unions

Task

1 Study Figure 9.7, which shows possible impacts of the arrival of a TNC on a poorer nation. Think about how these varying impacts can best be categorised into social, cultural, economic and environmental effects. Are any of the effects difficult to place in a single category?

2 Using Figure 9.7 and other information in this chapter, make a balanced assessment of the pros and cons of foreign investment by TNCs. Be prepared to use your own beliefs to form an opinion. Do you think that any one of these costs is particularly bad and negates all the other positives — or vice versa? What is your evidence for making this judgement? Back your impact assessment up with key facts.

Tip Up-to-date case studies can really help with exam success, so make sure you check that your facts are right. Firms like Shell and Tesco publish annual reports online, which contain information about their profits, locations and activities.

In addition, when TNCs locate within a trade bloc they can bring wealth to impoverished regions, even in richer countries, often by working in partnership with local governments that offer financial assistance (e.g. the Nissan factory in Sunderland). By sourcing parts locally within trade blocs, TNCs can generate more work and greater profits for local suppliers.

TNCs have more than a purely economic influence on the nations where they produce goods and services, and where their products are consumed. There are also social effects (they may help perpetuate inequality through giving unequal pay to men and women) and cultural effects (their products may alter local tastes and interfere with traditions). Adverse environmental impacts are commonplace, both locally and globally, with the global operations of large TNCs making a substantial contribution to carbon dioxide emissions and climate change (see Chapters 4–7).

TNCs could be far more effective at spreading wealth more fairly around the world. However, they are still one of the most effective mechanisms for wealth redistribution available to us (the value of FDI flows dwarfs that of international aid, for instance). In the future, TNCs could become more effective agents for transferring real wealth to developing societies if greater pressure were applied by government legislation. They might be persuaded to introduce a decent **minimum wage** for overseas workers and not just for staff at home. It is important to remember that each TNC should be assessed on its own track record, and not be seen as one of an undifferentiated mass of money-makers.

> ### Key term
>
> **Minimum wage** An hourly wage set by a nation's government that all companies must pay to their employees. The UK has a national minimum wage of more than £5 per hour, but most poorer countries have no such rules.

Review questions

1 Study Table 9.3. Compare the wealth of the world's most successful TNCs with that of middle-income and low-income nations.
2 Name two countries that it is difficult to place in an economic grouping and explain why this is the case.
3 Using examples, describe the varied types of 'middle-income' country.
4 Briefly outline the advantages that trade bloc membership brings to nations.
5 Using examples, describe ways in which the economies of different nations are becoming linked together by:
   a the activities of TNCs
   b trade bloc rules

Chapter 10

Global networks

Why, as places and societies become more interconnected, do places show extreme wealth and poverty?

By the end of this chapter you should have:

➤ *investigated how the world's economies, peoples and environments are connected to form networks, and explored the flows that link places together*
➤ *researched the important role of transport, telecommunications and the internet in helping flows to accelerate*
➤ *researched how natural resources (including energy) and human resources (with varying skills and culture) influence levels of connection*
➤ *understood why 'the rich get richer while the poor get poorer' in global networks*

Photograph 10.1 The world at night. City lights are yellow, oil flares red, burning forests purple and fishing fleets green. The aurora borealis over Greenland is pale blue

Photograph 10.1 shows our world at night as seen from space. The distribution of light gives an indication not just of how population is spread out, but also of

W. T. Sullivan III/SPL

where wealth is found — and where it is not. We can clearly identify the richest regions of Europe and North America, vast tracts of which are brightly lit. We can also identify rich **core** regions in states with far less impressive levels of overall national growth. These include the major cities of South Africa and South America, and the brightly illuminated coastline of Asia, signalling the locations of enormous cities in India, China and South Korea.

Brightly lit places are those where energy is in use, either to heat and light homes, offices and shopping malls, or to fuel the mass production of goods. They are the places that are most connected to other places in the world economy, through the consumption or production of goods and services. Lit up at night like this, they are, both metaphorically and literally, **switched-on places**.

This is not to suggest that all other places are 'switched off'. Almost nowhere is completely cut off from the rest of the global economy (the exception being some indigenous tribes in **wilderness** regions such as the Amazon, as discussed in Chapter 8). However, some areas make a far greater contribution than others to the twin economic processes of production and consumption that drive the global economy.

Key terms

Core The most developed and highly populated region of a country. The growth of core regions is fed by flows of labour from less well-developed regions.

Switched-on places Nations, regions or cities that are strongly connected to other places through the production and consumption of goods and services. In contrast, places that are poorly connected are said to be relatively switched off.

Wilderness An area of the planet that has remained relatively untouched by human activity and is home to only small numbers of indigenous people. Examples are the rainforests of Amazonia and Borneo as well as Antarctica, which is unpopulated.

Technology builds global networks

What might today seem like simple forms of transport, such as stagecoaches and canals, revolutionised the movement of goods and people during Britain's industrial age. Today, newer technologies — both transport and communications devices — allow these processes of change to continue, helping global networks to operate more efficiently (Figure 10.1).

Using these technologies, TNCs have played a major role in building bridges between countries, while air travel and tourism operators facilitate the

Figure 10.1
A communication timeline

200 AD	1500–1700s	Early 1800s	Late 1800s	Early 1900s	Late 1900s
World's first sailing ships	Industrial canals and stagecoach routes reduce land travel times	First steam ship crosses Atlantic in 1819 (29 days) with regular crossings by 1830s	Transatlantic telegraph cable laid in 1866, later to be superseded by telephone. Radio experiments begin in 1890s	Ford Motor Car Company launched in 1903. First television built in 1926. Boeing commercial flights by 1928	First mobile phones available in early 1980s. World wide web (internet) developed in 1989 using PC and modem

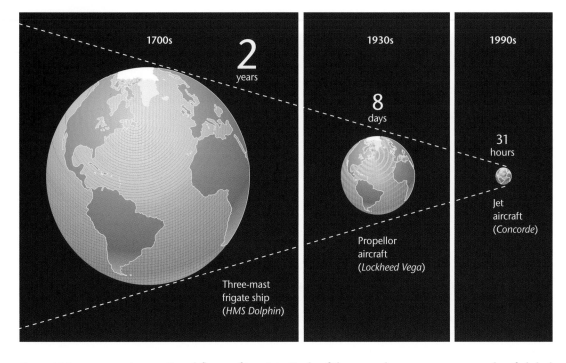

1700s

2
years

1930s

8
days

1990s

31
hours

Jet
aircraft
(*Concorde*)

Propellor
aircraft
(*Lockheed Vega*)

Three-mast
frigate ship
(*HMS Dolphin*)

Figure 10.2
A shrinking world:
the time taken to
navigate the globe

international flows of tourists. Each of these can be seen as an example of global network building. The travel firm easyJet is a good example of a global network builder whose success rests on recent innovations in jet air travel and online communications (see the case study on p. 115).

For increasing numbers of people, the effect is of living in a **shrinking world** (Figure 10.2). Some of the main ways of building networks through technology are as follows:

➤ *Telephones.* The first telephone and telegraph cables across the Atlantic replaced a 3-week boat journey with instantaneous communication. This revolutionised how business was conducted and laid the ground for TNCs to operate in different continents simultaneously. Telephone remains a core technology for communicating across distance. In parts of Africa where telephone lines have never been laid, people are technologically 'leap-frogging' straight to mobile phone use (Figure 10.3). In 2005, a system was introduced that allows people to buy cash vouchers and transfer credit to businesses, customers or family members via mobile phones.

➤ *The internet.* With the advent of broadband, large amounts of data can be quickly moved across cyberspace. This allows office staff to work from home as teleworkers. It enables firms to employ workers and consultants living in different countries. For instance, in the entertainment industry, firms like Disney can produce animated films using experts in different countries, all working at the same time. Music companies can e-mail sound recordings to be remixed by producers working in different countries.

Key terms

Shrinking world Thanks to technology, distant places start to feel closer and take less time to reach. This process is sometimes called 'time–space compression'.

Edexcel AS Geography

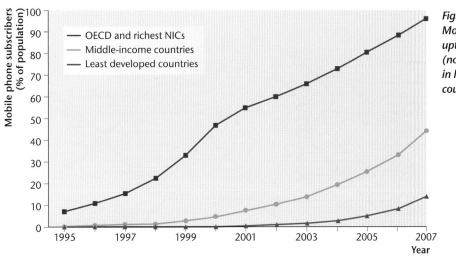

Figure 10.3 Mobile phone uptake over time (note increasing use in least developed countries)

➤ *Air travel.* Aerospace technology continues to evolve, allowing faster aeroplanes to be produced in greater numbers and with increased capacity. Firms like easyJet have pioneered low-cost no-frills mass air travel. Cutting-edge designs like the Airbus A380 (which can carry 550 people) are set to increase air passenger numbers even further.

➤ *GIS and GPS.* The first global positioning system (GPS) satellite was launched in the 1970s. There are now 24 in an orbit 10,000 km above the Earth. These satellites continuously broadcast position and time data to users throughout the world. Geographic information systems (GIS) are software systems that can collect, manage and analyse satellite data.

Networks and flows

Key concept

A **network** is an illustration or model that shows how different places are linked together. Geographers draw networks to emphasise the connections that exist between different places (Figure 10.4). Perhaps the most famous example of a network is the map of the London Underground (a transport network). We can imagine a global network of the most well-connected countries and cities laid out in similar terms (Photograph 10.2).

The points on a network map are called nodes. In global network theory, the term global hub is used to describe a node that is especially

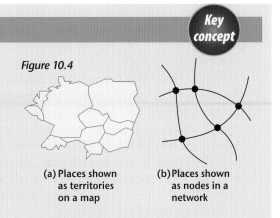

Figure 10.4

(a) Places shown as territories on a map

(b) Places shown as nodes in a network

well connected. Connections between nodes, or global hubs, are called **flows**.

Flows are movements of the following:

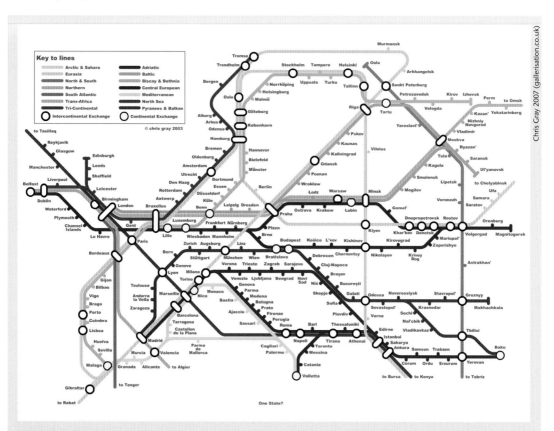

Photograph 10.2 An artist's impression of Europe redrawn as a network (based on the design of the London Underground)

▶ *Money.* Most credit cards now work internationally, allowing easier transfers of money than in the past. Major capital flows are routed through the global stock markets, numbers of which have increased in recent decades.

▶ *Raw materials.* Commodities such as food, minerals and oil have always been traded between nations.

▶ *Manufactured goods and services.* The value of world trade is now 70 trillion dollars. The figure rises by around 10% each year.

▶ *Information.* The internet has brought real-time communication between distant places, allowing services to be sold, while online communities have grown in size and influence (e.g. MySpace and FaceBook).

▶ *People.* Of all flows, the movement of people still faces the greatest number of obstacles because of border controls and immigration laws.

Geographical analysis at a global scale almost always involves some use of the term 'network', recognising that over time countries have become more:

▶ *interconnected* — trade and migration flows have increased due to technology, market forces and political decisions by some nations to open their borders

▶ *interdependent* — what happens in one place increasingly has impacts on other places. If a firm in one nation goes bust, then workers in branch plants in other nations will lose their jobs too

Case study   easyJet

The easyJet airline was founded in 1995 by Sir Stelios Haji-Ioannou (Photograph 10.3). It began as a small venture, running flights solely within the UK. Most of Europe's major cities are now interconnected via easyJet's cheap flight network.

At the start, the airline had just two aircraft. Inaugural flights from Luton to Edinburgh and Glasgow were supported by the advertising slogan 'Making flying as affordable as a pair of jeans — £29 one way'. In 1996, flights to Barcelona commenced and thereafter the company expanded at breakneck speed. It now has around 300 flight routes in the EU. Shortly after its 100 millionth passenger flight in 2005, easyJet announced another massive expansion, this time into new markets outside the EU (to Marrakech, Istanbul and Rijeka).

Clear signs of the firm evolving into a major TNC came early on in 1998 when easyJet acquired 40% of the Swiss air company TEA Basel AG, allowing it to establish its first European base in Geneva.

Photograph 10.4

Technology has helped to build the easyJet global network. It was one of the first airlines to embrace the opportunity of the internet, and the company's first online sale was made in April 1998. Now approximately 95% of flights are purchased in this way, making easyJet one of Europe's biggest internet retailers. By 2006, the company owned 122 aeroplanes (both Airbus and Boeing), carrying 33 million people to their destinations that year and bringing in revenues of nearly £2 billion.

Places that easyJet adds to its flight network become more 'switched on'. For instance, Tallinn in Estonia is home to 400,000 people. On 31 October 2004, easyJet started to fly British tourists there for just £40 each. Suddenly, the city became an affordable destination for UK citizens, especially groups of young men and women seeking a cheap but interesting destination for 'stag' and 'hen' weekends. There have been complaints of bad behaviour, and a rise in sexually transmitted diseases has been reported. However, the new route has brought more money to Tallinn and boosted trade for its hotels, restaurants, bars and nightclubs.

Table 10.1 Growth in easyJet passenger numbers, 1995–2006

Year	Passenger numbers
1995	30,000
1996	420,00
1998	1,880,000
2000	5,996,000
2002	11,400,000
2004	24,300,000
2006	32,953,000

Further research

www.easyjet.com/EN/About/
www.easyjet.com/EN/routemap/

Photograph 10.3 Sir Stelios Haji-Ioannou

What happens in global hubs?

Global hubs and other major network nodes are switched-on places possessing qualities that make other places want to connect with them. Generally, it is the presence of either **natural resources** or **human resources** that drives the process (Figure 10.5). Global hubs are often 'world cities' (Chapter 13) or may be **technopoles**. They also serve as core regions for their country's economy — places where wealth is created and spent, while ideas and innovation are shared as part of a **multiplier effect**, leading to a process called **cumulative causation** (Figure 10.6). Firms are able to make upstream and downstream linkages with other organisations, forming business **clusters** in such locations.

Figure 10.5 How natural resources and human resources help global hubs develop

Global hubs such as Beijing are places where the parent companies of major TNCs establish their subsidiary firms or forge alliances with local companies. For instance, Cadbury-Schweppes, which is headquartered in London, has established an Indian subsidiary (Cadbury India) in the global hub of Mumbai.

Flows of money, goods and workers connect the world's global hubs. The government of a country may establish an **export processing zone** (EPZ) to make movement even easier by removing import and export tariffs and giving tax breaks for firms.

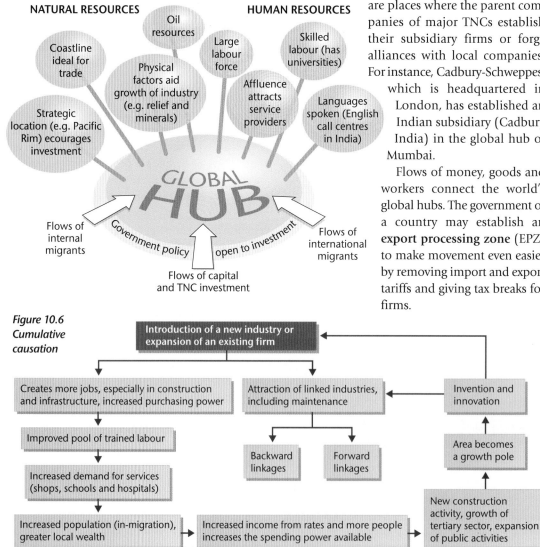

NATURAL RESOURCES

- Coastline ideal for trade
- Oil resources
- Physical factors aid growth of industry (e.g. relief and minerals)
- Large labour force
- Strategic location (e.g. Pacific Rim) ecourages investment

HUMAN RESOURCES

- Skilled labour (has universities)
- Affluence attracts service providers
- Languages spoken (English call centres in India)

GLOBAL HUB

- Flows of internal migrants
- Government policy open to investment
- Flows of capital and TNC investment
- Flows of international migrants

Figure 10.6 Cumulative causation

Introduction of a new industry or expansion of an existing firm

- Creates more jobs, especially in construction and infrastructure, increased purchasing power
- Attraction of linked industries, including maintenance
- Invention and innovation

- Improved pool of trained labour
- Backward linkages
- Forward linkages
- Area becomes a growth pole

- Increased demand for services (shops, schools and hospitals)
- New construction activity, growth of tertiary sector, expansion of public activities

- Increased population (in-migration), greater local wealth
- Increased income from rates and more people increases the spending power available

Key terms

Cluster A geographically concentrated group of connected industries and institutions, including firms, suppliers, financial backers, educational institutions and research agencies. For example, central London is home to clusters of television production companies and universities that deliver media courses.

Cumulative causation A model that explains why wealth becomes concentrated in certain places. Globalisation increases the chances of this, as local people can find global markets for their products or attract employers with their skills.

Export processing zone A small industrial area, often on the coast, where favourable conditions are created to attract foreign TNCs. These conditions include low tax rates and exemption from tariffs and export duties.

Global hub A settlement (or wider region) providing a focal point for activities that have a global influence. All megacities and world cities (see Chapter 13) are global hubs, along with some smaller settlements such as Cambridge, whose university and science park have a global reach.

Human resources The abilities and potential of the human population in terms of their educational levels, their skills, the languages they speak and their capacity to innovate and invent —

making them 'the ultimate resource' according to some commentators.

Multiplier effect The positive spin-offs that follow an initial investment (e.g. a branch plant) in a region. Other firms may gain business supplying parts, the increased spending power of workers stimulates the service sector, and higher tax revenues can be invested in education and infra-structure.

Natural resources Materials found in the environment that humans have the technological ability and desire to use. These change over time as technology develops (for instance, uranium became a fuel source after nuclear fission was first achieved).

Technopole A cluster of technologically innovative businesses and research institutes. Famous examples are Silicon Valley (California), Silicon Fen (Cambridge), Silicon Glen (Edinburgh and the Borders) and Seoul (South Korea).

Trickle-down The positive impacts on peripheral regions (and poorer people) of the creation of wealth in core regions (and among richer people). These impacts include the roll-out of national services (e.g. motorways, schools and hospitals), as well as regional aid and assistance for start-up businesses.

Global hubs in middle-income and low-income countries

In the world's richest nations, wealth has spread to rural and peripheral regions and is no longer concentrated solely in major cities. Economic theory suggests this is because the nations that industrialised first have had more time for wealth to **trickle down** from their core regions to the rest of the population. However, in middle-income countries, such as Brazil and South Africa, a great many people still live in poverty, despite the presence of global hubs such as São Paulo and Johannesburg.

Indeed, globalisation has made regional and social disparities in middle-income nations even greater than they used to be. In Nigeria, elites living in the core region of Lagos have experienced a huge growth in wealth in comparison with those living in poverty in rural areas. The Ogoni people of the Niger delta have received no benefits from the oil extracted from their lands, while suffering considerable environmental damage. The same story is repeated in other countries. Two-bedroom flats in the Vietnamese capital city of Hanoi now sell for up to £60,000, despite the massive poverty still found in some rural provinces.

Skills focus

Global hubs such as São Paulo in Brazil can seriously distort estimates of *typical* levels of wealth for a nation's people. A much higher proportion of extremely rich people (elites) live in these places than elsewhere, especially in low- and middle-income countries. This is because in any population a handful of very rich people — especially billionaires, of whom there are now over 70 in Asia — massively distort figures of average wealth.

Equally, statistics that show low average levels of national wealth may be concealing the presence of a rich elite living in a country.

Table 10.2 contains some facts about the distribution of wealth in ten nations that show varying levels of inequality. Slovakia has the greatest equality of income of any nation, although average levels of wealth there are relatively low compared with high-income nations like Denmark.

Tasks

1 Describe how levels of inequality vary between nations.

2 In the UK, anyone earning less than 60% of mean national income is said to live in relative poverty. Using this fact, can you explain why the following claims are *not* contradictory:

Table 10.2 Distribution of income in ten nations, 2005

Equality rank	Country	Average GDP per capita ($)	Total percentage of national wealth	
			Poorest 20% of population	Richest 20% of population
1	Slovakia	8,600	12	31
4	Denmark	47,600	10	34
5	Japan	35,600	10	36
19	Germany	33,800	8	38
23	Canada	35,000	7	39
157	Russia	5,400	4	54
165	Nigeria	860	4	56
178	South Africa	5,000	3	69
180	Brazil	4,200	2	64
183	Sierra Leone	210	1	64

Source: United Nations, 2005

- Billionaire wealth is on the rise in the UK.
- Earnings for low-paid workers are also on the rise.
- Statistics show that the number of Britons who live in *relative poverty* is increasing.

3 Discuss the relative merits of using mean, median and modal statistics to describe the typical level of wealth found among a population.

> **Tip** If you need to revise how mean, median and modal values are calculated, visit **www.geographypages.co.uk/asags. htm#mean**

Switched-off places

The very poorest nations of the world remain relatively switched off from global networks. They may lack a global hub or any strong flows of trade and investment with other places and economies. Conditions are poor for the overwhelming majority of people living in low-income nations such as Sudan, Chad and Myanmar (Burma), whether in urban or rural areas. If they do experience integration into the world economy, it is only in the most shallow form. For instance:

➤ Subsistence farmers in these regions may become dependent on flows of food aid from NGOs in OECD nations.

➤ Farmers may grow agricultural products for TNCs: for instance, the flower growers of Kenya's Lake Naivasha. However, wages are often so low that workers

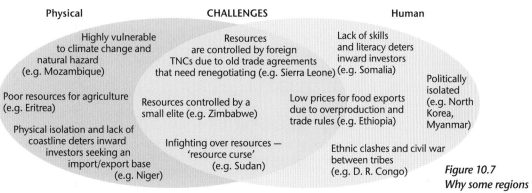

Physical	CHALLENGES	Human

Highly vulnerable to climate change and natural hazard (e.g. Mozambique)

Resources are controlled by foreign TNCs due to old trade agreements that need renegotiating (e.g. Sierra Leone)

Lack of skills and literacy deters inward investors (e.g. Somalia)

Poor resources for agriculture (e.g. Eritrea)

Resources controlled by a small elite (e.g. Zimbabwe)

Low prices for food exports due to overproduction and trade rules (e.g. Ethiopia)

Politically isolated (e.g. North Korea, Myanmar)

Physical isolation and lack of coastline deters inward investors seeking an import/export base (e.g. Niger)

Infighting over resources — 'resource curse' (e.g. Sudan)

Ethnic clashes and civil war between tribes (e.g. D. R. Congo)

Figure 10.7
Why some regions remain relatively switched off

have negligible spending power. As a result, no substantial local multiplier effects can develop. Low wages are often a result of cash crops being under-valued due to global overproduction. There is a global surplus of coffee, for instance, which is one of Ethiopia's major exports.

TNCs are unlikely to 'complete the circuit' by returning to such poverty-stricken places to sell their products (the way Tesco has done in rich parts of Asia — see Chapter 9). Incomes are so low in the world's poorest nations that TNCs do not see any market potential there. These are the least developed countries (LDCs) that were described in Chapter 9. They tend to be heavily indebted to the International Monetary Fund, the World Bank or commercial lenders.

What causes such extreme cases of global poverty? There are many possible explanations, and conditions in these countries are best investigated on a case-by-case basis. As a starting point, the mismanagement of natural resources and human resources should be looked at (Figure 10.7). We can make two final obser-vations about the nature of poverty in these relatively switched-off places:

➤ As other nations drive ahead faster, the gap between high-income and low-income countries is widening. Even where progress is being made, the poorest countries are being left behind as the richest pull further ahead of the field.
➤ The world's richest 1% of individuals (wherever they live) now own 40% of all wealth. The poorest 50% of adults own just 1% of global wealth.

Review questions

1 Describe the differences between a territorial map and a network map.
2 Study Photograph 10.2. Which cities has the artist chosen to represent as the most important global hubs? Suggest reasons why these choices were made.
3 Using Figures 10.1 and 10.2, draw a table that identifies *five* types of transport and explains how each has contributed to a 'shrinking world'.
4 Choose one example of a highly 'switched-on' nation and explain its success.
5 Explain the obstacles preventing some LDCs from becoming more fully integrated into global networks.

Chapter 11

Roots

How does evidence from personal, local and national sources help us understand the pattern of population change in the UK?

By the end of this chapter, you should have:
➤ *researched different ways in which local populations in the UK have changed and migrated since the start of the twentieth century*
➤ *examined the role of key social and economic factors in helping bring about these demographic and geographical changes*
➤ *explored the issue of a 'greying' population and considered how life in the UK is changing as a result of this trend*
➤ *understood some of the ways in which the demographic changes described in this chapter connect with the bigger picture of globalisation*

Demography is the study of population characteristics and movements. It is a core element of human geography. Chapter 8 explains important concepts and key terms for population studies, including migration and natural increase. This chapter explores twentieth-century demographic trends in the UK. You can gain additional information from daily newspapers, television programmes and population websites.

For instance, the rising challenge of the UK's **greying population** is one of the most important domestic political issues for the twenty-first century, and frequently makes newspaper headlines. Meeting the financial needs of the elderly, while also ensuring that the UK economy remains globally competitive, creates a massive headache for policy-makers. Another area of overlap between studies in geography and media interest is the growing field of **genealogy**. One of the greatest online success stories in recent years has been the publication of old family records and census data. Increasing numbers of people have discovered they can easily trace their own roots, both within and outside the UK, spurred on by programmes such as the BBC's *Who Do You Think You Are?* Geography students can draw on their own family histories, as well as televised accounts of celebrities researching their roots, to support this part of the course.

Analysing population change

During the twentieth century, populations in the UK changed both on a national scale and at the level of individual households and families. Data sources to support the study of these changes include:

Key terms

Genealogy The study of family history.

Greying population A population structure in which the proportion of people aged 65 and over is high and rising. This is caused by increasing life expectancy and can be further exaggerated by low birth rates.

> *National.* UK census data go back to 1801, with a good level of detail recorded from 1841 onwards.
> *Local.* Dating back to the Middle Ages, church records known as parish registers include information about baptisms/births, burials/deaths and marriages.
> *Personal.* Recollections of family members.

The picture that emerges from these different data sources reveals a series of profound changes. Since the 1901 census was conducted, several major demographic, economic and migratory shifts can be identified.

Family size

The total population of the UK rose from around 38 million in 1901 to 61 million in 2007. In contrast to this overall growth, individual household sizes have fallen markedly. In the early 1900s, four or five children might typically live under the same roof with their parents. Today, it is likely to be just two children. Many households consist of just one or two people, including pensioners, divorcees and gay couples. However, increased life expectancy has resulted in grandparents living longer, which can sometimes increase the size of **extended family** households. How has your own family size changed over time? How many brothers or sisters did your grandparents or great-grandparents have, compared to you and your friends?

> ### Key terms
>
> **Age-selective migration** A movement of a particular age-group or gender.
>
> **Extended family** Members of the family beyond the core of parents and children.
>
> **Social mobility** The movement of individuals between different levels of a social hierarchy, usually measured occupationally. Intergenerational mobility describes a social shift between parents and their children.

Population structure

The UK as a whole has developed a top-heavy population structure. Back in 1931, just 7% of the population were aged over 65, while 24% were under 16. Today, the figures are 16% and 19% respectively. Life expectancy has increased markedly over time. In 1901 the average age of death was 50 for men and 57 for women. By 2007 the figures were 77 for men and 82 for women, although considerable variations exist at the local level (Table 11.1). How old are the longest-lived members of your own family?

Table 11.1 Life expectancy for men by region, 2005 (years)

Highest	Years	Lowest	Years
Kensington	80.8	Glasgow City	69.3
East Dorset	80.8	Inverclyde	70.3
Hart (Hampshire)	80.1	West Dunbartonshire	70.7
Uttlesford (Essex)	79.9	Renfrewshire	71.8
South Norfolk	79.7	Western Isles	72.2
Wokingham	79.6	Manchester	72.3
Rutland	79.6	North Lanarkshire	72.4
Brentwood	79.5	Dundee City	72.5
Purbeck	79.4	Blackpool	72.8
Winchester	79.4	Liverpool	73.2

Migration

Over time, the mobility of the UK population has increased. One of the most important recent migrations has been movement away from manufacturing and mining towns, especially in the north of the England, and towards settlements with service-sector jobs. A general 'southeast drift' of the UK population has resulted, with 26% now living in London and the southeast.

Other major trends include counter-urbanisation — significant numbers of people have left towns and cities to live in surrounding rural areas (see

Figure 11.1 The UK's changing work structure during the twentieth century

Chapter 13). Important **age-selective migrations** include a move of retired people to seaside settlements and young adults leaving home and relocating to university towns. In addition, large amounts of international migration have taken place. What is the migratory history of your parents, family and friends?

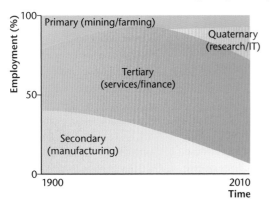

Employment

Employment structures for many settlements have changed beyond recognition in recent decades. The decline of traditional manufacturing, as well as job losses in farming and mine closures, has meant that increasing numbers of people have moved away from primary and secondary employment and have entered 'white-collar' work such as services, finance and media (Figure 11.1). What jobs did older members of your family do? How do you think your own career will differ?

Figure 11.2 The distribution of non-white ethnic groups in the UK, 2004

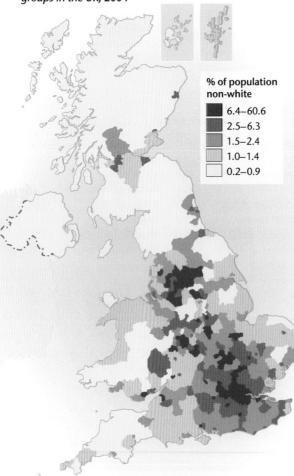

% of population non-white
- 6.4–60.6
- 2.5–6.3
- 1.5–2.4
- 1.0–1.4
- 0.2–0.9

Social status and aspirations

At the start of the twentieth century, most people in the UK were relatively poor and would have described themselves as 'working class'. During the twentieth century, average wages rose and more people entered higher education before graduating to non-manual work. As a result of this **social mobility**, more and more people have come to define themselves as 'middle class'. What are your own aspirations?

Ethnicity

The ethnic mix of people living in the UK (both British citizens and foreign nationals) has changed significantly over time, with minority groups now accounting for 8% overall. From the 1950s onwards, large-scale migration took place from the UK's former colonies of India, Pakistan and Bangladesh, as well as from Jamaica and African nations including Uganda and Kenya.

Significant numbers of Australians and white South Africans also relocated to the UK. Since the Maastricht Treaty of 1993 many European migrants have arrived and London is now home to 100,000 French nationals.

Segregation results in some districts having noticeably different ethnic profiles from others (Figure 11.2). Around 60% of people living in the

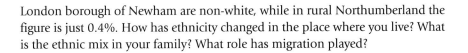

London borough of Newham are non-white, while in rural Northumberland the figure is just 0.4%. How has ethnicity changed in the place where you live? What is the ethnic mix in your family? What role has migration played?

Skills focus

This activity uses family history websites to discover how your own family background compares with national trends for the twentieth century. Some students may wish to share the findings of research that members of their own families have already undertaken.

During the national census (which is conducted every 10 years), all households in the UK are legally obliged to fill in a questionnaire giving details of ages, occupations and much more besides. Once these raw data have been analysed by government statisticians, statistics about population characteristics are published, such as the overall age and employment structure. Personal details from the original questionnaires remain confidential.

The raw data are made available for the public to view after 100 years. The actual household questionnaires — including the names and addresses of all the people living in the UK up to the time of the 1901 census — can be examined by anyone who wants to. After 2011, the data from the 1911 census will become publicly available.

If members of your own family were living in the UK in 1901, you may want to find out more about them. If you can locate the records of your great-grandparents (or even your great-great-grandparents), it will be interesting to find out how large their family was, where they lived and what their occupations were.

■ Begin by talking to your oldest living relatives. They will be able to give you background information, perhaps providing photographs. Hopefully they can give you the names of relatives who were alive in 1901 to get you started.

■ Consult any old birth or death certificates that have been kept by your family. Replacement copies can be ordered, for a small fee, from the General Register Office in Southport, which stores certificates from as far back as 1837.

Search online for relatives listed in the 1901 census (and even earlier, if you are interested), using the websites listed below.

If your family roots lie outside the UK, there are international genealogy sites (e.g. Family Search), while old passenger records for ships arriving in the UK are increasingly available for consultation online (e.g. Ancestry.co.uk).

Key websites for UK census information

National Statistics
The official government website: **www.statistics. gov.uk**
Regional demographic changes: **www.statistics. gov.uk/statbase/Product.asp?vlnk=14356**

ESRC Society Today
Part of the Economic and Social Research Council website: **www.esrcsocietytoday.ac.uk**

Useful websites for family research

1901 Census
Part of the national archives: **www.1901census online.com** (you have to pay to access parts of this and the next site).

Ancestry.co.uk
Hosts the 1901 census and birth, death and marriage certificates: **www.ancestry.co.uk**

BBC family history site
Helps the beginner with family research: **www. bbc.co.uk/history/familyhistory/**

Photograph 11.1 Extract from the 1901 census record for a Yorkshire village

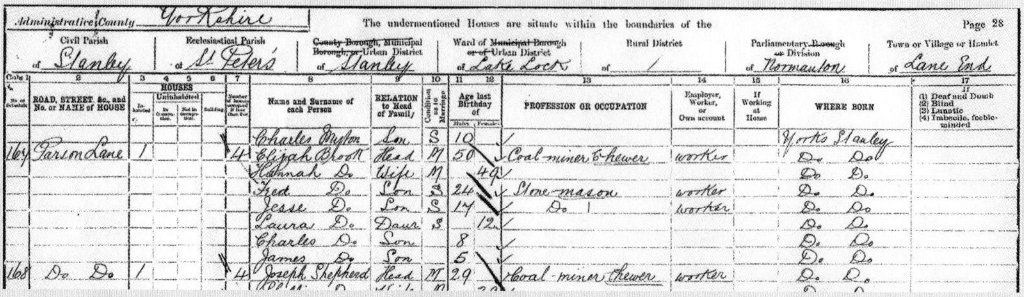

Census Online
Gives links to more online census records: www.censusonline.com

Find My Past
www.findmypast.com

Family Search
This site includes an International Genealogy Index to help with searches for relatives living overseas in 1901. It also has church records back to the middle ages: www.familysearch.org

Tracing family overseas
Moving Here website has 200 years of migration histories with a specific focus on south Asian, African Caribbean, Irish and Jewish communities that settled in the UK: www.movinghere. org.uk/galleries/histories/default.htm

Tips The data in old census records may be inaccurate. Names may be misspelt and ages misrecorded. You may have to look very carefully to spot your ancestors.

Table 11.2 The Brook family in 1901, as recorded by the census questionnaire shown in Photograph 11.1

Name	Relation to head of family	Age	Occupation	Place of birth
Elijah Brook	Head	50	Coal miner	Stanley
Hannah Brook	Wife	49	–	Stanley
Fred Brook	Son	24	Stone mason	Stanley
Jesse Brook	Son	17	Stone mason	Stanley
Laura Brook	Daughter	12	–	Stanley
Charles Brook	Son	8	–	Stanley
James Brook	Son	5	–	Stanley

Tasks
Photograph 11.1 shows part of a census record for 1901. The data have been transcribed in Table 11.2.

1 How does the family size differ from that of a typical family today?
2 What sector of industry are family members shown as working in?
3 What do the ages of the working members of the family tell us about different social values and laws in 1901 (think about the age you will be when you sit your AS/A2 exams).
4 Is there any evidence of migration in this family's recent past?

Explaining the pattern of population change

Changes in family size and population structure

Birth rates and death rates are the principal controls on population size and structure, both for the nation as a whole and for individual families. Both rates fell in the UK during the twentieth century, continuing a trend that dates back to

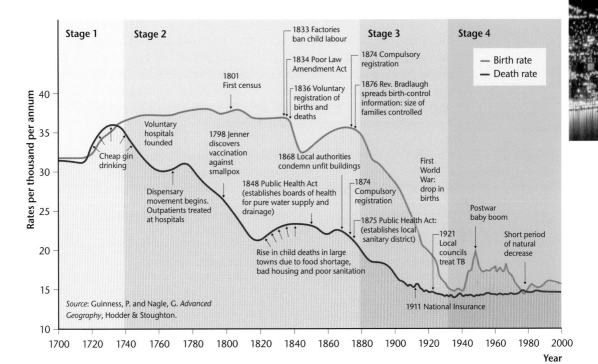

Figure 11.3
Changes in birth rate and death rate during the UK demographic transition

the 1700s and 1800s (Figure 11.3). Two important phases of population change stand out during the 1900s.

Phase 1: before the 1970s

Before the 1970s, population was still growing due to natural increase. The death rate had been falling since the 1800s, thanks to major improvements in food supply, health and hygiene. This trend continued during the early decades of the 1900s, bringing the death rate to its current low level by mid-century. However, it took until the 1970s, and the end of the postwar **baby boom**, for the declining birth rate to reach the same low level as the death rate, bringing natural increase almost to a halt. The total population grew from 38 million to 55 million between 1901 and 1971.

Phase 2: since the 1970s

Since the 1970s, total population has increased more slowly, and the growth has mostly been due to immigration, especially in recent years. Both the death rate and the birth rate have remained at a low and fairly constant level. As a result, family sizes are small while life expectancy keeps creeping upwards. Reports in 2007 suggested that the birth rate may now be slowly increasing again. This is because large numbers of migrant women of child-bearing age now live in the UK (a quarter of all new births are registered to foreign nationals). The total population grew from 55 million to 61 million between 1971 and 2007.

Key terms

Baby boom A brief increase in the birth rate. The UK experienced a baby boom at the end of the Second World War when returning soldiers started families, with an 'echo' of the event following in the 1960s.

Secularisation A general decline in the significance of religious beliefs. A secular society is one in which people are more likely to be tolerant of abortion and the use of contraception.

The factors which led to the twentieth century fall in fertility and increasing life expectancy are described in Table 11.3. Key to all of these has been education, helping people make informed decisions about child bearing and the risks of certain types of behaviour, such as smoking when pregnant. The UK's low birth rate owes much to **secularisation** and consumerism, with global forces, such as economic recessions, also playing a key role. Consumerism is a powerful force that helps explain many recent trends in human geography.

Table 11.3
Factors causing
changes in births
and life expectancy
in the UK

Falling births	Longer life expectancy
Women's status, pay and rights Women have enjoyed improved status and work opportunities. Middle-class and professional women are postponing the age at which they start a family (the average age is now 30). As a result, few women now have more than two children.	**Healthcare, treatment and prevention** The National Health Service (NHS) was introduced in the late 1940s. Accident and emergency departments provide immediate help for injured people. Vaccination against serious diseases has led to the disappearance of some from the UK (e.g. polio).
Contraception, abortion and education Oral contraceptive pills were legally made available in 1961. AIDS awareness campaigning in the 1980s resulted in condoms becoming far more widely available. Abortion was legalised in 1967, although it remains controversial. Sex education for young people ensures that risks of early pregnancy are well understood.	**Hygiene, sanitation and safety** Provision of universal education (the school-leaving age was raised to 15 in 1947) raised public awareness of the means by which diseases are transmitted. UK and EU health and safety laws regulate all hazardous aspects of people's lives (e.g. car seat-belt use, hygiene in restaurants and fire exits for all buildings).
Costs and consumerism The rising costs of living mean that parents may limit numbers of children in order to provide well for them and to maintain their own consumer lifestyles. The cost of bringing up a child is thought to be somewhere in the region of £150,000.	**Nutrition, diet and lifestyle** The risks associated with certain types of food, alcohol or lifestyle are widely publicised by the government. Fewer people now smoke, with a public ban finally introduced in 2007. However, obesity is on the rise, carrying with it a risk of type 2 diabetes (many schools are introducing healthier meals to help tackle this).
Global connections Some causes of falling births are external to the UK. For instance, the global depression of the 1930s (following the Wall Street Crash) led British people to limit family size. Rising energy costs in the 1970s (following the 400% rise in OPEC oil prices during 1973–74) also contributed to the UK's ongoing fertility decline.	**Global connections** Due to globalisation, the nature of work has changed. Many dangerous occupations have become automated, and most manufacturing and mining jobs have moved overseas. More people in the UK work in risk-free office environments. Improving health also owes much to the globalised nature of medical research.

Changes in employment, migration, ethnicity and social status

Along with changes in population size and structure, the social and economic characteristics of UK families have changed. Some of this can be attributed to government legislation: for instance, the opening up of higher education and policies encouraging regional and international migration. However, the role played by external (global) factors in bringing about change has also been significant (Table 11.4).

Table 11.4 Internal and external factors impacting on families in the UK

Evidence	Internal factors (for the UK)	External (global) factors
Migration trends	Postwar government slum clearance programmes, inner-city redevelopment schemes and New Town policies have all encouraged families to migrate since the 1950s. New Towns include Stevenage, Milton Keynes and Skelmersdale (outside Liverpool).	The global economic challenge set by NICs like China and South Korea has led to factory closures in northern UK cities such as Manchester and Liverpool. Many young workers migrated to southeast England looking for work during the 1980s and thereafter.
Employment and status changes	Increased A-level take-up has been encouraged by the government. The expansion of the UK's universities has enabled children in many families to become the first generation to gain the qualifications needed for middle-class occupations.	In the 1980s, the UK government ceased subsidies for industries that had become globally uncompetitive. Following the mine closures of the 1980s, fewer than 10,000 people now work in coal mining. The government has instead sought to enhance the UK's global comparative advantage in areas such as finance and media.
Changes in ethnicity	After the Second World War, more labour was needed to help with economic recovery. This led to the recruitment of workers from all over the British Commonwealth, notably Jamaicans and Indians.	Under EU legislation, citizens of other member states can live and work in the UK. Since 2004, around 600,000 Poles have come to the UK, as well as people from other EU states.

Consumption (and consumerism)

Key concept

The term **consumption** describes the purchase and use of commodities and services, including food, goods and leisure. Some geographers also write about the consumption of landscape and culture. **Consumerism** describes the growth of a way of life based around consumption, in which shopping and spending money are all-important. UK consumer spending reached £1 trillion in 2006.

Rising levels of consumption help to explain trends such as the spread of out-of-town shopping centres and the rise of TNCs. Consumption has also led to fertility decline in affluent nations. Raising children is expensive and people do not want to give up shopping, eating out and holidaying abroad.

The grey challenge

For reasons already outlined, the proportion of the UK's population aged over 65 is growing, leading to the 'greying' of British society (Figure 11.4). The country faces a growing burden of dependency. This can be shown mathematically using the dependency ratio, a shorthand measure that compares the proportion of a population that is economically non-productive with the proportion that (in theory) generates wealth. A high score of 70 or above suggests a lack of balance,

*Figure 11.4
The changing
dependent
population of the
UK, 1971–2021*

indicating that there are relatively high numbers of dependants in comparison with working taxpayers.

$$\text{dependency ratio} = \frac{(\text{population under 16}) + (\text{population over 65})}{(\text{population 15–64})} \times 100$$

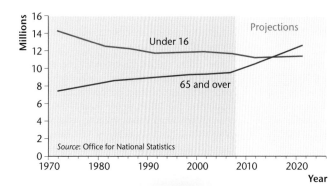

Source: Office for National Statistics

The dependency ratio is rising in the UK as the number of retired people increases (although a fall in the number of children being born means the ratio is not rising as fast as it might). Currently, 60% of Britons work and pay the state pensions of the 21% who are retired. By 2030, 56% of Britons will be working to support the 27% who are retired.

Economic costs

Financial provision must be made for the day-to-day living expenses of the elderly, as well as for health treatment and housing costs. By 2026, when the 1960s baby boom generation reaches retirement age, this will amount to about £30 billion per year. Local authorities with an unusually high proportion of elderly people must fund greater numbers of care homes and services which results in higher council taxes for working people.

Many older people retire to coastal regions (Figure 11.5). Properties remain occupied by elderly owners for much longer as life

*Table 11.5 House price rises in seaside
towns, 1995–2005*

Town	House price rise (%)
Falmouth, Cornwall	311.5
Penzance, Cornwall	302.2
Brancaster, Norfolk	287.0
Brighton, East Sussex	284.0
Mevagissey, Cornwall	265.4
Hastings, East Sussex	255.9
Bideford, Devon	251.1
Whitstable, Kent	250.3
Brixham, Devon	246.1
Hythe, Kent	242.5

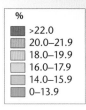

%	
■	>22.0
■	20.0–21.9
■	18.0–19.9
■	16.0–17.9
■	14.0–15.9
■	0–13.9

*Figure 11.5 The percentage of population in the
UK and Ireland aged over 65, by county*

expectancy rises. This can result in housing shortages, driving up prices for younger people. Between 1995 and 2005, average house prices in some UK seaside towns trebled, taking them well beyond the reach of many first-time buyers (Table 11.5).

Responsibility and care

In additional to the financial costs of an ageing population, rising longevity is placing an emotional burden on younger and middle-aged people who act as (unpaid) carers for older relatives. Thanks to improvements in healthcare, fewer people now die in their sixties and seventies from cancer, heart diseases or strokes. Instead, more people survive into their eighties and nineties and develop degenerative brain diseases such as Alzheimers.

Case study — Paying their own way? The UK's elderly population

Income for retired people in the UK can be complicated. The government pays a state pension to men over 65 and women over 60 (65 from 2020). This is little more than a subsistence wage. Additional state benefits include subsidised housing for those on very low incomes and free prescriptions. People need to have additional income sources if they want to continue living in the style they were accustomed to when working. Most retired people get their income from a variety of sources, which may include:

Photograph 11.2 Many people over retirement age contribute to the UK economy, including actor Michael Gambon

- *The state pension.* This is a universal entitlement that is available to everyone, whatever their income. It was introduced in 1946 as part of the National Insurance Act. In return for regular contributions from their wages (with additional contributions paid by the employer and the government), every worker is entitled to a weekly state pension upon retirement.
- *Other state benefits.* Housing costs are paid to those pensioners with no savings. The government gives free television licences to the over-75s, and a £200 winter fuel allowance is provided to the elderly. Local councils subsidise the cost of care homes for those who cannot look after themselves, and may issue free travel passes for trains and buses.
- *Company and personal pensions.* A company pension scheme may continue to pay a retiring employee a proportion of his or her final salary for as long as they live. Personal pensions can be built up through a lifetime of voluntary saving.
- *Continued employment.* Many elderly people who have worked in skilled occupations continue to work into their seventies and sometimes eighties. They may work as consultants.
- *Other investments.* Many older people own their own houses and can therefore borrow money from banks. The banks reclaim their money upon the owner's death and the sale of the house. This is known as 'equity release'. Older people may have stocks and shares and can continue to make fresh investments that yield new profits.
- *Family support.* In poorer families, children may

provide financial support for their aged parents. Of course, this works both ways. Older people with savings may also help support younger members of the family — grandparents might help with university fees, for instance.

The idea of an 'elderly population' is an oversimplification. There is a often a great difference — in terms of both physical health and ability to generate income independently — between highly active people in their seventies and more infirm and increasingly dependent people aged 80 and over.

It should be noted that younger people (under 40) may not be saving for old age in the way that their parents did, especially given the high costs of housing and the burden of student loans. As a result, financial dependency of the elderly may become even greater over time.

Benefits of a greying population
Elderly people make a range of contributions to society:
➤ voluntary charitable work
➤ spending money on goods and services
➤ earning money and paying tax
➤ bringing wisdom and experience to the worlds of politics and commerce

Global greying
The phenomenon of greying might be set to 'go global' in the future. Given the role that affluence and consumption play in reducing birth rates — not to mention the spread of modern healthcare, urban living, education and voting rights for women — it would be surprising if more countries did not begin to face the same demographic challenges as the UK.

Most OECD nations now have an ageing population, including some states whose main phase of economic growth occurred only relatively recently, such as South Korea. At the world level, the number of people aged over 60 is expected to exceed the number of children aged under 15 for the first time in 2047, helped by the long-term effects of China's one child policy. This has left the world's largest nation of 1.3 billion people with its own greying time-bomb. Compared to that, the UK's current demographic difficulties may one day appear minor.

Review questions
1 Study Table 11.1. Describe how life expectancy varies from place to place within the UK and suggest reasons for the differences shown.
2 Describe the varied data sources available to geographers studying population change over time in the UK.
3 Study Figure 11.5. Describe and suggest reasons for the pattern shown.
4 a Write down the names of as many elderly (over-65) celebrities as you can.
   b Making reference to your list, examine the claim that 'the grey challenge has been overstated'.

Chapter 12

On the move

How is migration changing the face of the European Union?

By the end of this chapter you should have:

➤ *examined the impact of international migration to Europe*

➤ *identified the patterns of recent movements within the EU, and examined the reasons for these movements*

➤ *assessed the social, economic, environmental and political consequences of migration*

Welcome to Europe?

The focus of this chapter is international migration: population movements between countries. Migration within a country (internal migration) is examined in Chapter 13.

International migration is a complex issue. It is important to draw distinctions between different types of migrant. Migrants may be voluntary or forced, temporary or permanent, legal or illegal (Figure 12.1).

Key terms

Displaced persons People who are forced to move, by war, famine, political persecution or natural disaster.

Illegal migrants People who avoid border and immigration controls and enter a new country illegally. Many are voluntary migrants seeking work, but some may be forced as part of 'human trafficking' to enter prostitution or other illegal activities.

Voluntary migrants People who move for quality of life reasons, usually economic gain (economic migrants). Many move temporarily (contract workers and professionals), returning home after months or years.

Figure 12.1 Types of migrant

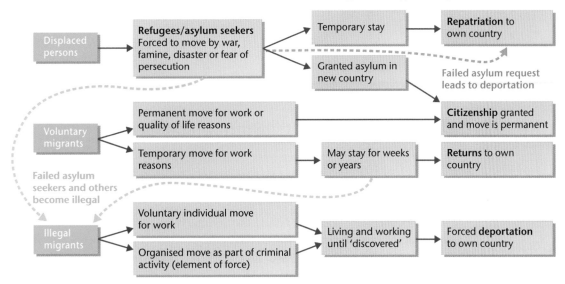

Migration theory

Key concept

A useful migration model is Lee's push–pull theory (1966). Lee explained the factors causing migration in terms of the positive and negative characteristics of origin and destination areas. Migrants have to perceive some benefit in moving from one place to another. They also take into account obstacles they might encounter including family pressures, government policy, costs of travel and language barriers (Figure 12.2).

Consider someone thinking of retiring to Spain from the UK:

push factors — poor weather, high house prices that generate income to finance the move, perceptions of rising crime

intervening obstacles — not speaking Spanish, red tape of obtaining visas and other legal requirements, family pressures to stay, distance

pull factors — better weather, lower housing and living costs, more relaxed lifestyle, many British migrants already living there, Spain being part of the EU

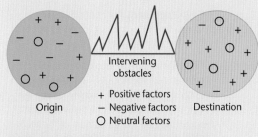

+ Positive factors
− Negative factors
○ Neutral factors

Origin   Intervening obstacles   Destination

Figure 12.2 Lee's push–pull migration model

TopFoto

Photograph 12.1 West Indians were encouraged to migrate to Britain in the 1950s to fill jobs

There is a key difference between migrants who are 'in the system' legally and those who are illegal. Accurate data on illegal immigration are hard to come by, and many migrants who are legal to begin with become illegal at the point when their leave to stay in a country expires.

Historic migration

Globalisation has made population movements easier than ever, and the volume of movements is increasing steadily. By 2005, 190 million people worldwide were living outside their country of birth — some 3% of the global population.

In the UK, successive waves of immigration since the Second World War have transformed the cultural landscape (Figure 12.3). By 2007, over 8% of the UK population was foreign born — more than double the global average. Table 12.1 illustrates the diversity of these migrants.

The links between the UK and its former colonies are important in explaining postwar migration. The UK relied on its colonies and dominions (Canada, Australia and New Zealand) during the Second World War. Small numbers of colonial soldiers, such as those from the Caribbean, stayed on in the UK after the war. They were joined by economic migrants from Jamaica, Trinidad and Tobago, and other island colonies as part of a deliberate policy to fill labour shortages in

Year 1950

Black Caribbean 566,000
Began 1948 — *SS Empire Windrush*
brought Jamaican economic migrants to
London to fill postwar worker shortages

▼ Economic migration

▼ Refugee migration

Figure 12.3
Migration to the UK
since 1950

1960

Pakistani (750,000) and Indian (1 million)
began late 1950s, peaked late 1960s. Many
migrants from poorer areas of Pakistan and
India. Initially men migrated alone

Bangladeshi (280,000) —
began in the mid 1960s,
but expanded rapidly
in 1980s as families
migrated to join men

1970

Expulsion of Asians
from Uganda in
1972. Around
30,000 sought
asylum in the UK

Black African
(480,000)
from former
colonies

The UK accepted around
20,000 Vietnamese 'boat
people' refugees. Many
came via Hong Kong

1980

Ethnic Chinese (243,000) —
began from colonies such as
Singapore and Malaysia in the
1950s, but has accelerated
from mainland China
since the late 1980s.
Many recent Chinese
migrants are students

1990

Conflict in the Balkans
caused forced migration
of Croatians, Bosnians
and Kosovans

Conflicts continue to generate
asylum seekers including Iraqis,
Kurds, Somalis and Zimbabweans

2000

Table 12.1
The geography of
UK postcolonial
immigration

Source: Data
from UK census,
2001

Opening of EU borders attracted large
numbers of eastern Europeans, especially
Poles, to UK for economic reasons

2010

Immigrant/ group	Location(s) within the UK	Population characteristics of the ethnic group
Chinese	47% live in London and the southeast. Many set up businesses such as takeaways in areas without competition, and so became more geographically widespread than other groups.	Average age is 27.
Black Caribbean	61% live in London, with a further 17% in the west midlands. London was often the place of arrival in the 1950s, and an area with acute labour shortages.	Three distinct age peaks at 60, 40 and 20.
Black African	78% live in London. A diverse range of communities from different African nations has developed within the capital.	Average age is 27, with 68% of working age.
Indian	Large concentrations in the west and east midlands, a lower percentage in London than most other groups. Geography reflects the availability of work in the 1960s.	Close to 50% were born in the UK. The majority are in the 20–50 age bracket.
Pakistani	London has the largest concentration, with the west midlands, Yorkshire and the northwest also high. Geography reflects the availability of work in the 1960s.	55% were born in the UK; 35% are under 16. A younger profile than the Indian group.
Bangladeshi	Over 75% live in London. Much of the work for Bangladeshis initially came from the garment industry in east London.	Just over half were born in the UK; the average age is 21, one of the youngest of all ethnic groups.

sectors such as the railways, buses and National Health Service (Photograph 12.1). This was encouraged by the 1948 British Nationality Act, which gave UK citizenship to people from the Commonwealth. Migration from Commonwealth countries was restricted by the 1962 Commonwealth Immigrants Act. By 1972 it had been tightened further to allow only those with work permits or people with grandparents and parents born in the UK to settle here.

Current trends: illegal migrants

Illegal immigration to Europe seems to be on the rise, although accurate data are hard to obtain. Some estimates suggest 4–8 million illegal African migrants may be in the EU. Total illegal immigration in the UK is estimated at 0.5 million. The appeal of the EU to Africans is obvious — it is an economic powerhouse virtually on the doorstep. Huge areas of Africa have been wracked by conflict, civil unrest, famine and poverty, so the push factors are strong.

Figure 12.4 shows the various routes taken by African migrants to the EU. Many migrants enter by boat through the Spanish Canary Islands, Malta and Italy, or through the Spanish enclaves of Ceuta and Melilla, which are on the African continent. However, migrating illegally to Europe has its costs:

➤ Migrants pay traffickers € 1,000–€ 4,000 each.
➤ The Sahara desert land route is dangerous and there are many heat-related deaths, and killings by bandits.
➤ Fishing boats used on the sea routes can be lethal.
➤ A common route, from Senegal to the Canaries, can take 8–10 days in potentially rough seas, in overcrowded boats.
➤ Being caught often leads to deportation.

Figure 12.4
Migrant routes from Africa to Europe

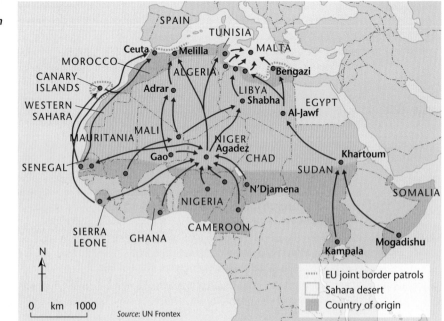

Case study **Malta under siege**

Tiny Malta (population 400,000), which joined the EU in 2004, increasingly finds itself on the front line of the battle to prevent illegal migration into Europe. The immigrants besieging Malta are from Africa, many coming via Libya.

In 2006, 1,700 illegal migrants arrived in Malta by boat, up from 500 in 2003. Most had 'missed' mainland Italy or Sicily and landed in Malta by mistake (Figure 12.5). The numbers may sound small, but given Malta's tiny size, 1,700 illegal immigrants is the equivalent of 400,000 arriving in Germany. EU patrol boats that find illegal immigrants in boats cannot turn them back, as international law obliges them to help. Maltese fishermen are often overwhelmed by migrants — many cling to tuna nets in the open sea (see Photograph 8.4, p. 96).

Malta has three detention centres and Maltese law states that all illegal immigrants should be detained for up to 18 months. The fear is that increasing numbers of African migrants will become 'trapped' on the tiny island, either awaiting hearing

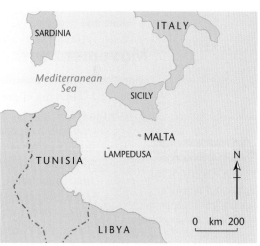

Figure 12.5 Location of Malta

of asylum claim cases, or housed in detention centres.

Key to reducing the migrant flow might be an agreement with Libya to police its waters more carefully.

Current trends: asylum seekers

A refugee is defined by the UN as someone who has

a well-founded fear of being persecuted for reasons of race, religion, nationality, membership of a particular social group, or political opinion, is outside the country of their nationality, and is unable to or, owing to such fear, is unwilling to avail him/herself of the protection of that country.

A person seeking to be classed as a refugee is an asylum seeker. If the claim for asylum is granted, the refugee is normally allowed to stay. If the claim is turned down, the immigrant may be deported.

Concern has been expressed about the numbers seeking asylum in the EU, amid fears that many are actually economic migrants. Asylum claims peaked in the early 1990s, and again in 2001–02, but have since fallen across

Figure 12.6 Asylum claims in developed countries, 1980–2006

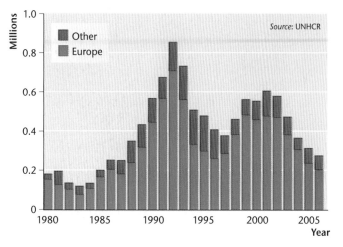

Europe (Figure 12.6). The majority of asylum seekers are from the middle and near east (notably Iraq, Afghanistan, Iran and Pakistan) or other countries where political and ethnic difficulties exist (Russia, Serbia and war-torn African states such as Sudan and Somalia).

Movement within Europe

Migration between countries within the EU has increased as the EU has grown. Figure 12.7 shows **net migration** in the whole of the EU between 2000 and 2004. What is noticeable is the negative net migration in east European countries. These countries have relatively low per capita incomes and since they joined the EU many of their workers have migrated west in search of work (post-accession migration). The core EU countries (the UK, Germany and France) have positive net migration. This results partly from the influx of eastern European workers, but also from immigrants from outside the EU. Countries around the Mediterranean basin (Spain, Italy, Greece and Cyprus) have the highest net migration. This results from the movement of 'sunseekers' from north to south (especially retirees), plus migration from Africa.

> **Key terms**
>
> **Net migration** The balance between immigration (people moving into a country) and emigration (people leaving a country).

Figure 12.7
Net migration
in the EU countries,
2000–04

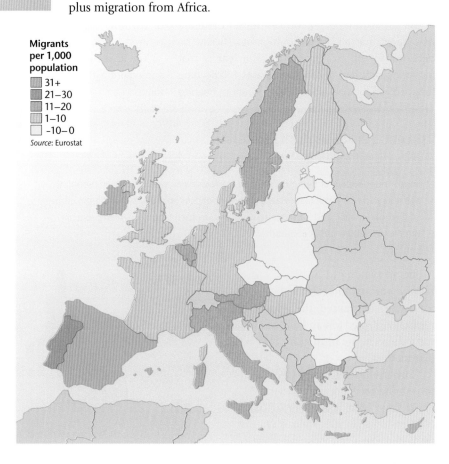

Migrants per 1,000 population
- 31+
- 21–30
- 11–20
- 1–10
- –10–0

Source: Eurostat

EU open borders

Most national border controls within the EU were removed in 1995 when the Schengen Agreement (Figure 12.8) was implemented. This enables easier movement of people and goods within the EU, and means that passports do not usually have to be shown at borders. The UK did not sign, preferring to keep its border controls. The new EU members in eastern Europe implemented this agreement in 2007–08.

In 2004, when eight lower-income eastern European countries joined the EU (Latvia, Lithuania, Estonia, Poland, Hungary, Slovenia, Slovakia and the Czech Republic), the UK (with Sweden and Ireland) decided to allow free migration of these people. The other EU member states imposed restrictions, for up to 7 years.

Schengen brings benefits, as EU labour can move to where there is demand, but also costs — once someone is in one EU country, they can move to most others with ease. The EU has set up Frontex, an external border control agency, to prevent illegal immigrants seeping in through borders with non-EU members.

Malta and Cyprus also joined the EU in 2004 and Bulgaria and Romania in 2007. Restrictions on migration of citizens from these countries were kept in place by the UK.

Figure 12.8
EU countries in the Schengen Agreement

Legend:
- ☐ Schengen members but not EU
- Implemented 1995
- Joined EU and Schengen 2007–08
- EU but not full Schengen members

A	Albania
B	Belgium
BO	Bosnia
C	Croatia
CZ	Czech Republic
L	Luxembourg
M	Moldova
MA	Macedonia
N	Netherlands
S	Slovenia
SE	Serbia
SL	Slovakia
SW	Switzerland

Table 12.2
Top ten source and host countries for UK migration, 2004–05

UK 2004/05 (numbers of migrants)	Top ten source countries of immigrants to the UK		Top ten host countries for emigrants from the UK	
EU countries	Poland	69,000	Spain	68,000
	Germany	43,000	France	52,000
	France	28,000	Germany	14,000
	Spain	27,000	Greece	12,000
Non-EU, Commonwealth countries	India	92,000	Australia	105,000
	Australia	78,000	New Zealand	43,000
	South Africa	63,000	Canada	24,000
	Pakistan	46,000	South Africa	23,000
Other non-EU countries	USA	56,000	USA	50,000
	China	49,000	China	19,000

Source: ONS, 2005

Table 12.2 shows the top source countries and host countries for UK migration:
➤ The large number of Polish immigrants are part of the UK Worker Registration Scheme for EU workers, and have come seeking work as plumbers, builders, hotel staff or in farming and food processing.
➤ Some sources and hosts almost balance (e.g. the USA), which is probably due to professionals moving to the UK for several years, then returning home.
➤ France, Greece and Spain receive high numbers of UK retirees and others seeking a new life in the sun. This is also true of Australia.
➤ Large immigration flows from India and Pakistan are probably family members of earlier migrants.

The UK has a huge temporary guest workforce. Numbers have risen steadily since the east European states joined the EU in 2004, but by late 2007 they were beginning to slow. One major difference from earlier migrations (see Table 12.1) is that these new migrants are not concentrated in one or two regions. Rural regions, such as East Anglia and the Scottish Highlands, have had significant immigration (Figure 12.9). The case study provides further detail.

Figure 12.9 UK distribution of eastern European migrants, 2006

Eastern European migration

'There's even an aisle for Polish food at Asda' ran a *Daily Telegraph* headline in 2007. The aisle in question is in Hereford, population 50,000. How does a town of this size support a Polish food aisle? The influx of eastern European migrant farm workers has made Herefordshire a rural migration 'hotspot'. An estimated 120,000 eastern European migrants registered in UK rural areas between 2004 and 2006, 8,100 of them in Herefordshire. Figure 12.10 shows the nationality of migrants in 2006.

Some migrants are seasonal agricultural workers (SAWs) whose numbers peak in early summer when the fruit harvest is at its height. Those from the eastern EU states have longer-term plans and may settle in the area. Problems associated with migrants in Herefordshire include:

- discrimination and distrust from local people
- variable migrant skill levels, with demands for training, especially in English
- high rents, as housing is in short supply

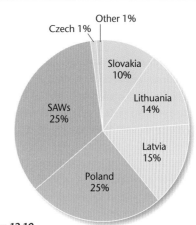

Figure 12.10
Nationality of Herefordshire's rural migrants, 2006

Note: 'Other' includes Estonia and Romania; SAWs = seasonal agricultural workers, for whom no nationality is given — mostly students from outside the EU.

Source: West Mercia Police

Photograph 12.2 A Polish restaurant in Oxford

- poor access to education and health, often as a result of the language barrier
- pressure on accident and emergency services, as few migrants register with a GP

There are also significant numbers of east European migrants in Scotland. Scotland's population was set to decline to under 5 million by 2014, but immigration has revised this date to 2026. The majority of migrants are Poles, and they are young (80% under 35), which is significant in a country that is ageing rapidly. Employers value the Polish work ethic and some businesses depend on migrants. Salmon processing in the Highlands, for example, has 30% migrants in its workforce.

There has been a Polish community in London for decades, centred in Hammersmith. Since 2004 this has swelled with up to 1,500 migrants arriving in the UK every day. Many arrive in the capital first, and find work as builders, plumbers, hotel receptionists, maids, cleaners and waiters even though they have university degrees. Wages are low, but better than in Poland. However, finding a job and somewhere to stay is not easy in the capital.

This has been the UK's largest mass migration ever. However, it is worth noting that between 2004 and 2007 the UK's unemployment rate varied between 4.5 and 5.5 % — one of the lowest in the world, despite the arrival of over 700,000 workers from eastern Europe.

Table 12.3 UK migrants in the EU

Country	Residents from UK
Spain	760,000
France	200,000
Germany	115,000
Ireland	290,000
Cyprus	60,000
Portugal	38,000

The major influx of migrants from eastern Europe since 2004 has been partly balanced by increasing numbers of people leaving the UK for good. This is a long-term trend and has resulted in an estimated 5.5 million Britons living abroad. There are now significant permanent British populations in several other EU countries (Table 12.3).

Spain is by far the most popular destination — the size of the 'ex-pat' community in Spain is similar to the population of Leeds.

The Costa living

The Spanish Costas have long been a draw for rain-soaked and windswept northern Europeans. Many, but not all, are British. Some 1.8 million properties in Spain are owned by foreign nationals, around 600,000 of them British. Many are holiday homes, but a significant number are owned by permanent residents — in other words, migrants. The British and Germans dominate the emigrant property market and 60% of migrants are over 45 years old (Figure 12.11). Among them are:
- a significant number of retirees
- those in their thirties and forties who have moved to set up businesses
- people who have moved partly as property speculators. They may still have business links with the UK, and some even 'commute'

Why have so many people migrated? Clearly the sun is the biggest draw, plus a perceived relaxed lifestyle. Property prices are lower than in the UK, as are taxes for ex-pats, and utility bills are around 50–60% of UK

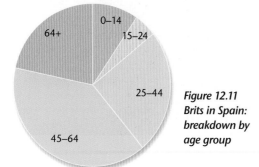

Figure 12.11 Brits in Spain: breakdown by age group

prices. In addition the distance between Spain and the UK has been 'shrunk' by:

■ the rise of low-cost airlines such as easyJet
■ a long-term road-building programme in Spain
■ the internet, which makes business and family communication with the UK much easier

However, there is a price. For retirees, ageing in Spain can become difficult — there is often a lack of care, healthcare costs can mount, and many of the purpose-built retirement communities are isolated and designed for people in good health, not those becoming frail.

Rampant coastal development has detracted from the natural beauty of the landscape and water supply is becoming a major issue as urbanisation exceeds available resources. Many Spaniards feel that the new arrivals fail to integrate, and live in ex-pat enclaves that have little economic impact other than to inflate property prices for locals.

The consequences of migration

Economic issues

Are migrants a net cost or net benefit to economies? This very much depends on who the migrants are and the type of work they can do. Young, single, skilled migrants are likely to boost economic growth, whereas migrating families with dependants, or asylum seekers, are likely to be a cost, at least initially.

Estimates from the UK Treasury suggest that migrants contribute 10% of taxes, but 'take' only 9% of government spending. Of the 700,000 or so eastern European workers who arrived in the UK between 2004 and 2007, only around 5,000 claimed any benefits such as income support, although some 70,000 claimed child benefit. The anti-migration group Migrationwatch argues that migration has little economic benefit — equivalent to 4p per week per person in added economic growth. However, in 2006, the financial firm Ernst & Young estimated that migration had added £12–18 billion in tax revenues since 1998. Table 12.4 examines the economic costs and benefits.

Table 12.4
The economic costs and benefits of migration

	Benefits	Costs
Host country	Fills skills gaps and shortages in the labour market. Reduces wage inflation, as labour supply equals demand. Economic growth, as migrants are also consumers. Entrepreneurship, as migrants bring new ideas. In the UK, provides a young, tax-paying workforce that helps balance an ageing population. Migrants can open new markets: for instance, demand for ethnic foods.	Reduces wages for domestic workers and, in the worst case, takes their jobs. Low-skilled migrants may not be very productive as they need training. Some migrants may be a burden on the state (education, health, housing). Demand for resources, such as housing, leads to shortages, rising prices and higher costs for everyone.
Source country	Migrants send remittances back home. This can amount to up to 10% of GDP. Returning migrants may have new skills they can use in their home country. Less pressure on resources, such as land. Unemployment may be reduced.	If key workers leave, economic growth may slow. If young people leave, the proportion of aged dependants rises. Innovation may slow if the young leave, and dependency on remittances rises.

Social, cultural and environmental issues

One in four children in the UK in 2007 was born to a foreign parent. The UK birth rate has increased since 2002, largely as a result of a growing young migrant population with higher fertility than the 'host' population. Migration is the root cause of the UK's gradual population growth. Many would argue that this is positive in a country with an ageing and declining population.

In host countries there are consequences such as:

➤ the creation of multicultural societies and the benefits of easy access to the music, food, tradition and ideas of other cultures
➤ language barriers, and the costs of providing education (which could equally be seen as an investment)
➤ migrants failing to integrate or experiencing prejudice. In some circumstances this can escalate into a major social problem. There is concern over the creation of 'parallel communities' which rarely mix
➤ the environmental impacts of increased population density, especially in crowded countries such as the UK and Holland, which suffer congestion, urban air pollution and urban sprawl

Migration has wider consequences for source countries, including:

➤ family break-up, as young men (generally) migrate, leaving families behind
➤ a culture of emigration, and a sense that leaving is a good thing — this can cause societies to undervalue themselves

It is important to distinguish between illegal immigrants, refugees and economic migrants and not be misled by tabloid headlines.

Managing migration

The poverty and racism suffered by some immigrant groups can lead to racial tensions and occasionally open conflict (for example the suburban riots in Paris in 2005). Governments have to manage migration to ensure that they:

➤ meet international obligations in accepting asylum seekers
➤ limit illegal migration
➤ match immigration to the needs of the economy and minimise emigration of key workers, and the resulting brain drain
➤ integrate immigrants into the host society

UK immigration policy is reviewed in the case study.

 Case study **UK policy on immigration**

UK immigration policy tries to balance the costs of migration with the benefits and only allows in certain migrants. Key elements are:

■ A tough policy on asylum seekers, accepting only genuine applicants. Numbers are steadily falling.

■ A points-based system which favours those with skills, education and earning potential.
■ The worker registration scheme (WRS), which allows migrants from some eastern European EU states to move to the UK to fill low-skill, low-wage employment gaps.

Table 12.5 The top ten UK visa application posts, 2006

Visa post	Received	Issued
Islamabad	177,056	109,268
Mumbai	170,299	138,227
Lagos	169,415	81,226
New Delhi	147,525	117,981
Moscow	128,261	121,754
Chennai	116,086	95,546
Beijing	77,138	69,041
Abuja	57,031	27,550
New York	56,831	53,048
Istanbul	56,341	52,772
Total for top ten posts	1,155,983	866,413
Total for all posts	2,753,078	2,235,857

Source: UK visas annual report, 2006, FCO

- Permanent residence is granted only when migrants have been resident in the UK for some years, and migrants who wish to become citizens of the UK must pass a 'Life in the UK' test.
- UK business visas favour those with money and ideas, and encourage investment in the UK.

In 2005/06, 2.75 million people applied for a visa to visit the UK — 57% more than in 2001/02. Around 20% of visa applications were refused, often because forged documents were used. Table 12.5 shows the number of visa applications made in the top ten 'posts' (UK visa offices abroad) in 2006. Note the dominance of developing world applications.

In 2008, the UK introduced a five-tier points-based system for non-EU immigrants:
- Tier 1: highly skilled individuals
- Tier 2: skilled workers with a job offer to fill gaps in the UK labour force
- Tier 3: limited numbers of low-skilled workers needed to fill specific temporary labour shortages
- Tier 4: students
- Tier 5: youth mobility and temporary workers allowed to work in the UK for a limited period of time

The idea is to make immigration easier to understand, and to target migrants that the country needs.

Review questions

1 Using examples, explain the difference between voluntary and forced migration.
2 Explain the data you would need to collect to calculate a country's net migration.
3 Using a table format, evaluate social, economic, cultural and environmental costs and benefits of the migration of eastern European workers to the UK.
4 Assess the extent to which the UK's immigration policy addresses the four points raised about managing migration on p. 142.

World cities

What is driving the new urbanisation and what are its consequences?

By the end of this chapter you should have:
➤ *considered how rural–urban migration feeds the growth of megacities*
➤ *contrasted a range of megacities, to appreciate their diversity and reasons for their differences*
➤ *examined the consequences of developing world urbanisation, and whether urbanisation can be made sustainable*

Rural–urban migration

How do cities grow? Two processes are key. The first is internal growth (natural increase), which results from city dwellers having a high birth rate. The second process is rural–urban migration. Most of those who move to cities from the countryside are young, fertile people who therefore cause a high birth rate within cities — migration fuels high internal growth.

The balance of these two processes is generally taken to be that internal growth accounts for some 60% of urban population growth, migration for around 30% and reclassification of rural areas to urban areas for the remaining 10%. Table 13.1 provides some data.

Table 13.1
Urban, slum and population growth rates, 2005

	Urban growth rate	Slum growth rate	General population growth rate	Comments
Latin America	2.2	1.3	1.4	Urban growth moderate; slum growth slow; megacities growing faster than other urban areas.
São Paulo	4.1		1.4 Brazil	
Mexico City	3.7		1.3 Mexico	
Asia	3.0	1.3	1.3	Rapid urban growth, driven by migration in particular. Slow slum growth.
Delhi	4.5		1.6 India	
Dhaka	6.6		1.9 Bangladesh	
Sub-Saharan Africa	4.5	4.5	2.3	Very rapid urbanisation, which for some cities is extreme; the vast majority is due to migration. Slum growth rapid.
Abidjan	8.0		1.6 Côte d'Ivoire	
Monrovia	8.2		1.4 Liberia	

Note: Growth rates are per cent per year

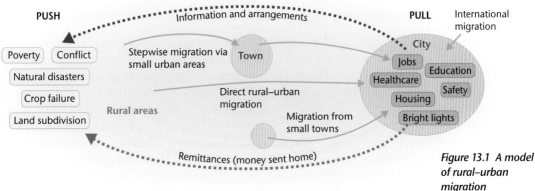

Figure 13.1 A model of rural–urban migration

The poorest areas of the world have the fastest urban growth rates, and migration tends to dominate internal growth. This is even more the case when one city dominates in a country, as these cities can grow at rates of 6–8% per year, with much of the growth consisting of **slums**. The population living in developing world slums is likely to reach 1.3–1.4 billion by 2020.

Why do people migrate to cities if the living conditions are so poor, for so many? Figure 13.1 is a model of push and pull factors, and types of migration, that contribute to urbanisation.

Many rural–urban migrants are well informed about the city to which they are migrating. The process is usually not 'blind' unless it involves an immediate crisis, such as war or natural disaster. Extended family or friends may have arranged jobs for the migrants. The majority who move are young and relatively well skilled. They may be aware that life in cities is not good, but are prepared to put up with the problems in the short term, knowing that in the long term their prospects are better than if they stayed in rural areas. Fundamentally, rural–urban migration is an economic decision.

Is it the right decision? The figures in Table 13.2 suggest that quality of life is better in urban Kenya, but not in Nairobi's slums. Many migrants will have to live in slums but they believe there are more opportunities in Nairobi than in rural areas.

Key term

Slum An urban settlement in which, according to the United Nations, over 50% of inhabitants lack one or more of the following: durable housing, sufficient living area, improved water supply, access to sanitation and secure tenure (ownership). Areas of slum housing built from waste materials are called shanty towns, and if they are illegally occupying land, squatter settlements.

Area	Infant mortality rate (per 1,000)	Poverty (% living on less than $1 per day)	Access to improved water supply (% of population)
Rural Kenya	76	53	46
Urban Kenya	57	49	89
Nairobi as a whole	39		
Slums in Nairobi	9		
Kibera slum in Nairobi	106		

Table 13.2 Urban–rural differences in Kenya, 2002

A study of migrants to Mexico City between 1995 and 2000, found that in-migrants numbered 521,000. Out-migration slightly exceeded this, so the city's population growth of 1.4% per year was a result of internal growth.

The majority of rural–urban migrants (flow 1 on Figure 13.2) come from poor farming states close to and south of Mexico City. Many of these are young women (average age 22), escaping rural poverty and seeking low-skill domestic work in Mexico City. These migrants are better educated than the population in general, having had 8–9 years in school compared to the national average of 7.6 years.

There is a large out-migration (flow 2) from Mexico City, but this is migration to the sprawling fringes of the city, in other states, so actually represents urbanisation. Equally, migration to Baja California in the north (flow 3) and the Caribbean coast (flow 4) mostly represents migration to urban areas. These include the manufacturing centres of Mexicali and Tijuana on the US border and the tourist centre of Cancún.

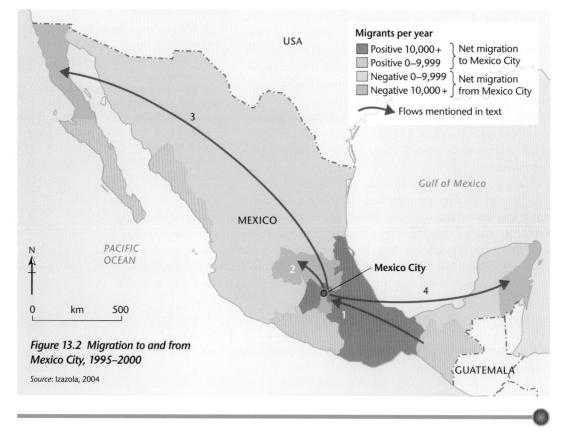

Figure 13.2 Migration to and from Mexico City, 1995–2000

Source: Izazola, 2004

New urbanisation

Figure 13.3 shows that the world's 25 fastest-growing cities of over 2 million people are in a belt stretching from Indonesia and China to the west coast of Africa. On average, the Asian cities are larger and growing slightly more slowly than their African counterparts.

Figure 13.3 The 25 fastest-growing cities (projection for 2005–15) which had over 2 million people in 2005

Annual growth rate (%)	
●	2.1 – 3.0
●	3.1 – 4.0
●	4.1+

2005 population	
●	2–5 million
●	5.1–10 million
●	10 million +

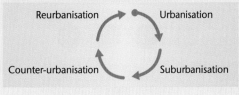

Contrasting megacities

It is important to recognise that rapidly growing cities and **megacities** are very diverse. This is for a number of reasons:

➤ *Level of development.* Many of Asia's cities are centres of wealth, many of Africa's are desperately poor.
➤ *Type of migrant.* Some migrants may be young, skilled and entrepreneurial, others may be older, poorer and perhaps forced to migrate.

> **Key term**
>
> **Megacity** An urban area with a population of over 8 million.

Urban processes

> **Key concept**

Urban growth refers to the growth in the physical size of a city, and is different from urbanisation. **Urban sprawl** occurs when urban areas grow outwards, usually in an uncontrolled way, on to surrounding rural land. In the developing world this often results from illegal slum growth.

In developing cities, **suburbanisation** occurs when the wealthy choose to live on the city edge to escape the poverty, crime, congestion and pollution of the city centre. A modern trend is for new suburbs to be **gated**, with walls, gates and security to keep non-residents out. This is common in Latin American and South African cities.

Counter-urbanisation refers to the movement of people out of cities and into rural areas.

It is mainly a developed world process, but the very rich in the developing world may also counter-urbanise.

Reurbanisation may follow attempts to regenerate areas of cities that have declined. Again, this is a developed world trend beginning to occur in Asian cities.

These urban processes are linked by the cycle of urbanisation (Figure 13.4).

Figure 13.4 The cycle of urbanisation

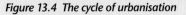

Reurbanisation → Urbanisation

Counter-urbanisation → Suburbanisation

> *Growth characteristics.* Some cities may be growing largely because of migration, others by internal growth.
> *Planning.* Many Asian cities are beginning to plan their growth (see case study of Chongqing), whereas in Africa planning is prevented by poverty and lack of planners.
> *Rate of population growth.* This varies from around 2–4% per year for Latin American cities, to 4–8% for some African and Asian cities.
> *Processes.* Different urban processes are occurring in different cities — these are explored in the 'Urban processes' key concept box (p. 147).

Figure 13.5 Life in contrasting cities (see Table 13.3, p. 150)

São Paulo (maturing)   20.4 37 98 88

Beatriz lives in Alphaville, a gated suburb of São Paulo. Her father owns car dealerships, and business is booming as Brazil's middle class grows. Her school, the mall, the country club and her friends are all close by. She rarely visits the centre of the city as the crime and pollution are too high, and there is no need. The gated community of 30,000 people is safe, and there is lots to do.

Cairo (consolidating)   15.9 57 99 88

Mounir lives in Moqattam, with 30,000 other 'recyclers' who make up Cairo's zabaleen (rubbish collectors). His father first came to the city 50 years ago. He is proud of the zabaleen's work, but fears that his livelihood could vanish as the city modernises and employs foreign waste-management companies to collect rubbish. His son works as a builder on the Greater Cairo Wastewater Project to improve the city's sewer system.

Beijing (maturing)   12.7 38 93 80

Wan Hu is an engineer who moved to the city when he graduated. He lives in the suburb of Wangjing and works for a German company based in Wangjing Science Park. Mr Wan lives in a high-rise apartment and his quality of life is good. He complains that air quality in the city is poor, but the pace of development means that work is not hard to come by.

Mumbai (consolidating)   21.3 60 99 97

Sarasa lives in Dharavi, Asia's largest slum in central Mumbai. Her family are leather workers and she is a maid – together they earn around £1,000 per month and have lived in the slum for 40 years. Water and sanitation are poor, but life is bearable. Sarasa's family fear eviction as upgrading of the slum began in 2004 and Mumbai is striving to rid the city of slums.

Johannesburg (maturing)   7.7 33 98 90

Jomo lives in Soweto, a black township. He earns about £100 per month as a miner. In 2001, he moved into a new house provided by the government, with water and electricity. Things have improved since apartheid ended, but only slowly. His two brothers are among the 40% of Soweto people who are unemployed, and he feels crime and the threat of AIDS are growing problems.

Lagos (immature)   10 79 88 74

Adeola lives in Makoko, a slum of 25,000 people in Lagos. Half of the slum is built on wooden stilts, and many inhabitants are fishermen. People sleep 6–8 to a room in the wooden shacks that pass for houses. Adeola has had no education, as it is too expensive. His life expectancy is about 40. Every few days he paddles 2 km in his canoe to get water. It costs 3p for 10 litres. There is no disposal system — everything is thrown into the same river that Adeola fishes in. Malaria and TB are common. Police never enter Makoko — it is too violent.

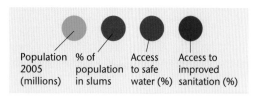

Population 2005 (millions)   % of population in slums   Access to safe water (%)   Access to improved sanitation (%)

Case study: Chongqing

Chongqing is China's fourth largest municipality. It is upstream of the Three Gorges dam and is a key inland port on the Yangtze River (Figure 13.6 and Photograph 13.1).

Many of China's 8.5 million annual rural–urban migrants head to cities like Chongqing. Chongqing city contains 4.1 million people, but the wider municipality (urban area) housed 31.5 million in 2005. Chongqing's vital statistics are staggering:

- Over 1,300 rural–urban migrants arrive every day.
- The urban economy grows by £7 million per day.
- Total population is growing by 500,000 per year.
- Around 130,000 m² of new buildings are constructed daily.
- Average income rose by 66% between 2000 and 2005, to £730 per year, almost three times the rural average.

Chongqing's growth is no accident. The city is core to the China Western Development Plan created in 2000 to spread development and industrialisation from the coastal zone and cities inland to lower-income areas. A great deal of infrastructure development is occurring, especially of transport, but the city has huge waste and pollution problems.

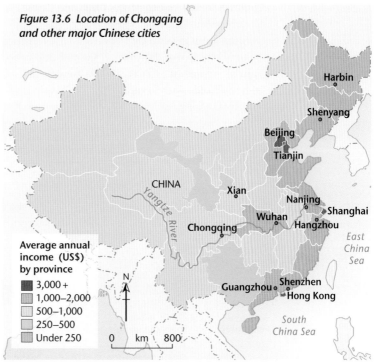

Figure 13.6 Location of Chongqing and other major Chinese cities

Average annual income (US$) by province
- 3,000 +
- 1,000–2,000
- 500–1,000
- 250–500
- Under 250

Photograph 13.1 Chongqing

The differences in experience revealed by Figure 13.5 result from different economic conditions in the countries concerned. The newly industrialising counties (Brazil, South Africa, India and China) are generating the wealth required to tackle slum housing.

Slum housing can be improved in a number of ways. In Brazil, household income has grown. Between 2000 and 2005 the number of households with an annual income of $6,000–22,000 grew from 14 to 22 million, while the number of households with annual incomes less than $3,000 more than halved. In these circumstances, people will improve their own homes, and new ones will be built. As taxes rise, governments can invest in social housing and improving water and sanitation. By contrast, in Nigeria per capita incomes are below 1960 levels and 57% of the population live on under $1 per day. There is little opportunity for self-improvement, or government programmes.

As new urbanisation progresses, the structure of cities changes (Table 13.3):

➤ Immature developing cities are dominated by slums on the urban fringes, and in city-centres. Both are areas where newcomers live — to be close to jobs, or

Table 13.3 World urbanisation types

	Urbanisation stage	Growth	Economy	Planning and cycle of urbanisation processes	Examples
Developing world	Immature	Very rapid: 3%+ per year. Largely migration growth.	Informal economy = 60%. Small-scale manufacturing, street trading, urban farming.	**Urbanisation** Little planning: uncontrolled sprawl. Squatter settlements dominate. Basic needs barely met. 60%+ live in slums. Environmental problems.	Kabul Lagos Kinshasa
Developing world	Consolidating	Rapid 2–3% per year. Balance of migration and internal growth.	Manufacturing important, some service industries. Informal economy around 50%.	**Urbanisation and suburbanisation** Attempts at planning, focused on waste, congestion and water supply. Upgrading of slums and some social housing. Most basic needs met.	Cairo Mumbai Jakarta Chongqing (see case study)
Developing world	Maturing	Slow: under 2% per year. Largely internal growth.	Service industry dominates, with some manufacturing. Informal economy under 40%.	**Suburbanisation** Effective attempts at housing, transport and land-use planning. Environmental problems being tackled. Quality of life satisfactory for many. Gated communities in suburbs.	Mexico City São Paulo Beijing
Developed world	Established	Very slow, under 1% per year. Some are stable.	Dominated by professional, services and retail. Formal economy.	**Counter-urbanisation and reurbanisation** Large-scale suburbanisation, with counter-urbanisation. Since 1980, most have regenerated inner-city and former industrial areas. Quality of life is high for most, and environmental quality is good.	London San Francisco Paris Birmingham

because there is no other land available. The rich are often confined in central business district (CBD) apartment blocks, surrounded by poverty.

➤ In the consolidating phase, government housing schemes and new towns are built, and housing conditions begin to improve. As wealth grows, individuals slowly improve their homes.

➤ In maturing cities, as the middle class swells and housing is improved, slums decline. Suburbanisation, often in the form of gated communities, becomes common.

World cities

So far, we have focused on big cities in the developing world, mostly megacities with a population of over 8 million. Some cities fall into a different category, that of **world cities**. London, New York and Tokyo are examples. A world city is defined not by size, but by influence. This might take the form of:

➤ political influence — for instance, New York is home to the United Nations

➤ transport and communications — Heathrow in London has more international passengers than any other airport

➤ economic power — the presence of stock exchanges and the headquarters of major TNCs

> ### Key terms
>
> **World city** (or global city) A city with major economic and political power. Examples are New York (also a megacity) and Paris (not a megacity).

Researchers at Loughborough University have attempted to rank cities into a world hierarchy, which is shown in Table 13.4.

It is noticeable that there are no 'full' developing world cities, and that only one African city is included (Johannesburg). Some minor world cities in the developed world have populations of only a few million (Melbourne, Stockholm) whereas some vast megacities (Cairo, Lagos) are not included. It is likely that some megacities will move rapidly up the list in the next few decades, as their economic and political influence grows. Are Shanghai, Seoul and São Paulo the leading world cities of tomorrow?

	Full world cities	Major world cities	Minor world cities
Developed world	London, New York City, Paris, Tokyo, Chicago, Frankfurt, Hong Kong, Los Angeles, Milan, Singapore	San Francisco, Sydney, Toronto, Zurich, Brussels, Madrid, Moscow	Amsterdam, Boston, Dallas, Düsseldorf, Geneva, Houston, Jakarta, Melbourne, Osaka, Prague, Washington, Montreal, Rome, Stockholm, Warsaw, Atlanta, Barcelona, Berlin, Budapest, Copenhagen, Hamburg, Miami, Minneapolis, Munich
Developing world		Mexico City, São Paulo, Seoul	Bangkok, Beijing, Buenos Aires, Istanbul, Kuala Lumpur, Manila, Shanghai, Caracas, Jakarta, Johannesburg, Santiago, Taipei

Table 13.4
World city hierarchy

Sustainable megacities?

Can developing world megacities be sustainable? To move up the urban hierarchy towards world city status, economic development needs to go hand in hand with social and environmental improvements. Many of the features of sustainable cities depend on good urban governance (Figure 13.7).

Growing cities in poorer countries can be unsustainable for several reasons:

➤ lack of adequate housing — due to rapid growth, poverty and lack of resources.
➤ poor health — linked to lack of water, sanitation and medical facilities
➤ weak urban governance — a lack of will, combined with a lack of resources, makes change difficult
➤ low environmental quality — resulting from poor transport infrastructure, lack of waste systems and industrial pollution
➤ poverty — resulting from low wages and underemployment

The Millennium Development Goals agreed by the United Nations in 2000 set clear targets for improving urban quality of life in developing countries. Goal 7 calls for a 'significant improvement in lives of at least 100 million slum dwellers, by 2020'. By 2007 there were 200 million more slum dwellers than in 2000, and by 2020 there are likely to be another 200 million.

Improving slum housing

Improving slums is an important step in making cities more socially and environmentally sustainable. Poor, unhealthy slum dwellers have a low capacity for work, and huge slum areas deter inward investment. There are many ways to improve housing conditions in slum areas and these are evaluated in Table 13.5.

Figure 13.7
A concept model for sustainable cities

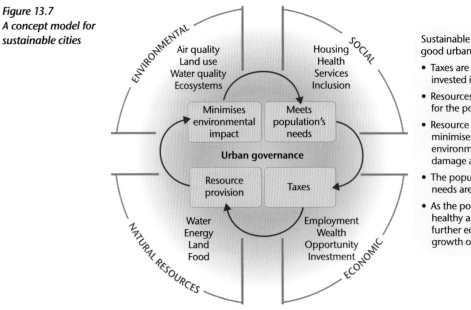

Sustainable cities have good urban governance:

- Taxes are collected and invested in the city
- Resources are provided for the population
- Resource provision minimises environmental damage and pollution
- The population's social needs are met
- As the population is healthy and educated, further economic growth occurs

Table 13.5 Strategies for improving slum housing

Strategy	Disadvantages	Advantages
Eviction The UN estimates that 6.7 million people were evicted from slums, 2000–02. High-profile evictions, such as those in Zimbabwe in 2005, keep the issue in the news. Eviction is an extreme solution that simply removes slums.	• International condemnation. • Slums may reappear in new locations. • Trust between people and authorities breaks down. • The process is often violent and chaotic. • People lose homes and businesses; economic activity may decline.	• A rapid solution with an immediate impact. • It may allow infrastructure projects to be completed. • If new housing is provided, it may work.
Security of tenure The UN suggests that 30–50% of people in developing cities have no legal right to occupy the land they inhabit. Tenure grants them that right.	• Compensation may have to be paid to landowners. • There is no guarantee that people will begin to improve their homes. • It may encourage further illegal land occupation.	• Utility companies (water, power) will connect areas that have secure tenure. • It is low cost. • Communities may choose to form groups to improve conditions.
Site and service It is possible to set out roads, sewers and water connections before slums develop. Low-income people move into these areas and construct their homes on prepared sites.	• It is expensive. • It requires careful planning and choosing of sites. • It often requires a rent to be paid, which can deter the poorest. • It is difficult to persuade residents to move in.	• It prevents urban sprawl. • Secure tenure is built in. • Sanitation and water have major health benefits.
Consolidation Residents gradually improve their homes.	• This only starts once tenure is secured. • It may take decades. • Quality of life is very poor in the early stages.	• It proceeds at a pace that can be afforded. • It is low cost.
Aided self-help (ASH) Local councils and NGOs provide building materials and training to help communities improve conditions.	• The process is slow, as it relies on spare-time work. • Standards of construction may be poor.	• Costs are low. • It can build community spirit and create a sense of ownership.
Social housing New homes are built for slum dwellers and slums are demolished.	• It may lead to eviction. • It is costly. • New housing may be too expensive for residents. • It is open to corruption as the sums of money are huge.	• It can create good-quality housing. • It removes slum housing quickly.

Social housing can be a solution. In the 1990s the Cingapura Project in São Paulo planned to build 10,000 low-cost housing units in 5–11-storey blocks and rent these to slum residents for $25 per month. In the end, only around 14,000 homes were built at a cost of around $300 million. This improved housing conditions for 45,000 people, but only those who could afford the rent. At least 2 million more people in São Paulo need improved housing.

Another common approach is participatory slum improvement. This is a form of slum upgrading that works with slum communities and is similar to aided self-help. It dates back to 1980 and the Orangi Pilot Project (OPP) in Karachi,

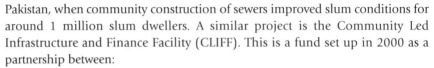

Pakistan, when community construction of sewers improved slum conditions for around 1 million slum dwellers. A similar project is the Community Led Infrastructure and Finance Facility (CLIFF). This is a fund set up in 2000 as a partnership between:

➤ the UK Department for International Development — £6.84 million
➤ the Swedish government international aid agency (SIDA) — £1.5 million
➤ the Homeless International Guarantee Fund — £0.6 million
➤ local funds approximating to £1.2 million in India and £0.5 million in Kenya

CLIFF works by providing small loans (micro-credit) to slum dwellers to improve their homes and infrastructure, and by building pilot projects (such as new houses) to show slum dwellers what they might achieve.

Improving health and environment

In cities such as Lagos, even the most basic needs of many citizens are not met. Improving water supply and sanitation are crucial if the cycle of poverty and deprivation is to be broken. Often external aid is required as the scale of the problem overwhelms developing cities. The Greater Cairo Wastewater Project began in 1983 and is still ongoing, costing over £2 billion. Much of the funding has come from USAID and the UK, and a great deal of the work has been carried out by major TNCs. Engineered solutions on this scale are unusual and costly. They can lead to debt, and may involve evictions from slums to put infrastructure in place. If the cost of water increases for the poor, the benefits are lost.

Small-scale water and sanitation projects are often implemented by NGOs. The case study of urban water supply in Dhaka illustrates one approach.

 Case study **Urban water supply in Dhaka, Bangladesh**

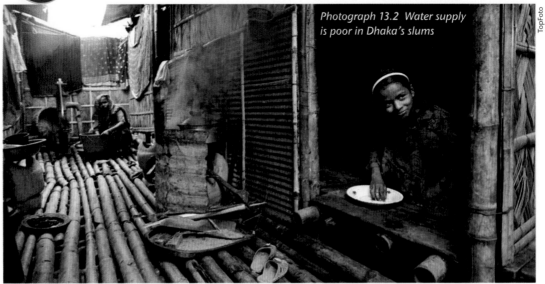

Photograph 13.2 Water supply is poor in Dhaka's slums

TopFoto

Dushtha Shasthya Kendra (DSK) is a Bangladeshi NGO working with WaterAid in the slums of Dhaka (Photograph 13.2). Water and sanitation are poor, and over 90% of slum dwellers have no security of tenure and therefore no 'official' water connection. Many slum dwellers buy water, at inflated prices, from people who are connected to the water supply.

DSK's approach has been to persuade the water company, DWASA, to connect the poor to the water network. It has worked mainly in established slum communities. From 1996 to 1999, 6,000 households benefited from the construction of 40 simple water pumps, at a cost of $26,000. The communities run the pumps, and an elected pump monitor is responsible for collecting payment and paying the water company. Households pay around $1 per month to use the water supply.

The NGO, DSK, acts as a mediator to persuade the water company to connect slum areas, and to raise the initial capital costs. Water costs for slum dwellers are dramatically lower once pumps are connected, and the water company makes money.

Transport and environment

Developing cities that have improved social conditions often begin to consider wider environmental improvement. Economic growth can lead to pollution as transport use and industry develop.

Many megacities, especially in Asia, have severe air pollution. In 2007, 70% of the residents of Calcutta were reported to have respiratory disorders, caused by levels of suspended particulate matter (SPM) which were double World Health Organization (WHO) guidelines. Pollution is so severe that a 'brown cloud' shrouds southeast Asia for much of the year. Reducing this level of pollution involves investment in new infrastructure and systems. Some examples of initiatives in cities around the world are:

➤ In Mexico City, private cars are banned from driving in the city on one day a week, according to the last digit of their number plate (the *Hoy no Circula* system). Beijing experimented with a similar system in 2007.
➤ In Delhi, all buses and rickshaws were converted to cleaner compressed natural gas in 2002. Strict emissions controls were applied to cars in 2000, and many old lorries were banned. Since 1997, sulphur dioxide levels have fallen by 35%.
➤ A zero-emission maglev railway opened in 2001, connecting Shanghai to its airport.
➤ In Brazil Curitiba's innovative approach to improving environmental quality includes low-cost express bus lanes (used by 85% of its population), community-led recycling and the provision of parks (see p. 310).

Ecocities?

A sustainable city meets the social and economic needs of its inhabitants while at the same time minimising environmental pollution and waste. This ideal is not achievable for many developing cities, especially in Africa. Their focus is likely to be improving basic social conditions, supported by NGOs and international aid. Maturing developing cities can afford to taker a broader approach to sustainability and begin to reduce resource use and pollution. The ideal is an 'ecocity' which meets social needs and minimises environmental problems.

Curitiba in Brazil gets closest to this ideal, but it is a relatively small city of around 3 million people and its growth has been carefully planned for over 20 years.

Dongtan, on the mouth of the Yangtze River in China, is being built as the world's first eco-city. The Shanghai Industrial Investment Corporate (SIIC) aims to create a low-energy city that is close to being 'carbon neutral'.

Review questions

1 Explain why 2007 was a key year for global urbanisation.
2 Divide a page into two columns labelled 'push' and 'pull', and list the social, economic and environmental factors that drive migration to developing world cities.
3 Using examples from your own research, outline ways in which developing cities might become more sustainable.
4 With reference to Table 13.5, identify the strategy which you think is the best way of improving slum housing. Give your reasons.

Chapter 14

Global challenges for the future

What are the social and environmental consequences of globalisation, and can we manage these changes for a better world?

By the end of this chapter, you should have:

➤ *understood how economic changes brought about by globalisation have serious knock-on effects for societies and environments*

➤ *explored the issue of worker exploitation in poorer nations and considered how lives are changing as a result of the exporting of jobs overseas*

➤ *researched the environmental costs of globalisation and examined the viability of green strategies available to consumers*

➤ *examined the actions that consumers and their countries can take to address the continuing poverty of poorer nations*

Globalisation is primarily an economic process. However, a series of social and environmental effects follows on from the economic changes. Economists call these additional effects **externalities**.

As economies become globalised, a whole raft of additional changes take place in national life. For instance, globalisation has resulted in a **global shift** of poorly paid manufacturing work from richer to poorer countries. With this industry comes social ills such as poor working conditions and child factory labour. An even greater concern is global carbon emissions. These have been greatly increased by economic growth and the growth of global trade networks.

Positive and negative effects of globalisation

Positive changes include the rise of new 'Tiger' economies, including China and India. In these newly industrialised countries (NICs), a growing number of individuals enjoy significantly higher incomes and **purchasing power parity** than in the past. South Korea was one of the first Asian nations to experience rapid industrial growth. During the 1960s, foreign investors began working with local firms called *chaebols*. As national revenues soared, so did levels of spending on education and health. Today, South Korea is a member of the Organisation

Key terms

Externalities The range of benefits and costs generated by economic activity that are not fully accounted for in the price-and-market system of economics, and need to be accounted for separately. Pollution is a prime example of a negative externality, while rising literacy is a positive externality.

Global shift The global-scale relocation of different types of industrial activity, especially manufacturing industries. As well as redrawing the world economic map, global shift has brought social, political and environmental changes to nations.

for Economic Cooperation and Development (OECD) and has the world's eleventh largest economy.

Longer-established OECD economies have been affected differently. Unable to maintain a competitive manufacturing sector due to high labour and land costs, the UK has striven to develop a **post-industrial economy** in order to remain globally competitive. This has meant raising levels of educational attainment. More people in the UK now work in the service sector or the **quaternary sector**. These kinds of employment tend to provide greater disposable income, bringing improved diet, healthcare and housing.

However, globalisation brings negative changes too. The economies of cities like Sheffield (steel), Manchester (textiles) and Liverpool (chemicals and machine assembly) entered a period of marked decline during the 1980s. **Deindustrialisation** meant that some of those who lost their jobs never returned to full-time employment. Serious social problems developed in inner cities, taking the form of a spiral of deprivation (Figure 14.1). Rising gun crime on estates in UK cities reminds us that 'losers' of globalisation can be found in all nations.

Globalisation is also responsible for the growth of a two-speed world. Global billionaire wealth is now at an all-time high (Table 14.1), and is on the rise in Asia, where two of the world's ten richest people live. Yet high numbers of people still live in poverty in

Key terms

Deindustrialisation
The decline of regionally important manufacturing industries. It can be charted in terms of workforce numbers or output and production measures.

Post-industrial economy
Replacement of traditional manufacturing or mining employment by an employment structure focused on services and technology (the tertiary and quaternary sectors).

Purchasing power parity
A measure of average wealth that takes into account the cost of a typical 'basket of goods' in a country. In low-income countries, goods often cost less, meaning that wages go further than might be expected (thus China's GDP per capita of around $2,000 per year generates a PPP closer to £7,000).

Quaternary sector
The component of a country's employment structure that includes research, information management and financial management. Quaternary activities span computing, bioresearch, defence industries and new media, among others.

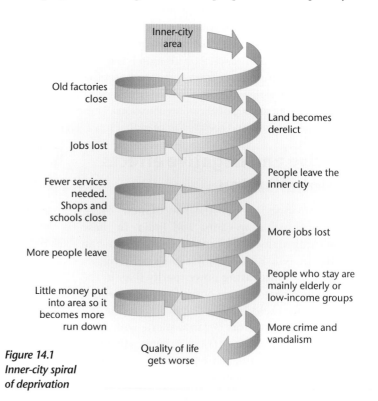

Figure 14.1
Inner-city spiral
of deprivation

nations such as India, China, Indonesia, Pakistan and Bangladesh. Globalisation has widened the gap between rich and poor. The wealthiest 1% of people in the world receive as much income as the bottom 57%.

Name	Sector	Citizenship	Wealth ($bn)
William Gates III	IT and software (Microsoft)	USA	56
Warren Buffett	Financial investments	USA	52
Carlos Slim Helú	Telecommunications	Mexico	49
Ingvar Kamprad	Retailing (IKEA)	Sweden	33
Lakshmi Mittal	Steel making	India	32
Sheldon Adelson	Casinos, hotels and tourism	USA	26
Bernard Arnault	Luxury retail goods	France	26
Amancio Ortega	Retailing (Zara)	Spain	24
Li Ka-shing	Mixed services	Hong Kong	23
David Thomson	Media and entertainment	Canada	22

Table 14.1
The ten richest people in 2007

 Case study Two-speed India

By 2040 India is expected to be the second largest economy in the world, with China in first place and the USA in third place. India has become an attractive site for TNCs to set up factories and, more recently, offices and call centres. In addition to the arrival of foreign firms, Indian entrepreneurs are

Photograph 14.1 Dharavi slum in Mumbai

learning to make globalisation work to their advantage. India's own companies are now establishing bases in other countries, boosting the nation's gross domestic product (GDP). For instance, Indian firm Tata recently bought Corus, the leading UK steel manufacturer.

Despite India's impressive overall growth, the gap between rich and poor has widened sharply. In this nation of 1.1 billion people, as many as one-third still live in absolute poverty. Around 375 million people live in urban slums or in poor and isolated rural regions. Levels of pay for agricultural and factory workers are as low as $1 a day. Yet India is now home to 32 billionaires. Steel billionaire Lakshmi Mittal is the world's fifth richest person, symbolising the new power and wealth found in India.

On the other side of the wealth divide, Dharavi slum in Mumbai is home to some of the poorest people in Asia. Some 600,000 people are crammed into just 1 square mile of land (Photograph 14.1). The Indian authorities now want to remove the slum as part of a programme of social and economic modernisation (the land is also worth billions of pounds to developers). It is unlikely that the slum dwellers will be rehoused, yet India's urban population is growing all the time due to in-migration from rural areas (Table 14.2).

Table 14.2 Changing demographics in India

	1945	2005
Population	340 million	1.1 billion
Urban population (%)	8.7	28.7
Life expectancy (years)	37.4	62.9
Death rate per 1,000	43	25

Further research

National Geographic

Multimedia films looking at Mumbai and Dharavi: www7.nationalgeographic.com/ngm/0705/feature3/multimedia.html

New Statesman

Special reports on India: www.newstatesman.com/200708020025

BBC

A large bank of reports on India: news.bbc.co.uk/1/hi/world/south_asia/country_profiles/1154019.stm

Moral and social consequences of globalisation

In China, many factory employees suffer conditions similar to those in the UK during the nineteenth century (Figure 14.2). They make the same textiles and electrical goods that used to be produced in Europe but without the same high levels of pay and safety at work that have made European manufacturing more expensive. In Indonesia and Costa Rica, people have faced persecution and imprisonment for trying to organise trade unions that campaign for improved pay and conditions at work.

Workers may live in shanty towns where living conditions are poor. Diseases such as dengue fever are rife in South American and Asian slums, mirroring the cholera and tuberculosis epidemics in London slums in the nineteenth century. Globalisation — especially the outsourcing of manufacturing — may be responsible for a great many people living and working in unacceptably poor conditions. Agricultural workers are no better off. Côte d'Ivoire cocoa farmers and Kenyan flower growers suffer long working hours in harsh conditions for appallingly low levels of pay.

Yet the case against globalisation is far from clear-cut. Many factory workers are migrants who have escaped lives of rural poverty that may have been even harsher.

Manchester, England, 1844

The work between the machinery gives rise to multitudes of accidents. The most common accident is the squeezing off of a single joint of a finger, somewhat less common the loss of the whole finger, half of a whole hand, an arm, etc., in the machinery. Lockjaw very often follows, even upon the lesser among these injuries, and brings death with it. Besides the deformed persons, a great number of maimed ones may be seen going about in Manchester; this one has lost an arm or a part of one, that one a foot, the third half a leg; it is like living in the midst of an army just returned from a campaign.

In the year 1842, the Manchester Infirmary treated 962 cases of wounds and mutilations caused by machinery, while the number of all other accidents within the district of the hospital was 2,426. What becomes of the operative afterwards, in case he cannot work, is no concern of the employer.

Frederick Engels, *The Condition of the Working Class in England in 1844*:

Yongkang, China, 2003

Yongkang, in prosperous Zhejiang Province just south of Shanghai, is the hardware capital of China. People all over the world use Yongkang-made parts. They are the nuts and bolts of hundreds of brand name products, like Bosch, Black & Decker, and Hitachi. Yongkang, which means 'eternal health' in Chinese, is also the dismemberment capital of China. Unofficial estimates run as high as 2,500 accidents here each year.

Some factories resemble operations at the dawn of the industrial age, where migrant labourers use rudimentary machines that can sever the limbs of those who succumb to momentary distractions.

Legally, the loss of all fingers on one hand is a sixth-degree injury, mandating compensation of 200,000 yuan, or about $24,000. In practice, most owners reach settlements with their employees for nominal amounts and pay their bus fare out of town.

'China's workers risk limbs in export drive', *New York Times*, 7 April 2003

For instance, 30 million people died of famine in rural China between 1958 and 1961. Despite poor conditions in the factories of cities like Yongkang and Chongqing, urban workers now have higher overall life expectancies than recent ancestors in rural areas.

Figure 14.2 The global shift of industrial injuries

There is also evidence that conditions at work are improving, albeit slowly. In 2006, India announced it was to ban child labour. A series of progressive new labour contract laws are being introduced in China, designed to give workers far better rights. However, if workers in China or Bangladesh are awarded significantly improved pay and conditions, TNCs might simply look elsewhere for a source of cheap labour. This practice is called 'capital flight'. What effect would it have on prospects for continued economic growth in these nations?

Environmental and social costs

Offsetting the environmental costs of global trade

Globalisation has resulted in masses of cheaply produced food and goods crossing continents. Low production costs have driven global levels of consumption to record levels. This has negative environmental impacts including air pollution and the creation of landfill sites for the burial of consumer waste. At a global level, the carbon emissions associated with this level of consumption, along with other environmental impacts, are headline news (Figure 14.3).

The Independent

*Figure 14.3
Environmental
headlines from
the* Independent
*newspaper,
2006–07*

The mass production and consumption of goods increases the **ecological footprint** of societies and individuals. The footprint of someone in the UK is about the size of six football pitches (the global average is one-third of this). The related concept of carbon footprints was introduced in Chapter 6.

Table 14.3 shows the typical carbon emissions profile for a UK citizen and highlights some of the ways in which globalisation contributes to this relatively high total of around 11 tonnes of carbon dioxide annually.

In order to achieve sustainable development, it is necessary to reduce these carbon emissions. Chapter 6 addressed a number of strategies in some detail, including those being pursued at national and international levels. Individual consumers can also help tackle the environmental costs of globalisation through the purchasing choices they make. Some key consumption strategies are examined below.

Recycling, reusing and refusing

Many local campaigns exist to raise awareness of recycling or refusing to buy items that carry too much packaging. In the village of Modbury in Devon, for example, plastic carrier bags have been banned. The viability of recycling schemes can be threatened by the energy used in shipping much of the paper and glass to China for reprocessing. Meanwhile, the cheap cost of imported goods encourages people to treat many items, such as clothes and even mobile phones as essentially disposable.

Local buying

Fiji water is a notorious brand of bottled water that is transported 16,000 km from Fiji to the UK. Drinking water is available from taps in

Key terms

Ecological footprint
A measurement of the area of land or water required to provide a person (or society) with the energy, food and resources they consume and the waste they produce.

Food miles The distance food travels from a farm to the consumer.

Table 14.3 Footprint facts for a typical UK citizen

Activity	Annual per capita carbon dioxide emissions	How globalisation contributes to large carbon and ecological footprints
Recreational purchases and foreign holidays	2.7 tonnes	Videos, stereos and DVDs are imported from China, increasing their carbon footprint. Disposal of packaging and waste in landfill sites increases a society's ecological footprint. A return flight to Malaga emits 400 kg of carbon dioxide per passenger.
Heating	1.5 tonnes	Every extra degree on a household thermostat accounts for an additional 25 kg of carbon dioxide per person per year. Much energy is derived from the global trade in fossil fuels, increasing a household's ecological footprint.
Food	1.4 tonnes	Carbon dioxide is released by energy used in cooking and the 'food miles' travelled by imported food and drink. TNCs have bought up large areas of land and oversupply food to high-consuming societies (e.g. the USA and some EU nations). The result is an even larger ecological footprint.
Household costs	1.4 tonnes	Emissions are generated by running electrical appliances and by the manufacture and importing of furnishings. Running a fridge releases 140 kg of carbon dioxide annually.
Hygiene	1.3 tonnes	Taking baths instead of showering releases an extra 50 kg a year of carbon dioxide. This figure would be high irrespective of globalisation.
Clothing	1.0 tonne	Carbon dioxide is released in producing and transporting clothes and shoes, often from overseas. Cheap prices due to low manufacturing costs overseas encourage 'throw-away' attitudes, which result in increased landfill and an enlarged ecological footprint.
Commuting and work travel	0.8 tonnes	Commuting to work releases carbon dioxide, as do business trips overseas.

the UK at far less cost to the environment. Locally produced meat and vegetables may clock up fewer **food miles** than imported food. However the energy used in producing winter crops in heated greenhouses in the UK can generate even more carbon emissions than importing food by air.

Organic buying

Organic farming attempts to reduce the environmental impacts of food production by avoiding the use of chemical fertilisers and pesticides. However, organic food is often imported from abroad, making it energy intensive. Organic asparagus from Peru may not be grown using pesticides, but it certainly flies a long way to reach the UK.

Carbon credits

Firms such as the UK's Carbon Neutral Company offer individuals and organisations the chance to erase the environmental damage caused by their greenhouse gas emissions. Trees soak up carbon dioxide, so paying for a tree to be planted after you have taken a flight abroad can neutralise some of the carbon produced. However, this is not a solution to climate change, and scientific doubts over the

Useful websites

The BBC website gives plenty of environmental coverage:
www.bbc.co.uk/nature/environment/conservationnow/global/

The *Guardian* and *Independent* newspapers provide good coverage of environmental action:
www.guardian.co.uk/environment
www.independent.co.uk/environment/

The important reports on climate change produced by the IPCC can be accessed via the Hadley Centre:
www.metoffice.gov.uk/research/hadleycentre/index.html

There is an interesting article on biofuels on the National Geographic site (click on 'Compare biofuels' too):
http://ngm.nationalgeographic.com/2007/10/biofuels/biofuels-text

Ludlow is promoting local food purchasing:
www.localtoludlow.org.uk

Modbury has banned plastic carrier bags:
www.plasticbagfree.com

DEFRA report on low-carbon initiatives (e.g. 'Low Carbon Wolvercote'):
www.defra.gov.uk/ENVIRONMENT//climatechange/uk/individual/pdf/study5-0707.pdf

value of carbon credits from forest projects led to their exclusion from the EU Emission Trading Scheme.

Biofuels and green technology

Oil from crops such as jatropha can be used instead of conventional fossil fuels. Cars which run on biofuels or a mixture of petrol and biofuel are intended to be 'greener'. However, although using biofuels saves on use of non-renewable fossil fuels like oil, it still emits carbon dioxide. Large amounts of energy are needed to process biofuels for use. Wide-scale removal of rainforest to clear land for palm oil production in Malaysia is starting to cause climatic damage in other ways and growing biofuel crops instead of food crops contributes to food shortages in the developing world.

Green taxes

Adding a 'green' tax to the cost of flights, or introducing road-pricing schemes such as London's congestion charge might reduce travel-related greenhouse-gas emissions. However, such policies may only penalise poor people, while the rich still pay to drive and fly around the world.

Further research

None of these courses of action offers consumers a simple way of offsetting their own contribution to the environmental costs of globalised mass consumption. Try to explore one or two of these suggested solutions in greater depth. Newspapers such as the *Guardian* and *Independent* have environmental supplements that regularly report on such topics. Key documents explaining the need to reduce carbon footprints are the *Stern Report* and the series of reports published by the Inter-governmental Panel on Climate Change (IPCC). Websites documenting local initiatives, such as those in Ludlow, Modbury and Wolvercote, are also worth a visit.

National environmental strategies

The UK government claims that the UK is responsible for just 2% of global carbon emissions. This does not include UK businesses' overseas operations. A report by Christian Aid suggests the figure becomes 15% when the emissions of UK industries operating overseas are included. This would represent nearly 4 billion tonnes of carbon dioxide annually, making the UK the world's seventh-largest polluter, responsible for more pollution than the 112 least polluting nations put together.

Even if nations like the UK can tackle their own high levels of carbon emissions, greater global challenges lie ahead. For instance, air travel is no longer the exclusive preserve of the world's richest nations. India is currently spending $12 billion on airport building and could have up to 2,000 planes in operation for domestic flights by 2020. If China can match US levels of car ownership, it will end up with 1.1 billion cars, requiring 99 million barrels of a oil a day (more than current global oil output). Allowing the aspirations of people in these nations to

Sustainable development

Key concept

Sustainable development means 'meeting the needs of the present without compromising the ability of future generations to meet their own needs'. It was one of the main aims agreed at the 1992 UN Conference on Environment and Development in Rio de Janeiro.

The suggestion is that future generations should not face serious resource shortages and a reduction in environmental quality, as a result of existing societies outstripping the carrying capacity of the planet. However, in the absence of any 'technological fix', a significant reduction in levels of economic growth would be needed to achieve this commitment.

Given that free-market economies measure success by their rate of economic growth, sustainable development is a radical proposition. Unsurprisingly then, the term is often watered-down. Minor improvements to a firm's 'green credentials' are often trumpeted as 'sustainable' initiatives — for example supermarkets charging for plastic carrier bags, or McDonald's using recycled chip oil to fuel its fleet of vehicles.

Far more will need to be done to guarantee future generations a quality of life that is at least equivalent to that enjoyed by affluent people today. Fish stocks, oil and forests must not diminish further. Are any significant changes in patterns of resource use likely to be adopted in the immediate future?

Sustainability can be compartmentalised in various ways (see Chapter 7, page 80). For example:

➤ *Economic sustainability* is when individuals and communities continue to have access to a reliable income over time.

➤ *Social sustainability* is when all individuals in a community can continue to claim a reasonable quality of life and have opportunities to maximise their potential.

➤ *Environmental sustainability* is when no lasting damage is done to the environment and resources are managed in ways that guarantee their continued use.

Further research

Sustainable Schools

The sustainability website for UK schools:
www.teachernet.gov.uk/sustainableschools

Dependency When a nation relies for income on outside sources and has only weak control of its own economic future.

Ethical purchase A financial exchange where the consumer has considered the social and environmental costs of production of the food, goods or services purchased.

be met, while achieving a global reduction in carbon emissions, is the greatest challenge that lies ahead.

Tackling the social costs of globalisation

Strategies to help the world's poor are often controversial (Table 14.4). For instance, international aid may create **dependency** in recipient nations. Another way in which individuals can act is by making **ethical purchases** (Photograph 14.2). Ethically sourced clothes or food cost more, but are distributed by organisations that have pledged to pay a fair price to the workers that produce them. This is known as fair trade.

Table 14.4 Taking action to create a more equitable world

Strategy	Example	Viability
Fair trade An attempt to reduce the economic unfairness of globalisation. By 2006, the total value of UK fair trade sales was £300 million and it is growing at 40% per annum.	Shoppers can choose to buy fair trade coffee and more of the money goes to the producers of the coffee beans. Other examples of fair trade produce are chocolate, bananas, wine and some clothing items such as jeans.	Buying fair trade goods means more money goes to poor workers. However, as the number of schemes grows, it becomes harder to monitor how 'fair' they are.
Ethically sourced goods Consumers can avoid purchasing goods produced under exploitative 'sweatshop' conditions. The work of the UK Ethical Trade Initiative (ETI) is worth researching.	Gap received bad publicity during the 1990s due to claims that Indonesian staff suffered poor working conditions. The firm has introduced stricter regulations for its overseas operations and guarantees workers 'dignity and respect'.	Outsourcing and supply chains among TNCs make codes of practice hard to enforce. Although firms such as Gap and Nike prohibit worker exploitation in their own factories, goods produced for them by a third party may have used 'sweatshop' labour.
Charitable donations and international aid Governments give aid and non-governmental organisations (NGOs) such as Oxfam and Christian Aid collect money directly from the public to help address the economic unfairness of globalisation.	In 1984–85 and again in 2004–05 Band Aid raised money for famine relief in Ethiopia. Around £100 million was raised in the 1980s. In 2004–05, money was also given to people living in Sudan's Darfur region.	Aid can result in dependency for poorer nations and can make it difficult for emerging businesses to profit. In Zambia, clothing manufacturers have gone bankrupt due to the free second-hand clothes donated by OECD charities — known locally as *salaula*.
Trade reforms Governments and international lobbying organisations have tried to improve terms of trade for poor nations, especially rules regulating the import and export of agricultural produce. Protesters gather at World Trade Organization and G8 conferences and make their case for change.	Huge subsidies paid to European farmers under the Common Agricultural Policy (CAP) and protective trade tariffs encircling the European Union (EU) force up the cost of imported African goods. Changing these rules would help African farmers.	The Commission for Africa has drawn attention to the need for reforms of subsidies, tariffs and non-tariff barriers for poorer countries. European farmers resist measures that open markets up to greater competition, as this could threaten their livelihoods.

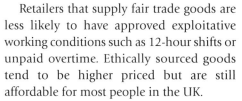

Retailers that supply fair trade goods are less likely to have approved exploitative working conditions such as 12-hour shifts or unpaid overtime. Ethically sourced goods tend to be higher priced but are still affordable for most people in the UK.

To demonstrate what a difference ethical purchasing can make, consider world coffee prices. They are now at a 30-year low, just 25% of the 1960 level. This is a result of global overproduction, tough competition and world trade rules that offer little protection to coffee growers. Ethiopia has lost an estimated $900 million export revenue over the last 5 years as a result. However, high street coffee prices have not fallen during the same period. What happens to the profits? Companies selling fair trade coffee send a higher proportion of sales profits back to coffee farmers. Critics of global trade laws claim that sweeping reforms of these laws would be even more beneficial to poor farmers.

Photograph 14.2 A coffee-picker in Nicaragua working on a fair trade plantation

Skills focus

Cost–benefit analysis (CBA) assesses the desirability of a project, scheme or course of action. It does so by tabulating the overall social and economic benefits to a community and comparing these with the social and economic costs of pressing ahead with the proposed course of action.

Task

Examine the content of the case study on the next page and then conduct a cost–benefit analysis for (a) purchasing locally produced goods and (b) purchasing air-freighted goods using the following steps:

1 Draw up a matrix with three columns and three rows (Table 14.5).
2 In columns 2 and 3, list the costs and benefits — in terms of levels of energy use and carbon

Table 14.5

Purchasing strategy	Costs	Benefits
Local buying		
Air-freighted goods		

emissions, or other social and economic considerations such as worker exploitation or the benefits of long-distance food exports for poor countries.

3 It is hard to quantify these factors (give them a numerical value). Some types of 'cost', such as worker exploitation, are not measured in monetary terms. You might therefore attempt to apply your own ranking or rating system to give a numerical score to each cost or benefit identified. This will allow you to make a calculation of the balance between total benefits and total costs for the two purchasing strategies.

Should we buy more local produce?

More and more people want to help reduce their carbon footprint by buying British food and avoiding imported foods. Unfortunately, the situation is more complex than it might seem. Locally produced food can end up travelling long distances if it is taken to central depots for storage before being delivered to retail outlets. People who are trying to shop ethically need to ask themselves some important questions.

First, was the transport efficient? Large aeroplanes may travel long distances but they are also efficiently loaded, which reduces the impact per tonne of food. Locally sourced food may have travelled shorter distances but in much smaller vehicles, meaning that carbon dioxide emissions per tonne are relatively high.

Second, how much energy did the food production system use? One recent study showed that it can be more sustainable (in energy-efficiency terms) to import tomatoes from Spain than to produce them in heated greenhouses or polytunnels in the UK during winter and spring.

Third, what are the economic and social benefits of buying overseas food? Many developing nations are dependent on food exports to countries such as the UK. Will it hurt Kenyan farmers if UK consumers stop buying Kenyan runner beans because of the high food miles attached to them?

Transport and trade of food has the potential to lead to economic and social benefits, for both developed and developing nations. Indeed, economic growth in the latter may well depend upon continued exporting.

However, the increasing reliance on air freighting of food products over vast distances is not environmentally sustainable. For people who are concerned with 'doing the right thing' there are no easy answers.

Further reading

The DEFRA website reports on food miles and other issues: http://statistics.defra.gov.uk/esg/reports/foodmiles/final.pdf

Review questions

1 Look at Table 14.1. Explain what it suggests to us about:
   a levels of inequality between nations
   b levels of inequality within nations.
2 Read the quotations in Figure 14.2. Suggest ways in which conditions have improved since 1844 for manufacturing workers based in Britain. What obstacles exist to improving current conditions for Chinese workers?
3 Choose one strategy, which you have personally participated in, designed to reduce the environmental costs of globalisation. Describe its strengths and weaknesses.
4 Describe the varied ways in which globalisation affects the lives of people living in poorer countries.

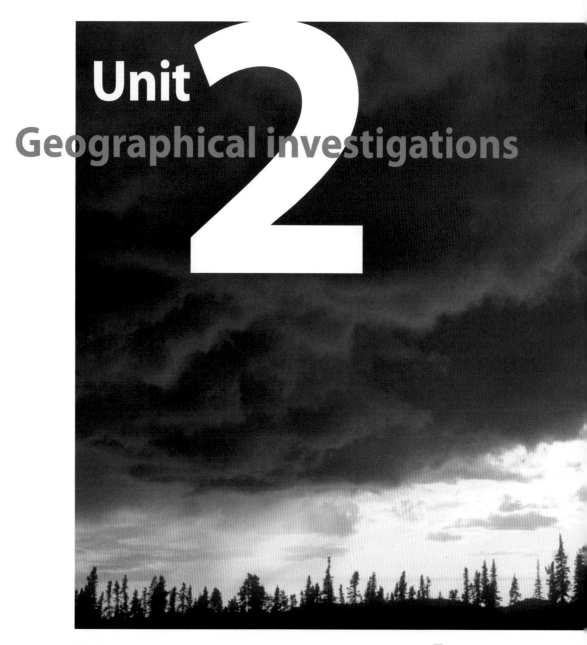

Unit 2

Geographical investigations

Extreme weather

Extreme weather watch

What are extreme weather conditions and how and why do they lead to extreme weather events?

By the end of this chapter you should have:

➤ *examined the nature and distribution of different types of extreme weather*

➤ *used your own observations, published information and research to understand how background conditions influence contrasting weather events*

➤ *researched how extreme weather develops using contrasting examples such as a hurricane sequence, snow and ice, and drought*

Table 15.1 The average annual impacts of extreme weather in the USA

Event	Cost ($bn)	Deaths
Hurricanes	5.1	20
Tornadoes	1.1	50
Floods	5.9	80
Drought	7.0	–
Lightning	1.0	175
Hail	2.3	–
Winter storms	1.0	47
Extreme cold	–	770
Extreme heat	–	384
Totals	23.4	1,526

Source: Catastrophic Risk Management, spring 2005

Table 15.2 How does UK weather compare with extreme records worldwide?

	UK records	World records
Wettest place	Sprinkling Tarn, Cumbria: 6,528 mm per year	Mt Wai-ale-ale, Hawaii: 11,680 mm per year
Driest place	St Osyth, Essex: 513 mm per year	Quillagua, Chile: 0.05 mm per year
Hottest place	Brogdale, Faversham, Kent: 38.5°C	Al'Aziziyah, Libya: 57.7°C
Coldest place	Braemar, Aberdeenshire: –27.2°C	Vostock, Antarctica: –89.2°C
Sunniest place	St Helier, Jersey: 1,915 hours per year	Yuma, Arizona: 4,300 hours per year

What do we mean by extreme weather?

Extreme weather events are usually defined as being severe or unexpected. Major hurricanes, such as Katrina, and large-scale flooding in Bangladesh grab the global headlines, but a mini-tornado in northwest London and a sudden downpour near Boscastle are examples of localised extreme weather events. Heatwaves and cold snaps may have severe short-term consequences, while the impacts of drought may be long-lasting.

Table 15.1 shows the annual impacts of extreme weather events in the USA. The pattern of economic and social losses depends on the type of event. Notice how the economic losses associated with drought are even larger than those of hurricanes and floods. High death rates are linked to extreme temperatures. Results may, of course, look very different in a less economically developed country.

Figure 15.1 can be applied to different types of extreme weather, by altering the variables on the vertical axis — temperature, rainfall, discharge or wind speed. The timescale can be hours (hydrograph), days (passage of a depression), or even years (drought). The graph also shows the links between extreme weather and hazardous conditions.

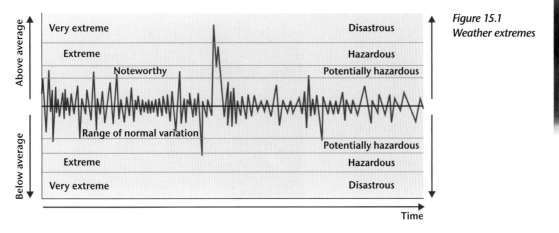

Figure 15.1
Weather extremes

Investigating extreme weather

UK weather

This section is designed to help you understand and investigate UK weather systems and their underlying meteorology.

Fieldwork and practical work should include:

- some observing and recording of weather data
- keeping a diary of weather conditions and events
- analysing the impacts of UK weather, using information from the media where possible

Research could focus on:

- why and how UK weather events occur
- the different weather systems and phases seen in UK weather
- case studies of recent extreme events, such as the UK floods in July 2007

The Meteorological Office website is a good place to start researching weather: www.metoffice.gov.uk/weather/uk. The 'Forecast' section helps set the scene for fieldwork with text and maps, 'Latest/recent past' shows what the current weather is like and 'Climate' looks back at past and extreme weather events using data, graphs and diaries.

Current and forecast weather is also on the BBC weather site: www.bbc.co.uk/weather/ukweather/ which has radar and satellite images as well as surface pressure maps.

Primary weather data can be recorded using a range of traditional instruments, in schools, colleges or field centres, supported by the large network of UK weather stations. Most weather stations collect monthly totals and averages, but over 200 stations now log data automatically and transmit weather changes and warnings continuously to the Meteorological Office using wireless and satellite links.

Keeping a weather diary

Keeping a diary allows you to see how the weather changes, showing up unexpected events and revealing weather impacts. Many amateur weather watchers have their own web pages (e.g. at www.greatweather.co.uk) or blogs, or post at sites such as www.youtube.com. There is a growing number of geographic information system (GIS) applications using Google maps to plot weather changes — some in real time. All of these enable patterns of weather to be identified and monitored over 4–10 days (the medium term), and the effects of storms, cold snaps, depressions and anticyclones to be clearly seen.

The BBC provides useful diary-type information about how current weather events (especially where they are extreme) affect people's lives, particularly via its online news pages. Understanding how these patterns come about is important. The Met Office education pages have sections headed 'For students' and 'Weather data' at: www.metoffice.gov.uk/ education/secondary/index.html. These are a valuable research and reference tool. A DVD entitled *Weatherbytes*, available from the Met Office, explores five key weather topics including fronts, air masses and depressions.

Some weather diary opportunities in 2007 were:

■ New Year began with winds over 110 km h⁻¹. Firework displays and concerts were cancelled.
■ February brought heavy snowfall across England and Wales. Schools closed, traffic was disrupted and homes were without power.
■ There were record high temperatures in April. Temperatures on 15 April reached 26.5°C in Sussex — 10°C above normal. Spring was dominated by high pressure and anticyclones.
■ In summer there was a change to low pressure. On 25 June phenomenal rainfall and severe flooding hit Sheffield, Doncaster and

Photograph 15.1 Flooding in Abingdon, 2007

Hull in Yorkshire and Lincolnshire. One-sixth of the average annual rainfall fell in 12 hours.
■ On 20 July, 3 months' rain fell in 4 hours in parts of southern England. Severe flooding occurred in the Severn catchment at Gloucester and Tewkesbury, and the upper Thames around Oxford and Abingdon (Photograph 15.1). Continued depressions made this our wettest summer since records began.

An ideal scenario would be to link fieldwork and research together. This means using weather forecasts, recording weather changes yourself, consulting synoptic maps and satellite photographs, researching the background meteorology and referring to the media.

Table 15.3 Potential weather hazards

Weather system	Possible hazards
Depression	• Floods from continuous rain • Gales from high winds (storms) • Blizzards from snow • Storm surges at coast
Anticyclone	• Summer anticyclone: drought, heatwave, wildfires • Winter anticyclone: cold, frost, fog (radiation), snow

Weather systems such as **depressions** and **anticyclones** are associated with weather hazards, as detailed in Table 15.3. The skills focus on p. 174 explains how to use synoptic weather maps.

The passage of a depression

The arrival of a depression brings a sequence of weather changes which can be observed and recorded using weather station equipment. This is shown in Figure 15.2 by a cross-section and table, which should both be read from right to left to understand the meteorological processes involved.

Depression A region of low atmospheric pressure which revolves in an anticlockwise direction (in the northern hemisphere). Its rising air brings unsettled weather — windy conditions and precipitation.

Anticyclone A region of high pressure bringing calm conditions. Subsiding air makes precipitation less likely, although temperatures can be extreme — winter frosts and summer heatwaves.

Figure 15.2 Weather associated with the passage of a depression

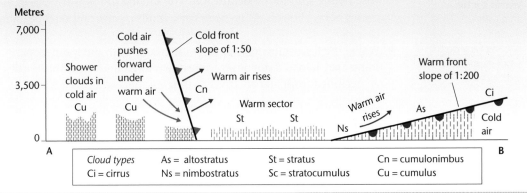

Weather element	Cold front			Warm front		
	In the rear	At passage	Ahead	In the rear	At passage	Ahead
Pressure	Continuous steady rise	Sudden rise	Steady or slight fall	Steady or slight fall	Fall stops	Continuous fall
Wind	Veering to northwest, decreasing speed	Sudden veer, southwest to west; increase in speed, with squalls	Southwest, but increasing in speed	Steady southwest, constant	Sudden veer from south to southwest	Slight backing ahead of front; increase in speed
Temperature	Little change	Significant drop	Slight fall, especially if raining	Little change	Marked rise	Steady, little change
Humidity	Variable in showers, but usually low	Decreases sharply	Steady	Little change	Rapid rise, often to near saturation	Gradual increase
Visibility	Very good	Poor in rain, but quickly improves	Often poor	Little change	Poor, often fog/mist	Good at first, but rapidly deteriorating
Clouds	Shower clouds, clear skies and cumulus clouds	Heavy cumulo-nimbus	Low stratus and strato-cumulus	Overcast, stratus and stratocumulus	Low nimbo-stratus	Becoming increasingly overcast, cirrus to altostratus to nimbostratus
Precipitation	Bright intervals and scattered showers	Heavy rain, hail and thunder-storms	Light rain, drizzle	Light rain, drizzle	Rain stops or reverts to drizzle	Light rain, becoming more continuous and heavy

Fronts Sloping surfaces in the atmosphere where different air masses meet. They may be **warm, cold** or **occluded.**

Warm sector An area (often tropical maritime air) between the fronts where temperatures are warmer.

We can summarise the events in the passage of a depression as follows:

➤ As the warmer maritime air approaches, it meets the cooler air already in place. Being lighter and warmer, it rises and triggers rain. This sloping surface where the two types of air meet is called the **warm front.**

➤ The middle of the depression is characterised by warmer temperatures. Here in the **warm sector**, pressure is low and the weather calmer, if drizzly.

➤ The **cold front** marks the return of colder air pushed around anticlockwise by the spin of the depression. The mixing of the two types of air causes heavy showers. As pressure rises, winds change and skies begin to clear.

➤ Where the faster-moving cold front catches up with the warm front, the fronts may join and no longer come down to ground level. This is called an **occluded front** and effectively wipes out the warm sector feature.

An extreme version of a depression, the 'storm of the century', is shown in Figure 15.9 on p. 179.

Skills focus

Synoptic maps (charts) use symbols to show data, together with surface pressure isobars. These are like contour lines on relief maps, but show pressure ridges and troughs instead of hills and valleys. Where isobars are close together, this means strong winds. Reading such maps is an important skill in forecasting and explaining weather.

The synoptic map in Figure 15.3 is typical of the forecast charts which preceded the torrential rain in July 2007 and caused flooding in the lower Severn and upper Thames catchments.

Task

Using the information in Figure 15.3:

1 Identify the two weather systems shown on the map.

2 Describe how they have brought different weather conditions to:

  a England and Wales

  b the north of Scotland

3 Suggest how conditions shown in England and Wales were not typical of summer weather.

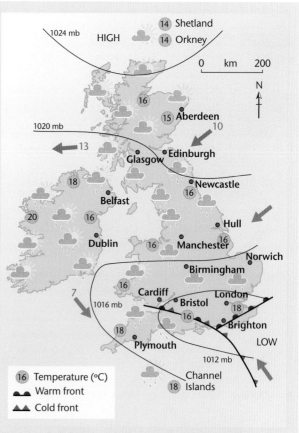

Figure 15.3 Synoptic map for 12 noon, 20 July 2007

What's behind UK weather?

The traditional view

Much of the time, westerly airstreams bring our weather to us from across the Atlantic. This maritime air is often unstable and when it meets with colder, dense air it rises and cools, bringing depressions and wet or windy weather.

At other times, continental air can produce stable conditions, in which air is subsiding, reducing the chances of rainfall. Such anticyclones often bring clear skies, which can result in heatwave summers or freezing winters.

More modern insights

Our increasing knowledge of the upper atmosphere reveals other processes at work. As the Earth spins, meandering flows of air move towards us from the west. Some 10 km above the polar front these waves drive the fast-moving current of air called the polar **jet stream**, which seems to determine the surface pattern of high- and low-pressure systems below (see Figure 15.4).

Recent research brings together ideas to explain how weather is becoming more extreme. Meteorologists suggest that conditions in the North Atlantic region oscillate between two phases:

➤ *Blocked phase*. In a 'normal' summer, westerlies are blocked by anticyclonic systems over Europe ('blocking highs') and the jet stream directs storms north of the UK, bringing us more settled, stable conditions (Figure 15.5). This situation led to the heatwave in France in 2003 and the dry conditions in 2006 in the UK.

➤ *A progressive phase*. The jet stream flows across the south of the UK, allowing deep Atlantic depressions to increase the risk of storms, storm surges and flooding (Figure 15.6). Examples are the great storm of October 1987 and the floods in the spring and summer of 2007.

Figure 15.4 Mechanisms behind extreme weather in the mid-latitudes

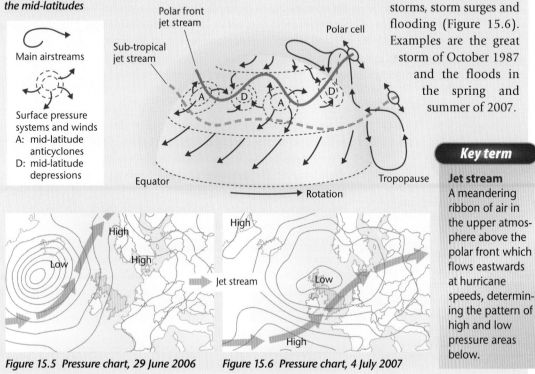

Figure 15.5 Pressure chart, 29 June 2006 *Figure 15.6 Pressure chart, 4 July 2007*

Key term

Jet stream
A meandering ribbon of air in the upper atmosphere above the polar front which flows eastwards at hurricane speeds, determining the pattern of high and low pressure areas below.

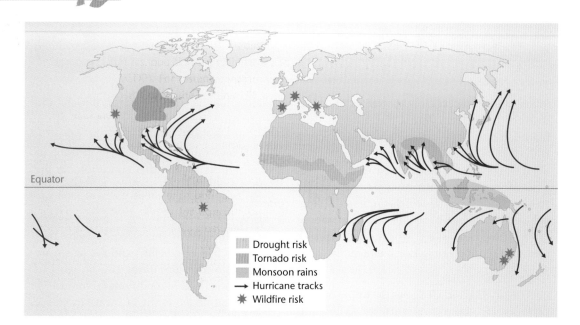

Figure 15.7
The global pattern of some kinds of extreme weather

Key:
Drought risk
Tornado risk
Monsoon rains
→ Hurricane tracks
✳ Wildfire risk

Equator

How extreme weather develops

Extreme weather occurs in response to differences in temperatures and humidity in the Earth's atmosphere. Hurricanes are created by the heat of the tropics, snow and ice by colder continental or polar air. Winds drive storms westwards from the tropics and eastwards across temperate latitudes. Blizzards and tornadoes occur typically in parts of North America and northern Europe. Torrential rain and floods are common in south and east Asia, while droughts are a recurring feature in many sub-Saharan African countries (Figure 15.7).

Hurricanes

Tropical storms are one of the most powerful types of extreme weather. In their various forms, which include **hurricanes**, they affect 80% of the Earth's landmass. They are even more frightening at sea, where there is little to modify their ferocity. The pressure gradient between different parts of the Earth's atmosphere generates the global pattern of winds. Warm air provides the energy for storms, while the warm water in the oceans is the source of the moisture that creates the heavy precipitation involved.

Every year, on average, about 60 storms develop over the tropical oceans. Once they reach over 120 km h^{-1}, they are classed as hurricanes. In the Indian Ocean, tropical storms are known as cyclones and in the eastern Pacific as typhoons.

How hurricanes form

Most hurricanes form north of the equator between July and October in the low pressure areas once known by sailors as the doldrums. Here the trade winds meet over the warm ocean. In this **inter-tropical convergence zone (ITCZ)**, where sea temperatures are above 26°C and air humidity over 75%, the unstable air begins to rise, triggering thunderstorms. These storms group together, forming a single hurricane with an enormous amount of energy (see Figure 15.8).

➤ Falling air pressure pulls in denser, colder air from surrounding areas, creating an anticlockwise (in the northern hemisphere) upward spiral of increasing wind speeds.

➤ Water vapour evaporated from the ocean below rises and cools rapidly, creating a massive wall of cumulonimbus cloud around the central eye.

➤ Condensation releases latent heat, which increases energy and wind speeds still further, pushing the rising air up to an altitude of 10 km above sea level.

➤ At the top of the hurricane, the cooling air spreads outwards, creating a thick canopy of cirrus clouds up to 1,500 km across.

➤ Besides strong winds, torrential rain and massive storm waves are produced.

Figure 15.8
Cross-section of a hurricane

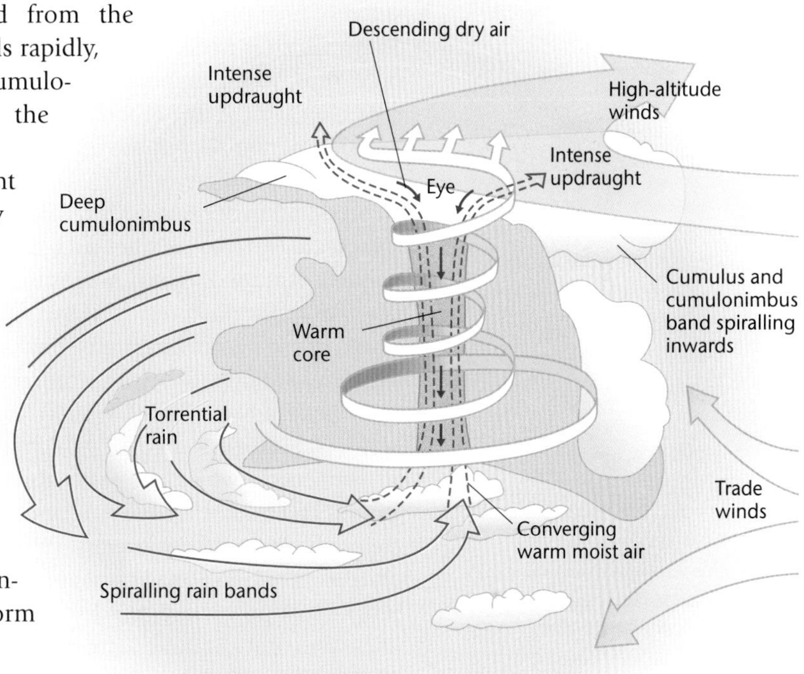

Labels: Descending dry air; Intense updraught; High-altitude winds; Intense updraught; Eye; Deep cumulonimbus; Cumulus and cumulonimbus band spiralling inwards; Warm core; Torrential rain; Trade winds; Converging warm moist air; Spiralling rain bands

In the southern hemisphere hurricanes spin in a clockwise spiral.

Hurricanes on the move

Tropical storms do not remain stationary and during the Atlantic hurricane season, officially from 15 May to 30 November, they move northwestwards across the Caribbean and the Gulf states, gathering strength and speed. They are deflected in this direction by the spin of the Earth — the **Coriolis effect**. Speed of travel varies from 8 to 32 km h^{-1} in the tropics, increasing to over 80 km h^{-1} in higher latitudes. Once they are over land, hurricanes begin to lose their strength, typically turning northeastwards. The strength of a hurricane is classified on a scale from 1 to 5.

The track of a hurricane is not always easy to predict as Hurricane Mitch (1998) showed when it took a quite unexpected path across central America, destroying large areas of Honduras and neighbouring countries.

Key term

Coriolis effect The way in which moving objects are deflected to the right in the northern hemisphere (and to the left in the south) by the spin of the Earth. This determines the general path of hurricanes and their internal rotation.

A hurricane's low pressure conditions also have a marked effect on sea level, every 1 mb of air pressure change relating to a sea level change of 1 cm — so a 960 mb storm will increase sea level by around 0.5 m. However, the total increase in wave heights caused by this **storm surge** may be much greater.

Blizzards and ice storms

In winter, when colder dense air from the poles meets the warmer moist air of the tropics along the Earth's polar front, it may trigger snowfall. If a period of high pressure occurs, frost and ice are likely.

> Snow, which is frozen water vapour that has turned into ice crystals, only forms when temperatures in the lower levels of the atmosphere fall below 4°C. A rule of thumb is that 10 mm of snow is equivalent to 1 mm of rainfall, but this ignores the fact that some types of snow are drier than others.

> A combination of heavy snowfall, low temperatures and strong winds can create extreme weather such as **blizzards**. Heavy snowfall is a frequent feature of North American winters because cold air moves down from the polar region. If this air is met by an opposing tropical storm, the result can be extreme blizzard conditions. This occurred in the USA in March 1993 (the 'storm of the century'), in January 1996, and again on New Year's Eve 2000 (the 'millennium blizzard').

> Major **ice storms**, five of which have hit Canada in the last 50 years, occur when rain passes through a layer of cold air near the ground and freezes as soon as it lands. Trees and structures like pylons are easily damaged. In January 1998 a severe storm brought 5 days of freezing rain to Canada and as far south as New York. Four million people lost power supplies for weeks as 129,000 km of electricity lines were brought down. The estimated costs were $4.7 million and 28 Canadians died, mostly from hypothermia.

Key terms

Blizzard A snowstorm becomes a blizzard when wind speeds reach more than 56 km h[-1]. Temperatures in these conditions can drop to −12°C and visibility is poor.

Ice storm This occurs when a rain-bearing warm front arrives in an area of cold dense air, and the rain freezes as soon as it lands.

Storm surge The combined effect of strong winds and low barometric pressure causing waves to 'pile up' against coasts. These effects may be amplified by local factors (e.g. high tides, shallow water, estuary/delta coastlines).

Case study The storm of the century, USA, March 1993

In March 1993, an intense pool of cold air moved southeastwards towards the east coast of the USA. When it reached the Gulf of Mexico, it collided with a tropical storm (warm tropical maritime air) heading north from the Gulf of Mexico. The result was hurricane-force winds, torrential rain and mountainous waves.

During the storm:
- Winds from Florida to Canada reached gale force 8–11, with gusts of storm force 12 common. A maximum of 232 km h[-1] was recorded in Nova Scotia.
- Snow fell at an average rate of 900 mm h[-1]. Drifts in many states reached over 3 m. Snow even fell in Florida.
- The National Weather Service estimated that the snowfall during this 4-day period was equal to 40 days of flow on the lower Mississippi River.
- Off Nova Scotia, waves up to 20 m high sank the carrier *Gold Bond Conveyor* with all hands (33 people).
- Inland Nova Scotia was flooded as 520 mm of snow were followed by 580 mm of rain, when the warm sector of the storm passed over.

- Parts of New England and the barrier islands of Carolina were badly flooded as tidal surges lifted water locally by up to 3 m above normal.
- Severe and unseasonal thunderstorms and tornadoes swept across Florida, triggered by the high sea temperatures.
- The lowest recorded temperature, at the cold front, was –12°C.
- The lowest air pressure recorded over the 3 days was 962.8 mb.

The human consequences were severe: every major airport on the east coast was closed at some point or another, Amtrak suspended all rail services from Chicago to the east coast, interstate highways 75, 77 and 81 were closed, and over 3 million people were left without electrical power. The storm caused 291 deaths (more than in the earlier Hurricane Andrew) and affected people in 26 states. The total damage was estimated at over $6 million and several states sought disaster relief from federal funds.

Figure 15.9 The storm of the century

Further research

Wikipedia
A good summary of the storm and satellite images:
http://en.wikipedia.org/wiki/1993_North_American_Storm_Complex

University of Illinois
Educational activities site:
http://ww2010.atmos.uiuc.edu/(Gh)/arch/cases/930312/home.rxml

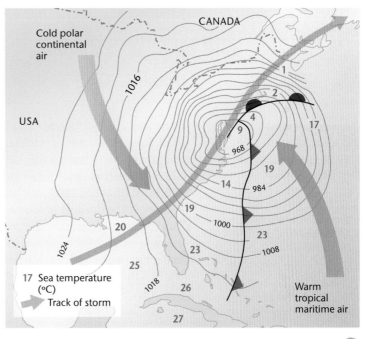

Drought

Severe **drought** is a greater hazard than storms because of the area it can cover. It is estimated that as many as 10 million people were killed by drought in China in 1878. Drought happens most in arid or semi-arid areas where the unreliable nature of rainfall is as much an issue as the low amount. Figure 15.10 shows the unpredictability of rainfall in the **Sahel** and the drought pattern of recent years. This region is perhaps the most drought-prone area of the world. The failure of the rains or the extension of the dry season in countries such as Ethiopia, Sudan and Chad leads to extreme conditions. Human actions such as deforestation, overgrazing and collecting firewood may also be contributing to desertification.

Key terms

Drought A lack or shortage of water for an unusually long period of time, involving 50% less than the usual rainfall over 3 months. Drought ranges from a dry spell to successive years of aridity.

Sahel A zone of semi-arid lands between Africa's Sahara Desert and the savanna grasslands to the south. Rain falls unreliably in the short rainy season.

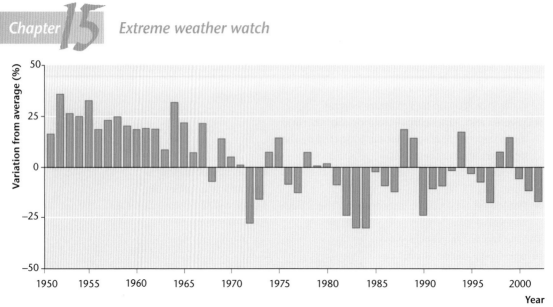

Figure 15.10 Rainfall unreliability in the Sahel, 1950–2005

Monsoon Seasonal winds, caused by the movement of the ITCZ, which bring alternately dry and rainy conditions to southeast Asia and west Africa. The term derives from the Arab word *mausim*, meaning 'season'.

The late arrival or failure of the heavy **monsoon** rainfall can bring severe drought conditions. Monsoon countries such as China, India, Bangladesh and Indonesia regularly top the Asian drought table.

In areas such as western Europe, persistent blocking anticyclones, as in the summer of 2003, can lead to the development of drought conditions. The drought in southeast England in 2006 resulted from a combination of a winter anticyclone in March 2006 and a series of summer anticyclones. This pattern of weather is likely to become more frequent in future. Such droughts are not as severe as those in tropical areas, but the high level of water use at such times can cause problems.

Review questions

1 Describe what you consider to be 'extreme weather'.
2 Summarise how *either*
   a weather recording or keeping a weather diary, *or*
   b some wider research has helped you to understand *one* aspect of the UK's weather.
3 Identify the different types of extreme weather shown in Figure 15.7 and annotate a world map or draw up a simple table to show where each type occurs, why it occurs in that place and one named example/event involved.
4 Describe some of the differences and similarities between drought and other types of extreme weather.

Chapter 16

Extreme impacts

What are the impacts of extreme weather on people, the economy and the environment?

By the end of this chapter you should have:

➤ *researched some of the reasons behind the varied impacts of extreme weather*

➤ *used your own investigations and research to understand how these impacts affect people, the economy and the environment*

➤ *examined the impacts of extreme weather events using contrasting examples, such as a hurricane or tornado, local river flooding and a drought or heatwave*

The impacts of extreme weather

The impacts of weather hazards depend upon the scale, intensity, predictability and duration of each hazard, but also on the nature of the places and communities involved. Figure 16.1 considers the role of hazard intensity, geographical location and degree of vulnerability in the impact of hurricanes. It shows that the worst-case scenario is a low-lying coastal location within a densely populated poor country, in the direct path of a category 5 hurricane. This diagram could be redrawn to represent other extreme weather events.

Hurricane Mitch in central America in 1998 seems to fit this pattern. The impacts were:

➤ damage caused by high winds — 290 km h⁻¹

➤ flooding — 60 cm of rain per day for a week meant that 85% of Honduras was flooded

➤ widespread damage to infrastructure — especially to road bridges over rivers

➤ loss of crops — most notably bananas and other export crops

➤ debt crisis — Honduras was unable to fund either hurricane protection or the cost of rebuilding

Figure 16.1
Factors affecting hurricane impacts

Location
➤ Caribbean or Atlantic coastal area, in likely path of hurricanes
➤ Low-lying coastal plain or river lowland/delta area
➤ Steeper inland area deforested and eroded (flood risk)

Intensity
The Saffir-Simpson scale

Category	Damage	Wind speed (km h⁻¹)	Storm surge (m)
1	Minimal	119–53	1.22–1.81
2	Moderate	154–77	1.82–2.73
3	Extensive	178–209	2.74–3.95
4	Extreme	210–49	3.96–5.48
5	Catastrophic	250+	5.49+

 Worst-case scenario

Vulnerability
➤ Economically poor/ageing population with little access to transport
➤ Ignorance of risk, prediction, forecasting and protection
➤ Limited public information or emergency capability

Table 16.1 The world's worst hurricanes

Name	Locations	Year	Category	Pressure (mb)	Deaths	Cost ($)
Wilma	Central America	2005	5	882	63	29bn
Labor Day	Florida, USA	1935	5	892	423	–
Mitch	Central America	1998	5	905	20,000	6bn
Camille	Mississippi, Louisiana and Virginia, USA	1969	5	909	256	1.4bn
Katrina	Mississippi, Louisiana, Alabama and Florida, USA	2005	4*	920	1400	81bn
Andrew	Florida and Louisiana, USA	1992	5	922	53	30/45bn
Charley	Florida and California, USA	2004	4	941	35	15bn
Galveston	Texas	1900	4	936	8,000	20m

* Experts downgrade Katrina to category 3 or 2 at landfall.

The pattern of impacts for the world's worst hurricanes shows more variation (Table 16.1).

Fieldwork and research

Extreme weather impacts

This section is designed to help you investigate and explain the impacts of extreme weather. You should explore contrasting events, which have (a) immediate, unfolding and (b) longer-term impacts, using a case-study approach.

- *Fieldwork* is most easily focused on how the impacts of river flooding unfold with time.
- *Research* into immediate and longer-term events is best directed at a specific hurricane, tornado or flood, and its economic, social and environmental impacts. A drought or heatwave event should be explored in connection with water resources, food supply and health issues.

Examples of the kinds of event you could investigate are given later in this chapter

Flood impact research

The opportunity to observe and record local flood events may arise, but it is safer to investigate the effects of previous flooding. A key location for investigation is the **floodplain**, which is often part of the built-up area in cities.

Sources of information include:

- *Maps.* The local Ordnance Survey (OS) map can be used to identify flat lowland areas.

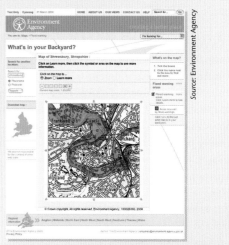

Figure 16.2 Flood map of Shrewsbury

An aerial photograph (www.blomasa.com/aerofilms/en) may also be useful. The mapping resource www.multimap.com links maps and photographs together. Google Earth at http://earth.google.com provides an even better resource that can be zoomed, tilted and annotated.

Key term

Floodplain The area adjacent to a river, formed by the deposition of sediment when the river floods.

*Photograph 16.1
Shrewsbury and
the River Severn
floodplain*

- *Environment Agency.* Entering the name or postcode of any location at www.environment-agency.gov.uk/subjects/flood/?lang=_e produces a crude map of likely flood risk (Figure 16.2). The agency's regional offices may help you to access flow data for a local river.
- *The media.* Local newspapers may provide useful secondary data
- *Other resources.* Online reports or reliable blogs, geographic magazines and Field Studies Council reports may also be useful, together with local history resources.

- Obtain data about variations in river flow.
- Organise group surveys (e.g. resident and business questionnaires) and conduct interviews with key persons (e.g. flood warden or Environment Agency officer).
- Make an appointment to visit the local newspaper office and view files of previous flood coverage. Check out its website too.
- Prepare log sheets, checklists, questionnaires and base maps to collect and present data.
- Use censuses to identify concentrations of vulnerable groups.
- Map the distribution of flood-proofing designs and defences.

Flood impacts investigation

Some suggested fieldwork tasks and uses of secondary data for an urban floodplain are:

- Land-use survey — use a base map to plot land use (residential, industry, open space, etc.)
- Land-use transect — sketch a cross-section away from the river, plotting building and land use. Add contours and likely flood levels.
- Pick out height contours and flood recurrence levels, using a large-scale OS map.
- Annotate photographs of floodplain features or previous flood events to show impacts.

Some of these tasks, such as a land-use survey and questionnaire, can be tackled in groups, pooling data. Other tasks, such as identifying areas vulnerable to flooding, and carrying out transects, can be done individually. The results of these investigations could be presented in a variety of ways (Figure 16.3), for example a PowerPoint presentation including annotated photographs, charts, diagrams and maps.

The fieldwork described in Figure 16.3 could be adapted to any settled floodplain location.

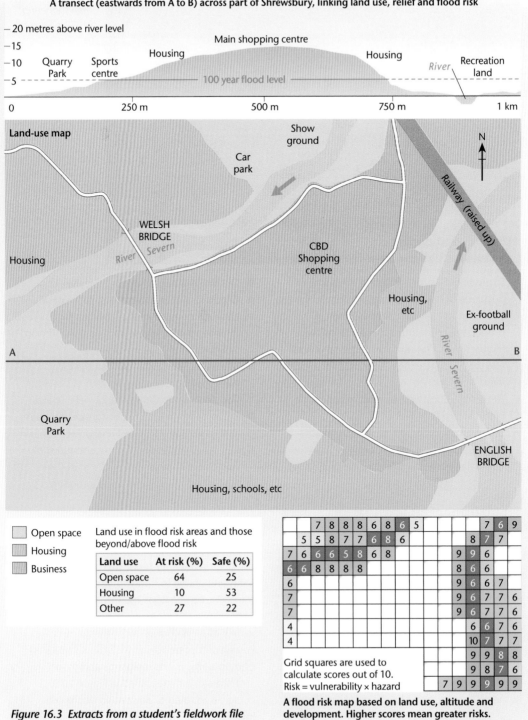

A transect (eastwards from A to B) across part of Shrewsbury, linking land use, relief and flood risk

— 20 metres above river level
—15
—10
—5
0

Main shopping centre

Housing

Quarry Park   Sports centre

Housing   River   Recreation land

100 year flood level

250 m   500 m   750 m   1 km

Land-use map

Show ground

Car park

WELSH BRIDGE

River Severn

Housing

CBD Shopping centre

Housing, etc

Ex-football ground

River Severn

Railway (raised up)

N

A   B

Quarry Park

ENGLISH BRIDGE

Housing, schools, etc

Open space
Housing
Business

Land use in flood risk areas and those beyond/above flood risk

Land use	At risk (%)	Safe (%)
Open space	64	25
Housing	10	53
Other	27	22

Grid squares are used to calculate scores out of 10.
Risk = vulnerability × hazard

Figure 16.3 Extracts from a student's fieldwork file

A flood risk map based on land use, altitude and development. Higher scores mean greater risks.

Impacts of Hurricane Katrina, USA, August 2005

Hurricane Katrina was the costliest and one of the deadliest hurricanes in history. It is estimated to have caused $84 billion in damage and claimed at least 1,836 lives, mostly in New Orleans, which flooded as the levée system protecting the city failed.

Katrina formed over the Bahamas in August 2005, moving westwards across southern Florida as a category 1 hurricane. It reached category 5 at sea by 1 p.m. on 25 August. The storm soon doubled in size, the pressure readings fell to 902 mb, wind speeds rose to 280 km h⁻¹ and gusts reached 344 km h⁻¹. Eventually it swung north-eastwards, weakening to category 3, and making landfall at 6 a.m. on 29 August.

A casual visitor to New Orleans today might be forgiven for thinking the city had regained its feet.

Wealthier neighbourhoods, where people were able to tap their own resources, have seen most progress. The poorest sections are still almost completely barren, with the removal of most of the storm's wreckage the only positive sign.

The federal government took a year to approve a $10 billion grant for flooded-out homeowners. The fund will soon run out, well before the last applicant is paid.

The federal government's attitude towards flood protection has also been less than reassuring. A top-notch levée system is surely the linchpin of the city's future. But many of the promised changes will not come to pass until 2011.

The state's 'Road Home' aid programme for homeowners is better known as the 'Road to Nowhere'. So far, less than a quarter of the roughly 180,000 applicants have had their money.

The city's population was recently estimated at 262,000, about 58% of what it was before Katrina. Some of the city's poor will not return. Many, if not most, cheap rented houses were underinsured and will not be rebuilt or restored. Some of the wealthier citizens are leaving too, because their jobs have moved away. Some of those who lend the city its unique character, musicians in particular, are struggling.

Source: Adapted from *The Economist*, 25 August 2007

Figure 16.4 New Orleans 2 years on

Table 16.2 The impacts of Katrina on the New Orleans area

Economic impacts	Social impacts	Environmental impacts
• 30 offshore oil platforms damaged or destroyed and 9 refineries shut down. This reduced oil production by 25% for 6 months. • Forestry, port trade and grain handling severely affected. • Hundreds of thousands of residents left unemployed. Trickle-down effect with less taxes being paid. • Total economic impact in Louisiana and Mississippi estimated at over $150 billion.	• Over a million people evacuated, displaced or made homeless. • Most major roads into and out of the city damaged as bridges collapsed. • Overhead power lines brought down by strong winds. Water and food supplies contaminated. • Worst-hit groups were those with no personal transport, less well off, non-white and vulnerable.	• Storm surge destroyed sections of the barrier islands and Gulf beaches. • 20% of wetland lost, affecting breeding of pelicans, turtles and fish. 16 National Wildlife Refuges damaged. • 5,300 km² of forest and woodland destroyed • Flood waters containing sewage, heavy metals, pesticides and 24.6 million litres of oil pumped into Lake Pontchartrain.

Effects

- The high winds destroyed many downtown buildings, such as the Hyat Regency Hotel, and damaged the roof of the Superdome, which was later used as an emergency centre.
- Katrina's storm surge caused severe damage along the Gulf coast, where 8 m waves overwhelmed the flood protection system in New Orleans. These high water levels caused breaches in the levées along the Mississippi Gulf outlet.
- The heavy rainfall increased the height of Lake Pontchartrain. This combined pressure broke the levées in 53 places, eventually flooding 80% of the city at depths of up to 6 m.

The economic, social and environmental impacts of Hurricane Katrina are summarised in Table 16.2.

Figure 16.4 summarises the seriousness of the impacts of Katrina 2 years on.

Further research

The websites listed below have animations, photographs, maps and links to other sites:

http://news.bbc.co.uk/2/shared/spl/hi/americas/05/katrina/html/default.stm

http://en.wikipedia.org/wiki/Effect_of_Hurricane_Katrina_on_New_Orleans#Damage_to_buildings_and_roads

www.metoffice.gov.uk/education/secondary/students/katrina/index.html

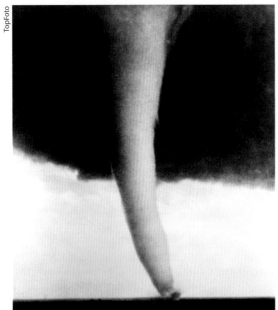

Photograph 16.2 A tornado in Kansas

Table 16.3 The (enhanced) Fujita scale for tornadoes

Category	Potential damage	Wind speed (km h^{-1})
EF0	Light	105–37
EF1	Moderate	138–78
EF2	Considerable	179–218
EF3	Severe	219–66
EF4	Devastating	267–322
EF5	Incredible	323+

The impacts of tornadoes and floods

Tornadoes, like hurricanes, have characteristic locations as well as differing scales of intensity. The original Fujita scale classified tornadoes by their speed of rotation. An 'enhanced' version of the Fujita scale was implemented in 2007 and is shown in Table 16.3. Tornadoes are difficult to record accurately as they are unpredictable, short-lived and relatively small.

Tornadoes are the least understood form of severe weather. Scientists use satellite data and doppler radar to track super cell storms (thunderstorms with a deep rotating updraft) and the tornadoes they produce.

Tornado formation

Most tornadoes have a characteristic funnel-shape (see Photograph 16.2). Winds can reach up to 350 km h^{-1} while the tornado itself moves at an average of about 60 km h^{-1}. Typically, buildings are damaged and in extreme cases vehicles are picked up and carried over small distances. Tornadoes are often short-lived and remain in one place for only a few seconds. Their internal structure is not unlike that of a hurricane (see Figure 16.5) and they too tend to develop from severe thunderstorm conditions. Research suggests they are linked to super cells on land or hurricanes at sea.

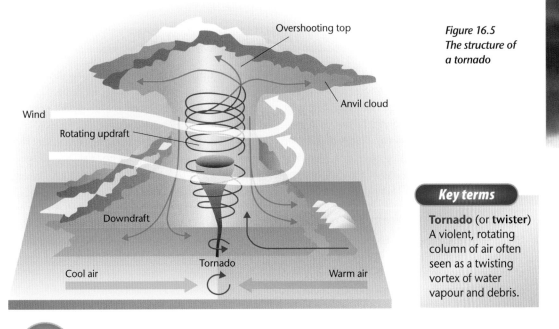

Overshooting top

Anvil cloud

Wind

Rotating updraft

Downdraft

Tornado

Cool air

Warm air

Figure 16.5
The structure of
a tornado

Case study: Impacts of tornadoes in the USA and UK

Tornado Alley

The most violent tornadoes often occur in what Americans call 'Tornado Alley', in the states of Texas, Oklahoma and Kansas. In spring and summer, warm moist (tropical maritime) air from the Gulf of Mexico moves northwards and inland, where it is met by dry (continental) cooler air moving eastwards from the Rockies. This triggers convection and strong winds. The jet stream accelerates these effects as it meanders eastwards across central USA.

Oklahoma City is the most tornado-prone city in this area and on 3 May 1999 a long-track EF5 tornado hit the city, leaving a trail of destruction over 1 km wide. It destroyed 1,800 homes and damaged a further 2,500, creating a $1.2 billion repair bill. On the same day, 40 tornadoes occurred elsewhere across the state and a top wind speed of 512 km h^{-1} was recorded in Moore, Oklahoma. Forty-three people died and 700 were injured

On 5 May 2007, a severe tornado hit Greensberg, Kansas (population 1,500), flattening 95% of the town. The EF5 tornado was around 2.5 km wide, making it one of the largest as well as most ferocious

ever recorded. The death toll was only eight people, mainly due to the 20-minute warning that forecasters were able to give.

UK tornadoes

There are around 40 tornadoes per year in the UK, mostly in rural areas.

On 7 December 2006 six people were hurt as a tornado hit London. 'It was literally like the Wizard of Oz,' said one shopkeeper, describing how roof tiles, chimneys and rubbish bins were thrown around. About 150 homes in northwest London were damaged, some severely. The EF2-intensity tornado formed suddenly with a path 20 m wide and was over in 15 seconds.

An even more extreme event took place in King's Heath, Birmingham, on 28 July 2005. Winds of 200 km h^{-1} wrecked cars, trees, homes and businesses, and injured 19 people.

Further research

www.tornadoproject.com
www.noaawatch.gov/themes/severe.php

Case study   Flood impacts in England and Wales, summer 2007

Met Office figures for the 3 months to 29 July 2007 showed 387 mm of rainfall in England and Wales, more than double the average rainfall of 186 mm. The north of England was badly hit by floods in June, while western and southern areas were most affected in July. This was the wettest July on record, recording 129 mm of rain in England and Wales (for meteorology, see Figures 15.5 and 15.6 in Chapter 15).

June: floods in South Yorkshire

- On 25 June, the rivers Don and Sheaf overtopped their banks, causing flooding in the Don valley area of Sheffield, the Meadowhall shopping centre and Sheffield Wednesday's football ground. There was damage to 1,273 homes, two people were killed, and many jobs were lost. The financial cost is estimated at £30 million. There was also widespread flooding in Barnsley, Doncaster and Rotherham.
- On 26 June, over 700 villagers near the Rotherham Ulley reservoir were evacuated after cracks appeared in the dam. Emergency services pumped millions of gallons of water from the reservoir to ease the pressure on the dam, and the nearby M1 motorway was closed as a precaution.
- On 27 June, the army moved into the Doncaster area after the River Don overtopped its banks and threatened the Thorpe Marsh power station.

Over the same period in Hull 17,000 homes were flooded, power supplies were lost and schools were forced to close.

July: floods on the Severn and Thames

Flooding in July was focused along the rivers Severn and Thames (Figure 16.7).

- On 20 July, rainfall along the course of the River Severn had already reached record levels, when a powerful storm sent the river into flood. In the days that followed, this had a devastating effect in many of the towns and villages downstream. A dozen people were killed and the financial costs amounted to £6 million.

- On the upper Severn at Shrewsbury, the scene of much flooding in the past (see Chapter 17), the flow was six times the normal level, but defences begun in 2003 largely did their job.
- On the mid-Severn around Worcester river levels rose to 4.5 m above normal. The village of Upton-upon-Severn was the first serious casualty. Flooding occurred here six times in 2007.
- The greatest impacts were felt on the lower Severn, in Tewkesbury, where the River Avon joins the Severn, and in Gloucester, with its waterfront developments. Homes were flooded, power supplies damaged and water supplies cut off.

Over the same period, Oxford, Abingdon and other towns along the upper Thames were flooded. Additional localised, unpredictable flash floods occurred (e.g. in Tenbury Wells).

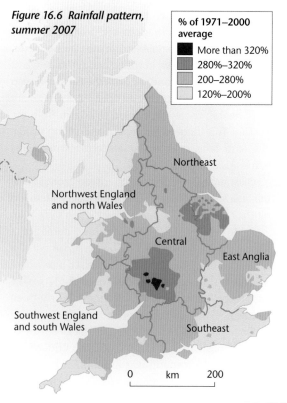

Figure 16.6 Rainfall pattern, summer 2007

% of 1971–2000 average
- More than 320%
- 280%–320%
- 200–280%
- 120%–200%

Northeast

Northwest England and north Wales

Central

East Anglia

Southwest England and south Wales

Southeast

0   km   200

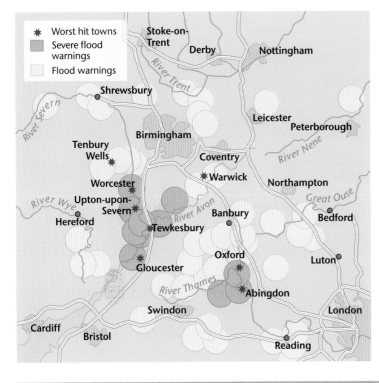

Worst hit towns
Severe flood warnings
Flood warnings

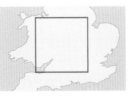

Figure 16.7 The areas of the UK worst affected by floods, July 2007

Further research

BBC

A good source for news of recent and past flood events is BBC news, which has a search facility:
http://news.bbc.co.uk/

Geographical Association

The GA website has a section of resources on managing flood risk:
www.geography.org.uk/
resources/flooding

Drought impacts

Drought is a cluster hazard (see Chapter 2). It is a natural trigger for malnutrition and famine, and a widespread problem in parts of Africa, southeast Asia and increasingly in temperate climates such as the central USA. Deaths resulting from famine are sometimes mistakenly attributed to drought when they have other underlying causes such as war or civil strife.

The impacts of drought can be categorised as direct and indirect, and are economic, environmental and social:

➤ Direct impacts include reduced crop and livestock production, water shortages, increased fire hazards, and damage to wildlife.
➤ Indirect impacts are the consequences for farmers and businesses, increased food and timber prices, unemployment, reduced tax revenues and migration.

Case study — **Drought in southeast Australia, April 2007**

In 2007 Australia, the world's driest inhabited continent, suffered its worst drought in 100 years. Arable land became a dustbowl and the Murray–Darling river system (Figure 16.8) was in crisis:

■ The lowest ever flow was recorded in the Murray River (Figure 16.9).
■ Algal blooms were triggered by warmer water.
■ Overgrazing and wind erosion damaged soils.

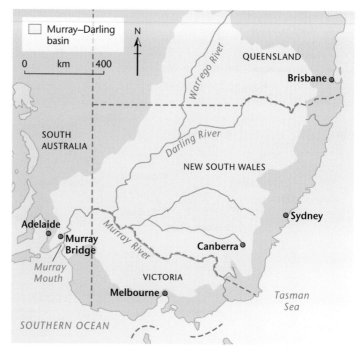

Figure 16.8 The Murray–Darling basin

- Forest fires endangered wildlife and people in the suburbs of Sydney.
- Water shortages threatened political agreements between the four Australian states.
- As water was diverted to the largest cities, irrigation supplies to livestock farmers were rationed.
- The downstream Murray River became over 1,000 parts per million saline.
- Low flow affected navigation up from the port of Adelaide.

With many regions in their sixth year of drought, Sydney's reservoirs were only 40% full. Wheat crops were the lowest in 12 years.

Australia has always had cycles of drought, but scientists fear that this is more than the usual El Niño cycle; it is the result of longer-term climate change.

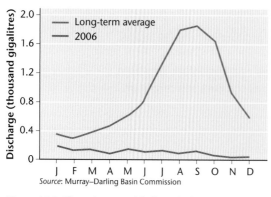

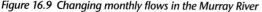
Source: Murray–Darling Basin Commission

Figure 16.9 Changing monthly flows in the Murray River

The issues

The drought problems of the Murray–Darling basin, like those in other places, concern decreasing water supplies and growing water demand. Increasing urbanisation, population growth and more intensive agriculture have degraded the once rich natural grasslands in the southeast of Australia. This region produces 40% of the country's farming output via livestock, vines, cereals and fruit, but only by using 84% of Australia's irrigation schemes. The drought is already showing marked economic and environmental impacts.

It is predicted that rainfall in the east will fall by 40% and temperatures will rise by 7°C by 2070 as a result of global warming.

Further research

www.bom.gov.au/lam/climate/levelthree/c20thc/drought.htm

http://search.bbc.co.uk/cgi-bin/search/results.pl?scope=all&edition=i&q=drought+australia&go.x=34&go.y=12

Review questions

1 Using Tables 15.1 (on p. 170) and 16.1, identify and justify what you think:
   a is the worst type of extreme weather in the USA
   b was the world's worst hurricane
2 Summarise how you might combine fieldwork and research to investigate the impacts of river flooding.
3 Choose *one* example of *either* a hurricane *or* a tornado. Using the information in this chapter and other sources, explain the types of impact involved. Be brief but include some detail.
4 Using one or more examples of *either* droughts *or* heatwaves, show how their impacts can be both direct and indirect.

Increasing risks

How are people and places increasingly at risk from, and vulnerable to, extreme weather?

By the end of this chapter you should have:

➤ *researched how the risks associated with extreme weather are increased by changes in climate and demographics, and by poor land management*

➤ *used your own fieldwork and research to investigate how river flooding at a local scale may have meteorological, hydrological and human causes*

Figure 17.1 Potential extent of flooding in Great Britain, 2080

The increasing flood risk

The threat of flooding is greater than that of any other natural disaster in the UK. Around 5 million people in 1.9 million properties (worth £214 billion) and 1.4 million hectares of agricultural land (worth £7 billion) are at risk from flooding. Some 65% of these properties are at risk from coastal flooding (and erosion) and the remaining 35% from rivers.

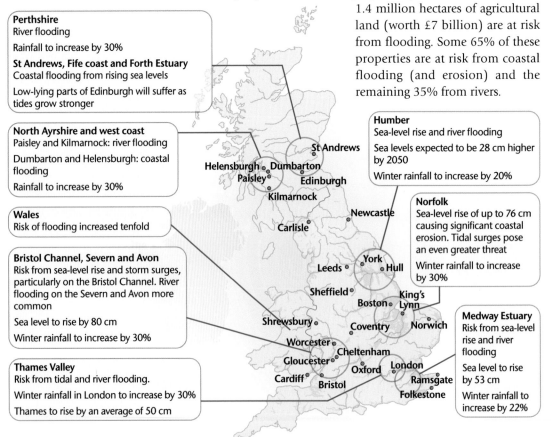

Perthshire
River flooding
Rainfall to increase by 30%

St Andrews, Fife coast and Forth Estuary
Coastal flooding from rising sea levels
Low-lying parts of Edinburgh will suffer as tides grow stronger

North Ayrshire and west coast
Paisley and Kilmarnock: river flooding
Dumbarton and Helensburgh: coastal flooding
Rainfall to increase by 30%

Wales
Risk of flooding increased tenfold

Bristol Channel, Severn and Avon
Risk from sea-level rise and storm surges, particularly on the Bristol Channel. River flooding on the Severn and Avon more common
Sea level to rise by 80 cm
Winter rainfall to increase by 30%

Thames Valley
Risk from tidal and river flooding.
Winter rainfall in London to increase by 30%
Thames to rise by an average of 50 cm

Humber
Sea-level rise and river flooding
Sea levels expected to be 28 cm higher by 2050
Winter rainfall to increase by 20%

Norfolk
Sea-level rise of up to 76 cm causing significant coastal erosion. Tidal surges pose an even greater threat
Winter rainfall to increase by 30%

Medway Estuary
Risk from sea-level rise and river flooding
Sea level to rise by 53 cm
Winter rainfall to increase by 22%

Flood risk is increasing because of:

➤ *Climate change.* Rainfall levels and intensity seem to be increasing, causing more river flooding. Storm surges and rising sea levels threaten our coasts.
➤ *Population migration.* As more houses are built on floodplains and in coastal areas, natural flooding that has always occurred turns into a hazard.
➤ *How we use land.* Urbanisation creates more impermeable surfaces and faster land drainage, all of which increase runoff rates and river discharge.

As demand for housing grows, river and coastal lowland areas are built on. The government's target of 3 million new homes by 2020 may not be achievable without building on flood-prone areas.

➤ Floodplains have long been sites for settlement. Today they attract industry and housing because the flat land has nearby infrastructure and is relatively cheap to build on. Riverside housing is attractive to buyers.
➤ Coastal lowlands have similar advantages, but with the added drivers of tourism and retirement. Population growth in some of these areas is a result of migration from other regions.

Figure 17.1 shows the areas of Great Britain expected to be at risk of flooding by 2080.

Flood risk and flood return periods

Key concept

Like all hazards, flooding has a frequency and magnitude, both of which are important in assessing the risks involved. The **flood return period**, also known as a **flood recurrence interval**, is an estimate of the likelihood of a flood of a certain size recurring. A flood likely to happen once in 10 years has a 10% chance of happening in any one year. However, this is not a forecast and such a flood may happen more than once in the same interval or not at all.

A river may flood on average every 2 or 3 years, with significant flooding only every 50 or 100 years. One way to illustrate this is shown in Figure 17.2. Floods may only reach the furthest edge of floodplain once in 500 years. Recent floods mean that our information on risk and recurrence needs updating.

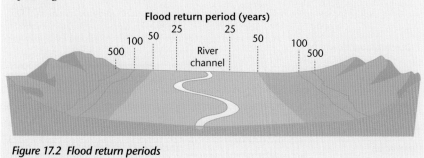

Figure 17.2 Flood return periods

Investigating increased river flood risks at a local scale

The focus for this work should be a small catchment or part of a larger river basin. You must do both your own fieldwork and research of secondary sources. Case studies of recent events, such as Shrewsbury, York, Carlisle, Boscastle or Sheffield could be used. The causes and severity of floods relate to the nature of the precipitation involved, the characteristics of the location and a variety of human and physical factors (see Figure 17.3).

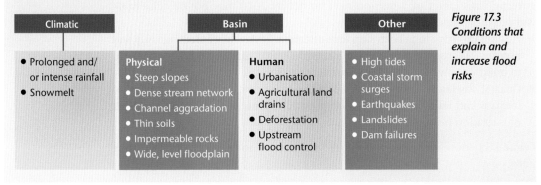

Climatic	Basin		Other
• Prolonged and/or intense rainfall • Snowmelt	**Physical** • Steep slopes • Dense stream network • Channel aggradation • Thin soils • Impermeable rocks • Wide, level floodplain	**Human** • Urbanisation • Agricultural land drains • Deforestation • Upstream flood control	• High tides • Coastal storm surges • Earthquakes • Landslides • Dam failures

Figure 17.3 Conditions that explain and increase flood risks

Skills focus

A **hydrograph** plots **discharge** or river level against time, showing how a river responds during and following a period of rainfall. The shape of the graph reflects how quickly the water reaches the river. The level of **infiltration** and the amount of surface runoff will be affected by the **antecedent** weather conditions, the landscape and the **interception** caused by vegetation.

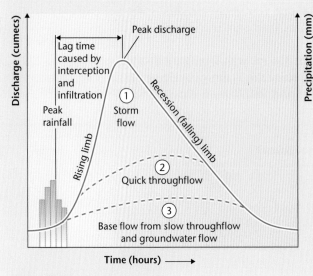

Figure 17.4 A storm hydrograph

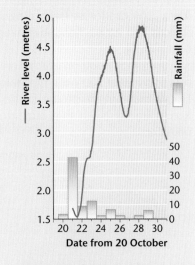

Figure 17.5 A storm hydrograph for Shrewsbury, October 1998

When analysing hydrographs it is helpful to use the terminology shown in Figure 17. 4.

Tasks

Figure 17.5 shows the hydrograph for a storm in Shrewsbury that led to severe flooding. Using the information in the graph:

1. State the values of the peak rainfall and peak river level.
2. Estimate and explain why there is a **lag time**.
3. Comment on the relationship between the pattern of rainfall and river level, using the vocabulary shown in Figure 17.4.

Key terms

Antecedent The previous weather, soil moisture or flow conditions.

Discharge The rate of river flow measured in cumecs.

Hydrograph A graph showing the changing pattern of discharge over time.

Infiltration The rate at which rainfall soaks into the ground, reducing runoff.

Interception The way in which trees and other vegetation prevent or delay runoff.

Lag time The delay between peak rainfall and peak discharge.

Case study

Flooding in Skipton, June 1982

Records for 6 June 1982 show that 30 mm of rain fell in 2 hours in this part of Yorkshire, much of it falling in quite a small area. Conditions in the previous week had also been wet.

Catchment area

Rombalds Moor rises steeply to a height of over 300 m. Its gritstone geology is largely impermeable, which encourages quick surface runoff. There are some trees but most of the land is grazed by livestock. Four or five small tributaries fall 200 m in about 1 km, before turning westwards into a steep-sided valley, alongside the A65 road, to become Skibeden Beck (see Figure 17.6 and Photographs 17.1 and 17.2). The bedload of the beck is limited in amount but is generally quite large in size. Evidence shows that some of the watercourse had been diverted or neglected and moorland paths were eroded.

Photograph 17.1 and 17.2 Rombalds Moor

Bob Hordern

Bob Hordern

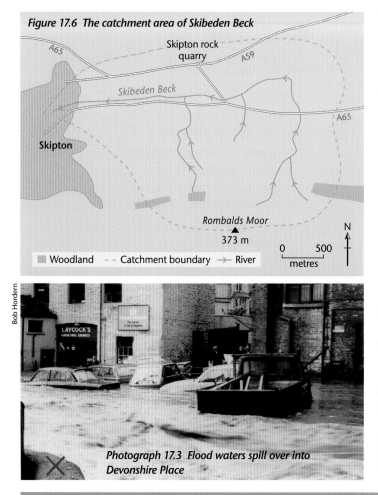

Figure 17.6 The catchment area of Skibeden Beck

Skipton rock quarry

A65

A59

Skibeden Beck

A65

Skipton

Rombalds Moor
▲
373 m

N

0   500
metres

■ Woodland   - - Catchment boundary   → River

Bob Hordern

Photograph 17.3 Flood waters spill over into Devonshire Place

The urban section

As it enters the built-up area of Skipton, the beck faces a number of obstacles. First, it is prevented from meandering by the sudden change in land use to housing and business. The use of culverts, open and covered, increases as the stream approaches the town centre. Add to this the increased runoff from car parks, drains and roads, and the potential flood risk becomes clearer. It was in this lower course that bedload and debris alongside the Otley Road forced flood water up into the main streets of Skipton in 1979 and again in 1982 (Photograph 17.3).

The ground floors of shops in Caroline Square and the (then) new Co-op department store were ruined. Hundreds of houses, including sheltered bungalows, were flooded. The 1982 floods were estimated to be a 1 in 400 year event but other devastating flood events in 1909, 1979 and 2002 suggest recurrence is more frequent.

Flood risks

You can undertake your own fieldwork to support a case study like the Skipton one. Primary data can be obtained by:

■ interviewing residents (will need to be aged at least 40 years)

Photograph 17.4 Students measuring discharge in Devonshire Place culvert. The wall top marked (x) here and in Photograph 17.3 gives an idea of the difference between flood level and low flow

Bob Hordern

- drawing up a land-use map along the course of the stream
- recording evidence of management (bed-load traps, channel widening, realignment, tree planting, etc.) and potential future problems
- measuring discharge and calculating bankfull discharge and flood levels (Photograph 17.4)
- investigating runoff and infiltration rates (see Photographs 17.4 and 17.5)

Additional research

- The local weekly newspaper is often a good source. In this case, the *Craven Herald* is available on microfilm at Skipton public library.
- An Ordnance Survey map of the area will help you better judge the scale of the stream.
- For online mapping you can use Multimap (www.multimap.com). BD23 6DR will find the closest location to Skipton. Zoom out once to see the full catchment area, then switch to aerial photo or map.
- Google Earth: http://earth.google.com. Remember you can zoom, rotate (try south) or tilt either the map or the aerial photograph.
- Geology can be researched using British Geological Survey maps, some of which are

Photograph 17.5 Students measuring infiltration rates

Bob Hordern

digitised: http://shop.bgs.ac.uk/bookshop/catalogue.cfm?id=2.

- Data for some UK river gauging stations, including average flow, are available from the National River Flow Archive: www.nwl.ac.uk/ih/nrfa/river_flow_data/nrfa_retrievals.htm

Review questions

1 Choose *one* riverside location in the UK (look it up on the Environment Agency's flood website) and describe the flood risk there.
2 Explain why a flood hydrograph is useful to people trying to investigate or deal with a flood event.
3 Describe some fieldwork and research activities that might help to explain the causes of flooding in *one* location you have researched.
4 For *one* named example of river flooding, identify which factors (human and physical) you think were to blame. Be brief but include some detail.

Managing extreme weather

How can we best respond to and cope with the impacts of extreme weather?

By the end of this chapter you should have:
➤ *used your own fieldwork and research to investigate the success of short- and longer-term strategies to manage river flooding and hurricanes*
➤ *researched how new technology can be applied to extreme weather management*
➤ *assessed the sustainability of attempts to alleviate drought and manage water supplies*

Approaches to managing extreme events

There are essentially three ways of managing extreme weather events as described below for floods and hurricanes and in Table 18.1 for other events. These can be used before, during and after the event.

Modifying the event

It is possible to modify a weather event by attempting to control the environment: that is, by modifying the causes of the event. For example, floods can be modified by afforestation or the building of control dams. It is difficult to modify the causes of hurricanes, although experiments to cool sea surface temperatures, or use cloud seeding to weaken the weather system, have taken place. Another option is to develop hazard-resistant technology, for example designing buildings to cope with high winds and flooding.

*Photograph 18.1
Flooding around
Tewkesbury, 2007*

Modifying vulnerability

A combination of technology to monitor and predict extreme weather events, and strategies to improve education and increase community preparedness can be used. GIS mapping of the risks from meteorological, river and tidal flood events is increasingly used in prediction. Satellites and radar can be used to track storms and provide warnings.

Table 18.1 Approaches to managing other extreme weather events

Extreme weather event	Modify the event		Modify vulnerability		Modify loss
	Control	Hazard-resistant design	Community preparedness	Prediction and warning	Aid before, during and after
Tornado	Not possible yet.	Hazard-resistant building design.	Evacuation procedures.	Analogue computer modelling of risk. Satellite technology combined with doppler radars to predict formation.	Federal and state aid, as well as international aid.
Drought	Rain-making strategies, technologically not proven. High-tech water management.	Genetic modification (GM) technology to breed drought-resistant crops.		Data analysis from computers should predict onset of drought in long term. Use of satellite imagery to assess onset of drought.	Agricultural research to develop moisture conservation schemes for Sahelian farmers.
Wildfire	Limited success from chemical/ water spraying and fire breaks.	House design: use of spark arrestors and clay/concrete.	Use of GIS to analyse fire tracks and occurrence, to identify risk areas.	Satellite (using infrared) to monitor. Night-time thermal emissive anomalies give temperature and size of fires.	

Modifying loss

Modifying loss involves using insurance in richer countries and both emergency and long-term aid in poorer countries. New technology can be used to target aid to vulnerable communities.

Fieldwork and research

Managing extreme weather events

You can carry out fieldwork to look at the choice of management strategies used and understand how some strategies can be more successful than others.

Flood protection

It is probably easiest to investigate flood protection in a small area or part of a river catchment, building on ideas of flood risk assessment in Chapter 17. One useful exercise would be to evaluate the success of a local flood management scheme and perhaps to suggest future strategies. Table 18.2 gives examples.

Information to support this could come from the Environment Agency website (www.

environment-agency.gov.uk/subjects/flood/). The National Flood Forum (www.floodforum.org.uk) has information about flood preparedness and useful links. Case studies of flood events in places like Shrewsbury, York and Carlisle could also be used to compare local and integrated catchment management using a wider mix of strategies.

Hurricane preparedness

Secondary research on the internet can provide insight into how successful warnings, engineering, technology and planning have been in hurricane preparedness. The management of major events like Hurricane Katrina is still being analysed.

Table 18.2 Flood management solutions

Structural measures

Method	Advantages	Disadvantages	Local UK examples
Flood storage (e.g. dams, washlands and relief channels)	Protects property Brings new development May be multipurpose	High economic costs Environmental losses Downstream impacts	Washland schemes, River Nene, Northampton Relief channel, River Thames, Maidenhead
Channelisation, realignment and flood barriers	Relatively cheap Little effect beyond local area Can be modified	High maintenance costs Environmental impacts	Channel, River Erewash, Derby Flood barrier, River Foss, York
Flood protection (e.g. flood proofing and embankments)	Reduces flood damage Separates river from property	Maintenance costs Limited scope May increase risks	Protection and embankments, River Ouse, York and downstream

Non-structural measures

Method	Advantages	Disadvantages	Local UK examples
Emergency action, warnings and flood relief	Cheap No changes to land use Only costly if floods	Damage costs potentially very high Individual losses	River Severn, Shrewsbury
Flood insurance	Raises awareness Gives financial support	Encourages risk Does not deal with causes Not available to some	Common throughout UK
Floodplain zoning	Low-cost strategy Regulates users Helps flood impacts	Does not protect existing users May deter developers	Wetland areas encouraged, River Soar, Leicester Parkland, Shrewsbury

Other strategies

Method	Advantages	Disadvantages	Local UK examples
Catchment approach (e.g. planting woodland)	Deals with cause (i.e. intercepts upstream)	Politically difficult (e.g. ownership issues)	Afforestation in Lake District National Park
River restoration	Allows rivers to return to natural state	Means some flooding Probably small scale	Meanders put back along River Cole, Oxfordshire

Fieldwork and research

Flood management

A useful plan and set of fieldwork activities could be based upon those for Shrewsbury used in Chapter 16. They might include:

- mapping the management strategies used along the river (see Figure 18.1)
- identifying any hard defences used
- plotting land use in the flood zone

A list of different methods could be checked against the structural measures shown in Table 18.2.

- Interviews with local Environment Agency staff might further identify the non-structural measures used, e.g. emergency actions, flood warning systems and planning decisions.

Wider actions in the catchment might also be investigated.

- Table 18.2 suggests likely advantages and disadvantages of the various measures. These could be used to design a questionnaire to survey the views of a sample of local residents on the success of the measures implemented.
- The advantages and disadvantages in Table 18.2 could also be used to draw up the costs

and benefits of various strategies, their environmental impacts and longer-term implications (see the case study below).

Further research

Some research opportunities were identified in Chapter 16. www.curriculum-press.co.uk/demo/a_geog/127_Flooding.pdf is another useful reference.

Case study | **Evaluating flood protection in Shrewsbury**

In response to floods in Shrewsbury in autumn 2000, the Environment Agency considered several approaches to protecting the town against future flooding:

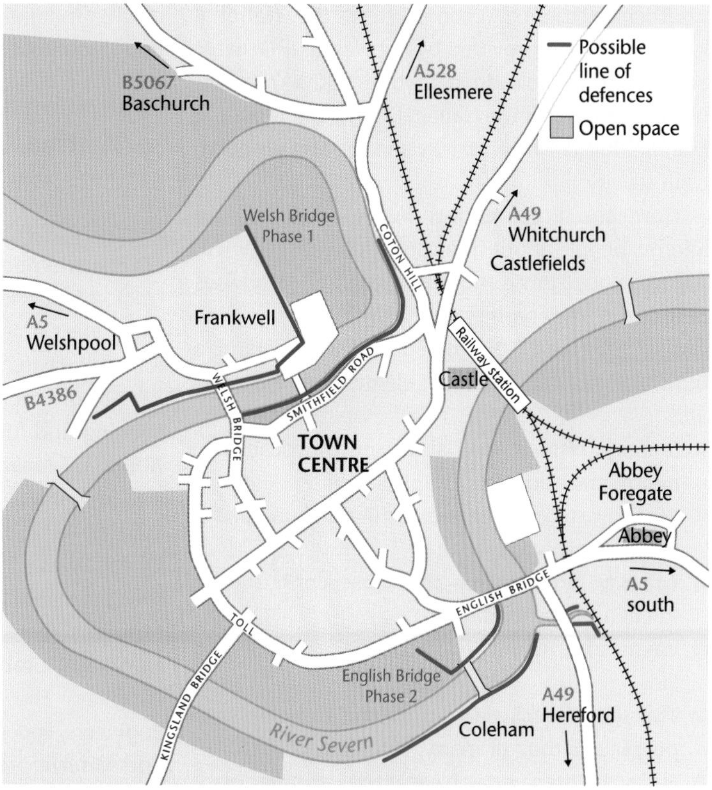

- *Upstream containment.* Allowing water from the River Severn's main tributary, the Vyrnwy, to flood land upstream (washland) rather than at Shrewsbury. This option is seen as too costly at present, as £18 million would need to be paid to landowners in compensation, but wetland could be environmentally beneficial. This type of sustainable, holistic solution, supported by wildlife groups, may need to be revisited in the future.

- *Channel dredging.* This traditional, hard engineering approach in the Shrewsbury meanders was not considered feasible as the channel would

Figure 18.1 Flood defence strategies for Shrewsbury

silt up again. It would be environmentally damaging and incur costs as high as £45 million.

- *Local defences and urban drainage modification.* This type of short-term, cost-effective management (£3.1 million) is likely to be used

increasingly in riverside towns, and was eventually favoured by the Environment Agency for Shrewsbury. It involved building defensive walls to protect key places, using floodgates, temporary barriers and inflatable dams, and improving sewer, surface runoff and urban drainage schemes. The scheme was introduced in two phases, starting at Welsh Bridge and moving on to English Bridge.

It was decided to continue two other strategies that were already in operation:

■ Control of riverside land use, to prevent inappro-priate building and to offer some areas in the town that could be allowed to flood.
■ Flood risk analysis, emergency support, flood monitoring and warning systems via the Environment Agency.

In the flood of July 2007, these schemes were mostly successful in Shrewsbury.

Case study — Evaluating hurricane preparedness, the USA

The main source of information about extreme weather in the USA comes from the National Weather Service provided by the National Oceanic and Atmospheric Administration (NOAA) (www.nws.noaa.gov) and the National Hurricane Center in Miami. This identifies, tracks and reports on hurricane activity.

Hurricane Preparedness Week educates and informs people about hurricanes. Its website (www.nhc.noaa.gov/HAW2/english/intro.shtml) advises people on their vulnerability, what actions they should take, and how to reduce the effects of a hurricane disaster. The main elements of the week are:

■ Sunday: history — a database of hurricanes to inform and educate.
■ Monday: storm surge — a useful graphic explains the risks involved.
■ Tuesday: high winds — the impacts of hurricane forces are described.
■ Wednesday: inland flooding — the greatest risk to life.
■ Thursday: forecasting — how this can help save people and their property.
■ Friday: be prepared — have a family disaster plan; is evacuation necessary?
■ Saturday: take action — make that checklist and rehearse it.

Another key source of information is the Federal Emergency Management Agency (FEMA, www.fema.gov/hazard/hurricane/index.shtm). Its work involves disaster mitigation, flood warnings and the national flood insurance programme.

Evaluating hurricane preparedness for Katrina

See the impacts already considered in Chapter 16.

Preparation

On the afternoon of 26 August 2005, the predicted track of Katrina was revised by the National Hurricane Center and a Hurricane Watch was issued for southeastern Louisiana, including New Orleans. A state of emergency was declared the following evening and 'devastating damage' was expected. About 1.2 million residents of the Gulf Coast were issued with evacuation orders in three phases, starting with the immediate coastal areas. New Orleans was scheduled in phase III (30 hours before the estimated time of arrival). About 80% of residents were evacuated, although there were significant problems with transportation and fuel supplies. The National Guard, Army Corp of Engineers, Federal Emergency Management Agency and disaster recovery agencies were all called into action.

How successful was it?

The plans were in place, the warnings were given and agencies were ready to act. However, the failure of the levées protecting the city, the loss of power and drinking water, and the slow response of FEMA

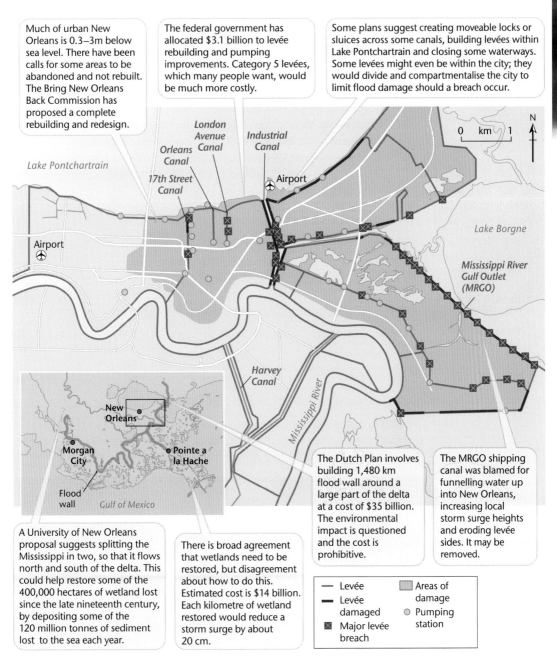

Much of urban New Orleans is 0.3–3m below sea level. There have been calls for some areas to be abandoned and not rebuilt. The Bring New Orleans Back Commission has proposed a complete rebuilding and redesign.

The federal government has allocated $3.1 billion to levée rebuilding and pumping improvements. Category 5 levées, which many people want, would be much more costly.

Some plans suggest creating moveable locks or sluices across some canals, building levées within Lake Pontchartrain and closing some waterways. Some levées might even be within the city; they would divide and compartmentalise the city to limit flood damage should a breach occur.

Lake Pontchartrain

London Avenue Canal

Orleans Canal

Industrial Canal

17th Street Canal

Airport

Airport

Lake Borgne

Mississippi River Gulf Outlet (MRGO)

Harvey Canal

Mississippi River

New Orleans

Morgan City

Pointe a la Hache

Flood wall

Gulf of Mexico

0   km   1

N

The Dutch Plan involves building 1,480 km flood wall around a large part of the delta at a cost of $35 billion. The environmental impact is questioned and the cost is prohibitive.

The MRGO shipping canal was blamed for funnelling water up into New Orleans, increasing local storm surge heights and eroding levée sides. It may be removed.

A University of New Orleans proposal suggests splitting the Mississippi in two, so that it flows north and south of the delta. This could help restore some of the 400,000 hectares of wetland lost since the late nineteenth century, by depositing some of the 120 million tonnes of sediment lost to the sea each year.

There is broad agreement that wetlands need to be restored, but disagreement about how to do this. Estimated cost is $14 billion. Each kilometre of wetland restored would reduce a storm surge by about 20 cm.

	Levée		Areas of damage
	Levée damaged	○	Pumping station
⊠	Major levée breach		

Figure 18.2 Proposals for rebuilding New Orleans

and other agencies do not suggest success. Recovery and regeneration are still slow and the political fallout continues (see also Table 16.2 on p. 185).

Post-Katrina strategies

Longer-term strategies are needed (Figure 18.2) so that New Orleans can stand up to future hurricanes.

The role of new technology

Key term

Appropriate technology
Tools suitable for less
economically developed
countries, which are
cheap to buy, simple to
build, and easy to use and
repair.

*Table 18.3 The role of new
technology: framework*

The use of new technology in managing extreme events includes
geographical information systems (GIS) to develop risk mapping,
global positioning systems (GPS) and remote sensing devices for
improving preparedness, as well as simple practical solutions, using
appropriate technology. High-tech methods are increasingly used in
flood and storm management, whereas drought management involves
a more varied range of solutions. Table 18.3 offers a framework for this
topic — your work should cover all rows and at least two columns. The
most useful website is www.noaawatch.gov.

	Hurricanes	River floods	Drought
Improving preparedness			
Event forecasting			
Reducing impacts			

Tropical storms

➤ Weather satellites are used to detect storm conditions.
➤ Ocean buoys detect changes that help predict hurricanes and El Niño patterns.
➤ Conventional radar can detect cloud and rainfall patterns.

*Photograph 18.2
A doppler radar
image of Hurricane
Charley
approaching
Florida, 2004*

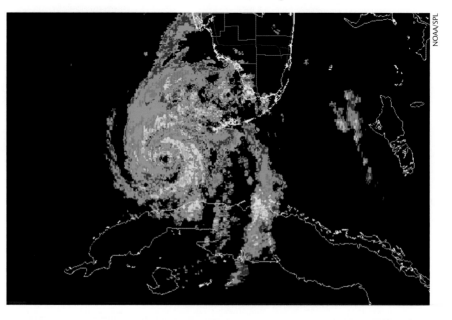

*Photograph 18.3
Flood defence
barriers in use on
the River Severn at
Ironbridge*

➤ Doppler radar can help with storm and tornado tracking (Photograph 18.2).
➤ Landfall prediction is the most important single element needed.
➤ Computer models are used to predict routes of hurricanes.

Floods

➤ Flood forecasting systems use a range of technology (Figure 18.3).
➤ Flood risk can be mapped using remote sensing and GIS.
➤ Environment Agency and Meteorological Office flood and weather warnings can be communicated by automated voice and text messaging and online.
➤ Floods can be simulated using software such as Flood Ranger.
➤ Flood protection devices have been developed to protect streets and properties (Photograph 18.3).

Drought

➤ Satellites can remotely assess drought in real time from environmental data (see Figure 18.4 and research at www.drought.unl.edu/dm/monitor.html).
➤ Gene technology can produce drought- and salt-resistant crops and livestock.
➤ Low, but innovative, technology can be used, such as drip irrigation or earth dams, agroforestry and 'stone piles' improving water conservation for farmers.
➤ Satellite data, GIS mapping and internet communication can provide up-to-date forecasts for drought in the USA.

*Figure 18.3
A flood forecasting
system in the USA*

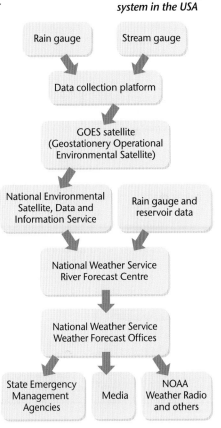

Case study   Flood forecasts of the future

The Meteorological Office will soon be able to issue detailed town-by-town forecasts that show precisely where extreme rain will fall. By 2011, new computers will allow forecasters to predict the exact path of downpours, or the location of flash floods, giving communities more accurate warnings of the risks they face.

A planned £120 million upgrade of the Met Office supercomputers in Exeter should mean that meteorologists will be able to predict more precisely how extreme rain will affect areas.

The improved processing power will provide warnings of severe weather three times as early, so that people can prepare.

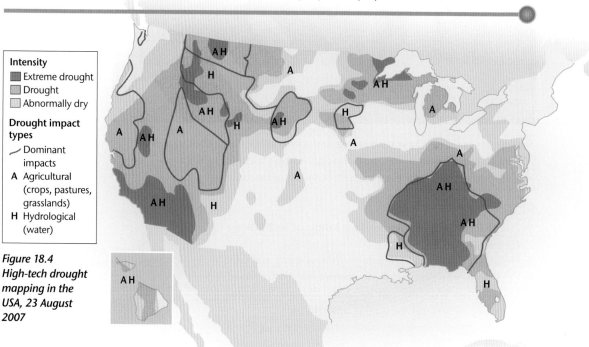

Intensity
- ■ Extreme drought
- ■ Drought
- □ Abnormally dry

Drought impact types
- ⁄ Dominant impacts
- **A** Agricultural (crops, pastures, grasslands)
- **H** Hydrological (water)

Figure 18.4
High-tech drought mapping in the USA, 23 August 2007

It should be noted that technology is only useful in managing extreme events if it is supported by a national and local framework. For example, hazard and risk maps need to be disseminated to and used by the communities for which they were developed. It is vital that information is standardised so that the results can be used by many agencies. Prediction is successful only if it is combined with education and community preparedness schemes.

Long-term solutions to drought

Key terms

Sustainable Dealing with both today's and tomorrow's needs.

Long-term solutions to any challenge need to be **sustainable**. Solutions to drought vary from country to country and often involve water management and adapting farming techniques. Somalia and Australia, discussed in the case study opposite, provide a useful contrast illustrating the physical, social, economic and political aspects of drought management.

Case study — Sustainable drought solutions in Somalia and Australia

Somalia

This drought-ridden, war-torn country is in east Africa. It has a population of around 10 million people, and cattle and bananas are its only exports.

Many nomads have become **subsistence farmers**, giving up their camels and goats for cattle and dry farming. *Enset* or false banana is an indigenous crop used for food, fodder and soil-improvement and is grown alongside cereals. It is drought resistant.

Conflict has led to neglect of farmland and water supplies, but with the help of NGOs like Oxfam and Candlelight, local *berkads* or storage wells have been restored. **Bunds** and terraces have been built to conserve soil and water. These improvements have sustainable credentials because:

- they have been planned and completed by the communities themselves, using local volunteer labour
- decisions are taken by village committees made up of elders, including at least one woman (women are traditionally the water managers and farmers)
- storing water from the wet season to the dry season involves conservation of a precious resource for the future

Figure 18.5 Map showing the location of Somalia

Key terms

Berkads Concrete- or stone-lined underground rainwater tanks, usually covered by natural roofing material to limit evaporation. They are gravity filled by channel-guided water runoff.

Bund Bank or line of stones designed to reduce surface water runoff and soil erosion.

Subsistence (farming) Producing food to eat, not to sell.

Australia

Farming in Australia, in contrast to Somalia, uses large quantities of water and takes place in a tough commercial environment. The water business around Goulburn, New South Wales, perhaps the driest place in southeast Australia, involves large-scale diversions from the Murray River and supply networks to Sydney. In January 2007 drought meant that local farmers lost 75% of their irrigation ration. In addition, swimming pools closed, parks went unwatered and each person was allowed only 120 litres per day.

This type of short-term drought response is typical in Western countries. The residents of Goulburn became the first in Australia to start drinking treated sewage water, as Australia began to

look for more sustainable solutions to drought.

Government spending of around £1 billion still goes mostly towards major projects, but new technologies and community grants for sustainable projects include:

■ *Water saving.* Bunbury, Western Australia, hopes to make a 30% water saving in its irrigation of city parks and ovals (30 hectares), using a new weather station which will automatically send instructions to a central control irrigation system. This will save 50 million litres of water each year.

■ *Water reuse.* Caritas College School, South Australia, engaged a consultant who recommended diverting rainwater to an existing (unused) underground tank. This water will be used to flush toilets. An analysis of annual rainfall data and the school surface area shows that the project will reduce total water use by 25%.

■ *Water treatment.* Ballarat Christian School in Sebastopol, Victoria, with local water authorities and environmental groups, developed a project to harvest water from a runoff drain. A pollutant trap collects rubbish before it enters the local river, and reed beds filter the water. This helps to stop the build-up of silt, improve river quality and has restored 0.5 hectares of land and waterway. The local church community provided labour.

The website of the Australian National Water Commission has well-illustrated case studies at all scales (www.nwc.gov.au).

Further research

The UNDP supports water projects in various countries and its website Waterfair looks at one such example in Somalia: www.waterfair.org/content. spring?contentItem=464 It has a downloadable video presentation and a short article on sustainable management of drought.

Review questions

1 Identify some short- and long-term strategies for managing extreme weather, and summarise their differences.
2 Using *one* specific flood management scheme, suggest why this scheme was chosen rather than the other options.
3 Identify ways in which new technology can help management of weather hazards.
4 Using examples, suggest why drought and flood managers are increasingly turning to sustainable solutions.

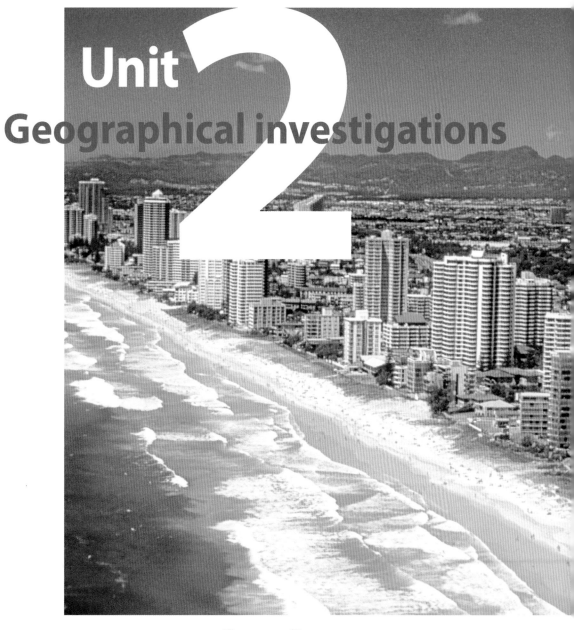

Unit 2

Geographical investigations

Crowded coasts

Competition for coasts

Why is the coastal zone so favoured for development?

By the end of this chapter you should have:
- ➤ *become aware of the natural diversity of the coast and the factors contributing to it*
- ➤ *developed an understanding of the factors leading to the concentration of population in coastal areas*
- ➤ *investigated and contrasted the development of two stretches of crowded coast, using your own observations and published sources*

Figure 19.1
The problems facing coasts — a global picture

The coastal zone is the most populated part of the world, containing many of the largest cities and manufacturing centres. Coastal lowlands are important food producers. Coastal ports play a leading role in world trade. The coast has become a popular place for leisure, recreation and tourism. The coastal zone is a battleground, not just between the land and sea, but also between competing land uses. This competition is creating development pressures that threaten the coast's natural environments. The dense coastal populations in Figure 19.1 confirm the attractiveness of the coast to people.

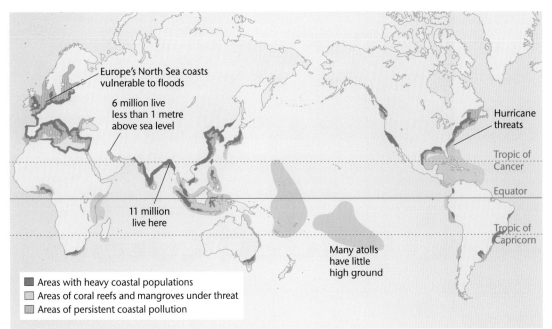

- Areas with heavy coastal populations
- Areas of coral reefs and mangroves under threat
- Areas of persistent coastal pollution

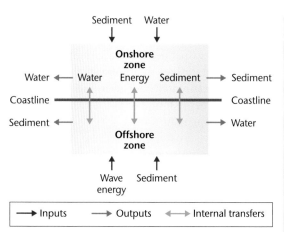

Figure 19.2 The coastal system

The coast is an open system involving inputs, internal transfers and outputs of water, sediment and energy (Figure 19.2) in a state of **dynamic equilibrium**. As we shall see in the next three chapters, this equilibrium is easily upset, particularly by human activities. Global warming means that increased storms and rising sea levels are accelerating coastal erosion and increasing the scale and frequency of coastal flooding.

Coastal diversity

A remarkable diversity of landscapes and ecosystems exists along the coast. Figure 19.3 identifies the main factors moulding the character of a stretch of coast. It also reminds us that coasts are a meeting point of land, sea and atmosphere. This unique combination produces a dynamic environment. Human settlement and development add to that dynamism.

The coast — Key concept

The **coast** is 'that part of the land most affected by its proximity to the sea and that part of the ocean most affected by its proximity to the land'. It is therefore a zone of transition. The coastline is the frontier between the sea and the land. Thus the coast is made up of two zones — onshore and offshore — located either side of the coastline (Figure 19.2). The onshore zone can extend up to 60 km inland. The offshore zone reaches as far as the outer limit of the economic exclusion zone (EEZ). This is currently set at 200 miles or 370.4 km. Within that limit, the coastal state has rights over the natural resources of the water as well as of the sea bed.

Key terms

Dynamic equilibrium The balanced state of a system when its inputs and outputs are equal. If one element changes because of some outside influence, this upsets the internal equilibrium and affects other components of the system. By a process of feedback, the system adjusts to the change and regains equilibrium.

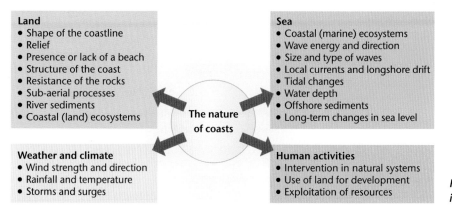

Figure 19.3 Factors influencing coasts

Coastal attractions

'Crowds flock to the coast' is a frequent newspaper headline seen during hot bank holiday weekends. However, the truth is that the crowds are already there. Indeed, they have been there for centuries. It is estimated that over half the world's population and two-thirds of its largest cities are found within 60 km of the sea. So what has made the coast so attractive to people?

 Case study   The coastal magnet

In 1990, around 30% of the world's population lived on the coast (60% in the 60 km-wide coastal zone). By 2002 that figure had risen to around 40%. Coastal populations are growing at a rate four times the global average. Some of the world's fastest-growing megacities, such as Lagos (Nigeria) and Shanghai (China), are on the coast. An economist has recently stated: 'People are attracted to the coasts because of the high density of ecosystem services, but then the concentration of population has the side effect of depleting those same services...It's like tourism: people are attracted to gorgeous natural settings until they become so full of people that the attraction is destroyed.'

Coastal ecosystem goods and services

The goods are the products that can be derived directly from terrestrial and marine coastal eco-systems (Figure 19.4). The services are the benefits that people obtain from these same ecosystems.

BASIC GOODS FOR SURVIVAL
Food crops, e.g. tree crops and seaweed
Food via agroecosystems and also indirectly for feeding livestock (fodder)
Meat and fish
Building materials (e.g. sand), timber etc.
Source of water
Energy via biomass, tides, HEP
Genetic resources for medicine etc.

COASTAL ECOSYSTEMS

VITAL SERVICES FOR SURVIVAL
Climate regeneration
Air purification: plants remove carbon dioxide (carbon sinks) and emit oxygen
Water control: vegetation exerts an impact on the water cycle
Flood protection and storm protection (mangroves and reefs)
Water purification: dilutes and carries away waste
Cycling of nutrients
Generation of humus to produce soil
Maintenance of biodiversity
Provision of wildlife habitats
Opportunities for aesthetic enjoyment and recreation
A gene pool for the future
Employment opportunities across all sectors

Figure 19.4 Basic goods and vital services provided by ecosystems. The items in blue boxes are those most relevant to coastal ecosystems

In middle and higher latitudes, the coast has a more equable climate than inland locations. This means more comfortable living conditions and may explain the early attraction of the coast to people. From the earliest times, however, much human movement between places was by sea rather than over land. There were no roads. Large areas of untouched wilderness impeded land transport. Instead, the inshore or coastal waters provided the 'roads' along which people moved to colonise and settle new areas. Coastal lowlands were often well suited to farming, while inshore waters provided additional food in the form of fish. So food security and transport were important reasons for the early concentration of population in the coastal zone.

Figure 19.5 presents a crude timeline setting out some of the major steps in the development of the coast since its early settlement.

Figure 19.5
A timeline of coastal settlement and development

c. 1000
Early concentration of population encouraged by food security and transport opportunities of coastal areas

— 1000 —

— 1100 —

c. 1300
Some coastal settlements become seats of political and economic power and are fortified. They offer security and attract more people and economic activities

— 1200 —

c. 1600
European colonisation of the Americas, Asia and Australia with first settlements established in coastal areas. Pioneer frontiers pushed inland, but coastal areas remain more populated

— 1300 —

— 1400 —

c. 1750
Industrialisation brings prosperity to ports handling raw materials and manufactured goods

c. 1800
Increased security of coast encourages settlement growth and acceleration of development

— 1500 —

c. 1850
Seaside resorts and coastal tourism take off

— 1600 —

c. 1930
Paid holidays from work give big boost to coastal tourism

— 1700 —

c. 1950
Large-scale expansion of port-related industries, such as steel, shipbuilding and oil refining

c. 1970
Exploitation of offshore oil and natural gas. Coastal settlements prosper as offshore bases and transshipment points

— 1800 —

c. 1980
Growth of water-based recreation in estuaries and inshore waters. Rising demand for second homes in coastal areas

— 1900 —

c. 2000
Coastal areas are possible providers of wind and tidal power. Greater leisure use. Development of deep-water specialised ports

— 2000 —

The Lancashire coastal plain stretches from the River Mersey in the south to the southern edge of the Lake District in the north. It is bounded by the Pennine Hills in the east and by a low-lying coastline in the west. The plain is very flat, and much of it is only a few metres above sea level. It has been continuously inhabited since prehistoric times.

Table 19.1 illustrates how exploitation of the plain's resource base and ecosystem services has changed over time.

Figure 19.6 Lancashire coastal plain

Table 19.1 The Lancashire coastal plain: changing resource exploitation

Resource	Use	Pre-industrial (pre-1750)	Industrial (1750–1950)	Post-industrial (post-1950)
Geology Sands and clays	Making glass and bricks	✓	✓	✓
Coal	Power for industry, railways and heating		✓	✓
Iron ore	Hardware goods	✓		
Climate Precipitation	High humidity important to cotton industry		✓	
Soils	Fertility good for farming and horticulture	✓	✓	✓
Vegetation Woodland	Charcoal and fuel	✓		
Peat	Fuel	✓		
Foreshore	Beach: recreation and tourism		✓	✓
	Cockles	✓	✓	✓
Sand dunes	Links golf courses		✓	✓
	Recreation			✓
Flat land	Urban and industrial sites		✓	✓
	Easy canal and railway construction		✓	✓
Rivers	Water power	✓	✓	✓
	Domestic and industrial water supply	✓	✓	✓
	Transport	✓	✓	
Estuaries	Defensive sites	✓		
	Sites for ports		✓	✓
	Sites for industry	✓	✓	✓
Inshore waters	Fish	✓	✓	✓
	Recreation		✓	✓
Wildlife	Food	✓		
	Protection and conservation			✓
Location	Involvement in the triangular trade with Africa (slaves) and North America (cotton)		✓	

But human resources also play their part in the development of coastal areas. In addition to the supply of labour, human resources include vision, skills and enterprise. These are critical in the transitions between phases. In the case of the Lancashire coast (Table 19.1), the most recent of its transitions is especially demanding. New uses need to be found for redundant buildings, and large areas of Liverpool, Preston, Southport and Blackpool need to be rebranded. Remember, too, that much of the modern economy is now about people providing services for other people.

So the attraction and value of the coast are largely to do with resources and opportunities (Figures 19.4 and 19.7) but nothing happens without people as the case studies below show.

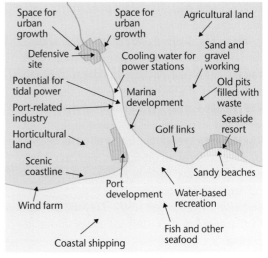

Figure 19.7 Coastal resources and opportunities

For over 100 years Blackpool was one of Europe's leading coastal resorts, renowned for its tower, lights and sticks of rock (Photograph 19.1).

During the eighteenth century, it became fashionable for well-to-do people in Britain to travel to the seaside in the summer. In those days, it was believed that bathing in sea water could cure diseases. Some people came to Blackpool on the Lancashire coast, but the settlement remained a hamlet until the first half of the nineteenth century (Figure 19.8).

The coming of the railway in 1846 made a huge impact on Blackpool. The train cut both the costs and time taken to reach the resort. Huge numbers of working-class visitors began coming to Blackpool every weekend.

Another boost came in the 1870s when each of the cotton textile towns of Lancashire began declaring its annual 'wakes week' when all the mills were shut. These holidays were not intended to give the workers a rest, but to allow time for textile machines to be serviced. Nonetheless, thousands of people from these towns were soon pouring into Blackpool during the holiday period. The tower, promenades, piers, amusement arcades, theatres and music halls were built. By the First World War, the number of visitors during the high season had mushroomed to 4 million. During the interwar years (1918–39), Blackpool's prosperity continued, helped by a law that gave workers

Photograph 19.1 Blackpool

holidays with pay. The town's permanent population reached nearly 150,000.

After the Second World War, Blackpool's fortunes began to decline. The main reasons were the advent of the package holiday and cheap air transport. The keenest competition came from the coastal resorts of the Mediterranean, which were able to deliver not just sea and sand, but also sun. Blackpool has tried to offset its decline by developing other attractions, such as conference facilities and casinos. However, the town is still struggling to survive.

See p. 243 for a case study of coastal defence in Blackpool and p. 298 for more about its decline.

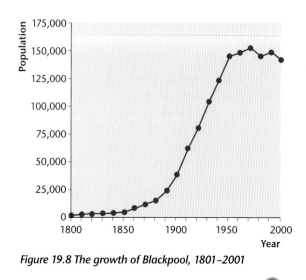

Figure 19.8 The growth of Blackpool, 1801–2001

Case study   Benidorm, Spain

Benidorm has a permanent population of 67,000, but during the summer peak season its population exceeds half a million.

The development of Benidorm as a coastal resort started in 1954 when its young mayor drew up an ambitious plan of urban development. This took off in the 1960s when it became popular with British tourists on summer package holidays. Its tourist season is now year long. The night-life, which revolves around bars and clubs in the centre of the resort, is a strong pull, particularly for younger visitors. Within a few decades, Benidorm has been transformed from a sleepy village to a pulsating urban area of skyscraper hotels and apartment blocks, theme parks, pubs, clubs and restaurants. It says much for the original plan that the built-up area today retains a lot of greenery. Benidorm remains proud of its three main beaches. All of them have 'blue flag' status. At the height of the season, they are some of the most densely populated parts of the world.

Many traditional seaside resorts in the UK are seeking to rebrand and find new ways of earning a living. The example of Boscombe in Dorset suggests that there may still be niches to be exploited in the leisure and tourism sector.

Case study   Making waves at Boscombe, UK

Boscombe, next-door to Bournemouth on the English south coast, will soon be the proud owner of Europe's first artificial surf reef. The reef, close to Boscombe pier, will occupy approximately 1 hectare. It will be made from large geotextile sand bags.

The land-based tourist facilities around Boscombe pier are tired and in need of rejuvenation. A surf survey has revealed that there are on average 77 good surfing days a year at Boscombe, although surfing takes place on 153 days, with a total of 5,000 surf visits a year. With the reef in place, the height of

waves along this part of the coast and the number of good surfing days will be doubled. Boscombe will be capable of hosting around 10,000 surf visits per annum.

The cost of constructing the artificial reef is around £1.1 million, but it is forecast that the business it brings to the resort will soon pay for that outlay. Indeed, it is estimated that the reef will generate an image value of £10 million per annum. It will create a demand for equipment shops and surf training schools, as well as accommodation and food and drink services. It is claimed that the environmental impact of the reef will, at worst, be neutral. Marine life should thrive on the reef and there will be no damaging effects to the beach. Indeed, it is thought that the reef will strengthen coastal defences.

Fieldwork and research

The growth of coastal resorts

This section is designed to help you investigate and understand how coastal settlements have developed over time. The natural factors and resources identified on pp. 211–214 should be borne in mind. The case studies of Blackpool and Benidorm should also help.

The most useful approach is to investigate two contrasting coastal resorts. Many traditional UK seaside resorts have seen better days and are struggling to rebrand themselves in the face of competition from foreign destinations. A UK resort can best be investigated using primary data and complementary research. You can use the internet and perhaps literature from a local travel agent to investigate an overseas resort.

Fieldwork and practical work should include:

■ mapping the location of tourist attractions and facilities (see the skills focus box on p. 218)

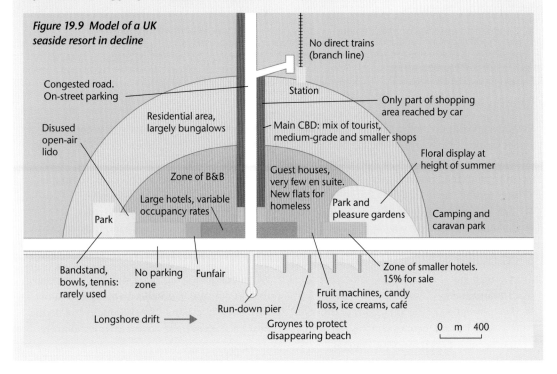

Figure 19.9 Model of a UK seaside resort in decline

No direct trains (branch line)

Congested road. On-street parking

Station

Only part of shopping area reached by car

Residential area, largely bungalows

Main CBD: mix of tourist, medium-grade and smaller shops

Disused open-air lido

Floral display at height of summer

Zone of B&B

Guest houses, very few en suite. New flats for homeless

Large hotels, variable occupancy rates

Park and pleasure gardens

Camping and caravan park

Park

Bandstand, bowls, tennis: rarely used

No parking zone

Funfair

Zone of smaller hotels. 15% for sale

Fruit machines, candy floss, ice creams, café

Longshore drift →

Run-down pier

Groynes to protect disappearing beach

0   m   400

- surveys of the age of buildings to establish the spatial pattern of the resort's growth
- visitor surveys (interviews or questionnaires) — see below
- carrying out pedestrian count, traffic flow and car parking surveys during the tourist season

and comparing them with similar surveys conducted out of season

- identifying other significant economic activities

You might find the model in Figure 19.9 useful. How does your chosen UK resort compare?

Skills focus

Mapping land use requires four things:

- A base map of suitable scale (OS 1:10,000 or 1:5,000 are good). Schools can often access free large-scale maps from the local authority. If not, try Google Maps.
- A simple classification of tourist amenities that can be easily applied in the field (hotels; boarding and guest houses; cafés and restaurants; information centres; car parks; amusement arcades, etc.)
- A strategic plan of action (e.g. whether to map the whole area or to sample it by means of transects — perhaps one along the seafront and others at right angles to the coast).
- Careful field observation of amenities.

Annotate your base map to give reasons for any clustering.

Complementary research into your chosen resorts could focus on:

- when and why tourism began
- population data from a run of censuses (perhaps accessed via your local authority or local library)
- different stages in the resort's development
- old maps (including early editions of large-scale OS maps, www.old-maps.co.uk)
- old photographs
- old guidebooks and newspapers from the local library or http://news.google.com.

Fieldwork and research

Visitor surveys

Research on visitors coming to a particular resort might focus on some or all of the following:

- their age — tactfully collected in terms of age groups (e.g. under 21; 21–40; 40–65, over 65)
- their home address — first part of the postcode
- duration of stay — day, weekend, 1 week, more than 1 week
- what type of accommodation they are staying in — B&B, guest house, hotel, self-catering, caravan, other
- their perception of the attractions of the resort (i.e. what caused them to visit this rather than another resort — accessibility, general

ambience, specific amenity or event, response to a particular promotion, etc.). Another way of finding out why people like a place is to search for geo-tagged photographs on the internet: try www.flickr.com/map.

- suggestions for improving the resort — car parking, tourist information, quality of accommodation, amenities, etc.

When designing your questionnaire, remember that, in this case, it is better to ask closed rather than open questions. The skills focus box on the next page gives more advice on questionnaire surveys.

Skills focus

The scale of any questionnaire survey depends on the number of interviewers available. Important issues to be resolved include:

Questionnaire design
- What is the information you require?
- Are your questions few in number, clear and unambiguous?
- Will your questions get the information you require?

Survey
- Where should the survey be conducted — at one location or more?
- On what day of the week and at what time of day should it be conducted?

- How many questionnaires need to completed to make your findings reliable?

It is usually better to design closed rather than open questions. These provide the respondent with a choice of answer from a list. Interviewees are asked to tick the relevant box(es) or to score or rank the items.

Before starting your survey, carry out a pilot with family and friends to check that the questions are clear and unambiguous, and that you are not missing out important lines of enquiry. Make sure there are no leading questions, as you need to avoid bias.

Review questions

1 Explain the difference between the *coastline* and the *coastal zone*.
2 a What is meant by dynamic equilibrium?
  b Suggest ways in which people might upset the dynamic equilibrium of the coast.
3 a For a named stretch of coast, identify what you think are its main physical attractions.
  b Are those attractions now stronger or weaker than they were in the past? Justify your answer.
4 a Give reasons for the decline of many British seaside resorts.
  b Suggest how management might bring about their revival.

Coping with the pressure

How do various coastal developments create competition and conflict? How can these pressures be resolved?

By the end of this chapter, you should be aware that:
➤ *development generates a rising demand for space*
➤ *competition for space creates conflicts and pressure on coastal environments*
➤ *the success of coastal developments hinges on achieving an acceptable compromise between economic benefits and environmental costs*

Figure 20.1 Development and its consequences

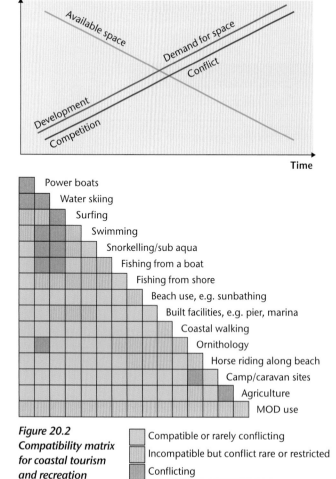

Figure 20.2 Compatibility matrix for coastal tourism and recreation

Development and use of the coast

Development is about exploiting resources. We often forget that land itself is a resource, but its supply can be increased artificially by reclamation. Until demand begins to exceed supply, the competition for land is usually resolved by sharing out land among competing users. Those who can pay most end up occupying the sites that suit them best.

Activities such as tourism, heavy industry, agriculture and fishing typically compete for coastal space. The expansion of these and other activities is likely to adversely affect both wildlife and the scenic appeal of stretches of coastline. Competition for land often results in conflict. The compatibility matrix (Figure 20.2) shows the conflicts that occur just within the coastal leisure, recreation and tourism sector.

Competition and conflict also occur in the offshore zone. This is illustrated by the key stakeholders in the sheltered waters of Lyme Bay, Dorset (Figure 20.3).

Stakeholders

Key concept

Stakeholders are individuals, groups or organisations that have an interest in the development or outcomes of a particular project. They may be involved financially or emotionally.

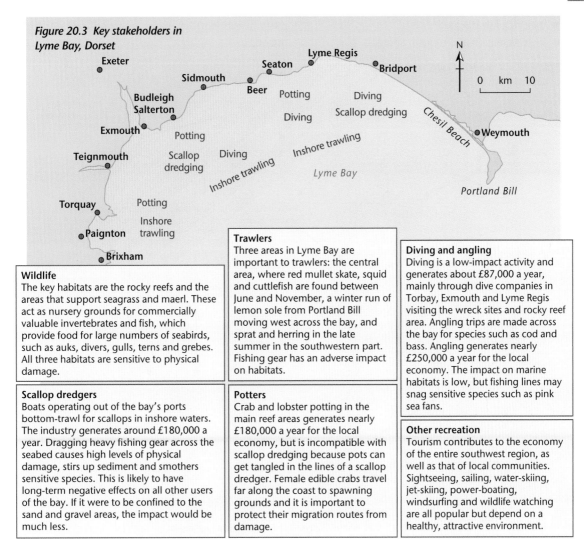

Figure 20.3 Key stakeholders in Lyme Bay, Dorset

Wildlife
The key habitats are the rocky reefs and the areas that support seagrass and maerl. These act as nursery grounds for commercially valuable invertebrates and fish, which provide food for large numbers of seabirds, such as auks, divers, gulls, terns and grebes. All three habitats are sensitive to physical damage.

Scallop dredgers
Boats operating out of the bay's ports bottom-trawl for scallops in inshore waters. The industry generates around £180,000 a year. Dragging heavy fishing gear across the seabed causes high levels of physical damage, stirs up sediment and smothers sensitive species. This is likely to have long-term negative effects on all other users of the bay. If it were to be confined to the sand and gravel areas, the impact would be much less.

Trawlers
Three areas in Lyme Bay are important to trawlers: the central area, where red mullet skate, squid and cuttlefish are found between June and November, a winter run of lemon sole from Portland Bill moving west across the bay, and sprat and herring in the late summer in the southwestern part. Fishing gear has an adverse impact on habitats.

Potters
Crab and lobster potting in the main reef areas generates nearly £180,000 a year for the local economy, but is incompatible with scallop dredging because pots can get tangled in the lines of a scallop dredger. Female edible crabs travel far along the coast to spawning grounds and it is important to protect their migration routes from damage.

Diving and angling
Diving is a low-impact activity and generates about £87,000 a year, mainly through dive companies in Torbay, Exmouth and Lyme Regis visiting the wreck sites and rocky reef area. Angling trips are made across the bay for species such as cod and bass. Angling generates nearly £250,000 a year for the local economy. The impact on marine habitats is low, but fishing lines may snag sensitive species such as pink sea fans.

Other recreation
Tourism contributes to the economy of the entire southwest region, as well as that of local communities. Sightseeing, sailing, water-skiing, jet-skiing, power-boating, windsurfing and wildlife watching are all popular but depend on a healthy, attractive environment.

Pressure on coastal environments

The intensity of the demand for coastal space puts particular pressure on the natural environment. There are at least three habitats or ecosystems that are becoming seriously degraded: coral reefs, mangroves and salt marshes.

Case study **Coral reefs**

Coral reefs are structures produced by living organisms. They are found in shallow, tropical marine waters, and support a great variety of animal and plant life. The value of coral reefs lies in:

■ their biodiversity
■ the protection they afford to low-lying coasts
■ their rich fish stocks
■ their recreation and tourism appeal

Coral is a living thing and is highly sensitive to changes in temperature and water quality. Reefs are easily stressed by a variety of human actions, and if the stress persists, decline leading to death soon sets in (Figure 20.4). Reefs are under threat from pollution, overfishing and ocean acidification. In some parts of the world they are quarried for building material.

Figure 20.4 A model of coral reef decline

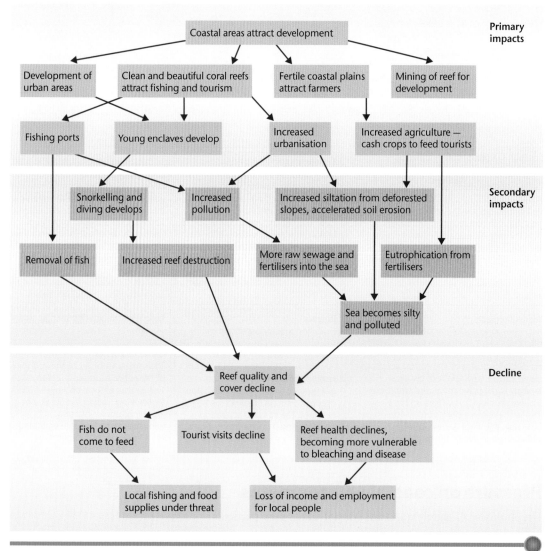

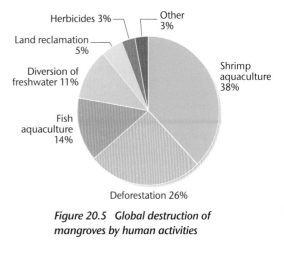

Case study   Mangroves

Mark Boulton/Ardea.com

Photograph 20.1 Mangroves on the Kenyan coast

Mangroves are trees and shrubs that grow in saline coastal habitats in the tropics and subtropics. They are vital nurseries for fish and crustaceans, and are rich in wildlife. Mangrove roots, which are exposed at low tide, trap silt and help to create new land. Mangrove timber provides fuel and building material. But perhaps the greatest value of mangroves in this age of rising sea levels is the protection from storm surges they give to low-lying coastal areas. The World Conservation Union (IUCN) compared the death toll from two villages in Sri Lanka that were hit by the 2004 Asian tsunami. Two people died in the settlement with dense mangrove and scrub forest, while up to 6,000 people died in the village without similar vegetation.

The popular perception of mangrove swamps is that they are disease-ridden. They are being cleared at a great rate to provide first timber, then sites for tourist resorts and shrimp aquaculture (Figure 20.5).

Herbicides 3%
Other 3%
Land reclamation 5%
Diversion of freshwater 11%
Shrimp aquaculture 38%
Fish aquaculture 14%
Deforestation 26%

Figure 20.5 Global destruction of mangroves by human activities

Further research

www.ejfoundation.org/pdf/tsunami_report.pdf

Coral reefs and mangroves are worth protecting for economic reasons. A recent United Nations report calculates the value of reefs and mangroves to fishing, tourism and coast protection. Their value varies between different regions but the report finds that overall reefs are worth between $100,000 and $600,000 km^{-2} yr^{-1}, rising to more than $1 million in parts of southeast Asia, where reef-based fisheries alone generate incomes of £2.5 billion annually. Mangroves can be even more valuable, with their worth to Thailand estimated at $3.5 million km^{-2}.

Case study   Salt marshes

Salt marshes are found along low coasts where boggy ground is flooded by sea water either daily or less frequently. Many UK salt marshes have been reclaimed for farm land, but those that remain provide valuable habitats where salt-tolerant plants grow and birds nest. In addition to their biodiversity, salt marshes play a vital role in coastal protection. Their meandering creeks, which allow tidal waters to flow in and out, reduce tidal energy. Marsh plants reduce wave energy. But salt marshes are among the most threatened ecosystems today. Specific threats include:
- reclamation — due to the perception that marshes are wasted space and can be drained for development
- industrial pollution — particularly of water, as

many marshes occur in estuaries which are hotspots of human activity
- agricultural pollution — leading to eutrophication
- shipping and pleasure boating, which cause 'wash' that leads to die-back of marsh vegetation
- pressure from developments such as marinas and recreational facilities

Salt marshes are also threatened by changes associated with global warming:
- the increasing frequency of high-impact storms
- changing temperature and rainfall regimes that can affect the tolerance of marsh plants
- sea-level rises that are occurring too quickly for the marsh ecosystem to adjust

One way of relieving the pressure on coastal space is to create land by draining wetlands, as described in the case study above, and reclaiming land from inshore waters and coastal lagoons. Such artificial land can be created relatively cheaply but not without environmental costs, as shown by the case study of Tokyo Bay.

Land reclamation   *Key concept*

Land reclamation is any process by which land can be substantially improved or made available for some use. Processes include:
- the treatment of derelict land
- drainage of land temporarily waterlogged by seasonal flooding
- drainage of lakes or shallow parts of the sea floor

In the last instance, an inshore area is enclosed by an embankment and the enclosure filled by rubble and rubbish or by material pumped from the sea bed.

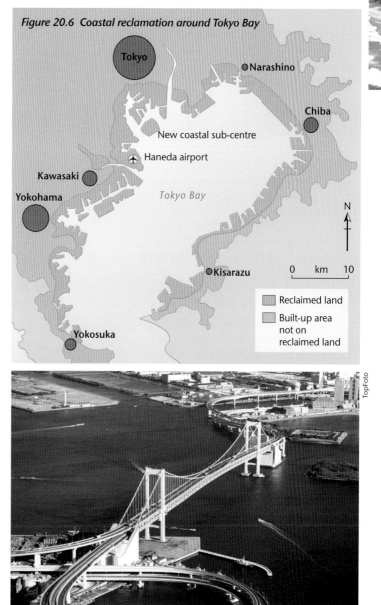

Case study   Land reclamation around Tokyo Bay

Around 75% of Japan's land surface is mountainous and unsuitable for settlement. Usable land is fragmented, occurring in small, detached coastal lowlands.

Until the twentieth century, wetland reclamation was undertaken mainly to provide land for agriculture. During the twentieth century, the prime motivators were urbanisation and industrial development. Between 1950 and the oil crisis of 1973, an estimated 110,000 hectares of new land were created around Tokyo Bay. This was to provide space for Tokyo and the other cities which make up the huge metropolitan area that now accommodates over 25 million people. The land was used for new port installations, heavy industrial developments such as oil refineries and steelworks, housing, commercial services, airport expansion (as at Haneda airport) and physical infrastructure in the form of sewage treatment works and electricity generating stations.

Since the mid-1970s, the scale of land reclamation has declined. The reasons include:

■ a slowdown in the rate of economic growth
■ pollution of water caused by the landfill used in some of the reclamation work
■ the discovery that during strong earthquakes, reclaimed land loses its load-bearing capacity
■ the vulnerability of low-lying ground to tsunamis in an era of rising sea levels

Figure 20.6 Coastal reclamation around Tokyo Bay

New coastal sub-centre

Haneda airport

Tokyo Bay

Tokyo

○Narashino

Chiba

Kawasaki

Yokohama

●Kisarazu

Yokosuka

N

0   km   10

▨ Reclaimed land
▨ Built-up area not on reclaimed land

Photograph 20.2 Much of the land around Tokyo Bay is reclaimed

■ environmental concern that the lost mudflat habitat and its wildlife should be restored
■ making the waterfront a place of leisure and recreation rather than development

Unit 2 Geographical investigations

Pollution

In this section, you are encouraged to explore two forms of coastal zone pollution, using fieldwork to look at one and research the other.

Beach pollution

Litter is a common form of beach pollution. It comes from two sources:

- It is left by beach visitors.
- It is deposited by high tides, having been carried from other beaches or dropped by passing boats.

A fieldwork project might involve comparing a number of beaches that differ in their accessibility to the general public. At each beach, collect the litter on, say, a 25 m stretch. Quantify your collected rubbish using the classification set out in Table 20.1. Compare the findings at each beach with the analysis in Table 20.1. Suggest reasons for any differences between your beaches. Such a project might be extended by repeating the exercise at a different time of the year.

It is possible to devise *beach quality surveys*, which record the size, natural beauty, safety, degree of sand, service provision etc. of a beach.

Further research

If you are interested in the quality of the beaches in your region, visit the websites of the Blue Flag and Quality Coast awards: www.blueflag.org and www.qcaguide.co.uk (download pdf). These will allow you to compare the beaches of different coastal resorts, as well as to compare resort and rural beaches. In addition to litter (also visit www.encams.org), you might wish to undertake an environmental enquiry to explore visual, noise and light pollution along the coast. If so, visit the following for some ideas: www.construction awards.co.uk/swingometer/vispol.php

Table 20.1 Top 20 litter items found during Beachwatch 2006 survey

Rank	Item	% of total litter	Items km^{-1}
1	Plastic pieces 1–50 cm	13.2	262.5
2	Cotton bud sticks	8.6	172.0
3	Plastic pieces < 1 cm	6.2	122.8
4	Crisp/sweet/lolly wrappers	5.6	110.9
5	Polystyrene pieces	5.5	108.6
6	Plastic caps/lids	5.4	108.4
7	Rope	4.3	85.3
8	Cigarette stubs	4.2	84.1
9	Plastic drinks bottles	3.9	76.7
10	Fishing net < 50 cm	3.3	65.4
11	Glass pieces	2.8	56.0
12	Cloth pieces/string	2.5	50.4
13	Fishing line	2.5	49.0
14	Metal drink cans	2.2	44.5
15	Plastic bags	2.0	39.9
16	Paper pieces	1.8	36.7
17	Cutlery/trays/straws	1.6	31.8
18	Rubber pieces < 50 cm	1.2	24.7
19	Foam/sponge	1.2	24.6
20	Metal pieces	1.1	22.8
	Total	**79.3**	**1,577.1**

Source: Marine Conservation Society

www.cpre.org.uk/campaigns/landscape/tranquillity
www.cpre.org.uk/campaigns/landscape/light-pollution

Impacts of aquaculture

Aquaculture seems an obvious way of increasing the world's food supply. However, the open net cage fish farms used in inshore and estuarine waters can discharge significant amounts of wastewater containing nutrients, chemicals and pharmaceuticals that impact on the environment and its wildlife. There is a need to balance these environmental risks against the benefits of aquaculture. Start your construction of the case for and against the spread of aquaculture in coastal waters by looking at the following websites:

www.panda.org/about_wwf/what_we_do/marine/

Photograph 20.3 A fish farm in El Salvador

problems/aquaculture/pollution/index.cfm
www.netregs.gov.uk/netregs/resources/278006/1238846/
www.york.ac.uk/depts/eeem/gsp/mem/issues/
aquaculture.htm
www.scotland.gov.uk/Publications/2007/03/29102058/5
www.onefish.org

Bear in mind two important questions:

■ Is the pollution threat of fish farms only to do with water?
■ Does coastal aquaculture do much to improve the food security of the poor?

Fieldwork and research

Destruction of high-value coastal areas

It is impossible to protect all coastal areas against development. Conservation needs to be targeted at 'high-value areas'.

Criteria to identify such areas include:

■ the presence of endemic species (i.e. plants and animals that are only found in this area)
■ the biodiversity of the area
■ its aesthetic value (its scenic beauty)
■ its amenity value as a place of recreation
■ its vulnerability to human impacts

For an appropriate fieldwork exercise:

■ Select two coastal areas which you think are of high value — a pristine one and a degraded one in need of management. They might be a sand dune, a salt marsh or a scenic area.

■ Take each of the last four criteria listed above in turn, and score your areas on a scale of 0 (no value) to 5 (great value).
■ Identify the ways in which your areas are threatened by human activities.
■ Try to evaluate the degree of environmental damage.
■ Compare your scores and other findings.
■ Find out what protection, if any, is afforded to your areas. For example, are they Sites of Special Scientific Interest (SSSIs)?

Interview stakeholders in your chosen areas. What do they want from the areas? What do they see as the main challenges facing those areas? Possible stakeholders are shown in Figure 20.7.

Economic
• Tourist industry   • Transport providers
• Fishing industry   • Port authorities
• Farmers   • Mineral industry

Political
• National and local • DEFRA
  government   • Landowners
• EU

Social
• Residents   • Health and
• Visitors   safety
• Special interest   • Museums
  groups   • Educationalists

Environmental
• English Nature   • Archaeological
• RSPB   NGOs
• Wildlife trusts   • Greenpeace
• National Trust

Figure 20.7 Some possible stakeholders in coastal Britain

Economic benefits versus environmental costs

Development brings economic benefits but has costs, particularly environmental impacts. In the UK and other developed countries there is a requirement to prepare an environmental impact assessment (EIA) before many proposals are given the go-ahead. The EIA aims to identify, predict and evaluate the significant effects of a development on the environment.

Case study Development costs and benefits: Dibden Bay, UK

Southampton, on the English south coast, is one of the country's leading ports, dealing mainly with containerised cargo and cruise-ship passengers (Figure 20.8). It is the UK's second busiest container port. The container-handling business has been booming in the UK for many years. Around 2000, it became clear that the country's container port capacity needed to be expanded or expected new business might be lost to mainland European ports, such Hamburg, Rotterdam and Le Havre.

Associated British Ports (ABP), the owner of Southampton's docks, had no room for expansion on the Southampton side of the Test estuary. However, a large area of land had been reclaimed for the purposes of port expansion on the opposite shore during the 1950s and 1960s. ABP submitted an application to build a new container terminal on this land at Dibden Bay.

Once the proposal was made public, various interest groups voiced their opposi-tion. The proposal was examined at a public inquiry, which lasted from November 2001 to December 2002. In April 2004, the transport minister upheld the inspector's recommendation that the new container terminal should not be given the go-ahead. The minister said: 'One important factor in

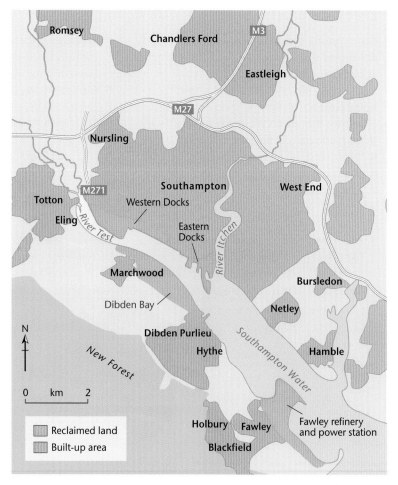

Figure 20.8 Dibden Bay and Southampton Water

Table 20.2 Stakeholders in the Dibden Bay proposal

Proponents of the project	Opponents of the project
Economic stakeholders	**Environmental stakeholders**
Associated British Ports, Southampton City Council, Confederation of British Industry, Transport and General Workers' Union.	Council for National Parks, English Nature and RSPB.
Reasons for support	*Reasons for objection*
• National need for more container-handling capacity.	• Threat to designated environmental areas.
• Southampton well placed for transatlantic container traffic.	• Dredging would be necessary to accommodate the super-container ships — more environmental damage.
• More jobs both during the construction phase and when port fully operational.	• Risk of oil spills.
• Increased efficiency of the port, using new container stacking techniques and new faster cranes.	• Proximity to the New Forest National Park.
	• Habitat loss.
	• Visual impact on landscape.
• Beneficial knock-on effects in linked port activities and marine industries.	**Local stakeholders**
• More money in local economy — good for a range of businesses and services in and around Southampton.	Hampshire County Council, local parish councils, local residents and New Forest District Council.
	Reasons for objection
	• Traffic congestion due to 50% increase in associated road traffic.
	• Transport links inadequate given that majority of container cargo business would be north of Birmingham.
	• Urbanisation of a rural area.
	• Adverse impact on quality of life for local residents — air, noise, water and light pollution.
	• Port expansion better in east coast ports with closer links to mainland Europe.

the making of this decision was the environmental impact on internationally protected sites.'

It seems odd that an area of reclaimed land, made up of sand, gravel and mud dredged from Southampton Water, could, in less than 40 years, become an internationally important site for wildlife. It is even stranger that no organisation objected to the initial reclamation of Dibden Bay in the 1950s and 1960s. At that time the mudflats of the bay were an important feeding area for migrant wetland birds.

To find the real reasons for the objection it helps to look at the proposal through the eyes of the proponents and opponents (Table 20.2).

The most telling argument made at the public inquiry did not concern the adverse environmental impacts. Rather it was that Southampton was not a strong candidate for a large-scale expansion of its container port. It was not well located on either the landward side (relatively poor transport links with the UK's main urban areas) or the seaward side (relatively far from the heartland of Europe). It is significant that since the minister made his decision, container port expansions have been approved for Thamesport, Felixstowe and Harwich — all east coast ports better located for trade with continental Europe. All three ports are owned by one company — Hutchison Port Holdings.

So in the case of Dibden Bay, it was not simply a matter of balancing economic benefits against environmental costs. *Economic costs* were also thrown into the equation, as well as arguments in favour of rival ports. Both helped to tip the balance against ABP. The company was unable to make a sufficiently strong case and lost out to a rival major port stakeholder.

Review questions

1 Explain how and why development increases pressure on coastal land.
2 Of the three coastal habitats illustrated in the section 'Pressure on coastal environments' (pp. 221–224), which do you think is the most threatened? Give your reasons.
3 a What is land reclamation?
   b Outline its costs and benefits in coastal areas.
4 a What is meant by the term 'stakeholder'?
   b Identify the stakeholders in a named coastal area that you know at first hand.
5 Examine the lessons to be learnt from the proposed container port at Dibden Bay.

Increasing risks

How is coastal development increasingly at risk from and vulnerable to physical processes?

By the end of this chapter, you should have:

➤ *understood that rising sea levels are increasing the risks of erosion and flooding in coastal areas*

➤ *become aware of the havoc that tsunamis and storm surges can cause along the coast*

➤ *grasped the scale and impacts of both coastal retreat and coastal flooding*

The devastating Asian tsunami of 2004 (see case study below) reminded the world that:

➤ The majority of the world's population lives in low-lying coastal areas.

➤ A significant proportion of those densely populated coastal areas are exposed to the tsunamis generated by earthquakes.

➤ The impact of storm surges is expected to worsen as a result of the rise in sea level due to global warming.

➤ The rise in level is global. Therefore, all coastal areas may expect higher rates of coastal erosion and a higher risk of flooding.

➤ The continuing concentration of settlement and development in coastal areas will make all the above problems even more serious and challenging.

Case study | **The 2004 Asian tsunami**

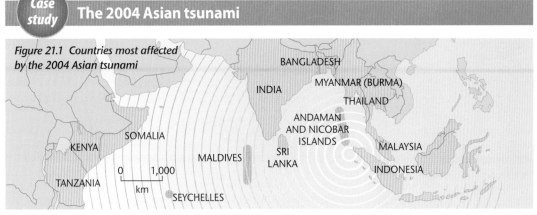

Figure 21.1 Countries most affected by the 2004 Asian tsunami

On 26 December 2004, an earthquake occurred under the Indian Ocean. Its epicentre was off the west coast of Sumatra, Indonesia. It triggered a series of devastating tsunamis along the coasts of most countries bordering the Indian Ocean (Figure 21.1). It killed around 280,000 people and inundated coastal communities across south and southeast Asia, including parts of Indonesia, Sri Lanka, India and Thailand. Hundreds of thousands of people were made homeless; settlements and their infrastructures were literally washed away. This was the ninth deadliest natural disaster in modern history.

The plight of the countries hit by the tsunami prompted a widespread humanitarian response. The worldwide community donated more than $7 billion in aid to those affected. No one has yet been able to put a cost to the total physical damage caused by the tsunami. However, the affected countries have come to realise the impact the event had on the mental health of those who survived. Aid programmes may quickly reconstruct homes, schools and hospitals, but rebuilding the shattered lives and minds of the people who lost friends, family, homes and livelihoods will take much longer. The World Health Organization estimates that 50% of the survivors may have problems and that between 5 and 10% have serious mental problems requiring treatment. Another survey found a 40% incidence of post-traumatic stress disorder in children affected by the tsunami.

Further research

www.tsunami2004.net

Increasing risk of coastal erosion

Coastal erosion is quite normal, and in most places it is unspectacular (Figure 21.2). However, there are some stretches of coastline which are eroding at alarming speeds. The cartoon in Figure 21.3 gives clues about the reasons for the disappearance of California's beaches. Essentially, as outputs increase and inputs decrease, the beach shore disappears.

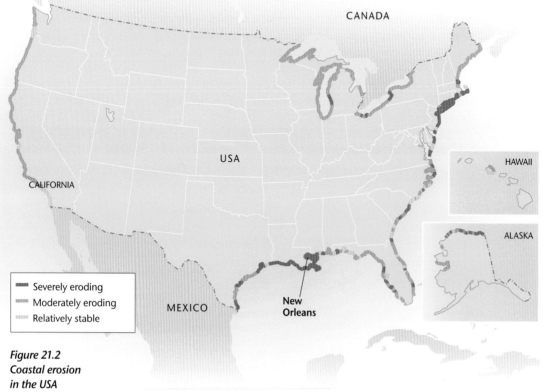

Figure 21.2
Coastal erosion
in the USA

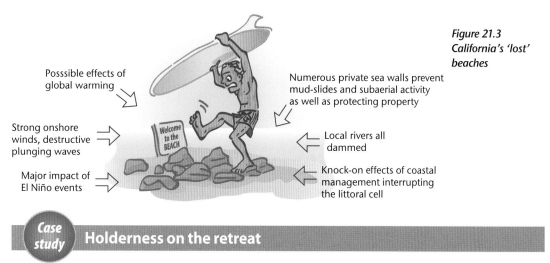

Figure 21.3 California's 'lost' beaches

Possible effects of global warming

Strong onshore winds, destructive plunging waves

Major impact of El Niño events

Welcome to the BEACH

Numerous private sea walls prevent mud-slides and subaerial activity as well as protecting property

Local rivers all dammed

Knock-on effects of coastal management interrupting the littoral cell

Case study **Holderness on the retreat**

Holderness on the northeast coast of England has the dubious distinction of suffering the fastest rate of coastal erosion in Europe (Figure 21.4). The coastline is mainly cliffs between 20 and 30 m high. They are made up soft, easily eroded glacial sands, gravels and boulder clay, and are currently retreating at a rate of more than 1 m per year — occasionally up to 10 m per year. Since Roman times, the coastline has been pushed back some 4 km. Many villages and much farmland have been lost to the sea. This area suffered badly in the 1953 storm surge (see the next case study).

The coast is very exposed, particularly to waves approaching from the northeast (Figure 21.5). This is

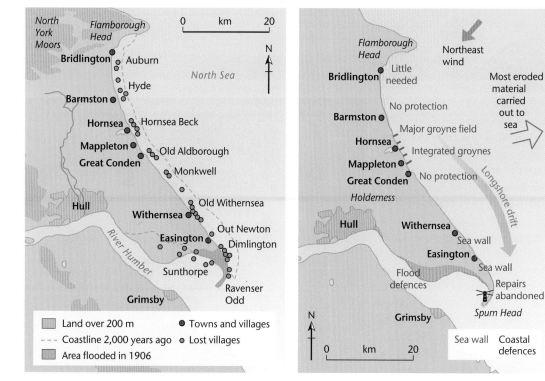

Figure 21.4 Retreat of the Holderness coast

Figure 21.5 Processes along the Holderness coast

the direction of longest fetch, which means that the waves are powerfully destructive. The cliffs are readily eroded by such waves. Much of the eroded cliff material is carried back out to sea and so does little to help protect the coastline. Some, however, is carried southwards by longshore drift and provides nourishment for Spurn Head, a spit at the entrance to the Humber estuary.

The prospects for the Holderness coast are bleak, particularly since a rising sea level is almost certain to accelerate the already alarming rate of coastal retreat. Attempts have been made to protect the coastline (Figure 21.5), but it is a losing battle. Given the costs of protection and the forces of nature, it looks as if coastal managers in the area will have to resign themselves to retreat of the coast.

Increasing risk of coastal flooding

There is a distinction between the gradual rolling back of a coastline by erosion and the breaching of a low-lying coastline by occasional, abnormally high sea levels. Although sea-level rise is an important influence on coastal flood risk, storm surges continue to pose the greatest threat. Storm surges are caused by low air pressure, which raises the height of the sea, combined with onshore winds. Shallow waters, as on the continental shelf, magnify these effects. In the case of the North Sea, its shape produces a funnelling effect, concentrating the surge in a decreasing area. The most extreme storm surges occur when the conditions just outlined coincide with high seasonal tides. Significant storm surges causing widespread damage and disruption along the east coast of England occurred eight times during the twentieth century. The most infamous of these was in 1953.

Case study — The 1953 east coast storm surge

On 31 January and 1 February 1953, weather and tidal conditions combined to produce an extreme storm surge, resulting in the worst natural disaster in northern Europe in 200 years (Photograph 21.1). A government inquiry into the causes of the floods identified that coastal defences were breached in 1,200 different places along the 1,600 km of the east coast of England. In total, 307 people died, 647 km² of land were flooded and 24,000 houses were damaged, of which 500 were totally destroyed. Around 200 industrial facilities were also damaged by flood water.

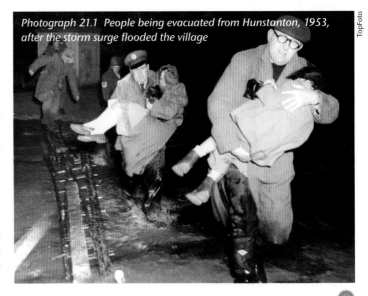

Photograph 21.1 People being evacuated from Hunstanton, 1953, after the storm surge flooded the village

TopFoto

The flooding caused by storm surges and tsunamis is occasional or periodic. However, there are some stretches of coastline where the risk of flooding is both sustained and increasing, as the case study on Venice explains.

Case study Venice

High water, or *acqua alta*, has been a persistent phenomenon throughout Venice's history. Over the centuries, the city has dealt with rising sea levels either by demolishing old buildings and erecting new ones on higher foundations made of impermeable stone, or by raising the entrances to buildings that line the dozens of canals. But Venice has an amazing architectural and cultural heritage and today, city leaders preserve historic buildings rather than rebuilding them.

When the city was founded 1,500 years ago, the Adriatic's standard sea level was almost 2 m below what it is today. All this time, the city has been slowly sinking. This has resulted mainly from the natural settling of lagoon sediments and the pumping of freshwater from a deep aquifer beneath the city. However, the rise in sea level, caused by global warming, promises still more trouble. Some experts believe that the continuous accumulation of silt in the lagoon is also helping to raise water levels. Others say the extraction of methane gas in the sea off Venice is undermining the islands on which Venice stands and contributing to the sinking. Today, Venice suffers some flooding on 200 days every year, compared with only 7 at the beginning of the twentieth century.

Further research

What can be done about this drowning of the city? Three proposals have been put forward. Visit the following websites to find out more:

www.pbs.org/wgbh/nova/venice/siege.html

www.guardian.co.uk/italy/story/0,,1838678,00.html

http://news.bbc.co.uk/1/hi/world/europe/4458910.stm

Case study Cotonou: a port city with a bleak future

Cotonou is the capital of Benin and, with a population in excess of 1 million, it is one of the largest cities in west Africa. It is on a narrow strip of land between the Atlantic Ocean and Lake Nokoué (Figure 21.6). A channel linking the lagoon to the sea runs through the middle of the city. A comparison of a map of 1963 and an aerial photograph taken in 1987 shows that the shoreline of eastern Cotonou retreated by 400 m in those 24 years, with a total loss of 112 hectares of land.

According to simulations based on increased temperature, sea level along this stretch of coast is expected

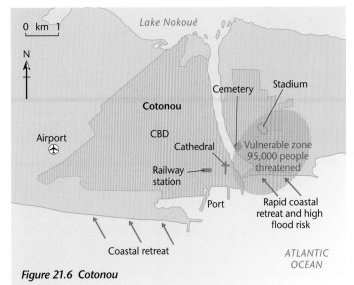

Figure 21.6 Cotonou

to continue to rise between now and 2050. Table 21.1 shows three possible scenarios for sea-level rise — 'basic', 'average' and 'extreme'. Figure 21.7 shows the expected impacts of the inevitable rise. Not only is part of Cotonou threatened, but the impacts on ecosystems will have serious consequences for the local population. Many impacts are already evident. These include the loss of fishermen's camps and a holiday village, poorer public health and increased soil salinisation.

What can a poor developing country, such as Benin, do to ensure the survival of its leading city? The short answer is 'little', unless there is help from outside agencies. The construction of groynes to stabilise the coastline may offer the city a breathing space, but will simply transfer the erosion problem further along the coast. Even then, it is estimated that another 195 hectares of land would be lost over the next 20 years. The following measures are being introduced to protect the health of Cotonou's residents:

■ using impregnated mosquito nets to protect against malaria
■ ensuring wider vaccination against tsetse fly
■ desalinising water for drinking purposes
■ recycling rainwater

The longer-term option is to disperse Cotonou and move key installations, such as the airport, factories, hotels and communications, to safer plateau areas. This option will require considerable financial investment, as well as technical assistance and the political will to make such radical changes.

Source: Based on *Environment and Urbanization*, Vol. 19, No. 1 (2007), pp. 65–79

Table 21.1 Forecasts of the rise in sea level at Cotonou

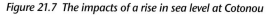

Timeframe	Sea-level rise (cm)	
	Year 2050	Year 2100
Basic scenario	7	20
Average scenario	20	49
Extreme scenario	39	59

Figure 21.7 The impacts of a rise in sea level at Cotonou

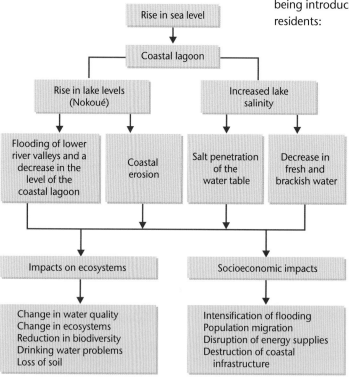

It is interesting to compare the likely futures of Venice and Cotonou. It would be ironic if the poor city of Cotonou were to survive by a pragmatic dispersal of its population and main activities, while the rich city of Venice and its priceless treasures were to perish because of indecision about the best course of action and a lack of finance. Closer to home, the issue of coastal flooding is becoming more pressing, as the case study on the Thames estuary shows.

The Thames estuary

Nowhere in the UK is coastal flood risk of more concern than in the Thames estuary. The Thames has a long history of flooding. Tide levels are steadily increasing, owing to a combination of factors. These include higher mean sea levels, more storms, increasing tide amplitude, the tilting of the British Isles (with the southeastern corner tipping downwards) and the settling of London on its bed of clay.

Tide levels are rising in the Thames estuary relative to the land by about 60 cm per century. Surge tides are a particular threat and occur under certain meteorological conditions. When a trough of low pressure moves across the Atlantic towards the British Isles, the sea beneath it rises above the normal level, thus creating a 'hump' of water, which moves eastwards with the depression.

The Thames Barrage (completed in 1984) was an important step in reducing the flood risk and protecting central London. However, with the Thames Gateway proposal to allow more development along the shores of the estuary (Figure 21.8), the flood risk issue once more comes to the fore. Can we afford to take the risk, bearing in mind the potentially large loss of life and property?

Further research

www.greenwich2000.com/info/tourism/barrier.htm
www.environment-agency.gov.uk/regions/thames/323150/335688/341764/
www.thamesweb.com/topic.php?topic_name=Flood%20Defence
www.thamesgateway.gov.uk

Figure 21.8 The Thames Gateway proposal

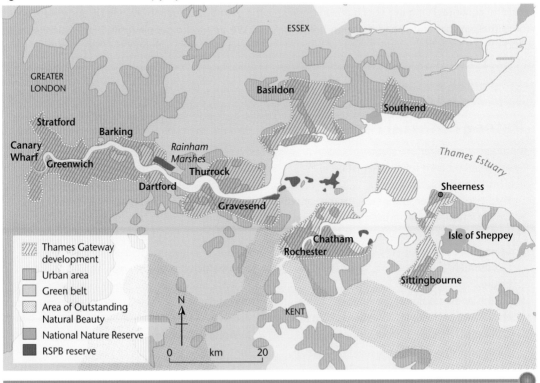

Finally, the case study of Grand Isle illustrates some worrying attitudes to risk.

Case study   **Grand Isle, Louisiana**

With 10 km of beaches, great fishing and a small-town atmosphere, Grand Isle in the Mississippi delta near New Orleans is the ideal refuge for people seeking a second home or a break from city life. In October 2005, Hurricane Katrina caused enormous wind damage and flooding around the shores of the Gulf of Mexico (Photograph 21.2). Within 2 years, however, Grand Isle was up and running again, thanks to aid and government help.

Photograph 21.2 A house devastated by Hurricane Katrina

For those who study coastal development, Grand Isle is a symbol not of hope, but of government folly. The island is regularly hit by storms, yet federal subsidies for coastal defence, housing and insurance continue to pour in. The US government is paying for people to continue living in risk-rich environments. Would the sensible and cheaper option not be to abandon such areas?

In the USA coastal areas now house 50% more people than in 1970. These coastal areas are also getting richer. The wealth of the 177 coastal counties in the USA is increasing by 4% per year. This means that even more expensive property is being built in the path of destruction. As one US engineer has put it: 'We are paying people to live in the hit zone....Did Katrina teach us anything?'

Fieldwork and research

Rates of coastal retreat

It is possible to undertake studies of coastline recession rates based on a combination of fieldwork and archival research.

Field evidence of coastal retreat can be varied:

- On the foreshore: the remains of old buildings and wartime defence installations; recently fallen debris at the base of cliffs; signs of active cliff slumping, undercutting, weakness and failure.
- On the landward side of the coastline: roads and field boundaries literally running out to sea; abandoned buildings; eroded cliff-top pathways. Refer to old maps: www.old-maps.co.uk.

Plot this evidence on a reasonably large-scale Ordnance Survey map — say, 1:25,000.

Archival research involves:

- Comparing the coastlines of maps drawn at different times. These are likely to be found in local museums and libraries or in your county record office. Plot the past coastline on the map which contains your field evidence. Knowing the dates of the various reconstructed coastlines, you should be able to work out an average rate of coastal retreat (metres per year).
- Analysing old photographs and newspapers. Photographs may be found in the same archives as the maps above. Old local newspapers might tell you about incidents or times when retreat was obviously occurring.

Coastal flooding

The issue of coastal flooding is best pursued by research into specific flood incidents. Among relatively recent UK coastal flood events, the following two are quite well documented.

East coast storm surge (1953)

www.metoffice.gov.uk/corporate/pressoffice/anniversary/floods1953.html

www.thamesweb.com/page.php?page_id=59&topic_id=9

http://www.environment-agency.gov.uk/subjects/flood/826674/882909/426221/426886/?lang=_e

Towyn (north Wales) floods (1990)

www.ngfl-cymru.org.uk/vtc/towyn_flood/eng/

www.conwy.gov.uk/section.asp?cat=4559

www.bbc.co.uk/wales/walesonair/database/towynfloods.shtml

http://web.anglia.ac.uk/geography/dsp/dividing-the-community.doc

Elsewhere in the world, none surpasses the scale and horror of the 2004 Asian tsunami in Aceh.

Aceh (Indonesia) (2004)

http://news.bbc.co.uk/1/hi/in_depth/world/2004/asia_quake_disaster/default.stm

www.asiantsunamivideos.com

www.tsunami2004.net

You might include interviews with local residents who remember particular flood events. YouTube may have video clips which document both UK and overseas coastal floods.

You can also carry out coastal flood risk mapping to see how existing land use is affected by flood risk and to work out who needs flood defences against the rising sea levels.

The following headings might provide a suitable framework for investigating one or more such incidents:

- vulnerability
- causes
- scale of impact — area affected
- scale of impact — damage
- duration
- lessons learnt

Review questions

1 *Either* outline the factors affecting the rate of coastal erosion *or* examine the factors causing widespread coastal flooding.

2 Distinguish between a *tsunami* and a *storm surge*.

3 Which do you think poses the greater threat in the UK — coastal erosion or coastal flooding? Give your reasons.

Coastal management

How is coastal management adapting to new ideas and situations?

By the end of this chapter, you should have:
➤ *understood the nature of, and difference between, hard and soft engineering coastal management techniques*
➤ *become aware of the challenges of coastal defence and coastal management*
➤ *learned about more recent approaches to coastal management*

Over the last 150 years or so, people have taken steps to protect 'valued' parts of the coastal zone from erosion and flooding. Much concrete, rock and timber has been used in the belief that these materials might be able to win the endless battle against the sea. All the management strategies used so far in this battle have involved either 'hard' or 'soft' engineering.

Hard-engineering management

Hard engineering involves building some type of sea defence, usually from rocks or concrete. It aims to protect the coast from erosion and the risk of flooding by working against the forces of nature. Figure 22.1 illustrates some of the techniques used at the foot of cliffs and on beaches. Table 22.1 gives more information and summarises their strength and weaknesses.

Hard engineering as a whole has several disadvantages:
➤ Structures can be expensive to build and maintain (to repair a sea wall can cost up to £3,000 per metre).

Figure 22.1
Examples of hard coastal engineering

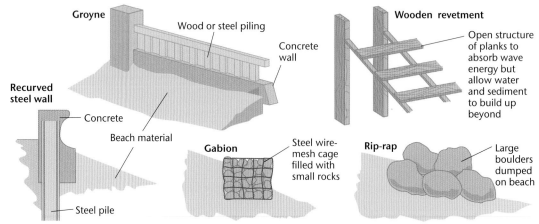

Table 22.1 Coastal hard-engineering techniques

Cliff-foot and beach strategies

Technique	Nature and purpose	Strengths	Weaknesses
Breakwaters offshore	Deflect and reduce the power of waves before they reach the shore.	Can be built from waste materials; mimic the protective nature of reefs.	Deflect waves along new paths, which may cause scouring of foundations or erosion else-where. Ecological impacts. Less effective on a large scale.
Embankments	Built from unconsolidated material (e.g. clay) above the spring mean high-tide level. Aim is to prevent sea from flooding low-lying areas.	Simple, relatively cheap and often quite effective.	**Coastal squeeze** reduces the width of, and protection provided by, salt marsh on the landward side.
Gabions	Smaller rocks than in revetments, held in metal cages (1 m cubes). May be stacked to build walls.	Have some of the strengths of the two techniques above, but cheaper.	Lightweight, small-scale solution. Metal cage may fail, spilling contents. If stacked, they can move during storms.
Groynes	Wooden or rock barriers, running perpendicular to the shore, trap beach material being moved by longshore drift.	Low capital cost and easily repaired.	Likely to interfere with sediment budget, causing deficit or even starvation downdrift.
Revetments	Massive sloping ramps across the beach to take the full force of wave energy. Made of rocks, concrete or timber. Large air spaces absorb wave energy.	As sea walls but cheaper to construct and less at risk of undermining.	Do not cope well with powerful storm waves. May damage foreshore ecosystems.
Rip-rap (rock armour)	Large rocks placed at foot of sea walls or cliffs, permeable and able to absorb wave energy.	Effective, cheaper than revetments. Can look natural.	May shift in heavy storm conditions or be under-scoured by backwash. Expensive.
Sea walls	Massive, made of concrete. Recurved version increasingly used to reflect rather than absorb wave energy. Used to inhibit erosion and protect against flooding.	Reasonably effective. Used to protect valuable or high-risk property.	Foundations can be undermined on beaches or where there is strong long-shore drift. Expensive to build and maintain.

Cliff-face strategies

Technique	Nature and purpose	Strengths	Weaknesses
Cliff drainage	Removal of water from rock strata by inserting piping reduces the risk of landslides and slumping.	Cost-effective.	Insertion of drains can weaken the cliff. Does nothing to pre-vent rock falls from dry cliffs.
Cliff fixing	Iron or steel bars driven into the cliff face to stabilise it and absorb wave energy.	Simple and reason-ably cheap.	Only suitable for some types of rock. Does not prevent wave erosion.
Cliff regrading	The cliff angle is lowered to reduce chances of collapse.	Works well on clay cliffs.	Retreat of the cliff line so uses up large areas of land.

➤ Defence in one place can have serious consequences for a nearby stretch of coastline, particularly in a downdrift direction.

➤ Defence structures cannot keep pace with rising sea levels.

➤ Structures can detract from the natural beauty of a coastline.

Table 22.2 Coastal soft-engineering techniques

Technique	Nature and purpose	Strengths	Weaknesses
Beach nourishment	Sand pumped from seabed to replace eroded beach.	'Natural'-looking process.	Expensive and never-ending. May have adverse ecological impacts.
Beach re-profiling	Shape of beach changed to reduce the effects of erosion.	Relatively cheap and simple.	Only works in low-energy environments.
Dune regeneration	Wooden structures erected to encourage sand deposition. Vegetation planted.	Effective if managed properly.	Only succeeds if public access controlled.
Developing natural defences of coral reefs and mangroves	Provide defence against erosion, storm surges and flooding.	Environmentally friendly.	Can prevent development.
Offshore reefs	Mining waste or old tyres fastened together and sunk. Act like wave 'speed bumps'.	Relatively cost-effective and low technology. Can be semi-natural.	Largely untested, but may have pollution implications.

Soft-engineering management

Soft engineering makes use of natural systems, such as beaches, sand dunes and salt marshes, to help with coastal defence. The advantage of these systems is that they can absorb and adjust to wave and tidal energy. Soft engineering techniques have been developed more recently than hard engineering and give the coastline a more natural appearance (Table 22.2).

Soft-engineering strategies are generally less expensive than hard-engineering ones but can involve a loss of property and land. The public tend to perceive them as giving up or taking the easy route.

The main task in coastal management is to decide whether the major coastal threat is erosion or flooding. In developing a shoreline management plan four broad options then become available:

➤ **Do nothing** — monitor the situation and let nature take its course.
➤ **Retreat the line** — pull back, setting up a new line further inland (see case study opposite of Abbotts Hall Farm).
➤ **Hold the line** — maintain or enhance the present line of coastal defence (see case study opposite of Blackpool).
➤ **Advance the line** — a rare decision to build forward of the present position.

'Do nothing' is cost effective and allows time for research to find new solutions, but is unpopular with local people and can lead to problems later. Managed retreat is also cost-effective — compensating people for loss of land is cheaper than defences in rural areas

Key terms

Advance the line A strategy to move the defence of an area seaward of its existing position.

Do nothing Carry out no coastal defence activity except for safety measures.

Hold the line A strategy to continue to hold the line of defence where it is.

Retreat the line A strategy to encourage the movement of the shoreline landward of its present position in a managed or controlled manner, hence the term 'managed retreat'.

— but leads to public protest and is again unpopular. In the final analysis, all management strategies should be judged on the basis of three simple criteria:

➤ feasibility — technically from an engineering viewpoint and in the light of a sound understanding of the coastal system
➤ cost-effectiveness — best tested by cost–benefit analysis
➤ appropriateness — best determined by environmental impact and risk assessments

 Case study **Blackpool: holding the line**

The Fylde section of the Lancashire coast contains a number of seaside resorts including Blackpool. Behind the coastline, the land is low lying and flooding rather than erosion is the major issue. Instead of taking the managed retreat option, the presence of these resorts has persuaded the decision-makers to opt for a 'hold the line' strategy.

Blackpool — with its promenade, piers, tower and pleasure beaches — has used massive concrete sea walls to protect its investment in the tourist industry (Photograph 22.1). The costs of building and repairs are high. Winter storms overtop the promenade and wave scour undermines foundations. Despite the decline in tourist numbers (see case study, p. 216), the resort has recently received £62 million of funding through DEFRA to develop the central promenade. The new sea wall will be designed to deflect and absorb wave energy rather than resist it. The promenade area will be increased by 5 hectares and access to the beach will be improved. The new sea front will give better protection to 1,500 business and residential properties.

This modern hard engineering contrasts with the soft-engineering management to the south of Blackpool. Here sand dune regeneration is the favoured mode of coastal protection.

Bob Hordern

Photograph 22.1 Blackpool's old and new sea walls

Case study **Abbotts Hall Farm, Essex: beating a retreat**

Southeast England is experiencing both a eustatic rise and an isostatic sinking (see Chapter 5). Sea level is rising at a rate of about 6 mm per year. This is placing pressure on stretches of low-lying coast. Many tens of kilometres of embankments have been built over the last few centuries as protection. In Essex, about 40% of salt marshes have been lost to coastal squeeze over the last 25 years. The mudflats and salt marshes here are important feeding and nesting areas for huge numbers of wading birds. Both habitats are being eroded at a rate of 2 m per year.

At Abbotts Hall Farm on the Blackwater estuary, a managed retreat scheme was implemented in 2002.

Five breaches were made in the embankments, allowing sea water to cover some 80 hectares of arable fields (Figure 22.2). This land will revert to what it was before it was cultivated — salt marsh.

The success of this scheme has persuaded the RSPB to embark on a much larger project. This will involve returning the whole of the nearby island of Wallasea (currently 65 km² of reclaimed arable land) to an extensive mosaic of marsh, creeks and mudflats.

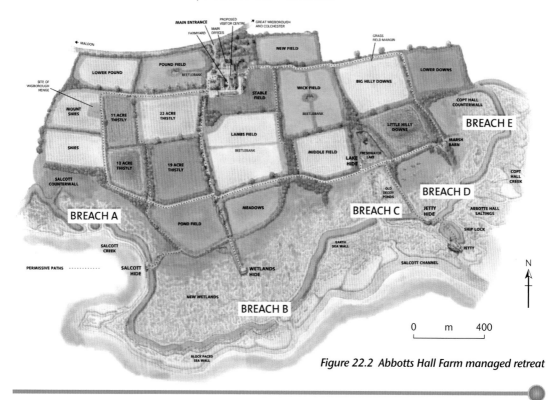

Figure 22.2 Abbotts Hall Farm managed retreat

Fieldwork and research

Assessing coastal defence schemes

Most of the UK coastline has some form of protective management. There is great scope for fieldwork surveys.

- Select a stretch of coast, say between 2 and 5 km long, which contains a range of management schemes.
- Research archive material, such as old photographs, newspapers and maps, to identify the coastal threat (erosion or flooding).
- Carry out your own survey of existing coastal protection schemes, using the following

criteria: date of implementation, cost and ease of construction, condition, effectiveness and visual impact (environment impact analysis). You might use a bipolar evaluation (Figure 22.3).

- For further information about the preparation of shoreline management plans, visit www. defra.gov.uk/environ/fcd/policy/smp.htm. Do a Google search for 'shoreline management plan' plus the name of your stretch of coastline to find out more about the local

Bipolar evaluation of coastal defences at:							

Location: .... **Type of defence:** ....

	Score						
Negative evaluation factor	**–3**	**–2**	**–1**	**1**	**2**	**3**	**Positive evaluation factor**
Vulnerable to erosion (unable to 'hold the line')							Effective protection against erosion (able to 'hold the line')
Vulnerable to overtopping (unable to control flooding)							Effective against overtopping (good flood defence)
Ugly (poor aesthetic value)							Enhances natural environment (high aesthetic value)
Poor access to beach							Good provision made for access to beach
High-risk safety hazard to general public							No obvious safety risk to general public
Short lifespan and/or high maintenance costs							Good life expectancy and/or low maintenance costs
High levels of disturbance caused to local people during construction							Low levels of disturbance caused to local people during construction
Disturbs natural coastal processes and habitats							Maintains natural coastal processes and habitats

Total score:

Figure 22.3 Booking sheet for a bipolar evaluation of coastal defences

management strategy. Is protection being given to the highest-value installations?

■ Undertake a questionnaire survey of residents and visitors to determine their awareness of: the coastal threat; the response by the authorities to that threat; the impact of the coastal defences.

■ Attempt a simple cost–benefit analysis of one or more of the schemes in your coastal strip. Compare the costs of a scheme with those that would have been incurred had the scheme not been implemented. Table 22.3 gives the approximate costs of different types of coastal protection, and Table 22.4 the criteria you might consider.

Table 22.3 Coastal protection techniques and their costs, 2006 prices

Protection technique	Approximate cost	Typical lifespan (years)
Concrete sea walls	£5,000–10,000 per metre	50–75
Earth embankments	£2,000–4,000 per metre	Variable
Revetments	£2,000–4,000 per metre	< 50
Groynes	£20,000 each	25–40
Gabions	£1,000 per metre	10–30
Rip-rap	£1,000 each rock	Short term
Beach feeding	Cheap	Short term

Table 22.4 Criteria for coastal cost–benefit analysis

Costs	Benefits
Construction of scheme	Protection of infrastructure
Ongoing maintenance	Protection of farmland/buildings
Purchase of land	Protection of tourist amenities (e.g. beaches)
Compensation	'Peace of mind' for residents
Knock-on effects	Reduced cost of emergency services

Remember that you are looking for answers to two basic questions:

■ What was the scheme meant to do?
■ Is it 'doing the business'?

Management of outstanding coastlines

Fieldwork investigating coastal management is likely to be restricted to field observation of management issues and environmental quality and visual surveys to assess why your coast is designated as outstanding. There are four important matters you need to understand:

- the need for, and value of, managing coasts
- that the management of any coast, be it high or low value, is normally shared between a range of authorities and organisations
- that there are two management 'battlefields' — between conservation and economic livelihoods and between different coastal stakeholders
- that it is difficult to assess the overall performance of most coastal management plans

Evaluating management plans really depends on your viewpoint and to whom you talk. Role-playing and interviews may help you make sense of the views of particular stakeholders. You will soon realise the potential divergence of opinion. One 'unbiased' indicator of management success might lie in the numbers of visitors to points along the coast and the distances they have travelled. These could be analysed using a questionnaire survey.

A recent survey has identified six different types of seaside visitor according to the experience they are looking for:

- quiet cups of tea
- unspoilt haven
- buckets and spades
- water play
- fun, fun, fun
- arcades and roller-coasters

You could use a questionnaire or interview survey to evaluate how well these different expectations are being satisfied along a stretch of coast. A high level of satisfaction might be taken as an indicator of successful management, as far as each particular interest group is concerned.

Further research

www.encams.org/views/ Click on *Research*, then *Beaches*, then *Beach Research 2005*.

Case study The Jurassic coast

The Jurassic coast — 155 km of coast in Dorset and east Devon — is England's only natural World Heritage site, designated in 2001 by UNESCO. The primary reasons for the designation were:

- the exposure along the coast of 185 million years of geological history
- the contribution the area has made to earth sciences, especially in its fossil beds
- remarkably varied coastal scenery

Photograph 22.2 A splendid stretch of the Jurassic coast

Kitchenham

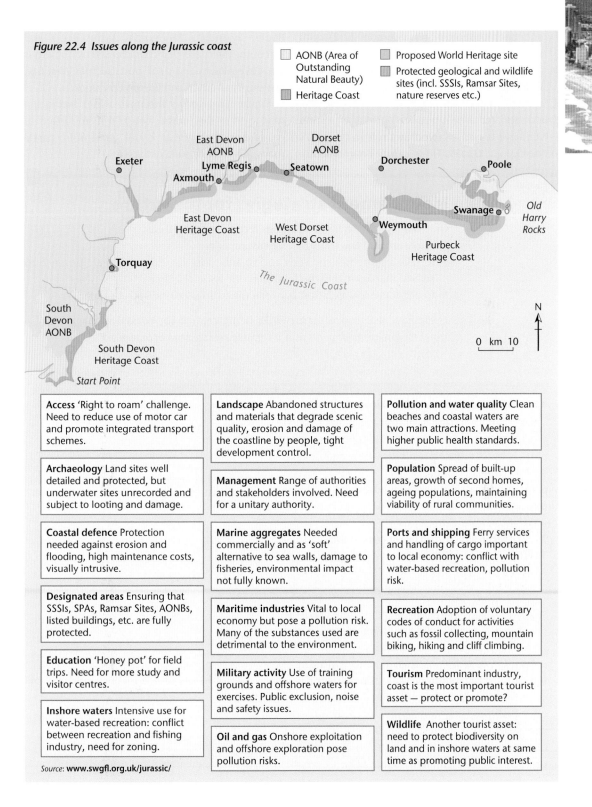

Figure 22.4 Issues along the Jurassic coast

Legend:
- ☐ AONB (Area of Outstanding Natural Beauty)
- ☐ Heritage Coast
- ☐ Proposed World Heritage site
- ☐ Protected geological and wildlife sites (incl. SSSIs, Ramsar Sites, nature reserves etc.)

Map labels: Exeter, East Devon AONB, Lyme Regis, Axmouth, East Devon Heritage Coast, Dorset AONB, Seatown, West Dorset Heritage Coast, The Jurassic Coast, Dorchester, Weymouth, Purbeck Heritage Coast, Swanage, Poole, Old Harry Rocks, Torquay, South Devon AONB, South Devon Heritage Coast, Start Point

N
0 km 10

Access 'Right to roam' challenge. Need to reduce use of motor car and promote integrated transport schemes.

Archaeology Land sites well detailed and protected, but underwater sites unrecorded and subject to looting and damage.

Coastal defence Protection needed against erosion and flooding, high maintenance costs, visually intrusive.

Designated areas Ensuring that SSSIs, SPAs, Ramsar Sites, AONBs, listed buildings, etc. are fully protected.

Education 'Honey pot' for field trips. Need for more study and visitor centres.

Inshore waters Intensive use for water-based recreation: conflict between recreation and fishing industry, need for zoning.

Source: **www.swgfl.org.uk/jurassic/**

Landscape Abandoned structures and materials that degrade scenic quality, erosion and damage of the coastline by people, tight development control.

Management Range of authorities and stakeholders involved. Need for a unitary authority.

Marine aggregates Needed commercially and as 'soft' alternative to sea walls, damage to fisheries, environmental impact not fully known.

Maritime industries Vital to local economy but pose a pollution risk. Many of the substances used are detrimental to the environment.

Military activity Use of training grounds and offshore waters for exercises. Public exclusion, noise and safety issues.

Oil and gas Onshore exploitation and offshore exploration pose pollution risks.

Pollution and water quality Clean beaches and coastal waters are two main attractions. Meeting higher public health standards.

Population Spread of built-up areas, growth of second homes, ageing populations, maintaining viability of rural communities.

Ports and shipping Ferry services and handling of cargo important to local economy: conflict with water-based recreation, pollution risk.

Recreation Adoption of voluntary codes of conduct for activities such as fossil collecting, mountain biking, hiking and cliff climbing.

Tourism Predominant industry, coast is the most important tourist asset — protect or promote?

Wildlife Another tourist asset: need to protect biodiversity on land and in inshore waters at same time as promoting public interest.

and geomorphology (Photograph 22.2) with unique features such as Chesil Bank
■ a combination of important habitats and conservation features

The designated area includes a number of resorts which have played an important role in the area's economy for 200 years. These include Bournemouth, Poole, Swanage, Weymouth, Lyme Regis and Exmouth. The coastline is characterised by numerous attractive villages and small ports such as West Bay, Seaton, Charmouth and Burton Bradstock.

Figure 22.4 shows the main issues facing the managers of the Jurassic coast. It is important to remember that these issues confront coastal managers in many parts of the world.

Management strategies for the future

New coastal management strategies recognise three needs:
➤ to ensure that the strategies are sustainable
➤ to take a more holistic view and to abandon the old piecemeal approach to coastal management which tackled one issue at a time
➤ to encourage cooperation between the various coastal stakeholders

These have led to new frameworks being created for coastal management — *shoreline management plans* and *integrated coastal zone management*.

Shoreline management plans

Key concept

The idea of **shoreline management plans** (SMPs) was first made public in 1995. The intention of the SMP is to coordinate activities between coastal authorities and address the conflicts between competing coastal interests, establishing a coastal defence strategy that:
➤ is sustainable
➤ is compatible with adjacent coastal areas
➤ takes account of natural coastal processes as well as the needs of people

For effective management, the coast is best subdivided into its sediment cells. There are 11 of these around the coast of England and Wales (Figure 22.5). Each is self-contained in terms of the movement of sediment, such as sand and shingle. Interrupting the movement of sediment within one cell should not have a significant effect on adjacent cells. Sediment cells are divided up into sub-cells and SMPs are prepared for each of these. Numerous organisations are involved in the preparation of these plans (see Figure 20.7 on p. 227).

Figure 22.5 The sediment cells of England and Wales

Integrated coastal zone management

The objective of **integrated coastal zone management** (ICZM) is to establish sustainable levels of economic and social activity in Britain's coastal areas, while at the same time protecting the coastal environment. It brings together all those stakeholders involved in the development, management and use of the coast within a framework that facilitates the inte-gration of their interests and responsibilities. This overcomes the old piecemeal approach to coastal management. It recognises that the geographical context of a coastline includes not only the cliffs, beaches, dunes, marshes and estuaries, but also the river catchments draining into coastal areas. The importance of sediment cells is recognised.

Case study The Isle of Wight

When it comes to preparing an SMP, each coastal sub-cell is divided into a number of management units (MUs). The Isle of Wight comprises seven such units. The Isle of Wight Council, like all others on the British coast, has four coastal defence options (see p. 242).

Figure 22.6 shows the distribution of the options chosen by the MUs.

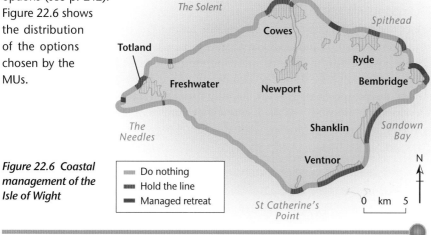

Figure 22.6 Coastal management of the Isle of Wight

- Do nothing
- Hold the line
- Managed retreat

One coastal management issue is likely to come more to the fore in the near future. As the world looks for alternative energy sources to the burning of fossil fuels, attention will turn to estuaries and their tidal power potential.

Case study The Severn barrage: to build or not

The Severn estuary has a phenomenal 12.8 m tidal range. Many proposals have been made to harness this potential power and two are now being actively discussed. One is to build a 16 km barrage between Cardiff and Weston-super-Mare (Figure 22.7). Estimated as likely to cost £15 billion and be up-and-running by 2020, it would provide clean and sustain-able energy for the next 120 years. The second scheme would involve constructing a barrage much further up the Severn estuary. It would cost one-tenth of the Cardiff–Weston proposal, but it would produce only 1.05 GW of electricity compared with 8.64 GW.

Environmentalists are supportive of any scheme that promises to deliver renewable, carbon-free energy. But Greenpeace and the RSPB point out that any barrage scheme would permanently inundate mudflats, sandbanks and salt marshes that are vital to huge numbers of wading birds and other wildlife. The green lobby finds itself in a dilemma.

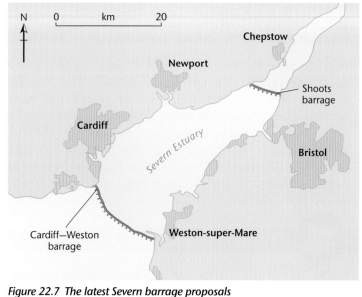

Figure 22.7 The latest Severn barrage proposals

A sustainable future?

Does the crowded coast have a sustainable future? There are limited stretches of the global coastline today where, thanks to new types of management, it may prove possible for future generations to enjoy the same coastal resources and opportunities that we do today. Equally, there are many long stretches of coast where the prospects are gloomy. Rapidly rising population numbers, relentless development pressures and the increasing dynamism of the coastline in an era of global warming are putting a sustainable future beyond reach.

Review questions

1. Illustrate the difference between hard and soft engineering in coastal protection schemes.
2. Is the appeal of soft engineering over hard simply that it is a cheaper form of coastal protection? Justify your answer.
3. Examine the case for and against allowing the coastline to retreat.
4. Outline the main arguments in favour of managing the coast.
5. Explain why sediment cells are so important in coastal management.

Unit 2
Geographical investigations

Unequal spaces

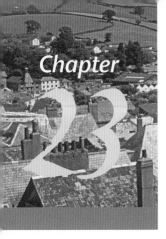

Recognising inequality

What are unequal spaces and what causes them?

By the end of this chapter you should have:
➤ *developed an awareness of the range of inequalities that exist*
➤ *used your own observations, published information and research to explore the processes that lead to different levels of inequality among people*
➤ *used a range of field-based and research sources to investigate patterns of spatial inequality*

What do we mean by inequality?

Inequality between different groups of people can be measured and thought of in different ways. Often it includes ideas about quality of life and standard of living, as well as income distribution, matters of health and access to opportunity of different kinds. Inequality is about unevenness — the 'haves' and the 'have-nots'.

Researchers split inequality into four areas:
➤ *Economic inequality* is the unequal distribution of wealth in society. This means that the things money and wealth buys are also unfairly distributed: housing, healthcare, education, career prospects, status. Access to all these things is largely dependent on wealth.
➤ *Social inequality* is about a lack of access to housing, healthcare, education, employment opportunities and status. It is the exclusion of some people from full and equal participation in what other members of the community perceive as being important.
➤ *Institutionalised inequality* is where unequal access is built into some of the social and political structures that support and maintain society. We see evidence of this kind of inequality in the workplace, the government, legislation (Acts of Parliament that become the law) and the legislature (the police and the courts system).
➤ *Technological inequality* is the idea that different people have different opportunity of access to technology, in particular communications technology such as computers and the availability of a fast internet connection.

Inequality matters

There are more rich people in the world than ever before, including around 7 million millionaires and over 400 billionaires. The UN Development Report 2006 describes a world of extremes:

The poorest 40% of the world's population account for 5% of global income, while the richest 10% account for 54%...more than 800 million people suffer from hunger and malnutrition, 1.1 billion people do not have access to clean drinking water and, every hour, 1,200 children die from preventable diseases.

Standard of living and quality of life are important concepts in this discussion (see Table 23.1).

Standard of living is about the ability to obtain goods and services, but quality of life cannot be measured simply in terms of income and wealth. On the other hand, standard of living does have an *influence* on quality of life. Higher-income households have more choice and flexibility in where and how they live. People may be disadvantaged by the place in which they live, for example if political and ethnic tensions undermine social and political stability. The processes that lead to uneven levels of quality of life and social opportunity are discussed later in this chapter.

Table 23.1
Defining standard of living and quality of life

Standard of living	Quality of life
Employment	Access to services
Income and wealth	Personal satisfaction
Number of foreign holidays	Environment
Quality and size of house	Peacefulness
Car ownership	Sense of community

Inequality at a range of scales

The global picture

Some facts about inequality at a global scale:

➤ 1.1 billion people live on less than $1 per day and 2.7 billion live on less than $2 per day.

➤ 1% of what the world spends each year on weapons would have funded primary school education for every child by 2005.

➤ The richest 50 million people in Europe and North America have the same total income as 2.7 billion poor people.

➤ The 48 poorest countries account for less than 0.4% of global exports.

➤ 20% of the population in the developed nations consumes 86% of the world's goods.

➤ 12% of the world's population uses approximately 85% of its water, and this 12% does not live in the developing world.

➤ Of the 1.9 billion children in the developing world, 1 in 3 are without adequate shelter, 1 in 5 have no access to safe water, and 1 in 7 have no access to health services (Photograph 23.1).

➤ 2.2 million children die each year because they are not immunised.

➤ Just under 1 billion people entered the twenty-first century unable to read a book or sign their names.

Photograph 23.1
School children washing their hands as part of a programme to improve health and hygiene

GlaxoSmithKline

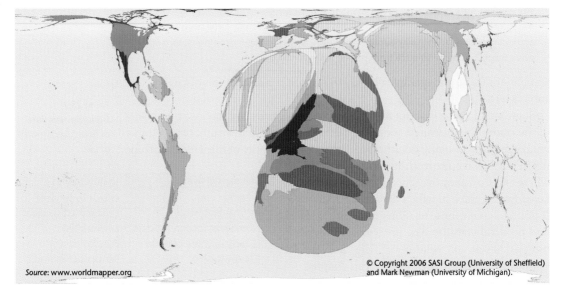

Source: www.worldmapper.org

© Copyright 2006 SASI Group (University of Sheffield) and Mark Newman (University of Michigan).

Figure 23.1
Inequality in HIV
prevalence, 2003

Figure 23.1 reveals another pattern of global inequality. The colours on the map indicate the different countries but the size of each country shows the proportion of all people aged 15–49 with HIV who were living there in 2003. The highest HIV prevalence was in Swaziland, where 38%, or almost four in every ten people aged 15–49 years, were HIV positive. All ten territories with the highest prevalence of HIV are in central and southeast Africa.

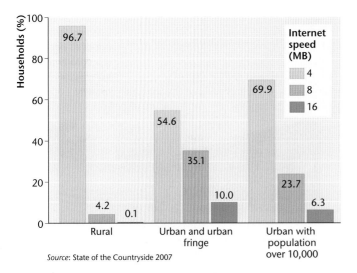

Source: State of the Countryside 2007

Figure 23.2
Differences in
internet speed in
England, 2006

Personal inequalities

Various factors may affect inequality at the level of the individual. One example relates to technology and the availability of a fast internet connection. An increasing number of services are being made available through the internet and interactive digital television, such as distance learning and online banking.

Critical to the quality and equity of the internet service is the speed of connection. As recently as 2006 there was a digital divide between rural and urban areas. Almost all areas of the UK had access to broadband, but inequalities existed in the range and speed of services. Figure 23.2 shows the differences between available broadband services in rural areas and towns in England. Remote rural areas may be able to get broadband, but the speed of that service is lagging behind that of their city counterparts.

Processes leading to inequality

Spatial inequality refers to the uneven distribution of income or other variables across different locations. A number of factors may come together to produce inequality (as shown in Figure 23.4). Three factors are especially important:

➤ access to services
➤ quality of life
➤ economic opportunity

Case study — **Spatial inequality and development in India**

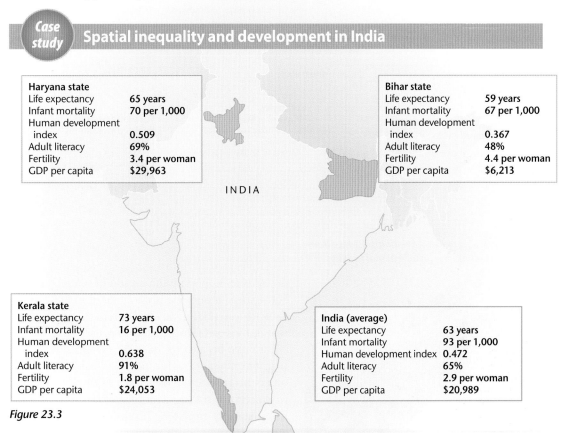

Haryana state
Life expectancy	**65 years**
Infant mortality	**70 per 1,000**
Human development index	**0.509**
Adult literacy	**69%**
Fertility	**3.4 per woman**
GDP per capita	**$29,963**

Bihar state
Life expectancy	**59 years**
Infant mortality	**67 per 1,000**
Human development index	**0.367**
Adult literacy	**48%**
Fertility	**4.4 per woman**
GDP per capita	**$6,213**

INDIA

Kerala state
Life expectancy	**73 years**
Infant mortality	**16 per 1,000**
Human development index	**0.638**
Adult literacy	**91%**
Fertility	**1.8 per woman**
GDP per capita	**$24,053**

India (average)
Life expectancy	**63 years**
Infant mortality	**93 per 1,000**
Human development index	**0.472**
Adult literacy	**65%**
Fertility	**2.9 per woman**
GDP per capita	**$20,989**

Figure 23.3

India is the world's largest democracy, with over 1 billion people, 17% of the world's population. The Indian government has halved the percentage of the population living in poverty in the last 30 years. It was down to 29% in 2000. However, 52% of people live on under $2 a day and 35% live on under $1 a day. The richest 20% of the population have 43% of the national income.

These figures mask significant inequalities *within the country* (Figure 23.3). Kerala state, for example, is often held up as an example of a commitment to development policies focused on equity and poverty reduction. As a result, people in Kerala enjoy levels of development higher even than those in wealthy states such as Haryana. In contrast, Bihar has much lower levels of life expectancy and adult literacy.

Figure 23.4
Spatial inequality

Context   Community attributes

Natural environment
Climate and weather
Air and water quality
Topography and soil
Animals and plants
Environmental
  contaminants

Built environment
Housing quality and
  affordability
Workspace
Nature of infrastructure
School
Transportation
Accessibility/remoteness

**Biological
characteristics**
Community age
  distribution
Community sex
  distribution
Genetic make-up
Ethnicity

Social
Cohesion
Influence
Network
Support
Social change

Cultural context
Norms and values
Religion
Racism and sexism
Competition and cooperation

Economic
Type and level of employment
Available technology
Income
Income distribution
Education

**Population
and spatial
inequality**

Political context
Public policies and laws
Political culture
Level of political participation

Lifestyles
Physical activity
Sexual practices
Smoking
Access to health information

**Population-based
health programmes**
Quality, availability and
  cleanliness of water supply
Quality of waste disposal
Air pollution control
Public health programmes

Photograph 23.2 Tesco at Evesham: distance from a large supermarket is an indicator of rurality

Access to services

Access is an important dimension of spatial equality. Some social groups are disadvantaged in their ability to reach essential goods and services. Disadvantage may have several causes. Some people may be disadvantaged because of the lack of services in an area (e.g. employment, education or health facilities), others because of the difficulty of getting to services (e.g. access to transport and the effects of geographical distance) and some because of social barriers and the ways in which society is structured (e.g. the effects of income, age, ethnicity, disability and social

Skills focus

In 1971 Cloke identified ten key indicators of rural life (and inequality) that could be used to categorise how 'rural' a place was. These included household amenities, population density, occupational structure and distance from the nearest urban centre of over 50,000 people.

A more modern interpretation of this index is shown in Figure 23.5. The range of indicators can be used to work out the degree of rurality of different neighbourhoods, both rural and urban. Inequality between places in terms of access to services can be assessed in this way.

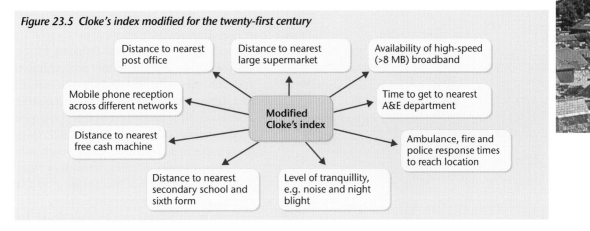

Figure 23.5 Cloke's index modified for the twenty-first century

Distance to nearest post office

Distance to nearest large supermarket

Availability of high-speed (>8 MB) broadband

Mobile phone reception across different networks

Modified Cloke's index

Time to get to nearest A&E department

Distance to nearest free cash machine

Ambulance, fire and police response times to reach location

Distance to nearest secondary school and sixth form

Level of tranquillity, e.g. noise and night blight

class). It is important to recognise that each of these conditions (availability of services, mobility and social inequality) plays a part in an individual's access to services.

Uneven levels of quality of life

Quality of life is multidimensional. In essence, it is the level of social and economic wellbeing experienced by individuals and groups, either as they perceive it or as it is identified by indicators that can be quantified.

Case study **Quality of life in Bristol**

Bristol City Council has undertaken an annual detailed survey of quality of life since 1996. Reports are available for download at www.bristol.gov. uk/ccm/content/Council-Democracy/Statistics -Census-Information/indicators-of-the-quality-of -life-in-bristol.en. The survey uses 180 indicators

divided among five key themes: a high-quality environment, a thriving economy, learning and achievement, health and wellbeing, and balanced communities. While there are significant spatial differences, recent findings also reveal gender differences (for example in health, Figure 23.6).

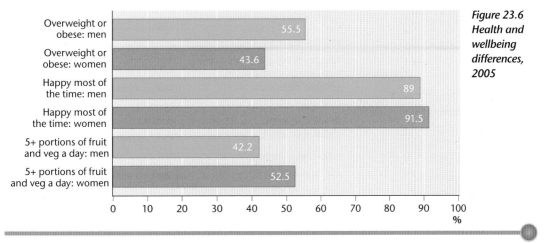

Figure 23.6 Health and wellbeing differences, 2005

	%
Overweight or obese: men	55.5
Overweight or obese: women	43.6
Happy most of the time: men	89
Happy most of the time: women	91.5
5+ portions of fruit and veg a day: men	42.2
5+ portions of fruit and veg a day: women	52.5

Unequal economic opportunity

The majority of the world's people are poor (Figure 23.7). Regional trends relating to inequality and income distribution in Latin America, sub-Saharan Africa, eastern Europe and the former Soviet Union, and east and southeast Asia indicate a marked and rising inequality between these countries and those of the developed world. The largest concentrations of poverty and underdevelopment occur in sub-Saharan Africa, south Asia and Latin America. In countries such as Niger and Sierra Leone, *not* being poor is the exception rather than the rule.

Even at a regional or city scale there are vast differences in wealth and income opportunity (see the case study on India, p. 255). The processes leading to local variation in deprivation (which is strongly linked to economic opportunity) are related to:

➤ income
➤ health deprivation
➤ employment
➤ crime
➤ education, skills and training
➤ barriers to housing and services

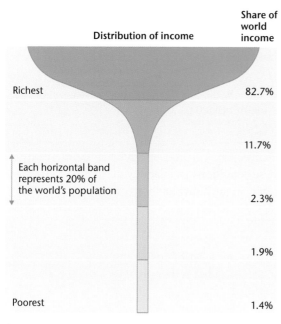

Figure 23.7 Inequality of world income distribution

Distribution of income — Share of world income

	Share of world income
Richest	82.7%
	11.7%
	2.3%
	1.9%
Poorest	1.4%

Each horizontal band represents 20% of the world's population

Fieldwork and research

Exploring patterns of spatial inequality

A range of tools and techniques can be used to explore local patterns of spatial inequality. Table 23.2 gives some examples of primary and secondary methods.

Research often generates the most interesting data and conclusions when two different types of area are contrasted, such as 'accessible' rural versus 'remote' rural locations.

Table 23.2 Primary and secondary methods of analysing spatial inequality

	Rural	Urban
Primary	Bus transport routes, time taken, frequency, etc.	Maps of accessibility, e.g. for wheelchair users in town centres.
	Village survey questionnaires, e.g. time to access shops, schools, cashpoint.	Maps of night-time facilities (zones of exclusion).
	Extended interviews with different groups, e.g. teenagers, single mothers, the elderly.	Shop diversity/cloning (see p. 324).
		Parking restrictions.
Secondary	Deprivation indices.	GIS maps of sports facilities.
	GIS health maps.	Data on deprivation.
	Google Local for the location of services.	Data on educational achievement.

Urban research

An example of an issue you can investigate is night-time exclusion from town centres. Many older people feel they cannot visit town centres at night, and use them less frequently than other groups. You can investigate patterns of use of the night-time economy using a daytime questionnaire survey. This should ask questions about age, gender and ethnicity coupled with frequency and patterns of use at different times of day and night. You can investigate how these compare with the overall age, gender and ethnicity profile for the area using census data from http://neighbourhood.statistics.gov.uk (see the skills focus below).

Additional questions can be used to establish a more detailed profile of people who use night-time facilities. You can ask questions about frequency of nights out, mode of transport, time spent, size of groups and type of venue visited. You could collect this information using a face-to-face survey or a drop-and-collect approach. Local authorities may publish maps showing pedestrian densities for selected areas at different times of day and night.

Rural research

A useful method for studying access for rural settlements is to develop a public transport index and use it to compare the status of different settlements.

For example a simple bus index can be used:

$$\text{bus index} = \text{number of routes} \times \text{daily frequency}$$

Table 23.3 shows the results for a village in Derbyshire. You can compare index numbers for different settlements as a measure of how their access to services differs.

Table 23.3 Calculating a bus index

Bus route	Daily frequency (Mon–Fri)
65	15
66	9
67	9
174	1
175	7
Totals 5	41

Bus index for this settlement = 5 × 41 = 205

Skills focus

Geo-demographic data

Geo-demographic data are pieces of information about people related to where they live. The term refers to a range of characteristics of income, lifestyle, employment — even the type of newspaper that you are likely to read!

There are a number of websites where you can obtain this type of information. It is always a good idea to read about the way in which data have been collected and manipulated. ACORN profiles (for example, at www.caci.co.uk/acorn) give detailed geo-demographic data (Figure 23.8).

Websites such as www.upmystreet.com and www.checkmyfile.com give access to this type of profiling through a postcode search. Similar data

Wealthy achievers: category 1		
Wealthy executives A	Type 1	Affluent mature professionals, large houses
	Type 2	Affluent working families with mortgages
	Type 3	Villages with wealthy commuters
	Type 4	Well-off managers, larger houses
Affluent greys B	Type 5	Older affluent professionals
	Type 6	Farming communities
	Type 7	Old people, detached homes
	Type 8	Mature couples, smaller detached homes
Flourishing families C	Type 9	Larger families, prosperous suburbs
	Type 10	Well-off working families with mortgages
	Type 11	Well-off managers, detached houses
	Type 12	Large families and houses in rural areas

Figure 23.8 Extract from an ACORN profile

Photograph 23.3 Detailed street-by-street demographic data can be obtained online

can also be viewed spatially at Dan Vickers Output Area Classification: www.casa.ucl.ac.uk/googlemaps/OAC-super-EngScotWales.html. This is an example of a basic type of geographic information system (GIS) that can be obtained from the internet.

A contrasting geo-demographic profiler is available at www.nhs.uk/healthprofile/Pages/HealthProfiler.aspx. By typing in the age, sex and postcode of a person in a particular area, their average health profile can be obtained.

Neighbourhood statistics

Neighbourhood statistics derived from census data are probably the most reliable source of information and are available for easily selected areas which are spatially small. It is important to understand the census hierarchy (see Figure 23.9).

The census allows data to be retrieved in graphical and numerical format. The website is very large and takes some getting used to, but it is an essential piece of equipment in the researcher's tool-kit. Explore the website and try to extract different types of data at different scales. http://neighbourhood.statistics.gov.uk

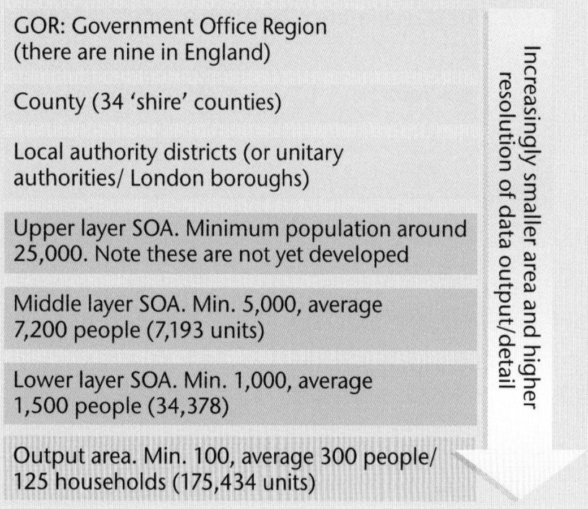

GOR: Government Office Region (there are nine in England)

County (34 'shire' counties)

Local authority districts (or unitary authorities/ London boroughs)

Upper layer SOA. Minimum population around 25,000. Note these are not yet developed

Middle layer SOA. Min. 5,000, average 7,200 people (7,193 units)

Lower layer SOA. Min. 1,000, average 1,500 people (34,378)

Output area. Min. 100, average 300 people/ 125 households (175,434 units)

Increasingly smaller area and higher resolution of data output/detail

Figure 23.9 Census hierarchy

Review questions

1 a Distinguish between the terms: 'standard of living' and 'quality of life'.
   b Give examples of spatial inequalities at a local level *and* a global scale.
2 In small groups, discuss the main causes of inequality. For rural and urban areas separately, put the causes into what you think is an appropriate rank order.
3 Discuss the advantages and disadvantages of primary and secondary fieldwork techniques that can be used to reveal patterns of spatial inequality.
4 Comment on the reliability and usefulness of geo-demographic data.

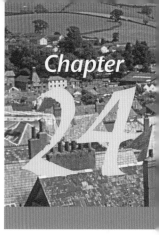

Inequality for whom?

What impact do unequal spaces have on people?

By the end of this chapter you should have:
➤ *investigated the impacts of reduced opportunities and facilities in rural and urban areas*
➤ *recognised that inequality creates marginalised groups in both urban and rural areas*
➤ *used a range of field-based and research sources to investigate the patterns of spatial inequality*
➤ *carried out an audit of a scheme to reduce inequality*

Inequality in the UK exists at a range of scales and in rural, urban and coastal districts. The highest wealth and lowest poverty rates tend to be clustered in the southeast of England (with the exception of most of inner London). Conversely, the lowest wealth and highest poverty rates are concentrated in large cities and the industrialised/deindustrialising areas of the UK. There are also smaller pockets of rural and coastal wealth and poverty.

Such inequalities have varying impacts on different members of society, yet we all have personal experience of inequality. Some researchers regard inequality as divisive and socially damaging.

Exclusion and polarisation in rural areas

In their book, *The Myth of the Rural Idyll* (1983), Fabes, Worsley and Howard stated that:

> The rural idyll conceals poverty...the poor unwittingly conspire with the more affluent to hide their poverty by denying its existence. Those values which are at the heart of the rural idyll result in the poor tolerating their material deprivation because of the priority given to those symbols of the rural idyll: the family, the work ethic and good health.

The following quotations from a DVD entitled *Rural Disadvantage: Hidden Voices*, produced in 2006, highlight the contrast between the idealised rural picture and the reality of rural life:
'It is beautiful, but we feel like we have been forgotten out here.'
'It's a lot more expensive to live out here than the city.'
'I can't see a way in which my children would be able to afford to live here.'

'There's nothing. Just the pub. That's all that's left in the village of any type of business at all.'

'The bottom line is that is that there is no well-paid work.'

Defining and classifying rural areas

Key concept

The most widely accepted classification for rural areas was devised in 2004 by the Office for National Statistics. It defines settlements of over 10,000 people as 'urban', and smaller settlements as 'rural'. Rural settlements are then divided into three categories:

➤ small town and fringe
➤ villages
➤ dispersed

In addition, settlements can be defined by whether they are in 'sparse' or 'less sparse' areas.

According to the 2001 census, approximately 9.5 million people in England (19.3% of the population) were living in rural areas, while the remaining 39.6 million (80.7%) lived in urban areas.

Around 80,000 people per year migrate into rural areas (with associated population increases), but there are clear and growing differences between the age profiles of rural and urban England, with rural areas showing more older people and a reduction in the proportion of people aged 20–35.

A number of social and economic barriers have contributed to rural inequality, as outlined in Table 24.1.

In the 1980s it was realised that the countryside was facing a jigsaw of deprivation and inequality. There were three main interrelated problems:

➤ *Household deprivation.* This relates to factors such as income and housing, and is about the hardships of individual households trying to maintain a reasonable standard of living (see case study, p. 264).
➤ *Opportunity deprivation.* This relates to the loss of particular aspects of rural life, such as jobs and services. Many rural families have to face the expense and difficulty of travelling longer distances even for basic services (see case study opposite).
➤ *Mobility inequality.* This concerns problems for some rural people in gaining access to jobs, services and facilities owing to lack of transport. Owning a car or motorbike is expensive, and is particularly difficult for low-income families.

Table 24.1 Causes of rural inequality

Social	Economic
• Out-migration of young people for better opportunities.	• Reduced access to employment opportunities. Additional costs of participating in the labour market (transport).
• The low priority given by policy-makers to exclusion in the rural UK.	• Low pay, especially in the small workplaces that dominate rural economies, and which may trap people in a lifetime of low-paid work.
• Limited access to healthcare provision (doctors, hospitals) and long travel times involved.	• The detachment from labour markets of older people in the workforce.
• Varying provision of education and limited choice. This extends to childcare provision.	• Barriers of tied housing, gang labour and seasonality in employment.

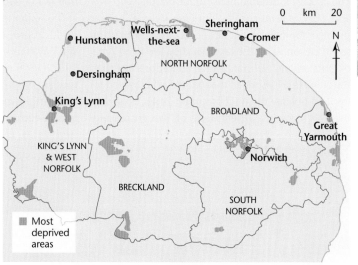

Case study   'Hidden' rural poverty in north Norfolk

Many small settlements across Norfolk are home to vulnerable groups experiencing deprivation. The principal groups affected by poverty are:

- older people living alone (predominantly older widows) and older couples, often relying solely on the state pension
- low-paid manual workers' households — rural areas contain a disproportionate number of people in low-wage sectors, notably agriculture and tourism
- those detached from labour markets, either formally unemployed or registered as long-term sick or disabled
- self-employed people — a major source of rural poverty among those of working age

Figure 24.1 Rural deprivation in Norfolk

Figure 24.1 shows hidden pockets of deprivation in Norfolk.

Skills focus

Measuring economic activity

Being out of work can have a severe impact on an individual's quality of life — in terms of both the economic implications and wider social exclusion. The impacts will be felt not only by individuals, but also by their partners and dependent children.

Task

Table 24.2 shows the level of economic activity in one rural community, Langham in north Norfolk. Describe the characteristics of the population in Langham compared to Norfolk and east of England. Use figures to support your answers.

Table 24.2 Economic activity in the population of Langham, north Norfolk

	Langham		Norfolk		East of England	
	No.	%	No.	%	No.	%
Total population aged 16–74	292	–	575,558	–	3,883,987	–
Economically active	162	55.5	377,578	65.6	2,689,563	69.2
Full-time	78	26.7	218,045	37.9	1,654,887	42.6
Part-time	24	8.2	75,989	13.2	484,731	12.5
Self-employed	52	17.8	54,404	9.5	359,110	9.2
Economically inactive	132	45.2	197,822	34.4	1,194,218	30.7
Working more than 49 hours per week	32	11.0	65,114	11.3	458,223	11.8

Case study **Lack of affordable housing, Kingsbridge, south Devon**

The lack of affordable housing for people who live and work in rural communities has been a serious problem for many years. Residents of Kingsbridge in south Devon value the fact that they live in an Area of Outstanding Natural Beauty, and appreciate that the area's qualities mean that people are attracted to live and holiday there (Photograph 24.1). However, there is growing resentment of the increasing number of people owning second or holiday homes in the settlement, who are perceived to be pushing up local property prices and limiting the housing stock available to local people.

The local economy is sustained mainly through tourism, which primarily offers low-paid and seasonal employment. As house prices go up, few local people earn enough to buy or rent one. The median household income in the local area is £20,103 (2006 data), while the average house price is £330,068.

In Kingsbridge, there is a great sense of frustration over the lack of progress on extending affordable and appropriate housing to all. Many local people feel that they have been working on possible solutions for a long time, but that they have not received enough support to implement them from the authorities who influence funding and policy.

Photograph 24.1 Kingsbridge is an attractive place

Exclusion and polarisation in urban areas

**Figure 24.2
Variation in quality of life across a typical UK city**

At one end of Canon St Road, London E1, you can pay £4 for a two-course meal.
At the other end of the street, less than 500 m away, the same £4 will buy you a small cocktail in Henry's Wine Bar.

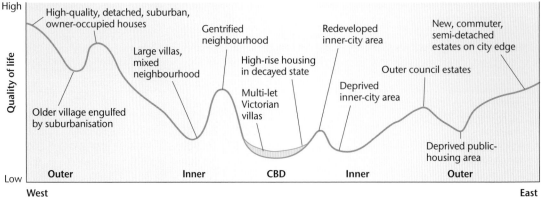

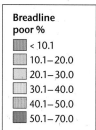

Urban areas also face challenges in terms of inequality, exclusion and segregation. Figure 24.2, for example, is an idealised cross-section showing how quality of life may vary along a transect of a city in the UK.

Patterns of inequality in cities are similar. In societies like ours based on competition, personal income is probably the single most significant indicator of inequality. Some groups of people are economically marginalised in the urban setting and suffer reduced opportunities (Figure 24.3).

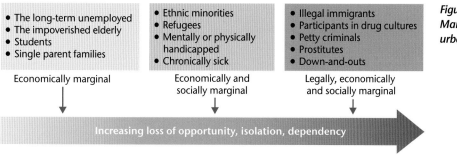

Figure 24.3 Marginalisation in urban areas

- The long-term unemployed
- The impoverished elderly
- Students
- Single parent families

Economically marginal

- Ethnic minorities
- Refugees
- Mentally or physically handicapped
- Chronically sick

Economically and socially marginal

- Illegal immigrants
- Participants in drug cultures
- Petty criminals
- Prostitutes
- Down-and-outs

Legally, economically and socially marginal

Increasing loss of opportunity, isolation, dependency

Case study   'Bull's-eye' London

The map of London (Figure 24.4) demonstrates clearly the development of an increasingly intense 'bull's-eye' effect, with 15 areas in 2000 having breadline poverty rates greater than 50%. Asset

Figure 24.4 The bull's-eye effect in London, 2000

CBD

0   km   10

Source: Joseph Rowntree Foundation (2007) *Poverty, Wealth and Place in Britain 1968 to 2005*, The Policy Press.

Breadline poor %
- < 10.1
- 10.1–20.0
- 20.1–30.0
- 30.1–40.0
- 40.1–50.0
- 50.1–70.0

wealth (property ownership) in London is clearly polarised. It ranges from 'low asset wealth' in the East End to higher levels in the west of the city where more wealthy people live.

Table 24.3 shows the degree of correlation between poverty and other census variables (2000 data), expressed as an index value. The closer the value is to 1, the stronger the association. Note how the highest levels of correlation are between poverty and unemployment, social housing and no car. Correlation values are in rank order.

Table 24.3 Correlation between poverty and selected variables in London, 2000

Factor	Degree of correlation (index)
% unemployed	0.95
% in social housing	0.94
% no car	0.93
% overcrowding	0.79
% low social class	0.77
% lone parent	0.74
% sharing amenities	0.44
% long-term illness	0.40
% private renting	0.30

Marginalised groups in the suburbs

Suburban residential areas often have a certain character and profile (Photograph 24.2). They are associated with respectability and stability. People who do not conform to these characteristics tend to be regarded as 'out of place' in the suburbs. Examples of people who may feel marginalised are transient populations, such as students, whose lifestyles and behaviour are sometimes seen as conforming to a different set of values from those of other suburban households.

Yet these 'place identities' are rarely descriptions of the truth. Such 'myths' about the character of a place can be used to justify exclusionary behaviour, as happened in Selly Oak, Birmingham. The myth about Selly Oak was that its resident population was well thought of and steady. When, in the 1990s, tensions developed between students and other residents, the newspapers held the students responsible, even though the area had a long history of transient student populations (from the University of Birmingham and nursing students from the nearby hospital). The accusation that students did not fit with the character of Selly Oak was a myth but was being used as the basis for exclusion.

Photograph 24.2 A typical suburban neighbourhood

David Holmes

The danger with simplistic notions of place identity is that they can result in exclusionary behaviour. They tend to support the conservative values associated with white, middle-class society. Groups which do not share these characteristics and values (e.g. other racial groups) tend to be treated as outsiders, and action may be taken to exclude them, even though they have a legitimate claim to inclusion.

Myth and exclusion

It is possible to do fieldwork and research into myth and exclusion. Select a nearby area, such as a neighbourhood in an urban area, town or village. Use a variety of research resources (internet blogs, interviews to find out personal histories, searches of newspaper archives, etc.) to build up a profile of myth and exclusion. Think about the following ideas:

- What is the supposed character of the area and is there evidence to suggest this is a myth in any way?

- Who or what groups are being excluded?
- Who might be doing the excluding, how and why?
- Try to consider who or what is 'included' (the norm or expected) and in turn who or what is considered inappropriate. For example, in middle-class residential areas it might be home owners versus travellers, while at the rural–urban fringe it might be landowners or farm workers versus second home owners or developers.

Skills focus

Task

Working in small groups, discuss members of society who may be disadvantaged through inequalities. These might include age, religion, health, income, ethnic background, or access to services, employment, education or transport.

Choose one of the affected groups and use the internet as a social research tool to establish the particular concerns, issues and challenges that

the chosen group may face. Search through blogs and forums for people's ideas. Pressure groups are a good source of information.

> **Tip** Other sources of information might be www.youtube.com and www.bbc.co.uk/videonation/. On these sites you can search by location and topic area.

Case study · Segregated schooling in the UK

A 2007 government report described how segregation of schools along racial lines is happening, as many towns are developing schools which are overwhelmingly white, Asian or black.

The majority of pupils in some areas of the country — particularly in deprived former mill towns in the north of England — have little contact with students from different ethnic backgrounds, even though they live in close proximity.

There are towns where social, ethnic and religious divisions are aligned, dividing the population and creating enormous tensions. Schools in these towns are becoming more and more segregated. In

Blackburn, for example, four secondary schools out of nine take more than 90% of their pupils from just one ethnic community. There are three overwhelmingly white schools: Darwen Vale High (95.5% white), Darwen Moorland High (91.6% white) and St Bede's Roman Catholic High (96.3% white). The segregation is matched on the other side of the racial divide: at Beardwood High 94.5% of pupils are Asian and just 2.5% of the school's pupils are white. Only one school in the borough reflects the ethnic mix. Separate communities are growing up alongside each other with little common point of contact and reference.

'White flight'

Key concept

The term **white flight** is used to describe the way in which some white families move area in order to be able to remove their children from schools where the intake is predominantly of Asian children. The resulting split in communities can increase segregation and racial tensions.

Fieldwork and research

Identifying the 'haves' and 'have-nots'

Quality surveys can be used to compare areas and identify the pattern of location of the 'haves' and 'have-nots'. You first need to select the areas you wish to compare — two or more contrasting rural or urban areas. You can base these on administrative or neighbourhood districts from the Office for National Statistics website (http://neighbourhood.statistics. gov.uk/).

Types of index

You next need to choose the factors you want to survey. Many different types of survey are available. Most of them involve using your own perception and assessment. Table 24.4 lists a few examples, and the criteria they use. Taking an existing published survey from a book or website and adapting it for your own use demonstrates initiative and can produce a survey of higher quality. However, you must take time to adapt the survey to your needs — lifting methods from another source or using an existing survey without thinking it through will reduce the quality of the data you collect and make

it harder to draw conclusions. See the tips in the skills focus on the next page.

Try to use numerical ranking s (e.g. bipolar scales) for ease of comparison and use more than one survey type in each area. In this way you can create an index of multiple deprivation (see key concept box on p. 269).

Table 24.4 Criteria for various survey types

Survey type	Criteria
General landscape evaluation	Based on your own 'gut feelings', e.g. boring vs stimulating, ugly vs attractive, crowded vs peaceful, threatening vs welcoming, drab vs colourful.
Scale of visual pollution	Scores from 0 to 3: no pollution to badly polluted. Criteria might include: obviousness of pollution, litter, smells, state of buildings, impact on surrounding area.
Index of ease of burgling	Based on penalty points. Absence of burglar alarm, security cameras, metal bars on windows, metal shutters, neighbourhood watch stickers, etc.
Graffiti assessment	Criteria include: size of words, size of pictures, style of writing, where visible from, method of writing (pen, paint, etc.)
Physical condition of buildings/index of decay	Criteria: deterioration of walls, peeling paint, slipped tiles, broken glass, broken gutters, etc. Range of ranking options: none, little, some, much.
Shopping survey	Quality of shops: type, other land use, quality of goods, no. of vacant shops, etc. Street appearance: safety for pedestrians, how crowded, street cleanliness, etc.

Skills focus

Tips

A range of strategies can be used to maximise the quality and value of any 'inequality' survey:

■ *Try to be as objective as possible* when devising scoring criteria. It will help if you: (a) work in a group that is mixed in terms of gender and cultural background, and (b) discuss your scoring differences and the reasons for them. 'Pre-calibrating' the scoring system can improve the quality of responses. This can be achieved in a group discussion by matching a series of photographs to scoring criteria.

■ *Use a mix of criteria* that together represent a fair way of measuring whatever you are interested in. These could cover a wide range of socioeconomic factors, such as employment, family structure, mobility and health.

■ *Criteria may be weighted* to reflect their relative importance. For example, unemployment rates have a direct bearing on levels of deprivation, so the 'weight' given to this factor should reflect its importance.

■ *Give written examples* (known as 'descriptors') for the polar values on a scale. For example, in an assessment of garden quality as part of a residential survey, if your scale is 0–5, you might describe 0 as meaning 'a neglected, overgrown rubbish tip'. If possible, do the same for the intermediate points on your scale (e.g. the descriptor for category 3 gardens might be 'reasonably maintained, not detracting from the overall environmental quality').

Complementary secondary data and information should be used to build up the portfolio of criteria that can be used to identify patterns of inequality.

Multiple deprivation index

Key concept

Indices of Deprivation (ID) were first introduced by the government in 2004. They are used to measure relative levels of deprivation in each administrative area of the UK. This should allow the government to rank areas according to need, and to ensure that the most deprived areas receive most help.

Seven different indicators of deprivation are combined to give a measure of **multiple deprivation**. Each of these indicators is itself made up of a number of different measures. The seven basic indicators are:

Income Proportion of people in the area who are deprived because they have a very low income.

Employment Proportion of people of working age who cannot work, because of unemployment, ill health or family circumstances. Unemployment is likely to lead to poverty.

Health and disability Proportion of people who die prematurely or whose quality of life is reduced because of poor health. Poor health often leads to unemployment and low income

Education, skills and training Inability of local people to get education, skills and training. Lack of education means that people are more likely to be poorly paid.

Barriers to housing and services Barriers to services include difficulty in reaching services such as shops and doctors because of their location and the lack of transport. Barriers to housing include affordability — the cost of housing being beyond the reach of local people.

Living environment This includes the 'indoors' living environment, in other words quality of housing, and the 'outdoors' living environment, for example air quality and level of road traffic accidents.

Crime The rate of recorded crime in an area including: burglary, theft, criminal damage and violence. Levels of crime tend to be higher in areas of poverty.

These indicators have since been updated by The English Indices of Deprivation 2007, downloadable at www.communities.gov.uk/communities/neighbourhoodrenewal/deprivation/deprivation07. Try looking for your local area.

Fieldwork and research

Checklist for evaluating schemes

Chapters 25 and 26 deal in detail with the difficulties of trying to evaluate schemes to tackle inequality. By way of introduction, Table 24.5 offers some initial suggestions for criteria.

Additional research can include the use of various economic measures obtained from local authority websites or the Office for National Statistics. In particular, look out for indicators such as levels of income, number of lone parent families, percentage of lone pensioners and number of people on state benefits.

Table 24.5 Criteria for evaluating schemes tackling inequality

Evidence	Qualitative	Quantitative
Social	Types and ages of cars, clothing worn (general photographic evidence). Interviews with focus groups, informal discussions.	Level of disposable incomes/purchasing power; changes in the shopping basket of local shops.
Economic	Evidence of prosperity (e.g. comparing current and historical photos).	Level of unemployment; range and type of employment (census data).
Environmental	General 'feel', cleanliness, safety of the area; general audit of place.	Litter surveys, level of biodiversity, street cleanliness.

Review questions

1 a Distinguish between exclusion and polarisation.
  b In what ways do rural and urban areas differ in terms of the outcomes of these two processes?
2 Using examples, summarise the impacts of reduced opportunities in rural and urban districts.
3 Discuss why it is difficult to evaluate schemes that tackle inequality.
4 What factors should be considered when designing a checklist to evaluate schemes to tackle inequality?

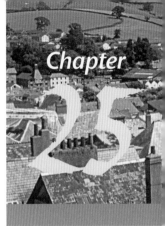

Chapter 25

Managing rural inequalities

How can we manage rural inequality and improve the lives of the rural poor? How successful have particular schemes been?

By the end of this chapter you should have:
➤ *recognised that there are serious social, economic and environmental problems and barriers that must be overcome to reduce rural inequality*
➤ *used a range of field-based and secondary research sources to investigate the success of contrasting schemes to reduce rural inequality*

Understanding the problems in rural areas

Chapter 24 outlined some of the inequalities faced by people living in rural areas, so you will already be aware that rural living is not without its problems. For many people, rural life is far from the idyllic vision portrayed in images such as Photograph 25.1. In rural areas, inequality is often hidden (Figure 25.1).

Photograph 25.1 The rural idyll

Corel

 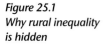
*Figure 25.1
Why rural inequality
is hidden*

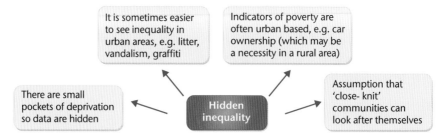

However, in recent years there have been attempts to highlight rural problems: huge media coverage of the impacts of foot and mouth outbreaks, fuel protests by farmers and Countryside Alliance marches have all raised the profile of countryside living.

Measures to manage rural inequality

People living in rural areas are not passive victims. Management of rural inequality has recently placed greater emphasis on enabling and empowering rural people to take greater control over their own lives through 'bottom-up' and sustainable development approaches that involve local people in their planning. Community development is at the heart of such approaches. Figure 25.2 illustrates some of these ideas.

Investigating access to services

Access to services continues to be an important issue for rural residents. Distances to service outlets tend to be longer than those in urban areas, and public transport provision is usually worse. The list below summaries some key ideas:

➤ The proportions of rural households that are close to key services such as banks, jobcentres and petrol stations are decreasing.
➤ Cars are essential for rural people who wish to access services. One-third of the poorest households in rural areas have two or more cars — in urban areas, the figure is less than 1 in 12.

*Figure 25.2
Measures to
manage rural
inequality*

Transport, economy and services • Encouraging local diversification and enterprise, e.g. farm diversification • Providing outreach employment • Using technology to support local home workers • Grants for transport and childcare	**Affordable housing** • Changes in housing policy and planning • Controlling the housing market (stopping affluent incomers?) • Gaining local support for new social housing projects • Encouraging inclusive communities with a mixture of housing types and prices
Tackling social exclusion • Improving pay • Integrating all people into work • Increasing benefit take-up • Improving access to further education and training • Using 'joined-up policies' at a local level	**Regeneration, partnerships and rural development** • Longer-term commitment to regeneration • Community-based partnerships and empowerment • Integration of sustainable approaches, using appropriate technology • Modification of 'top-down' agendas

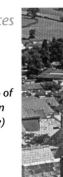

Service	Hamlet/ isolated dwelling	Village	Small town and fringe	Urban (more than 10,000 population)
Banks and building societies (4 km)	30.5	29.0	94.4	99.9
Cashpoints (all) (4 km)	59.6	67.4	99.2	100.0
Cashpoints (free) (4 km)	38.5	38.7	95.4	100.0
GP surgeries (principal sites) (4 km)	38.2	40.8	94.7	98.3
GP surgeries (all sites) (4 km)	43.8	51.2	97.1	100.0
Jobcentres (8 km)	17.3	25.2	35.7	87.0
NHS dentists (4 km)	27.4	25.9	88.5	100.0
Petrol stations (4 km)	52.8	62.2	93.5	100.0
Post offices (2 km)	45.0	74.4	99.6	99.4
Primary schools (2 km)	41.9	71.2	99.7	99.6
Public houses (2 km)	52.0	78.1	96.0	99.6
Secondary schools (4 km)	25.3	25.0	79.2	98.8
Supermarkets (4 km)	27.3	27.7	90.4	98.7

*Table 25.1
Availability of
services, 2007 (% of
households within
specified distance)*

Source: Government statistics

➤ The proportion of fee-paying cashpoints remains higher in rural areas than it is in urban areas.

➤ There are significant differences in accessibility to fast broadband for internet and e-mail. Access to broadband has improved significantly in rural areas, but it lags behind urban areas in terms of speed.

Table 25.1 shows the level of service availability across England in 2007, measured by the percentage of households that have a particular type of service outlet within a set number of kilometres. These are straight-line distances which ignore the transport network or other physical barriers such as rivers or mountains. Primary schools and post offices tend to be more widely distributed, hence the 2 km criterion, whereas jobcentres are fewer in number and therefore 8 km is used. Almost all households in urban areas have services readily available, but a much smaller proportion of those in villages and hamlets have similar provision.

Many of the differences in accessibility to services in rural areas can be explained by the availability of bus services. Hourly bus services have long been used as an indicator of a 'good' level of service (Figure 25.3).

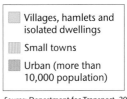

Figure 25.3 Percentage of households within 13 minutes' walk of a bus stop with a service at least once an hour, 2002–05

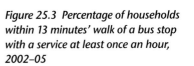

Villages, hamlets and isolated dwellings

Small towns

Urban (more than 10,000 population)

Source: Department for Transport, 2007

Public transport provision

Figure 25.4 Skipton bus service

(a) Rose diagram

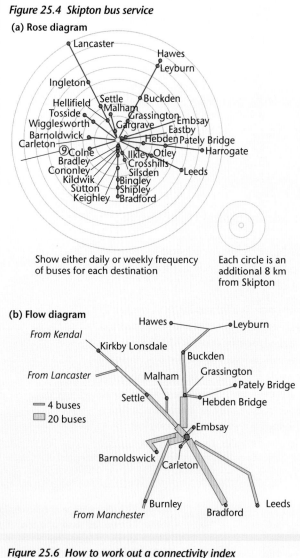

Show either daily or weekly frequency of buses for each destination

Each circle is an additional 8 km from Skipton

(b) Flow diagram

Hawes • — • Leyburn

From Kendal

Kirkby Lonsdale

Buckden

From Lancaster

Malham

Grassington

• Pately Bridge

Settle

Hebden Bridge

• Embsay

Barnoldswick

Carleton

• Leeds

Burnley

Bradford

From Manchester

— = 4 buses

▭ 20 buses

You can research public transport provision by focusing on the frequency of bus services. Figure 25.4 shows a survey of the main areas served by the Skipton bus service. Timetables and maps of bus routes (including GIS-based versions) can be found for most regions on the internet. Such research can be supplemented by questionnaire surveys to reveal how local people view the rural bus service.

Other research alternatives include calculating detour indices: 'journey time by bus' divided by 'journey time by car' (Figure 25.5) and connectivity indices (Figure 25.6). See also p. 259.

Figure 25.5 Example of a detour index

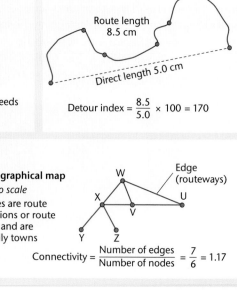

0 km 5

Route length 8.5 cm

Direct length 5.0 cm

Detour index = $\dfrac{8.5}{5.0} \times 100 = 170$

Figure 25.6 How to work out a connectivity index

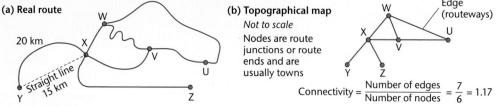

(a) Real route

20 km

Straight line 15 km

(b) Topographical map

Not to scale

Nodes are route junctions or route ends and are usually towns

Edge (routeways)

Connectivity = $\dfrac{\text{Number of edges}}{\text{Number of nodes}} = \dfrac{7}{6} = 1.17$

Case study: The Northern Fells Group

The Northern Fells Rural Project (www.northernfells-group.org/about/background/index.php) is a good example of an attempt to manage rural poverty, deprivation and inequality (see Figure 25.7). It has had a number of key project objectives:

- to pilot methods for the development of services in rural areas by using healthcare as an entry point
- to identify the unmet health and social care needs of rural residents
- to identify causes of social exclusion
- to map the provision of existing support services and identify any gaps
- to prioritise and implement actions to meet unmet needs

This was one of the Prince of Wales's three 'Rural Revival Projects'.

The Northern Fells Group took over from the Northern Fells Rural Project in November 2002. The group currently runs the following services:

- Administration, research, development and fundraising.
- Minibuses providing a flexible, accessible door-to-door service and group hire for people of any age who do not have their own transport.

- The Lend a Hand Group, which provides neighbourly support to people who are ill or less able and to their carers.
- Youth Initiative, which runs a range of activities, including cycling, first aid, babysitting, arts and sport as well as networking with local, county and national youth schemes.
- The Benefits Awareness Scheme, which assists the elderly, those with disabilities and families on low incomes.

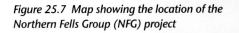

Figure 25.7 Map showing the location of the Northern Fells Group (NFG) project

Project appraisal

It is possible to take a basic local inequality profile and compare it with data from an area which has undergone some attempt to reduce inequality.

Programmes to tackle rural inequality can be assessed by asking the following:

- Are the programmes 'top-down', 'bottom-up' or 'partnership' based (see Chapter 28)?
- Are they targeted at specific geographical areas and locations? How are these areas selected?
- What are the particular aims of a programme?
- What do you think has been good or bad about particular approaches?
- What might be the impacts of a particular project in terms of improving sustainability?

Primary fieldwork opportunities may involve surveys of villages in a rural area which demonstrate contrasting solutions to the inequality issue. Such fieldwork could involve the use of video and still images to document change, or the use of recorded interviews (e.g. production of a podcast) to evaluate the positive and negative aspects of change as seen through the eyes of villagers from different settlements. Alternatively, you could find out about any focus groups that have been used to plan for particular projects. In some parts of the country, 'village hubs' have been established where a shop or pub has diversified its business (e.g. to offer internet access).

Land-use and functional surveys could also be used to record the location and type of service provision. A wide range of services, for instance, may indicate a revival in the fortunes of a place and a reduction in inequality.

Census data can be used to reveal changes in an area's demographics, as well as to contrast the levels of deprivation (http://neighbourhood. statistics.gov.uk/). The raw census data can be downloaded in the form of an Excel spreadsheet and analysed (see the skills focus box below). The typical indicators of poverty and inequality are:

- poverty rate
- child poverty rate
- unemployment rate
- percentage of people aged 18 and over with no post-school qualifications
- level of limiting long-term illness/disability rate
- percentage of households with no central heating
- percentage of households with no car

Skills focus

Spreadsheets such as Excel can be used to manage and manipulate large data sets, such as the indices of deprivation available from the Neighbourhood Statistics website. Data can be downloaded on to a spreadsheet and then analysed using a range of techniques.

Task

Download an example of a large spreadsheet and practise using the autofilter to 'filter' geographical areas and items from the data set.

Shopping basket survey

Shopping basket surveys can be used to compare the price and range of products offered by different retailers. They are a useful tool for surveying rural areas because there is a perception that smaller shops are more expensive and that they have a limited range of products. In fact, however, shops in rural centres that have undergone economic revival may stock a surprisingly large range of goods, including a choice of local produce.

Mechanisms for reducing rural inequality

Changes in farming

Attempts to revitalise farm profits have been characterised by diversification, environmental protection and intensification (see Chapter 29).

➤ What are the main kinds of activity that farmers have diversified into?

➤ Who are the activities aimed at and how is the notion of 'rurality' used to promote them?

➤ Is there a geography of diversification by region: that is, are some areas more enterprising than others?

Photograph 25.2
Farm diversification: this maize maze created by a farmer near York was first a visitor attraction and then harvested and fed to his cattle

TopFoto

Farm diversification

Visit one of the attractions of a diversified farm. If possible, carry out a visitor survey to measure patterns of usage and sphere of influence of the attraction. Try to determine through research the extent to which the scheme has provided employment opportunities and reduced rural inequality.

This idea can be extended further to look at rural sports. Over a period of 2 weeks, investigate a range of newspapers, magazines, television and radio programmes for advertising of rural sports. On a map, mark the location of each activity and add annotations regarding its setting (e.g. paintballing takes place in woodlands). Is the activity a permanent or temporary feature (e.g. the Glastonbury Festival)? What are the benefits and disadvantages of rural events and sports? Are there likely to be any conflicts between different user groups?

Figure 25.8
The Egan Wheel

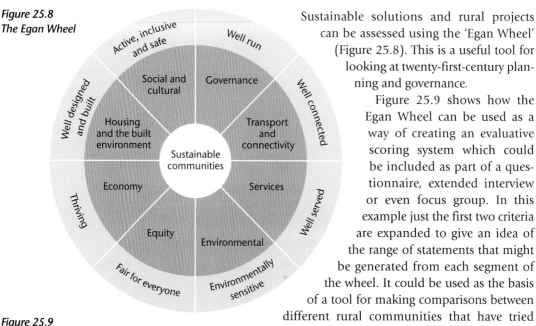

Sustainable solutions and rural projects can be assessed using the 'Egan Wheel' (Figure 25.8). This is a useful tool for looking at twenty-first-century planning and governance.

Figure 25.9 shows how the Egan Wheel can be used as a way of creating an evaluative scoring system which could be included as part of a questionnaire, extended interview or even focus group. In this example just the first two criteria are expanded to give an idea of the range of statements that might be generated from each segment of the wheel. It could be used as the basis of a tool for making comparisons between different rural communities that have tried contrasting sustainable solutions to reduce inequality.

Figure 25.9
Applying the Egan Wheel to a rural community

The website www.ruralcommunities.gov.uk provides a range of detail on innovative schemes designed to manage rural inequalities.

Name of the community/rural location _____

Is it a sustainable community?   1 = very good   6 = very poor

Ring a score for each of the following:

(1) Well run?
People are:

Included in decision making	1	2	3	4	5	6	Not included
Feel responsible	1	2	3	4	5	6	Don't care
Proud of local community	1	2	3	4	5	6	Not proud

(2) Well connected?
Getting in/out and around your community:

Excellent bus service	1	2	3	4	5	6	Non-existent bus service
Easy access to rail service	1	2	3	4	5	6	No access to rail service
Safe local walking routes	1	2	3	4	5	6	Lack of safe pathways
Safe local cycle-ways	1	2	3	4	5	6	Lack of safe local cycle-ways
Roads clear	1	2	3	4	5	6	Roads congested
Off-road parking	1	2	3	4	5	6	Parking on roads

New technology

Governments and other policy-makers at the local, national and European level see new technology and ICT as key resources for reducing inequality and improving quality of life and economic opportunity in rural areas.

Case study: Communications technology in the Highlands and Islands

Developments in communications technology (e.g. broadband and video conferencing) have been used in the remoter regions of Scotland as a regional development tool for the last 25 years. In particular, technology has been developed to tackle problems of unemployment and population loss. **Teleworking** allows people to work from home in remote locations.

There are a range of clear indicators of success:

■ ICT-led education at the UHI Millennium Institute, which is a virtual university with students based at a variety of 'academic partners' in the Highlands and Islands (see Figure 25.10)

■ the rapid growth of community-run websites utilising the area's excellent technology backbone

■ a significant increase in the number of new ICT-related jobs — estimates suggest that about 3,000 people work in this sector

However, some challenges still remain: physical remoteness, the high costs of replacing and upgrading software and equipment, difficulties in maintaining business networks and continued dependence on state subsidies.

Key term

Teleworking Working remotely using e-mail, phone and internet communication.

Further research

See www.hie.co.uk for more details on enterprise in the Highlands and Islands.

The 'Samknows' website (www.samknows.com/broadband) can be used to check the availability of high-end broadband in any UK location.

'FreeTV' (www.ukfree.tv/starthere.php) can be used to obtain maps of Freeview television coverage.

These last two are indicators of rural inequality and technology availability.

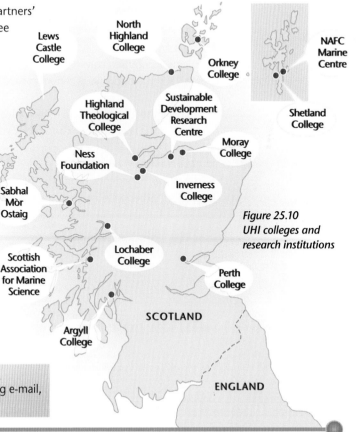

Figure 25.10 UHI colleges and research institutions

Rural employment schemes

Select a rural area and first examine its employment profile. This can be done at a variety of scales using census data supplemented by job advertisements in local papers and on websites.

- What are the dominant types of employment and what kind of work is available for local people?
- What are the levels of pay and is the work temporary or seasonal?

Rural employment schemes can be deemed successful if they tackle the problems of employment deprivation — low wages, seasonality, lack of transport, etc. You could use this type of approach to investigate rural industrial estates (use www.yell.com to locate them) with a questionnaire survey. Possible survey questions are:

- What kind of business is it?
- How many people does the business employ?
- What is the proportion of full-time to part-time, men and women?
- What are the strengths and weaknesses of the local workforce?
- If this is a new business start-up, how is it financed?

Review questions

1 Devise a simple table to illustrate the social, economic and environmental problems facing *rural* communities.
2 Figure 25.2 sets out ways of reducing rural inequalities. Giving your reasons, state
  a which of the four boxes you think is most important.
  b which of the ways in your chosen box you think is most important.
3 What are the challenges and opportunities for new high-tech businesses that locate in remote rural areas?
4 How can the 'experience economy' (businesses that offer customers such as tourists an 'experience') help in the reduction of rural inequalities?

Managing urban inequalities

What strategies can be used to combat urban inequality? How successful have particular schemes been?

By the end of this chapter you should have:
- ➤ *recognised that there are serious social, economic and environmental problems and barriers that must be overcome to reduce urban inequality*
- ➤ *learned that there are certain key players involved in the delivery of solutions*
- ➤ *used a range of field-based and secondary research sources to investigate the success of contrasting schemes to reduce urban inequality*

Understanding the problems in the urban zone

Social, economic and environmental inequalities occur in all urban areas, and enormous contrasts of wealth, opportunity and deprivation can be found over quite small distances. By carrying out fieldwork and research, it is possible to determine whether a neighbourhood is 'desirable' or not, and whether it is improving or deteriorating.

The wealthy and the poor tend to concentrate in different places. There are a number of reasons for this:
- ➤ *Housing.* Developers and builders tend to build housing on parcels of land with a particular market in mind. Wealthier groups, with their income flexibility, can choose where they live. This is often away from poorer areas.
- ➤ *Changes over time.* Many houses that were built for large middle-class families about 150 years ago have now been converted into multi-occupancy dwellings. Often these are privately rented to people on low incomes. At the same time, former poor areas are being 'infiltrated' by richer people who buy up cheaper housing stock and improve it. This process of 'gentrification' means that there is less affordable housing available in an area.
- ➤ *New migrants.* Migrant groups come to the host country in search of economic opportunity. However, low and unskilled migrant workers may only be able to find low-paid jobs and therefore have to live in the cheapest and lowest-quality housing. Migrants from particular countries tend to concentrate in the same place.

Causes of inequality in urban areas

In towns and cities, the quality of life varies from one area to another. Patterns of inequality develop as a result of the decisions taken by individual families in the housing market. People with more money tend to move to areas with a better

Urban deprivation

Key concept

Deprivation occurs for a number of reasons:

- *Culture of poverty* — problems arising from marginality, helplessness, dependancy and exclusion of certain groups that get trapped in poverty.
- *Institutional malfunctioning* — problems arising from failures of government planning, management or administration.
- *Uneven distribution of resources and opportunity* — some people have less access to resources, e.g. education
- *Structural class conflict* — problems arising from the divisions of labour (and power) which are part of the way a Western capitalist or market-based society works.
- *Underclass* — minority groups isolated from employment and other opportunities available to mainstream society.

quality of life; people who are less well-off can only afford to live in neighbourhoods with a poorer quality of life. In this way the pattern is reinforced.

There are social, economic and environmental elements of urban inequality, as shown in Figure 26.1. Physical features such as relief, and land uses such as transport and industry have an impact on quality of life. For example poorer neighbourhoods may be closer to polluting industry or built on steep hillsides (think of slums in developing countries). In economic and social terms wealthier people tend to live in areas with better access to shops and employment, more pleasant and healthy environments and greater provision for health and education. All of these issues are linked to factors of government and image (the dotted arrows on Figure 26.1). Government planning regulations in the UK can indirectly affect inequality. Local authorities, for example, may allow social housing in certain parts of a town or city but not in others. This impacts on the lives of people who live in, or near, clusters of social housing.

Figure 26.1 Issues in urban areas

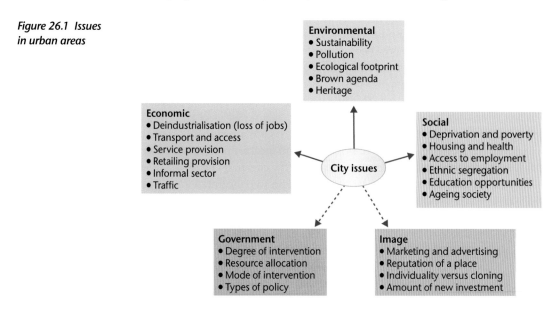

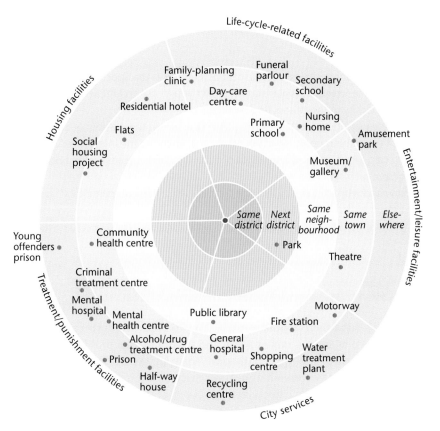

Figure 26.2
Preferred residential distance from selected public facilities

Access to services and amenities

Access to urban facilities such as parks, schools, libraries and hospitals is an important dimension of quality of life and equity. Figure 26.2 shows the preferred residential distance from different public facilities. Some social groups have less access to essential services because of:

➤ the lack of services in an area (e.g. employment, education or health facilities)
➤ the difficulty of getting to services (e.g. access to transport)
➤ social barriers and the ways in which society is structured (e.g. the effects of income, age, ethnicity, disability and social class)

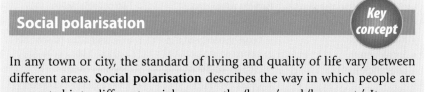

Social polarisation

Key concept

In any town or city, the standard of living and quality of life vary between different areas. **Social polarisation** describes the way in which people are segregated into different social groups: the 'haves' and 'have-nots'. It occurs because of differences in income which affect where people can afford to live and therefore what amenities and opportunities (e.g. jobs and schools) they have access to. Lack of opportunity means that inequality is perpetuated: people are unable to move into a more affluent social group.

Skills focus

Access to sporting facilities is one aspect of inequality. The Sport England Active Places website (**www.activeplaces.com**) allows you to use an interactive GIS mapping facility to locate sporting facilities.

Use the website to locate a sub-region and work out the number of facilities present (swimming pools, sports centres, etc.). Then use the interactive 'Sports facility calculator' (**www.sportengland.org/sportsfc.htm**) spreadsheet to obtain the suggested provision for a particular area.

- How and why are there differences in actual provision compared to recommended provision?
- Where should new facilities be built to reduce inequality?

The brown agenda

Key concept

Some cities (and their populations) in less developed countries are affected by the **brown agenda**, a mix of social and environmental problems brought on by rapid growth and industrialisation. There are two distinct issues:

➤ challenges of environmental health caused by limited land, shelter and services (e.g. access to clean water)

➤ problems of rapid industrialisation (e.g. hazardous waste, water and air pollution, and industrial accidents caused by poor standards of health and safety)

As might be expected, lower-income groups suffer most disadvantage from the brown agenda.

Aspects of inequality will vary from place to place. Table 26.1, for example shows components of inequality from some research carried out in Rosario, Argentina. The study found that the people of Rosario ranked access to the internet and green spaces as the most important elements in their quality of life.

Table 26.1 Components of inequality in Rosario, Argentina

Factors related to the household and its members	Factors related to the dwelling	Factors related to accessibility
• Income level • Employment • Education level	• Legal tenancy of the house and plot • Quality of the house • Overcrowding • Water connections • Electricity connections • Gas connections • Sewage connections	• Accessibility to schools • Accessibility to public health centres • Accessibility to green public spaces • Accessibility to 'new information networks' (e.g. internet)

Quality of life survey

You could use fieldwork in your local area to find out how people rate certain elements of quality of life. You can use a questionnaire survey in which you ask people to rank the importance of different factors. The results can be compiled to give an overall ranking.
In a survey of environmental inequalities in Macclesfield, the respondents ranked 'cleanliness' first, while 'dog fouling' was deemed least important (see Table 26.2).

Table 26.2 Environmental factors in Macclesfield

Rank	Factor
1	The standard of cleanliness in the borough as a whole
2	Waste recycling/composting services
3	The cleanliness of the neighbourhood
4	The cleanliness of town centres
5	Conservation of historic buildings
6	Nature conservation
7	Preservation of local heritage
8	The design of new buildings
9	Local landscapes
10	Air quality in the borough
11	Dog fouling

Key players in solving urban inequality

Management of urban inequality has a number of strands. As in rural areas, in recent years there has been greater emphasis on enabling and empowering people to take greater control over their own lives. Figure 26.3 illustrates some of the ideas intended by government and other agencies to reduce inequality.

National policies
- Reducing in inequalities in health ('postcode lottery') and education provision
- Distribution of central government funds to urban areas that are in most need
- Availability of new technologies, e.g. to support home and teleworking
- Changes to planning laws

Economic incentives
- Development of more social housing schemes combined with partnership schemes
- Tackling issues of low pay and unemployment, e.g. Pathways to Work programme
- More affordable public transport schemes, e.g. Oystercards

Partnerships and development agencies
- Role of sustainable futures, e.g. renewable waste management and partnerships
- 'Joined up' policies at the local level, using a range of agencies integrated together
- Community/residents' empowerment and involvement, especially with regeneration projects

Figure 26.3 Managing urban inequality

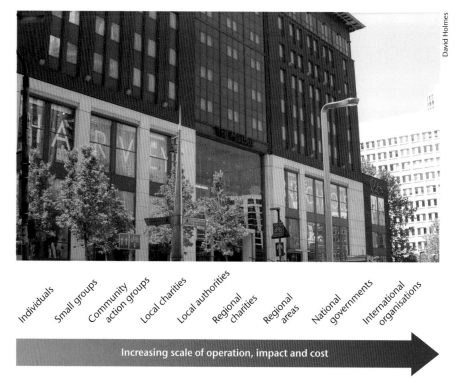

Photograph 26.1
How important is the design of new urban buildings for quality of life?

David Holmes

Figure 26.4
Urban stakeholders

Individuals | Small groups | Community action groups | Local charities | Local authorities | Regional charities | Regional areas | National governments | International organisations

→ Increasing scale of operation, impact and cost

Figure 26.4 shows the range of people, agencies and organisations involved in managing and reducing urban inequality. They may be described as stakeholders.

Different projects and partners have different approaches. Figure 26.5 demonstrates the ways in which crime, for example, can be managed and reduced at a local level through policies concerned with environmental or social issues, and aimed at individuals or groups. Policies in quadrant 1 of the diagram are environmental issues aimed at the individual whereas policies in quadrant 4, for example, are 'social' approaches which target groups rather than individuals. Notice that all the policies are positive ideas aimed at improving the living environment, education, or opportunities of individuals or groups, and thereby breaking the cycle of inequality. A reduction in inequality helps to decrease levels of crime and this in turn improves quality of life.

Figure 26.5 Policies aimed at crime prevention and community safety

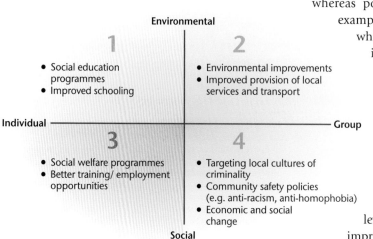

Environmental

1
• Social education programmes
• Improved schooling

2
• Environmental improvements
• Improved provision of local services and transport

Individual ──────────── Group

3
• Social welfare programmes
• Better training/ employment opportunities

4
• Targeting local cultures of criminality
• Community safety policies (e.g. anti-racism, anti-homophobia)
• Economic and social change

Social

One of the significant inequalities in many urban areas is transport. Its availability, cost and travel times are all important. See www.tom-carden.co.uk/ p5/tube_map_travel_times/applet/ for an interesting representation of the London Tube map and travel times displayed as concentric circles.

The central London congestion charging scheme introduced by the mayor of London is one mechanism for managing traffic and therefore reducing travel/access inequalities. Nearly all motorists have to pay a daily fee of £8 to enter central parts of the city, although the congestion area has grown since its initial development in 2003.

There has been great interest in the London experiment, and generally the scheme is regarded as successful. Some of the headline statistics are as follows:

- Congestion levels have been lowered by 30% in central London.
- There has been a reduction of 16% in the number vehicles on the road.
- Journey times in central London have fallen by 14%.

However, disadvantages have also been identified, such as some shops losing income and the fact that the charge unfairly hits people who are less well off and car dependent. London blogs and internet forums reveal that some people are not convinced by the scheme. Websites like these can be a useful source of evidence.

TopFoto

Photograph 26.2

Skills focus

Shanty towns in developing countries are one of the most recognisable consequences of rapid urbanisation and deprivation. The internet can be used to make a virtual visit to a shanty town of your choice — Google Earth has high-resolution imagery for some locations, such as Rio de Janeiro, Brazil.

You can also use the web to conduct a comparative research exercise about contrasting locations, such as towns and cities with and without improvement schemes. Table 26.3 could be used as a framework to investigate the degree of success or failure. The words in italics might be used as internet search terms if you enter the words 'shanty towns' at the same time.

Table 26.3
Evaluating progress
in shanty towns

Shanty towns in need of help	Shanty towns demonstrating improvement
Limited employment opportunities, high unemployment	*Mixed employment* opportunities, including some *formal work*
Poorly built housing and little ongoing improvement	*Housing improvement* through individual and group action
Poor *water supply* and sewage — infections and disease easily spread	Improvements in water supply (reliability and quality); minimises risk of disease
Limited electricity supply and dangerous illegal mains hook-ups	Legal electricity connections gradually replacing illicit supplies
Range of common *social problems*, including *crime*, prostitution and general lack of authority	*Strong social structures* and cooperation between *community and police* reduce illegal activities
Houses and environment appear untidy and poorly organised, with lots of *rubbish* present	Increasing order and tidiness of settlement; evidence of *recycling* activities in the informal economy
City authorities oppose informal settlement — residents feel insecure for fear of threat to *bulldoze*	More cooperation between residents and authorities. Small amounts of *infrastructure* being developed to support communities, e.g. schools, healthcare

Fieldwork and research

Assessing schemes to reduce urban inequalities

It is difficult to measure the success of individual schemes to reduce inequality. However, there is a range of local primary fieldwork opportunities for comparing neighbourhoods that have experienced a particular scheme and those which have not. In addition to quality of life surveys (p. 284), techniques include the following:

Photograph 26.3 Urban security camera

TopFoto

■ *Mapping the distribution and location of security cameras in an urban area* (Photograph 26.3). Why are there 'hotspots'? This can be linked to a land-use map showing the distribution of facilities that may attract 'trouble' and are open late at night (e.g. pubs, bars, late-night fast-food outlets). What might be the reasons for a limited number of cameras?
■ *Mapping the distribution of neighbourhood watch stickers and evidence of neighbourhood*

policing. Consider the use of a index of 'burglarability' (see Table 26.4).
■ *Mapping the distribution of gated communities within an urban area.* There are now more than 1,000 gated communities in England alone. It is possible to look at the evolution of such neighbourhoods over time — are they associated with either wealth or fear of crime? What areas are they found in? In urban areas they tend to be secluded

houses in the suburbs or blocks of flats in built-up districts.

■ *Conducting a survey of street cleanliness.* This may reveal something about the quality of the environment and could be used as an indicator of a scheme's success. A very basic street condition survey is shown in Table 26.5,

although more sophisticated versions are available.

■ *Investigating improvements in accessibility.* The 1995 Disability Discrimination Act gives disabled people rights in the areas of employment, education, access to goods, facilities and services, and buying or renting land or property. A range of examples of accessibility maps can be found on the internet. Table 26.6 shows the results of a survey of disabled users about car parking.

■ *Interviewing 'key players' (e.g. town centre managers, planners, local charity workers or recipients of help).* Blogs, forums and chat rooms can also provide evidence of residents' reactions to and concerns about schemes, particularly those which are controversial, such as airport expansion or new road development.

Case studies can also be drawn from further afield: for example, studies of World Health Organization initiatives. Look out for self-help schemes, traffic and public transport developments, and crime and policing initiatives.

Table 26.4 A 'burglarability index' giving points awarded for each feature

Feature	House	Retail/ commercial premises
Burglar alarm	10	10
External lighting system	5	10
Security cameras		10
Security doors with shutters		10
Security windows with shutters	5	10
Metal bars across windows	5	10
Other security design features (e.g. blocking off alleyways)		10
Security system at entrance — guard/dogs		10
Neighbourhood watch sticker	5	
Backing on to open space	−5	
Quiet street	−5	
Secluded entrance — bushes, etc.	−5	

Table 26.5 Basic street condition survey

Grade	Description of street condition
A	Absence of litter, detritus and waste
B	Small accumulations of detritus, small pieces of litter
C	Large accumulations of litter and detritus, small quantities of waste
D	Widespread accumulations of small and large pieces of litter, larger quantities of waste

Table 26.6 Car parking in the town centre: survey results for disabled users

Statement	Strongly agree	Agree	Neither agree nor disagree	Disagree	Strongly disagree
Not enough car parks in the town centre	10	10	20	50	10
Not enough disabled parking bays in the car parks	30	12	36	12	10
Disabled parking bays are poorly signed	24	46	24	5	1
Disabled parking bays are too narrow	32	32	29	6	1
Not enough lifts in the car park	5	15	55	20	5
Getting from car parks to shops is difficult	32	46	12	5	5
Not enough disabled toilets in the car parks	78	12	7	3	0

Skills focus

Deprivation is a complex and relative concept (see the key concepts box on p. 282). In 2004 a new *multiple deprivation index* (MDI) was drawn up, based on 2001 census data (see p. 269). Raw data relating to seven key indicators or 'domains' were collected and calculated for small spatial units called *super output areas* (SOAs), which contain about 100 households. There are 32,482 SOAs in England in total. Each of the domains is weighted as indicated in Table 26.7.

Table 26.7 Weightings in the multiple deprivation index

Domain	Weighting (%)
Income deprivation	22.5
Employment deprivation	22.5
Health deprivation and disability	13.5
Education, skills and training deprivation	13.5
Barriers to housing and services	9.3
Crime	9.3
Living environment deprivation	9.3

Task

Log into the Neighbourhood Statistics website (http://neighbourhood.statistics. gov.uk) and download MDI values for the SOAs of a town or city near you. Plot the values and identify the most deprived areas. Describe the overall pattern and the physical characteristics of the most deprived areas.

Review questions

1 Work in a group to discuss the range of inequalities that exist in urban areas. Which are the most important and which are the least significant?

2 Discuss the range of primary and secondary fieldwork that can be used to evaluate schemes to address urban inequality.

3 a Who are the urban stakeholders?

   b Do you agree that, as implied in Figure 26.4, the larger the stakeholder, the more influential it is? Give your reasons.

4 Make a table to identify the advantages and disadvantages of different ways of managing urban inequality.

Unit
Geographical investigations
2

Rebranding places

Chapter 27

Time to rebrand

What is rebranding and why is it needed in some places?

By the end of this chapter you should have:
➤ *investigated the different approaches towards rebranding and reimaging*
➤ *understood why rebranding is necessary in some places*
➤ *used a range of research tools to investigate the profile of areas in need of rebranding*

Key terms

Rebranding Developing a place to reposition its image and change people's idea of it, helping to 'sell' the place to a target audience.

Regenerating Positively transforming the economy of a place that has displayed symptoms of decline.

Reimaging Positively changing the standing and reputation of a place through specific improvements, e.g. increasing cultural identity or sporting excellence.

Regeneration, **rebranding** and **reimaging** of places has become increasingly prominent on government agendas in recent years, particularly in areas that have experienced significant economic or industrial decline. There has been some confusion about defining ideas and processes, but the idea of 'remaking' and 'improvement' is central.

The process of renewing places is costly and often involves the physical redevelopment of worn-out or outmoded facilities. But rebranding and reimaging mean more than making cosmetic improvements to the appearance of a place. They are also concerned with its reputation, spirit and identity. How people regard a particular place, both as internal users (residents) and as external customers (visitors and tourists), is important to its future and affects quality of life.

At the heart of any rebranding exercise, there is:
➤ an *environmental* focus — to improve derelict infrastructure and the quality of the environment
➤ a *social* focus — to overcome the spiral of decline and deprivation (Figure 27.1) and the cycle of poverty
➤ an *economic* focus — to improve job opportunities and bring income to the area
➤ a *political* dimension — to raise money for projects through the 'bid industry', which is necessary for successful rebranding

The need to rebrand

Rebranding may be required in a variety of locations: urban areas (both central zones and residential districts), former coal mining or industrial regions, parts of the countryside and coastal areas.

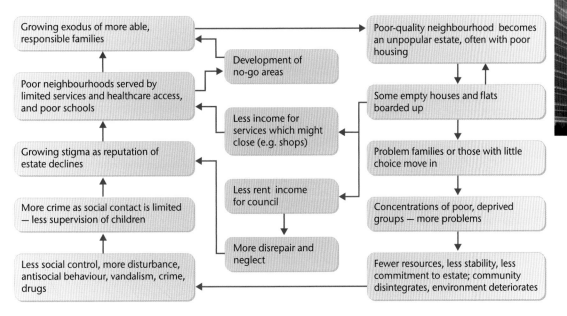

Growing exodus of more able, responsible families			Poor-quality neighbourhood becomes an unpopular estate, often with poor housing	
	Development of no-go areas			
Poor neighbourhoods served by limited services and healthcare access, and poor schools			Some empty houses and flats boarded up	
	Less income for services which might close (e.g. shops)			
Growing stigma as reputation of estate declines			Problem families or those with little choice move in	
	Less rent income for council			
More crime as social contact is limited — less supervision of children			Concentrations of poor, deprived groups — more problems	
	More disrepair and neglect			
Less social control, more disturbance, antisocial behaviour, vandalism, crime, drugs			Fewer resources, less stability, less commitment to estate; community disintegrates, environment deteriorates	

Figure 27.1 Spiral of decline on poor estates

Cities in decline

There is a range of reasons why cities may need rebranding. These might include:

➤ The increasing costs of upkeep, development and remodelling of central business districts (CBDs). Many CBDs are becoming increasingly congested, inaccessible and expensive.
➤ Loss of retailing function (particularly food retailing, electrical goods and do-it-yourself outlets) from CBDs to out-of-town shopping centres.
➤ Loss of offices and commercial functions from city centres to suburban and edge-of-town (peripheral) locations, such as prestige science parks.

Space versus place

Key concept

'Space' and 'place' are terms that often get used interchangeably, but it is important to appreciate that there can be differences in their meanings and interpretation:

➤ **Space** refers to the physical location and the distribution of geographical features such as football clubs or post offices.
➤ **Place** is a 'space' that has been given meaning by people. Individuals can make places significant through personal memories of events and experiences. Places may also be significant because of fame or tradition (e.g. Stratford-upon-Avon and Shakespeare or Cheddar and cheese). This association is particularly important when it comes to giving an identity and brand to a place so that it can be marketed and promoted.

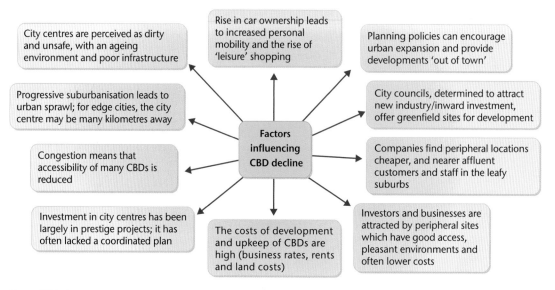

Figure 27.2 Factors in CBD decline

Figure 27.2 shows some additional factors in CBD decline.

Decision-makers and planners are worried about city areas in decline, since they can act as catalysts for further problems such as crime and loss of revenue from tourism in an area. A downward spiral can quickly follow. The CBD is an important social and cultural meeting point. A declining CBD is likely to accelerate the success of out-of-town shopping centres. In order for the CBD to find itself again, a range of rebranding initiatives must be used.

Case study   Birmingham

Economic history often forms an important component of regional identity – this has certainly been true of Birmingham and the midlands. The image of Birmingham was for many years determined by events at the British Leyland factory at Longbridge (which later became the ill-fated Rover). The impression was that of a city wedded to a disruptive and powerful workforce, constantly at odds with a weak management. The reconstruction of the city's image in the 1990s was therefore caught between two competing factors:

- the historical importance of the car industry to the identity of the city and region
- a series of negative associations that had become linked to that industry

Birmingham has also been closely identified with the failures of the 'modernist' project. Modernism is a style of architecture that became popular in the 1950s and 1960s. It relies on a simplistic and often angular form, using iron, steel, concrete and glass. Birmingham now offers a rich visual example of a modernist city striving to build a new city image. Others include Bristol and Coventry.

However, the city has begun a journey of significant and remarkable change. Table 27.1 shows a timeline of events, starting with the 'catalyst' events of the 1970s and 1980s.

Birmingham's current wave of remaking is not just producing impressive new buildings. Rather, along with many urban centres, it is using culture and identity to drive regeneration and advertise an image that will attract investment and tourism. Planners and urban architects have also established an interconnecting map of housing, workplaces and education that has redefined the quality of the city.

Table 27.1 Timeline of selected regeneration projects in Birmingham

1976	The National Exhibition Centre (NEC) opened on greenbelt land near to Birmingham International Airport, west of the city of Birmingham.
Late 1980s	The International Convention Centre (ICC) and Symphony Hall opened (1991). Development of the areas around Broad Street, including the Hyatt Regency Hotel (1990). Extension and refurbishment of the Birmingham Repertory Theatre (1991).
1993	Initial development by the Argent Group of the area called Brindley Place — a large 7 ha development costing £350 million. Now home to the Sea Life Centre, Ikon Gallery and Royal Bank of Scotland.
2002	Millennium Point opened — part of the Eastside redevelopment of the city; construction cost over £115 million. Completion of Phase 2 of the Custard Factory redevelopment — 100 studio offices and shops near Digbeth; seen as a good example of arts and media regeneration.
2003	Bullring development opened at a cost of £530 million, creating 8,000 new jobs; over 35 million visitors in the year of opening (second busiest shopping centre apart from London's West End). Redevelopment of the Quayside Tower, originally constructed in the 1960s.
2005	Completion of £40 million redevelopment of Matthew Boulton College, teaching over 500 courses to 7,000 students.
The future?	Big plans for the redevelopment of New Street Station and continued investment in the Eastside area of the city.

Photograph 27.1 Bullring shopping centre

Coalfield communities

The UK coal industry has been in decline for years and during the last two decades of the twentieth century most coal mines in Britain were closed. Between 1984 and 1997, 170,000 coal mining jobs were lost in England. This created serious problems for communities which had grown up around coal mining in earlier decades. In addition to job losses, coalfield areas faced their own particular set of challenges:

➤ The areas were characterised by high levels of dereliction and ground contamination, which were mostly the legacy of mining.
➤ There was not a strong tradition of self-employment and business start-ups.
➤ There was a lack of education and training in the population of coalfield areas.
➤ The proportion of the population in 1991 who were classified as having a long-term limiting illness was 15% in the coalfield regions, compared with 12% in England as a whole. Proportionately more people (44%) in households with a mining employment history claimed long-term illness than in other households (27%).

Countryside in crisis?

In recent years, the view that rural life is difficult and under threat has become prominent. This has partly arisen from media coverage of farming crises, especially the 2001 foot-and-mouth outbreak when there were daily reports of distraught farmers and horrifying footage of burning pyres of dead animals.

In addition a number of rural pressure groups and interest groups such as the Countryside Alliance have sought to highlight the difficulties faced by rural residents. This has to some extent created an anti-idyllic view of the countryside as:

➤ backward
➤ unsophisticated
➤ unfriendly, especially to incomers
➤ environmentally damaged
➤ boring
➤ sleepy and slow

Image of place

Key concept

Geographers spend a lot of time working with images, although we may not always call them 'images' — they may be referred to as figures, charts, graphs or even maps. The term 'image' is sometimes used in a negative way to suggest something superficial or not factual, or even to imply a distortion of the truth.

Image of place is important and can be shown through a variety of media: websites, pictures, poetry, paintings, cartoons. What image says about a place may determine how successful that place is.

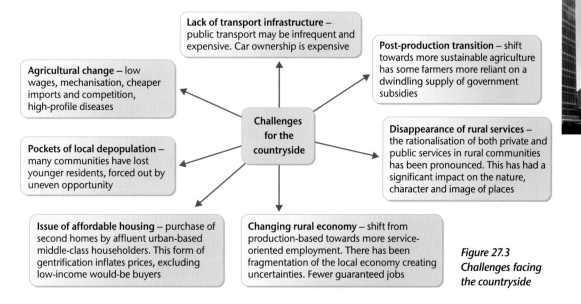

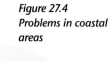

*Figure 27.3
Challenges facing
the countryside*

These viewpoints have been reinforced by media representation. For example, television shows such as *Father Ted* and *The League of Gentlemen* as well as the *Viz* character Farmer Palmer all portray rural people as simple, backward or hostile.

Apart from negative images and issues of inequality (see Chapter 24), there are other problems which particularly affect the countryside. Figure 27.3 shows some of the broader countryside issues associated with change.

Problems at the seaside

Most coastal settlements are dependent on a seasonal, resort economy, which is shrinking and moving unavoidably towards decline. The symptoms of this decline may be evident in the physical environment and the secondary statistics that describe the social and economic condition of a place. Many coastal areas have also experienced a decline in their traditional fishing industries coupled with the challenges of high concentrations of migrant labour.

Coastal areas are also problematic as a result of their physical geography. Their location means they can only be accessed from one direction and they tend to be remote and hard to get to. Figure 27.4 summarises the issues.

> ### Key term
>
> **Post-productionism** Changes in agricultural policy and practice shifting the emphasis away from maximum yields and towards a more sustainable agriculture. Post-productionism has been characterised by diversification and more organic production.

*Figure 27.4
Problems in coastal
areas*

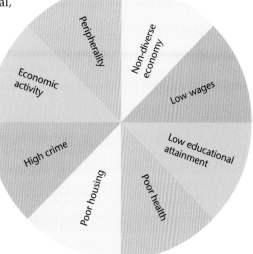

Photograph 27.2 Cromer on the north Norfolk coast is a resort that has needed investment from the local authority

David Holmes

Case study Blackpool in decline

Less than two decades ago, the Victorian working-class town of Blackpool drew as many as 17 million visitors a year, but these days it struggles to attract more than 10 million. Cheap package holidays sucked away many families in the 1980s, and big northern cities such as Leeds and Newcastle cornered the 'weekend-break' market in the 1990s (see the case study on p. 215).

Fewer tourists have also meant fewer jobs. Between 1994 and 2005, the number of registered businesses in Blackpool fell by 6%, although the number of businesses across the country increased by 15%. Most of the victims were small guesthouses. Unemployment now stands at 7% and wages have fallen. In 2002 the average Blackpudlian was paid 17% less than the average Briton; by 2006 the gap was 23%. Figure 27.5 shows levels of multiple deprivation in 2004 for super output areas in Blackpool. Note how a significant number of the super output areas are in the top 10% of deprivation nationally.

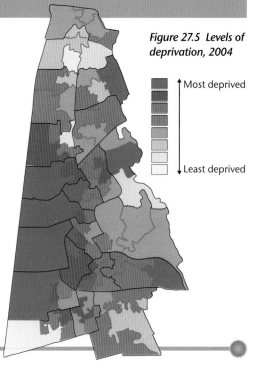

Figure 27.5 Levels of deprivation, 2004

↑ Most deprived

↓ Least deprived

Fieldwork and research

Establishing the profile of a place

A range of fieldwork surveys and secondary research sources can be used to establish the 'profile' of an area. The profile is a description of what a place is currently like. The more evidence that can be collected, the better the quality of the profile.

Examples of primary surveys are given in Table 27.2. Surveys will need to be customised depending on the type of place visited, for example urban, rural or coastal.

Secondary sources

Use the internet and other sources to find out more about places. The websites below give a good introduction to 'place':

■ www.flickr.com/map. Scroll around the map to get photographs of places. Zoom in and out and see what imagery people have uploaded. Google Earth has a similar facility.

Table 27.2 Primary surveys

Survey	Description
Environmental quality surveys	There are a range of possible surveys, such as street quality, shopping quality, landscape quality and litter. One possibility is to map the incidence and type of graffiti or create your own index of decay (see p. 268).
'Place check' forms	At a range of predetermined locations, record what you like and don't like. Support your written findings with photographs and video and audio recordings.
Questionnaire surveys	Conduct a survey about the image of a place, its reputation and problems. An example of this type of approach is given in Figure 27.6, which shows an identity (image) audit for Barcelona.
Recording the 'drosscape'	'Drosscape' is an American term to describe parts of a town where there is significant decay and dereliction. When these areas are mapped, they can form the focus of regeneration. Find out more at: www.newscientist.com/channel/opinion/mg19426062.100-the-word-drosscape.html
Internet blogs and forums	These can be a rich source of attitudes and opinions about a place and a good starting point to evidence profiles.

■ www.geograph.org.uk. This site has photographs for map grid squares all over the UK. Find and explore the area in question.

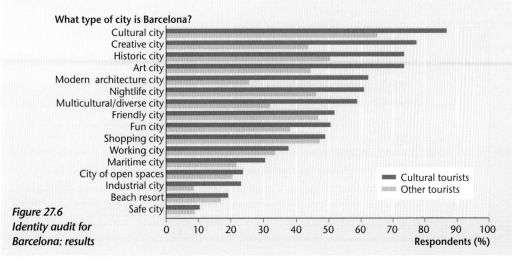

What type of city is Barcelona?

Figure 27.6 Identity audit for Barcelona: results

■ www.checkmyfile.co.uk. Use the free postcode checker to find out what a place is like.
■ http://upmystreet.com. See what the Acorn profile is for an area that you choose.
■ http://maps.google.co.uk. Google Maps lets you see satellite imagery of what your place is like, together with maps of roads etc.

Other sources may also help to establish the profile of a place. Tourist information brochures, for instance, can show how places are trying to market themselves. The Office for National Statistics has data on housing, health and employment, which can be downloaded (http://neighbourhood.statistics.gov.uk/).

Skills focus

Task

Figure 27.7 shows environmental quality scores for two contrasting urban districts. These could have been calculated using a number of approaches such as: landscape and street evaluation, litter and cleanliness, upkeep and state of buildings. A 'penalty' scoring system is often used, where a higher number indicates worse conditions. In Figure 27.7 Walverden has a worse **median** score than Cloverhill. However the higher **inter-quartile range** of data for Walverden may indicate that the area is more varied in overall quality. It could also show that the results are less reliable since there is less agreement in quality scores.

■ Why is it better to use a variety of techniques for measuring environmental quality rather than just one?
■ Which area is more in need of rebranding?

Key terms

Inter-quartile range This contains 50% of all the scores of data.

Mean The arithmetic average of all the data.

Median The middle point in a data set.

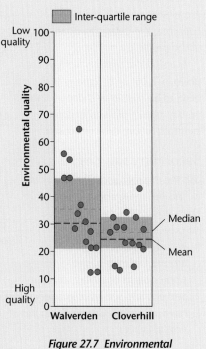

Figure 27.7 Environmental quality results

Review questions

1 What is the purpose of rebranding?
2 What is the profile of an area?
3 How do urban, rural and coastal areas in decline differ from each other?
4 A number of strategies are used for rebranding places: development of heritage tourism, sports cities, farm diversification schemes, new retailing facilities, etc. In groups, choose one of the strategies and research the pros and cons of your selected strategy.

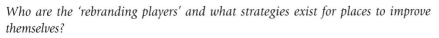

Rebranding strategies

Who are the 'rebranding players' and what strategies exist for places to improve themselves?

By the end of this chapter you should have:
➤ *carried out fieldwork and research into who the 'rebranding players' are*
➤ *reviewed the range of strategies for places (rural and urban) to improve themselves*

The rebranding players

Rebranding players are the **stakeholders** in the rebranding process. There is a range of possible stakeholders, including public partners, private firms, sponsors, not-for-profit organisations and government departments. These different groups and individuals get involved at different stages of the project development process. Figure 28.1 shows examples of different key players.

Stakeholders are likely to be different in urban and rural contexts. Table 28.1 provides some examples. Note how some funders and stakeholders apply to both contexts.

> ### Key term
>
> **Stakeholders**
> Individuals, groups or organisations that have an interest in a particular project. They may be involved financially or emotionally because the development is in their neighbourhood.

Figure 28.1
Key players in rebranding projects

Table 28.1
Examples of rebranding stakeholders

Urban	Rural
Advantage West Midlands — Development Agency (www.advantagewm.co.uk). The home page of all of the Development Agencies is at www.englandsrdas.com	European Union, e.g. Objective 1 programme and Leader programme (www.defra.gov.uk/rural/structure/obj1.htm, www.defra.gov.uk/rural/leader/index.htm).
English Partnerships — its principal aim is to 'deliver high-quality sustainable growth in England' (www.englishpartnerships.co.uk).	Action with Communities in Rural England, ACRE (www.acre.org.uk) — promotes local rural initiatives.
The Arts Council (www.artscouncil.org.uk/funding/index.php) offers various funding opportunities for arts-linked projects.	Natural England — gives grants to farmers for various environmental agriculture schemes (www.naturalengland.org.uk/planning/grants-funding/default.htm)
Big Lottery Fund (www.biglotteryfund.org.uk/index/)	
Heritage Lottery (www.hlf.org.uk/English/)	

Questioning the stakeholders

Secondary research can be carried out on the internet to find out the purpose and activities of individuals and organisations involved in rebranding strategies.

Primary fieldwork could involve questionnaires, extended interviews and the establishment of focus groups with key players. Typical lines of questioning might include:

■ aims and nature of the project or proposal (e.g. its location and scale)
■ reasons for involvement in the project (e.g. a personal connection, a business opportunity

or part of a wider rebranding strategy)
■ level and type of involvement (e.g. substantial financial input, consultant, community adviser)
■ other partners and partnerships connected to the project, and the relationship to them
■ length of project and length of involvement
■ overall costs of the project and funding streams
■ legacy opportunities

It may be useful to video the interview or digitally record the responses for future reference.

Top-down, bottom-up and partnership approaches

Players, stakeholders and policy-makers have adopted three main strategies to tackle rebranding projects:

➤ *The top-down approach.* In this approach, rebranding decisions are made by authorities or agencies and imposed on particular people and places. The advantage of this approach is that it is strategic in nature and offers a coordinated strategy. However, local communities in both rural and urban environments may feel isolated from the decision-making process and refuse to engage with the project. This approach also ignores local knowledge, which may lead to obvious mistakes being made.

➤ *The bottom-up approach.* This is based on listening to local opinion and devising local solutions to problems rather than producing an overarching strategic

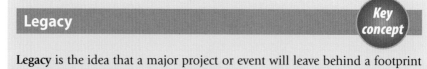

Legacy

Key concept

Legacy is the idea that a major project or event will leave behind a footprint of infrastructure and initiatives which will have a positive impact on the local community, economy and environment.

The London 2012 Olympic legacy, for example, boasts:

➤ impressive sporting facilities, including swimming pools, cycling tracks and tennis courts
➤ 9,000 new homes (many of them affordable) in the Olympic Park
➤ new schools, family health services and other community facilities
➤ permanent jobs in such diverse sectors as tourism and hospitality, food and media, and the construction industry

plan. The advantage is that local people are closely involved in developments and are empowered. However, such approaches may lack the 'teeth' or power to make substantial changes; they often rely on volunteers.

➤ *The partnership approach.* This approach, which aims to combine the best features of the top-down and bottom-up approaches, is increasingly being adopted. Partnerships are made up of representatives from the state, private and voluntary sectors, so that a range of voices is heard. Partnerships may also be well placed to draw on funding — for example, from the National Lottery, which requires matched funding from elsewhere. However, partnerships are not without problems. Because of the number of partners involved, decision making can sometimes be bureaucratic and longwinded.

Rural rebranding strategies

The countryside offers a range of rebranding possibilities (see Figure 28.2). Some of these draw on identity, culture and heritage, others utilise **farm diversification** and some are linked to new technologies.

Building on what's there

An important aspect of rebranding rural places is the celebration of local distinctiveness. Increasingly, local producers have to make and market something specialised in order to differentiate themselves from the competition. A 'resource audit' is important for determining the probable success of the rebranding process, as there is a range of factors that support the strategy of championing rural and local distinctiveness:

➤ *Location* — proximity to an urban market may be a commercial advantage, while remoteness may attract people seeking peace and tranquillity.

Key term

Farm diversification
Setting up by farmers of new, sometimes non-agricultural enterprises to increase farm incomes. In the UK an estimated 40% of farm income now comes from diversification.

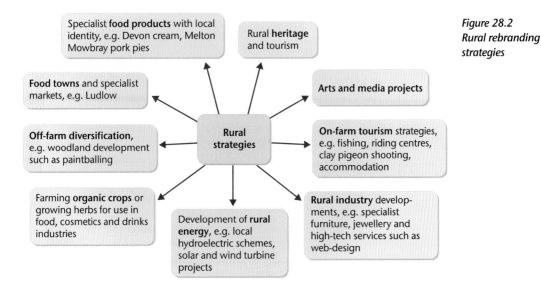

Figure 28.2
Rural rebranding strategies

David Holmes

*Photograph 28.1
Rural heritage
includes food
associated with
particular areas*

> *Physical environment* — attractive landscape, terrain suitable for certain activities (e.g. hillwalking), climate etc.
> *Cultural heritage* — historic buildings, redundant mines and railways, local history and traditions, cuisine, festivals, etc. (see Photograph 28.1).
> *Human capital* — skills, attitude and capacity for risk taking/leadership in the population of an area.
> *Social capital* — the ability of local institutions and people to take effective action together at the local level.

This is all part of a bigger picture of 'commodification' of the countryside (making it into something to sell), which has led to the economic restructuring of rural

Valorisation

Key concept

Valorisation (adding value) is the sustainable exploitation of a previously underused local resource so that it generates wealth and employment in the area. Rebranding is often at the heart of adding value in the rural economy.

If a farmer decides no longer to sell his crop of cherries directly for final consumption, but instead to buy the plant and machinery necessary to make the cherries into cherry brandy and to sell the brandy rather than the unprocessed fruit, then the farmer is adding value. If the farmer then opens a shop in the nearby town to sell the brandy to tourists, rather than at wholesale prices to other retailers, he is adding still more value to the original cherry resource. The Prince of Wales is doing this with the Duchy brand by opening a shop in Cirencester.

areas. As traditional production-based economic activities such as farming and mining have declined in many rural areas, diversification has occurred. This means that the countryside now has many 'buyers' — these include not only tourists, but also relocating businesses, adventure-seekers, film production companies, recreationists and consumers of specialised rural foods.

The role of technology

Technology can be an important ingredient in the rural rebranding recipe. It allows individuals and businesses in physically remote locations to share ideas and reach customers, as well as opening up a range of new business ideas based on technology, as the case study of Cornwall shows.

> ### Case study The broadband revolution in Cornwall
>
> The non-profit making partnership actnow (www.actnowcornwall.co.uk/home.asp) aims to promote economic development in Cornwall through the use of broadband and IT. It has been a key driver in the Cornwall economy since 1992. The £12.5 million scheme was established through a range of partners including BT, Cornwall Enterprise and the South West Regional Development Agency. Of this funding, £5.5 million came from EU Objective 1 money. Figure 28.3 gives some examples of innovative ideas that have been made possible.

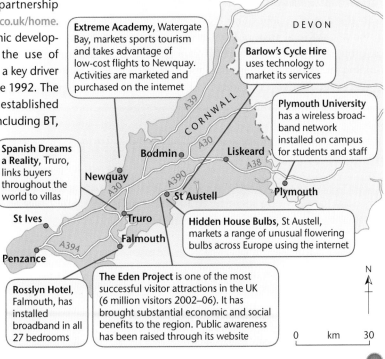

Figure 28.3 Effects of the broadband revolution in Cornwall

Extreme Academy, Watergate Bay, markets sports tourism and takes advantage of low-cost flights to Newquay. Activities are marketed and purchased on the internet

Barlow's Cycle Hire uses technology to market its services

Plymouth University has a wireless broadband network installed on campus for students and staff

Spanish Dreams a Reality, Truro, links buyers throughout the world to villas

Hidden House Bulbs, St Austell, markets a range of unusual flowering bulbs across Europe using the internet

The Eden Project is one of the most successful visitor attractions in the UK (6 million visitors 2002–06). It has brought substantial economic and social benefits to the region. Public awareness has been raised through its website

Rosslyn Hotel, Falmouth, has installed broadband in all 27 bedrooms

'Flix in the Stix' is a pioneering project that uses the latest in digital technology to take cinema films to local venues throughout Shropshire and Herefordshire (www.artsalive.co.uk/default.asp_Q_intContentID_E_6). It is the biggest film touring scheme in Europe, offering nearly 600 films a year, and partnering with 80 or more communities. Working with local promoters, using existing venues and employing low-cost technology, big screen films can be shown for those in rural areas who, because of their geographical remoteness, do not normally get the opportunity to see them.

Farm diversification

As incomes from farming have declined, farmers have been encouraged to diversify into other ways of making money such as accommodation (B&B, campsites, holiday cottages), farm shops and leisure activities such as clay pigeon shooting. The 'Earthly Ideas' website provides clear information about diversification and promoting the 'rural brand' — see www.earthlyideas.co.uk/marketing. html for advice on marketing. 'Best Rural Retailer' (www.bestruralretailer.co.uk) is a competition for shops that promote local produce and diversification.

Case study — The Leader Programme

The European Union Leader Programme (translated as 'link between actions for the development of the rural economy') is a good example of partnership working. Leader was started in 1991 with the aim of regenerating local communities in the poorest rural areas of Europe. Organisations or groups in these communities can apply for funding according to a specific set of criteria. Leader has funded a number of innovative projects across Europe (see http://ec.europa.eu/agriculture/rur/leaderplus/index_en.htm for more information). Types of project eligible for funding include:

- craft-type activities
- local heritage initiatives
- tourism-related activities
- marketing of local produce
- promotion of local events

Urban rebranding strategies

Urban areas, both towns and cities, have a range of rebranding strategies available (see Figure 28.4). Some are similar to rural strategies in that they draw on identity, culture and heritage, while other approaches act as catalysts for development (e.g. technology and sport).

Figure 28.4 Urban rebranding strategies

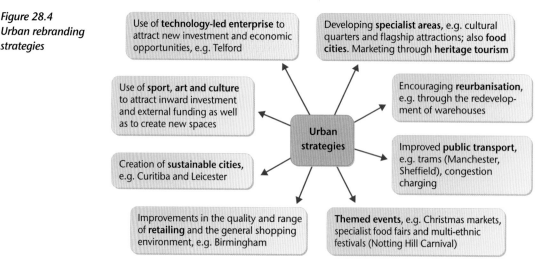

Use of **technology-led enterprise** to attract new investment and economic opportunities, e.g. Telford

Developing **specialist areas**, e.g. cultural quarters and flagship attractions; also **food cities**. Marketing through **heritage tourism**

Use of **sport, art and culture** to attract inward investment and external funding as well as to create new spaces

Encouraging **reurbanisation**, e.g. through the redevelopment of warehouses

Creation of **sustainable cities**, e.g. Curitiba and Leicester

Improved **public transport**, e.g. trams (Manchester, Sheffield), congestion charging

Urban strategies

Improvements in the quality and range of **retailing** and the general shopping environment, e.g. Birmingham

Themed events, e.g. Christmas markets, specialist food fairs and multi-ethnic festivals (Notting Hill Carnival)

Cities of sport and culture

Many cities have recognised that a large sporting event, and the improvements in infrastructure it brings, can act as a major catalyst for regeneration. There may be additional paybacks including investment in tourism, public services, hotel accommodation and environmental improvement. The media attention both before and during an event usually acts as a form of marketing. This can create longer-term spinoffs as business and visitors are attracted to the city long after the sporting event has finished.

Case study Manchester: Commonwealth Games 2002

One of Manchester's key motivations for hosting the Commonwealth Games in 2002 was to make a giant stride towards becoming a successful twenty-first-century city. Central to achieving this objective was the notion of enhancing the city's 'brand' to allow it to compete more effectively for international business and tourists. The Games provided significant positive outcomes:

- They were used as a catalyst in other regeneration projects such as Sport City, which has become part of the Institute for Sport and involved the reclamation of a large area of brownfield land.
- Businesses benefited from the high attendance at the Games events.
- The inhabitants of Manchester derived an ongoing 'feel-good factor' from hosting the Games.

The key to making high-profile schemes work for local areas is to ensure they are part of an overall improvement strategy — including social regeneration. Most urban regeneration programmes and government policies now adopt the partnership approach. This involves getting the public sector, such as local councils and local and central government agencies, to work with private sector firms, community groups and voluntary sector organisations. In the case of the London 2012 Olympics, a partnership approach is key to its success.

In 2008 Liverpool was awarded the title 'European Capital of Culture' (www.liverpool08.com). Culture has been an important way of defining the rebranding process in many cities, and Liverpool has used this as a catalyst for development. The city has, for example, capitalised on its musical roots, especially

Photo-tourism *Key concept*

What sometimes defines the image of a place are the photographs people take. This 'tourist gaze' is an interesting area of geography, which enables researchers to identify buildings or other spaces that are significant to the visitor. In essence, such photographs are digital postcards featuring idealised and stereotypical representations of the place being visited.

North West Development Agency

*Photograph 28.2
The opening of
Liverpool's
celebration of its
European Capital of
Culture*

its connection with the Beatles. As part of its celebration of culture, the city council has produced its own 'sound map' (www.liverpool08.com/Images/sound_tcm 79-82276.pdf). Local culture can be exploited in this way to create or reinforce a city's identity.

Innovative architecture

Design of new buildings is important and is often handled as a competition (e.g. Tate Modern, London). Sometimes this use of iconic buildings to add to the appeal and identity of a place is called 'signature architecture'.

Use of public art

A wide variety of art may be used in public spaces. This is not a new idea. Sculptures and other forms of public art such as murals (Photograph 28.3) are used to introduce talking points, create meeting places and add a different dimension to urban spaces. A less formal and non-commissioned type of public art is graffiti.

*Photograph 28.3
Art such as murals
can create a talking
point or add to the
character of
a place*

David Holmes

David Holmes

*Photograph 28.4
Café culture in
Brindley Place,
Birmingham*

Café-bar culture

A significant feature of recent city-centre development is the rise in the number
of cafés and bars, which is linked to the idea of the city being 'open' 24 hours
a day. Typically, in the UK, modern cafés and bars are found in premises that
were formerly occupied by
high street banks, or are
part of a wider regeneration
scheme (Photograph 28.4).
The rise of this so-called
'cappuccino culture' has
played a significant part in
revitalising parts of cities
that were previously in
decline.

Cultural diversity

It is commonplace in cities
to find 'quarters' associated
with a particular ethnic
group, such as 'Chinatown'
or 'Little Italy'. Such distinctive areas provide special
character and quality which
is attractive to tourists and
investors.

Fieldwork and research

Graffiti

Fieldwork can be used to
map the distribution of graffiti
in an urban space. A graffiti
assessment chart (Table 28.2)
can be used to record and
quantify the type of graffiti
displayed. On a broader scale,
consider what type of urban
issue(s) this geography of
graffiti reflects. Does it, for
example, represent gang
culture, social exclusion,
racial tension, property
development or community
art schemes, or is it 'pure'
vandalism?

Table 28.2 Graffiti assessment chart

		Score
Maximum size of words	0–10 cm	+1
	11–25 cm	+2
	26–50 cm	+3
	>50 cm	+4
Maximum size of pictures	0–10 cm	+1
	11–25 cm	+2
	26–50 cm	+3
	>50 cm	+4
Nature	Obscene/racist	+5
Method	Ink/pencil	+1
	Felt pen	+3
	Aerosol	+5
	Wood carving	+8
	Concrete drilling	+10
Visible from	1–5 m	+1
	6–10 m	+2
	11–30 m	+3
	31–50 m	+4
	>50 m	+6

Figure 28.5 A model of sustainable development

Rebranding for a sustainable future

Many rebranding strategies accommodate elements of sustainable development. This is sometimes depicted as a three-legged stool in which sustainability is supported by all three 'legs' (Figure 28.5):

➤ *Economy.* Economic activity should serve the common good, be self-renewing, and build local assets and self-reliance.
➤ *Environment.* Humans are part of nature, nature has limits, and communities are responsible for protecting and building natural assets.
➤ *Society.* The opportunity should be available to everyone to participate fully in all the activities, benefits and decision making of a society.

Examples of sustainable approaches in rural and urban contexts are given in Table 28.3. The case study below looks at two 'sustainable' cities.

Table 28.3 Sustainable development in urban and rural areas

Urban	Rural
• Employment opportunities close to communities, reducing transport footprint • Preservation of heritage and culture • Innovative design, minimising waste energy and resources • Respect for and enhancement of the natural environment	• Economically viable, providing a range of employment opportunities (social equity) • Limited use of artificial chemicals in any production methods (ideally organic) • Local foods and produce, reducing food miles and adding value • Using technology to support agriculture, e.g. Farmwizard (http://www.farmwizard.com/public/main.aspx)

Case study **Leicester and Curitiba: different sustainable approaches**

Figure 28.6 Leicester's Environment City strategy

Cutting waste by effective recycling

Saving energy

Cleaner air by cutting emissions

Better mobility, less traffic

Noise reduction aiming for quiet city status

Protecting wildlife habitats

Slowing climate change by efficient energy use

'Greening' the city by tree planting

Leicester became The UK's first 'Environment City' in 1990, and in 1996 it received a European sustainability award. Sustainability is a tool to improve the quality of life for citizens, enhancing their health, safety and general well-being. There is also a responsibility not to cause environmental damage to other parts of the world. Figure 28.6 illustrates the components of Leicester's environmental strategy.

The situation in Leicester is in stark contrast to that in the city of Curitiba, in southeastern Brazil. Curitiba faces the problems of all developing world cities: rural dwellers pushed off the land and the building of slums and shanty towns by the migrant poor on the edge of the city. Despite these challenges, Curitiba has the reputation of a sustainable city for its particularly good recycling and transportation developments, many of which utilise low-technology approaches. The city's sustainability projects are multi-purpose, cost-effective, people-centred, fast, simple, home grown, and based on local initiatives and skills.

Curitiba stands out as a model of voluntary sustainability. Leicester, in contrast, shows a more top-down approach in which an 'Environment Strategy' has been put in place by a partnership of organisations.

Further research

Leicester: www.environmentcity.org.uk
Curitiba: www.pce.govt.nz/news/speeches/speech_01_09_18.pdf

Skills focus

Task

Design an interview with a DJ of a local community radio station. The purpose of the discussion is to find out about the history and impact of the community radio station in the local area. You expect the interview to last about 5 minutes. Think about how you will use:

- open versus closed questions
- single versus multiple responses
- question sequencing
- layout and design
- style of questions (e.g. ensuring no ambiguity)

Work in small groups to develop the questionnaire.

Review questions

1 Who are the players and stakeholders in the rebranding process?
2 Create a table which outlines the advantages and disadvantages of top-down, bottom-up and partnership approaches to managing rebranding.
3 For both rural and urban contexts, research the similarities and differences between the main rebranding strategies.
4 In what ways might coastal rebranding strategies vary from those for either an urban or a rural environment?

Chapter 29

Managing rural rebranding

How successful has rebranding been in the countryside?

By the end of this chapter you should have:

➤ *carried out fieldwork and research into the success of contrasting rural rebranding schemes, such as rural food markets, farm diversification and heritage tourism*

An assessment of the success of rural rebranding strategies requires a range of economic, environmental and social evaluations. Some types of evidence are harder to collect than others (Table 29.1). If collection of **quantitative data** to support ideas is difficult, it might be necessary to rely on 'softer' or anecdotal evidence of success. A range of basic primary survey techniques could be applied:

➤ questionnaire surveys — for example, finding out more about why people are there by using an 'attraction survey' (see the skills focus on p. 326); or finding out where people have travelled from using a 'sphere of influence survey'

➤ facilities/shopping surveys — analysing the range and type of retail provision and how this has changed

➤ various bipolar/quality surveys (e.g. litter, environment) plus specialised quality surveys for a particular facility, in which researchers devise their own criteria

➤ capacity surveys — assessing the patterns of usage of a facility over a set period of time (e.g. morning or afternoon)

In each instance, recording sheets must be appropriate, customised and fit for purpose.

In addition to using primary techniques, a number of secondary research sources (e.g. census data, 'Upmystreet' and 'Geograph') can be used alongside various 'texts' (see p. 314) which identify and promote rebranded places.

Key term

Quantitative data
Information that can be counted or expressed numerically (e.g. number of visitors in 1 hour). This type of data is often collected through observation, then processed and statistically analysed. It can be represented visually in graphs and charts.

Table 29.1 Evidence for evaluating rural rebranding schemes

Evidence	Easy	Moderate	Difficult
Economic	Census statistics, e.g. population figures; functions/ services	Tourism statistics, e.g. seasonal visitor rates; change in house prices	Historical tourism data (may be anecdotal); change in services
Social	Short questionnaires; footfall and catchment surveys	Interviews/extended questionnaires	Focus groups; oral histories; place reputation
Environmental	Basic litter surveys; biodiversity	Change in environmental quality, land use, etc.	Air quality and general pollution statistics

Investigating adding value locally

Promoting local produce and specialised food products traditional to the area can be an important part of the rebranding process. It often involves emphasis on direct sales by farmers and local producers, for example at farmers' markets. The sites of local food production, such as farms, dairies, cheesemakers, vineyards and breweries, can be marketed too as tourist attractions, creating a second income stream.

Farmers' markets are increasingly common and are an important part of rural development. They contribute towards the rebranding process on three levels:

- They directly encourage food tourism.
- They help support locally based small-scale food processing.
- They can increase incomes for farmers by removing the 'middlemen' — the commission taken by wholesalers and retailers.

Fieldwork and research into such rebranding activities may take a number of forms, but they will initially require a scoping activity to find out about the place, its products, history and activities. Questionnaires, for example, can be designed to yield the following information:

- who uses the facility: age, gender, ethnicity, economic status
- where the visitors come from
- what visitors like or dislike about the facility and its products, etc.

Permission is needed, e.g. from the organisers of a farmer's market, to carry out this type of survey. Making contact to gain permission may be an opportunity to conduct more in-depth interviews with the facility's staff. Here you can get detailed information about the history of a place and its rebranding process.

Photograph 29.1 Hexham farmers' market, Northumberland

Peter Atkins

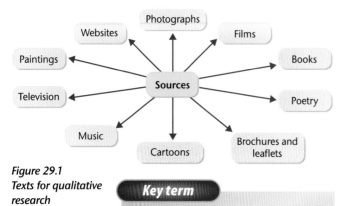

Figure 29.1
Texts for qualitative research

Qualitative research: analysis of texts

Geographers can analyse a range of **qualitative** sources or 'texts' to find out about the image of a place and the way in which it is marketed or promoted. A variety of texts can be studied (Figure 29.1).

Some of these texts (e.g. leaflets, films) may be consciously used to help rebrand a place. By studying them you can see how certain organisations attempt to influence ideas and feelings about a place.

Fieldwork and research

Rebranding for tourism

Choose a rural place and examine how its image has been marketed to encourage tourism. Evidence can be obtained from a variety of research sources, such as those shown in Figure 29.1. Try to evaluate how successfully each chosen text portrays the area to encourage visitors. Figure 29.2 gives an idea of the types of question you can ask about individual texts.

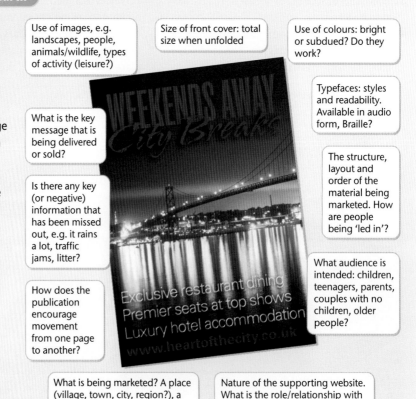

Use of images, e.g. landscapes, people, animals/wildlife, types of activity (leisure?)

Size of front cover: total size when unfolded

Use of colours: bright or subdued? Do they work?

Typefaces: styles and readability. Available in audio form, Braille?

What is the key message that is being delivered or sold?

The structure, layout and order of the material being marketed. How are people being 'led in'?

Is there any key (or negative) information that has been missed out, e.g. it rains a lot, traffic jams, litter?

What audience is intended: children, teenagers, parents, couples with no children, older people?

How does the publication encourage movement from one page to another?

What is being marketed? A place (village, town, city, region?), a theme park, a shop?

Nature of the supporting website. What is the role/relationship with this document?

Figure 29.2 Analysis of texts

Case study The Lake District

Before the eighteenth century the Lake District was viewed as a wild and inhospitable place that should be avoided. This opinion was changed by poets like Wordsworth and Coleridge. It became fashionable to admire landscape and to visit 'picturesque' parts of Britain like the Lakes. Since that time, the Lake District has changed its image to appeal to a range of people – this is shown in the timeline in Figure 29.3.

> Late eighteenth century: Lake District inspired romantic poets, notably Wordsworth

> Mid nineteenth century: better transport and holiday from work marked the start of mass tourism. Area continued to inspire poets and writers, e.g. Beatrix Potter and Arthur Ransome

> Changing image to appeal to different audiences and markets

> 1950s and 1960s: publication of Wainwright's *Pictorial Guides* encouraged more visitors to the fells for walking and hill climbing

> 1980s onwards: Beatrix Potter and Wordsworth tourism. Wide range of other attractions. Landscape of National Park

Figure 29.3 Image in the Lake District

Fieldwork and research

Investigating representations of the countryside

Choose a part of countryside that is strongly associated with a particular author, poet, artist, musician or television or radio programme. Examine the work of one writer or a particular television programme and then consider the following points:

- How is the area portrayed? What does the work make you feel about it?
- What particular local features or qualities are celebrated?
- How does this work compare with other pieces about the area?
- Is this work used to promote and market the area?

Example: Coleridge and Exmoor

The Coleridge Way in Somerset is an example of how a poet has been used as a brand to attract

Figure 29.4 The Coleridge Way website

visitors through heritage marketing (see www. coleridgeway.co.uk). Although Samuel Taylor Coleridge did not write a poem about Exmoor, it is clear that the 'studies' he made on Exmoor appeared in some works.

One of his most famous works was 'Kubla

Khan', in which the sacred River Alph ran into the 'sunless sea'. There is such a sea at Culbone (north Somerset), where the high cliffs shade the shore. The Culbone area probably also inspired the lines:

But oh! That deep romantic chasm which slanted
Down the green hill athwart a cedarn cover!
A savage place! As holy and enchanted
As e'er beneath the a waning moon was haunted
By woman wailing for her demon-lover!

Studying rural recreation and farm diversification

As we have seen, one strand of the rebranding process can involve a new approach to farming, not through a modernisation of methods, but rather through a diversification of activities. One way of diversifying is to sell produce directly to customers through farm shops or farmers' markets (as described earlier in this chapter). Farmers can also use their resources (i.e. their farms) to make money from sporting and horse-riding activities, tourist accommodation and organic farming or other 'green' initiatives, as outlined in Figure 29.5.

Figure 29.5 Farm diversification opportunities

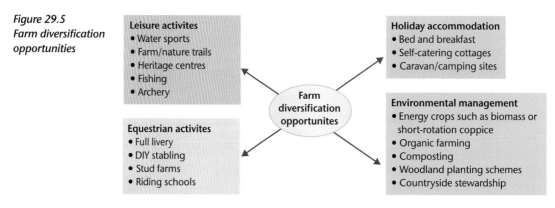

Leisure activites
- Water sports
- Farm/nature trails
- Heritage centres
- Fishing
- Archery

Holiday accommodation
- Bed and breakfast
- Self-catering cottages
- Caravan/camping sites

Farm diversification opportunites

Equestrian activites
- Full livery
- DIY stabling
- Stud farms
- Riding schools

Environmental management
- Energy crops such as biomass or short-rotation coppice
- Organic farming
- Composting
- Woodland planting schemes
- Countryside stewardship

Farm diversification

Visitor surveys make excellent fieldwork activities in places where initiatives set up by enterprising farmers attract large numbers of tourists (Photograph 29.2).

Given enough time and working in groups, it is possible to build up a detailed picture of activity patterns — that is, the flows within a site and the number of users at particular places (Figure 29.6). You can record numbers or flows of users at particular attractions at different

Photo 29.2 Sheep racing in north Devon

David Holmes

times through the day by positioning researchers at those points and counting at set times. This is called **participant observation**. These quantitative data can be backed up with qualitative impressions about the level of crowding and atmosphere using photographs to create a 'photo-essay'.

This type of work can be combined with more detailed evaluations of the location, involving:

➤ Analysing the types of people visiting the site either by observation or by questionnaire surveys. Do some age/social/gender groups use the facility more than others? What activities are preferred by different people?

➤ Studying how the site is marketed and managed. How is rurality 'sold'?

➤ Researching information on activities and events (e.g. mountain-bike trails).

➤ Conducting an in-depth interview with the

manager about the site's history and likely future.

➤ Setting up focus groups of visitors and local residents. Have changes (social, economic and environmental) to the local area and its communities as a result of the attraction been beneficial or otherwise?

Digital maps (e.g. RAC or AA Routefinder) can be used to calculate accessibility and travel times to the site from particular locations. Isochrones on maps indicate how long it takes to travel from the isochrone line to a particular location. These tend to be much more useful than straight-line distances.

This type of information can help in piecing together the rebranding story, especially if new transport infrastructure has been put in place to help reduce journey times.

Figure 29.6 Mapping activity patterns

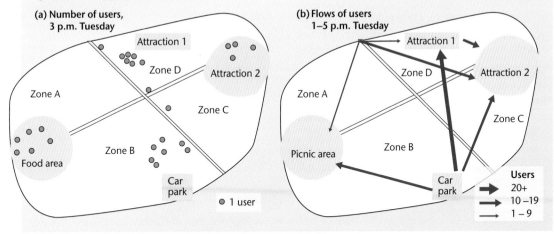

Participant observation

Information can be gathered through careful observation of participants at a site, for example tourists at a farm-based activity centre. This may involve actually undertaking the same activity as the participants in order to collect data. It is a form of 'ethnography', which is the study of people and their actions.

Photograph 29.3 The social function of forests is important in European countries

Traditionally, the main function of forests in Europe has been wood production. Over the last few decades, management of forests as nature reserves has become an important secondary objective, sometimes surpassing wood production as the primary function. The social functions of forests, such as recreation, have also started to move up the political agenda in many countries in recent years.

Thetford Forest Park covers 7,900 ha and is the largest man-made lowland forest in England. It is estimated that there are over 2 million visitors to the Forest Park each year, making it one of the top visitor destinations in the east of England (see Figure 29.7). High Lodge Forest Centre in the park is a major east of England attraction — 300,000 people used it in 2006. There were also 10,000 visits by school children carrying out educational activities. The park offers a range of diversified activities:

- Bike Art — cycle hire and shop
- giant maze
- giant play sculpture trail
- deer safaris
- fungal forays

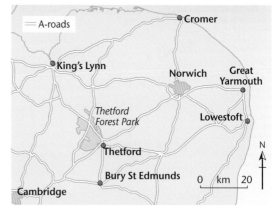

Figure 29.7 Location of Thetford Forest Park

- willow weaving
- rustic furniture making
- watercolour painting
- outdoor concerts
- kids' activity days

Other special uses of the park include car rallies, motorcycle enduros, mountain bike championships, field archery contests and husky-dog racing.

The development of this type of 'nature tourism' is one of the ingredients in rural development and rebranding. However, there are severe pressures on many forest areas and they are in danger of being degraded ecologically and physically due to high recreational use. This is likely to affect people's enjoyment of the environment and landscape, and therefore the demand for nature-based tourism. Tourists' expectations of the environment differ: some look for cultural landscapes and a traditional use of the land, some want facilities for activities such as cycling, others hope to be able to find nature in a pure and original condition.

Further research

Find out more at 'Woodland for Life': www. woodlandforlife.net/wfl-action/ and also at www.forestry.gov.uk/thetfordforestpark.

Evaluating rural festivals

Festivals based on music, food, art and culture are a familiar part of the summer and autumn calendar for many rural areas. These one-off events can be part of the economic development strategy of rural areas. Examples of festivals include:

➤ music, e.g. folk music, classical music (Orkney's St Magnus Festival), rock music (Glastonbury)
➤ food, e.g. Sturminster Newton Cheese Festival
➤ wine, e.g. Christchurch Food and Wine Festival
➤ sport, e.g. Wenlock Olympic Games
➤ comedy, e.g. Newbury Festival
➤ literature, e.g. Hay on Wye Literary Festival
➤ craft, e.g. Shrewsbury Craft Festival
➤ airshows, e.g. Abingdon Air and Country Show

Table 29.2 considers the impacts of festivals, both positive and negative. The size of the economic impact depends on characteristics of both the festival (e.g. number of days) and the local economy (other attractions and linkages).

Table 29.2
Evaluating festivals

Advantages	Disadvantages
Short term	*Short term*
• Local restaurants, hotels, B&Bs benefit from increased visitor numbers	• Cost of staging event
• Attracts tourists who would not normally visit the area	• Risk of weather-related failure
• Possible additional funding from local authority or sponsorship from local business	• Diversion of resources such as police from normal duties
• Can encourage community cohesion and celebrate distinctiveness	• Overcrowding, congestion and noise disrupting residents' lives
	• Strain on community infrastructure
	• Environmental impacts and eco-footprint
Long term	*Long term*
• Sustained visitor numbers and repeat visits bring economic benefit	• Possible legacy of financial debt
• Creation of jobs and diversification of local economy	• Underutilisation of infrastructure following event ('white elephant legacy'). Costs of maintaining empty buildings and facilities
• Development of new tourism-related enterprises	• Economic benefits of staging event not felt by local community but go outside
• Developments in infrastructure and sustainable planning initiatives	
• Increased local tax income	

Skills focus

An attraction survey is an in-depth survey in which you should:

- Ask up to 25 people what they are planning to do, or have done, at a particular site.
- Evaluate and discuss with the respondents their opinions about the quality of particular sites, or elements/features within one particular locality.
- Devise a questionnaire with maps and images. Ask people to mark on a large-scale map which route they took to reach the site. Ask them to rank the pictures of the site's facilities in order of preference.

Task

Develop a basic questionnaire that you might use to evaluate a rural festival as described above or an attraction such as the Eden Project: www.edenproject.com.

Look at the 'virtual tour' on the Eden Project website. How does this attract people to different zones and how could you monitor activity patterns?

Review questions

1 What are the difficulties in evaluating rural rebranding?
2 How can analysis of texts help us to understand rebranding?
3 Devise a table to compare the different approaches to qualitative and quantitative fieldwork.

Managing urban rebranding

Chapter 30

How successful have urban areas been in rebranding themselves?

By the end of this chapter you should have:

➤ *carried out fieldwork and research into the success of various urban rebranding attempts, such as flagship schemes, waterfront regeneration and heritage tourism*

A context for change

Many urban environments in developed countries are undergoing rapid, dramatic and distinctive change. The character of city centres, for instance, is shifting from a traditional association with production and finance to a domination by culture (e.g. museums) and consumption (shops and restaurants). Figure 30.1 shows how some of these elements interact. Tourism, in particular, can lead to investment in physical, economic and social regeneration (Figure 30.2).

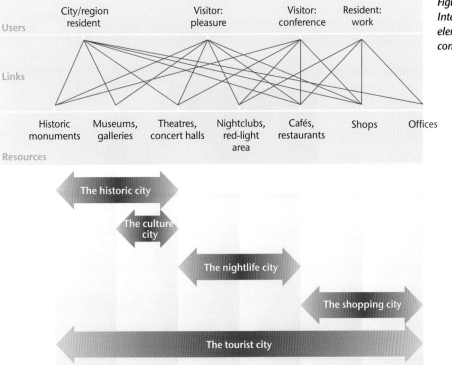

Figure 30.1 Interaction of elements in the contemporary city

Figure 30.2
Regenerative
aspects of
tourism

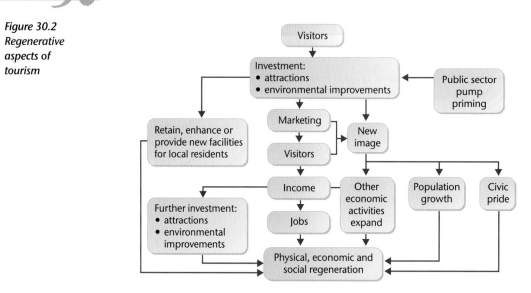

The evidence for rebranding and reimaging is perhaps more obvious in the urban environment than in rural places. It is possible to think of many examples of cities with big new buildings, innovative use of materials and design, and a new focus on tourism and culture.

Figure 30.3 shows the key ingredients in the urban rebranding 'recipe'.

Flagship developments

Key concept

One of the key means of encouraging the economic revival of city centres is through the development of **flagship developments**. These are usually large-scale, high-profile and high-investment projects, such as major new museums, art galleries, theatres or sports facilities (see Photograph 30.1). Iconic 'signature' buildings designed by well-known architects may also be part of the new image.

Sometimes the flagship developments are part of a wider scheme of improvements funded by a mixture of private and public money. The idea is that these projects improve the image and reputation of an area, and help to attract people and other activities.

Photograph 30.1 Bridgewater concert hall, the exhibition centre in the former railway station and the 'signature' Beetham Tower in Manchester

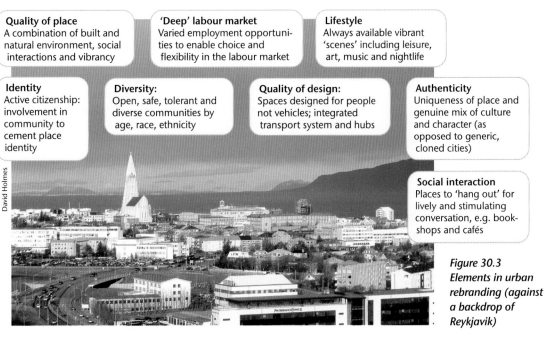

Quality of place
A combination of built and natural environment, social interactions and vibrancy

'Deep' labour market
Varied employment opportunities to enable choice and flexibility in the labour market

Lifestyle
Always available vibrant 'scenes' including leisure, art, music and nightlife

Identity
Active citizenship: involvement in community to cement place identity

Diversity:
Open, safe, tolerant and diverse communities by age, race, ethnicity

Quality of design:
Spaces designed for people not vehicles; integrated transport system and hubs

Authenticity
Uniqueness of place and genuine mix of culture and character (as opposed to generic, cloned cities)

Social interaction
Places to 'hang out' for lively and stimulating conversation, e.g. bookshops and cafés

David Holmes

Figure 30.3
Elements in urban rebranding (against a backdrop of Reykjavik)

Investigating the 24-hour city

A significant feature of recent urban and town-centre development has been a rapid expansion in the number of cafés, bars and clubs. While café-club culture is well established in many European cities, it is a newer phenomenon in the UK. Along with this changing emphasis on leisure has come the development of the '24-hour city'. This is characterised by expensive inner-city apartments, innovative restaurants, late-night bookshops and other retailing, and a lively club scene.

Fieldwork and research

Urban rebranding and the 24-hour city

Various types of fieldwork can be conducted to find out more about the impact of rebranding and the 24-hour city. A detailed questionnaire survey (undertaken during the day) can be geared to find out about the following:

■ *Exclusion.* Many older people and especially older women can feel excluded from town centres at night, particularly at the weekend. About 45% of 16–34-year-olds go out 'on the town' at least one evening a week, while only 15% of the over-55s do, and 71% of over-55s would not go out in a town centre in the evening (Camden Town Survey 2005).

■ *Activities undertaken.* Your survey might ask where people go, the size of their group, how much money they spend, the time they return home, how often they go out and the transport they use.

In addition to questionnaires, surveys of land use can reveal to what extent a town or city has become more '24-hour' through the process of regeneration and reimaging. Table 30.1 compares services suited to daytime or night-time provision.

Using this as a starting point, create a land-use map of the town/city centre and calculate what proportion of facilities are 'day' or 'night'. Then try to work out how many of the night-time facilities are features of a rebranding/local improvement scheme.

Table 30.1 Day and night services

Daytime facility	24-hour/night-time facility
• Professional services, e.g. solicitors • Swimming pool • Specialist food shops • Banks and building societies • Department stores	• Clubs • Supermarkets • Some pharmacists • Restaurants and take aways • Hotels

Skills focus

According to the New Economics Foundation (NEF) many of the UK's towns are becoming like 'clones' of each other. In place of independent local shops there is a near-identical package of chain stores on most of the nation's high streets. This is one of the negative impacts of urban rebranding, causing the individual character of many town centres to be lost.

Some fieldwork data collected in Shrewsbury and Telford (Table 30.2) show the number of chain stores compared to independents.

Task

Using the formula below, from the New Economics Foundation, calculate the degree of cloning.

- Award 5 points for each *type* of shop in the town.
- Award 50 points for each *independent* shop.
- Award 5 points for each *chain* store.

Table 30.2 Comparison of shops in Shrewsbury and Telford

	Shrewsbury	Telford
No. of types of shop	25	23
Independent shops	321	35
Chain stores	152	103
Total shops	473	138

These are primary data from Shrewsbury, which we suspect is *not* a clone town

These are primary data from Telford — a suspected clone town

Add up the total points for each town.

$$\text{clone town score} = \frac{\text{total points}}{\text{number of shops}}$$

Figure 30.4 shows clone town ratings according to the score.

More information on cloning can be found at: www.neweconomics.org/gen/z_sys_publicationdetail.aspx?pid=189

Figure 30.4 Clone town rating scale

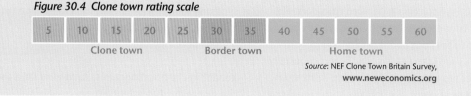

5	10	15	20	25	30	35	40	45	50	55	60

Clone town   Border town   Home town

Source: NEF Clone Town Britain Survey, www.neweconomics.org

Waterfront regeneration

Since the 1980s, waterfront regeneration has become a significant strand of urban regeneration strategies. In many places, derelict waterfronts (both coastal and inland, adjacent to rivers) have been transformed into vibrant flagship

developments which have helped stimulate economic growth in the area. Other advantages of waterfront regeneration include:
➤ the provision of new employment opportunities
➤ new facilities and attractive public spaces for local people and tourists
➤ the provision of new homes

Case study   Waterfront regeneration in Plymouth

Plymouth is the regional capital of the southwest peninsula of England, and has approximately 250,000 residents. Since the 1980s, the city has been energetically pursuing a strategy to revitalise its waterfront. This has been supported by the Urban Development Corporation and more recently English Partnerships and the South West of England Regional Development Agency. The first sites to be redevel-

oped were Royal William Yard, Mount Wise and Mount Batten. The city council has also invested in revitalising the historic Barbican and Sutton Harbour area. This has included the relocation of the fish market and the opening of the new national Marine Aquarium. Figure 30.5 shows the main locations in Plymouth where waterfront and linked regeneration have taken place.

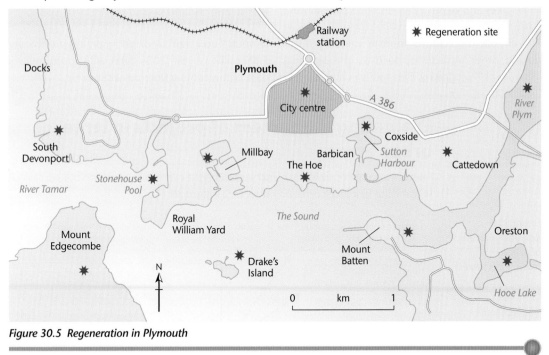

Figure 30.5 Regeneration in Plymouth

Urban heritage tourism

Heritage tourism means visiting places because of their interesting history. This includes industrial archaeology such as old factories and docks, canals and railways, as well as historical buildings and former homes of historic figures. These features, when regenerated and marketed, can act as a magnet for the increasing number of urban tourists visiting cities for day trips and short breaks.

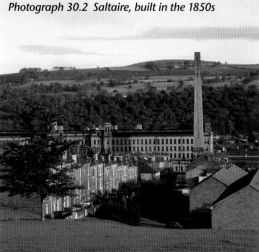

Case study — Heritage tourism in Bradford and West Yorkshire

Bradford's tourist industry attracted nearly 10 million visitors in 2006 and employs over 15,000 people. The city council has been forward thinking in establishing a rich heritage tourism market for visitors. Attractions in Bradford and the surrounding area include:

- the Industrial Museum — recreating life in Bradford in the late nineteenth century
- the Alhambra Theatre — a fine example of an Edwardian theatre
- Saltaire 'model' Victorian industrial village (Photograph 30.2) — a World Heritage site
- the village of Haworth — home of the Brontë sisters
- Keighley and Worth Valley historic steam railway

Photograph 30.2 Saltaire, built in the 1850s

The city has also added tourism value by introducing other attractions, such as the National Museum of Photography, Film and Television and the famous 'curry trail'. Tourism income is worth over £400 million a year (2006 data), with approximately 65% of this coming from day-visitors.

Evaluating the success of projects in large urban areas

There is a range of fieldwork and research you can use to evaluate the success of rebranding in a large urban context (see Figure 30.6).

*Figure 30.6
Research indicators
of urban
rebranding success*

Economic
Environmental
Social

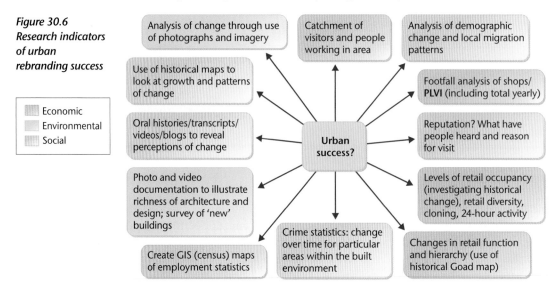

- Analysis of change through use of photographs and imagery
- Catchment of visitors and people working in area
- Analysis of demographic change and local migration patterns
- Use of historical maps to look at growth and patterns of change
- Footfall analysis of shops/ **PLVI** (including total yearly)
- Oral histories/transcripts/ videos/blogs to reveal perceptions of change
- Reputation? What have people heard and reason for visit
- Photo and video documentation to illustrate richness of architecture and design; survey of 'new' buildings
- Levels of retail occupancy (investigating historical change), retail diversity, cloning, 24-hour activity
- Create GIS (census) maps of employment statistics
- Crime statistics: change over time for particular areas within the built environment
- Changes in retail function and hierarchy (use of historical Goad map)

Urban success?

Fieldwork and research

Coastal rebranding: success or failure?

The research ideas suggested in Figure 30.6 can be applied to coastal sites:

- *Economic* — retail occupancy/retail health (look at types of shops), footfall, levels of employment (seasonal, casual, part time, full time); compare economically with other locations using census statistics or Acorn profiles; affordability of housing.
- *Social* — crime statistics, graffiti assessment, use of Wikipedia/YouTube to reveal identity and issues; research local media, forums, community action groups, etc.
- *Environmental* — beach quality surveys, incorporating 'Blue Flag' criteria (the Marine Conservation Society has a good litter survey plan: www.adoptabeach.org.uk), route quality surveys (especially in locations where pedestrianisation has taken place); visitor surveys — catchment, average spend, impressions of change.

Case study — Regenerating Cromer, Norfolk

Cromer is a resort on the north Norfolk coast. Enhancing Cromer's seafront was the focus of a £6.1 million investment programme by North Norfolk District Council in 2002. The project involved refurbishing Cromer Pier and the Pier Pavilion Theatre, regenerating the promenade and creating a new museum celebrating the 200-year history of the Royal National Lifeboat Institution (RNLI) in Cromer.

One of the notable successes of the scheme was the use of sustainable building technologies. The Rocket House is home of the RNLI museum dedicated to Henry Blogg, the most decorated lifeboatman in Britain. The museum building (Photograph 30.3) is mostly naturally ventilated, using cross ventilation. Conservation heating in the museum maintains constant humidity levels by varying the temperature within a band of 5–22°C, outside of which it maintains a minimum temperature for frost protection in very cold weather or a maximum temperature for comfort and energy-efficiency reasons during the summer. This system maintains humidity and saves energy.

Photograph 30.3 The Rocket House, Cromer

David Holmes

Researching the impact of flagship developments

Begin by researching the history of a chosen flagship project. A good website to look at is that of the company Urban Splash (www. urbansplash.co.uk). It has completed a number of major reimaging and rebranding projects around the country. Using Table 30.3 as an example, compile a table of research information.

You should illustrate any research activity with images and maps to support the process. Internet blogs and forums, as well as letters and editorial comment in local papers, can reveal attitudes towards developments. Try to answer two central questions:

- How has a flagship development been used to redevelop an area and change its 'image'?
- Has the flagship been a catalyst for other developments?

Responses to these questions will help with answering the bigger question of how successful a particular scheme has been.

Table 30.3 Research data: flagship developments

Name and location of flagship	Date of beginning and end of project	Development company/main contractors	Cost of project	Funding streams	Function, usage and nature of architectural style	Peoples' opinions/ reputation of development/ project

Assessing rebranding 'images'

Images of rebranding can come from a variety of sources, such as websites, visitor guides and information packs. Information produced by organisations such as developers, city councils or arts centres to attract tourists or businesses often illustrates recent changes in image.

For a particular place you are studying, collect a range of publicity material to analyse how important image is to the rebranding process. Consider the following evidence:

- How is the historic nature of the place used?
- Which types of tourist are targeted?
- What is the range and type of visitor attractions?
- What evidence is there of sustainability and eco-friendly innovation?
- How have new technology and products been used in buildings and architecture?
- Have major businesses been attracted as part of the rebranding process?
- Are there distinctive areas, such as a specialist shopping street?
- Have sculptures or other art been used in public spaces?

This activity could be developed further to compare 'before' and 'after' images of the areas that have been redeveloped.

London 2012

Photograph 30.4 An artist's impression of the aquatic centre for London 2012 Olympics

Evaluating sport as an agent of rebranding

The use of sport events and developments to act as a catalyst of regeneration was discussed in Chapter 28. The likely benefits of regeneration caused by sport include:

➤ new sporting facilities (Photograph 30.4)
➤ increased tourism
➤ economic benefits (e.g. reduction in unemployment)
➤ enhanced infrastructure (e.g. transport)
➤ increased reputation and higher profile for the city
➤ general improvement to the area (e.g. rise in quality of life)

Some of these data can be obtained by primary research, for example using questionnaires to look at the quality of life before and after a development, surveys of infrastructure, or comparisons of local sporting facilities before and after the event. Some historical data will be available for making comparisons (e.g. levels of employment before and after the sporting event from the local authority or from the Office for National Statistics website, http://neighbourhood.statistics.gov.uk).

It may also be worth enquiring about any negative impacts of rebranding, such as the cost of the event, overcrowding during the event and unused facilities. Good sources of information are local newspaper archives and local forums. These can be an excellent way of finding out how local people really value sporting developments. The World Student Games held in Sheffield in 2006 created a big debt for the city but raised its profile on an international scale. Two contrasting opinions from the Sheffield Forum (www.sheffieldforum.co.uk) about the Games were as follows:

The WSG have been a financial disaster for this city and left us with facilities we have to pay for, then pay full price to use, higher council taxes, less money to spend on council services and for what? So we can have a week of glory on Channel 4 once a year. Some price tag and regeneration that!

I was in Sheffield at the time of the World Student Games. I was working the track as a volunteer at Don Valley Stadium. Lots of people benefited. Why do you think so many sports events locate themselves in the city? For Sheffielders at the time, the city was known for the amount of jobless steelworkers there were. I don't regard the games as a big debt.

Review questions

1 Describe the range of urban rebranding strategies.
2 How can the use of culture help in the rebranding of urban places?
3 How is gentrification linked to rebranding?
4 Explain why evaluating *either* urban *or* coastal rebranding is difficult.
5 Does urban rebranding always bring success?

Index

Bold page numbers indicate definitions of key terms